Introduction to Hospitality Operations

Introduction to Hospitality Operations

EDITED BY
PETER JONES
Head of Service Sector Management, University of Brighton

CASSELL

Cassell
Wellington House, 125 Strand, London WC2R 0BB, England
215 Park Avenue South, New York, NY 10003, USA

First published 1996

British Library Cataloguing-in-Publication Data
A catalogue record for this book is available from the British Library.

Library of Congress Cataloging-in-Publication Data
Introduction to hospitality operations / edited by Peter Jones.
        p.   cm.
    Includes bibliographical references and index.
    ISBN 0-304-33444-8. — ISBN 0-304-32902-9
    1. Hospitality industry.   2. Food service management.   3. Hotel
management.   I. Jones, Peter, 1951–   .
    TX911.I68   1995
    647.94′068—dc20   95-18387
                                                                          CIP

ISBN 0-304-33444-8 (hb)
ISBN 0-304-32902-9 (pb)

Typeset by Action Typesetting, Gloucester
Printed and bound in Great Britain by The Bath Press, Avon

ACKNOWLEDGEMENTS

The editor would like to thank all those people who have assisted in the production of this
text by explaining how their businesses operate, by providing photographs and other
materials, or through their general encouragement and support. Amongst the many who
have done so are the following: Mr L. Bainbridge, Catering Manager, P & O European
Ferries; Pauline Brown, Human Resources Manager, Jarvis Hotels; Adrian Carpenter,
University of Brighton; David Costa, General Manager, Benihana, London; Chris Cowls,
BurgerKing; Simon Chrichton, Director of Catering and Retail, Forte Posthouse; Michael
Collyer, Owner, Netherfield Place Hotel; Bob Cotton, Director of Corporate Affairs,
Gardner Merchant Ltd; Michael Dent, Forte PLC; Gill Doxford, Marketing Services
Manager, Swallow Hotels Ltd; Bill Flavell, Proprietor, White Horse Caterers; Phil
Gassman, Catering Manager, University of Sussex; David Hayes, Chief Executive, Con-
sort Hotels; Mr R. Hoffmann, Corporate Executive Chef, Stena Sealink Limited; Jarvis
Hotel Sales and Marketing Department; Hamish Johnston, Head of Support Services,
University of St Andrews; Alan Jones, Chief Executive, AJs Restaurants; Andrew Lock-
wood, University of Surrey; Diane Miller, General Manager, Heathrow Marriott Hotel;
Mr B. Muldoon, Trains Manager, InterCity East Coast; Ms Elaine Rawlins, De Vere
Hotels; Chris Ripper, Personnel Director, Scottish & Newcastle; Jenny Sharpe, General
Manager, British Airways; Sarah Taylor, Marketing Assistant, Scott's Hotels Limited;
Nicola White, Sales Executive, Hanbury Manor Hotel; Jonathan Wilde, Marketing Ser-
vices Executive, Gardner Merchant Ltd.

Contents

ACKNOWLEDGEMENTS   iv

CONTRIBUTORS   vii

PREFACE   ix

1   The Hospitality Industry   1
    Peter Jones

PART A   The Accommodation Industry

2   The Accommodation Sector   21
    Steven Goss-Turner

3   Business and Conference Hotels   36
    Steven Goss-Turner

4   Resort Hotels   50
    Angela Roper

5   Budget Hotels   61
    Keith Johnson and Warwick Clifton

6   Guest Houses and Small Hotels   73
    Alison Morrison

7   Hospital Hotel Services and Residential Care   86
    Judith Brown

8   Hostels and Halls of Residence   96
    Michael Deakin

PART B   The Foodservice Industry

9   The Foodservice Sector   107
    Peter Jones

10 Restaurants   122
    Peter Jones

11 Foodservice in Hotels   138
    Peter Jones

12　Motorway and Roadside Restaurants　153
　　Peter Jones

13　Licensed Trade Foodservice　161
　　Hadyn Ingram

14　Fast Food　172
　　Stephen Ball

15　Employee Feeding　190
　　Cliff Goodwin

16　Welfare Catering　209
　　Nigel Hemmington

17　Travel Catering　234
　　David Kirk and Trevor Laffin

18　Outdoor Catering　252
　　Peter Jones

INDEX　261

Contributors

The Editor, **Peter Jones**, is Head of the Department of Service Sector Management at the University of Brighton. He is the author, co-author or editor of seven textbooks. He has also authored several chapter contributions to other texts and numerous articles in the area of operations management. His research interest lies in discovering what influences effective operational activity, and especially the role of innovation in achieving successful performance.

Stephen Ball is Senior Lecturer in the Department of Food, Nutrition and Hospitality Management at the University of Huddersfield. He has a wide range of industrial experience and has acted as a consultant for a number of national and international hotel and catering organizations. He was the creator of the Fast Food Database and has researched and published extensively on the fast food industry. He was a major contributor to the Jordans Survey *Britain's Fast Food Industry* and is editor and chief contributor to the text *Fast Food Operations and Their Management*.

Judith E. Brown is a Senior Lecturer in the Department of Leisure Management at Cheltenham and Gloucester College of Higher Education. She has a wide variety of experience in the hospitality industry and has taught in both the UK and Switzerland. Her interests relate to the management of accommodation and the cultural and social aspects of the industry.

Warwick J. Clifton is a graduate of the University of Huddersfield's Hotel and Catering Business degree. He is currently completing a doctoral study on the growth of transnational hotel groups in Europe.

Michael Kent Deakin is Field Chair of Hotel Management at Cheltenham & Gloucester College of Higher Education. Having graduated with a Master's Degree from the University of Huddersfield, he has had a long-standing interest in the structural changes within the European Hotel sector with special interest in locational and ownership strategies of major groups. He has extensive experience as consultant to a wide range of accommodation providers, specializing in all aspects of operational management.

Cliff Goodwin is Senior Lecturer in Operations Management in the Department of Service Sector Management at the University of Brighton. A former area manager with both a major contract caterer and restaurant chain, he is the author of the HCIMA's open learning resource on operations management.

Steven Goss-Turner is a former senior human resource manager of a major international hotel chain, with 15 years' experience of the hotel industry. He is currently a Senior Lecturer at the University of Brighton. He is the author of *Managing People in the Hotel and Catering Industry*.

Dr Nigel Hemmington is Head of Division of Hospitality Management at Cheltenham & Gloucester College of Higher Education. Dr Hemmington's interests are mainly in consumer behaviour related to strategic management of hospitality operations, especially in the public sector. He has published a number of articles and reports in this area.

Hadyn Ingram was a third-generation publican, having been the licensee of a large west London pub for fifteen years after training in hotel management. He is currently a Senior Lecturer at Bournemouth University. He also owns a hotel in the city of Salisbury, as well as writing books and articles on operations and strategic management for the hospitality industry.

Keith Johnson is a Principal Lecturer in the Department of Food, Nutrition and Hospitality at the University of Huddersfield. He has written extensively on a variety of aspects of hospitality management. His research interests include the human resource management strategies of global hotel companies and the dynamics of the European hotel industry.

Professor David Kirk is Head of Department of Hospitality and Tourism Management at Queen Margaret College, Edinburgh. His teaching and research interests relate to the use of technology in the hospitality industry, particularly in relation to the design and management of catering facilities.

Trevor Laffin is a lecturer in the Department of Hospitality and Tourism Management at Queen Margaret College, Edinburgh. After twelve years' experience in the luxury hotel sector, his specialist interest is in food and beverage management. Current research interests include the role of the chef in country house hotels and foodservice provision in training restaurants.

Alison Morrison is currently a lecturer at The Scottish Hotel School, University of Strathclyde, with specialized interest in small businesses within the hospitality industry. She has spent over twenty years in the industry, fifteen of which have been in the ownership of small hotels and restaurants. Current research is focused on small firm strategic alliance towards the award of a Ph.D. which is due for completion by the end of 1995.

Dr Angela Roper is a Senior Lecturer in Marketing and Business Development in the School of Hotel and Catering Management at Oxford Brookes University. She specializes in developing and leading strategic management teaching, as applied to the hospitality industry, at both undergraduate and postgraduate levels. Both her Ph.D. thesis and recent publications have focused on the competitiveness of hotel groups, in particular hotel consortia as strategic alliances. Angela is currently working on a three-year inter-disciplinary research project entitled 'What makes a successful international hotel group?'

Preface

When I wrote *Foodservice Operations* in 1981, little did I realize that it would still be in print 13 years later and be used throughout the world to teach hospitality students. In 1988, I updated the text without making any significant changes to the structure. However, this text is a major revision – so much so that the book has a new title, *Introduction to Hospitality Operations*. There are two basic changes. Firstly, the book looks not only at foodservice operations but also accommodation. Secondly, all the chapters are written in the style of those chapters from Part A of the original text. That is to say they define the type of operation, describe the size and nature of the industry sector, identify markets served and typical locations, outline the nature of the product/service, explain how the operation is organized and staffed, describe 'standard operating procedures', and they identify current issues and future trends.

Why have these changes been made? When the original text was written there was a very good book that outlined the scope and nature of the hotel and catering industry, albeit from an economic perspective. This book is now out of print. So there is a need for one which covers all of the hospitality industry. Secondly, I have co-authored and edited two other textbooks that specifically look at operations management – *The Management of Hotel Operations* (1989) and *The Management of Foodservice Operations* (1994). *Introduction to Hospitality Operations* is intended to underpin these two texts by introducing students to broad principles before looking in detail at management.

At first sight it might appear relatively easy to write a book about the hotel and catering industry. After all, hotels, restaurants, pubs, travel catering, and so on happens all around us. It is a tangible activity that can be directly observed and experienced. In fact, writing about the industry is quite difficult. There is not even common agreement about the use of terms to describe the industry and its component sectors. Thus in the UK the most common usage has been to describe it as the 'hotel and catering industry'. In the USA, 'lodging and foodservice' is the more common terminology. Both of these approaches also tend to exclude a significant part of the industry, usually referred to as the 'institutional' sector, which provides both accommodation and meals in places such as schools, universities, hospitals, prisons and so on. In both countries, the term 'hospitality' is being adopted as a more concise and 'up-market' descriptor of the whole industry.

In this text, the hospitality industry is seen as being made up of two main sectors – the accommodation sector (which includes both hotels and institutions) and the foodservice sector. The term 'foodservice' is preferred to 'catering' for similar reasons to the adoption of 'hospitality' – the word 'foodservice' has a better image than 'catering'. In addition the development of some new styles of foodservice, such as fast food or cook-chill, have more similarity with food retailing or food manufacturing than traditional catering.

Finally, we need to be clear about at what *level* this review of hospitality operations is taking place. This book examines hospitality operations at the 'operating management system' level. Along with Andrew Lockwood, I have suggested that there are four different levels at which the industry can be understood.[1] The simplest level is at the operating system level, which largely looks at the technology of the operation. For instance, such technology can be traditional production equipment, or cook-chill, or hospital tray systems. The next level is the 'operating management system' (which is the main concern of this text). This explains how the technology is organized and the delivery process is managed. Above this is the 'operational management system' (which is the focus of the two texts referred to above). This is concerned with the effective management of the total operation based around the integration of key result areas. And finally, there is the operations management level which takes a strategic perspective of management.

There is of course one other major change between this text and the original text. Many of the chapters in this book have been written by people other than myself. There are many reasons why colleagues have become involved in this project. But two are most important. Firstly, the contributors to this text know much more than I about the topic in their chapters. This book is therefore of a much higher standard than if I had written it all. And secondly, it is a pleasure to collaborate with colleagues who are enthusiastic, knowledgeable, and conscientious. My sincere thanks to them for their hard work and contribution. All that is good about this book is due to them; anything that is not as good as it might be, is due to me as the editor.

Peter Jones
March 1995

1. Jones, P. and Lockwood, A. (1994) 'Hospitality Operating Systems', *New Visions for Hospitality Operations Management Conference*, Chelmsford, November 4.

ONE

The Hospitality Industry

PETER JONES

INTRODUCTION

The term 'hospitality' has emerged as the way hoteliers and caterers would like their industry to be perceived. It conveys an image that reflects the tradition of service that goes back over many centuries to the earliest days of inn-keeping. Thus in 1987, the Hotel, Catering and Institutional Management Association – the industry's professional association – changed the name of its journal to *Hospitality*. Likewise in 1991, the British Hoteliers, Restaurateurs and Caterers Association – the industry's main trade association – changed its name to the British Hospitality Association. The term has also been adopted by educators, so that many universities and colleges now offer courses in hospitality management.

In essence hospitality is made up two distinct services – the provision of overnight accommodation for people staying away from home, and the provision of sustenance for people eating away from home. Both of these services meet very basic human needs – the need to sleep and the need to eat. It is perhaps because these two things are so fundamental to human existence, that many people, especially in the UK, consider the industry to be straightforward and unsophisticated. Hence a great many people enter the business as small hoteliers, licensees, guest house owners and restaurateurs without any previous experience of the industry. Often these entrepreneurs are not as successful as they thought they would be. Indeed the hospitality industry has one of the highest level of bankruptcies of any industry in the UK. The situation in the early 1990s has been so bad, that firms of accountants (acting as receivers) own more hotels than the largest hotel chains in the UK. The prevalence of many small operators also tends to reinforce the argument that quality standards in the industry are poor. Their lack of expertise leads to low standards, and their lack of success leads to little or no investment in their businesses. This also contributes to the industry's image problem.

However, the industry has changed significantly over the last decade. In the earlier editions of this text, I argued[1] that this was due largely to the impact of ideas and concepts developed in the USA. Probably a more significant factor, related to American influences, has been the growth of large chains. Throughout the 1980s, there has been the consistent growth of hospitality companies across all sectors of the industry. For instance, roadside dining saw the development of two very strong brands in Little Chef and Happy Eater, along with numerous other smaller operators. On every high street or in shopping centres there are quick service restaurant chains such as Kentucky Fried Chicken, Burger-King and McDonald's. The large brewers significantly altered their policies towards their licensed premises, developing managed retail outlets rather than tenanted houses. Hotel chains developed strongly branded properties, such as Forte's Travelodge and the Stakis Court hotels. Contract foodservice also saw the emergence of three large companies – Sutcliffes, Gardner Merchant and Compass – which have also greatly increased their branding. These large chains have transformed the hospitality industry because they have introduced more professionalism to the business than ever before.Their size, and hence their financial and manpower resources, enables them to adopt the highest possible standards and increased competition motivates them to deliver these standards.

In this chapter, the hospitality industry is defined. The historical background and development of the industry is then described, prior to identifying the current size and scale of the industry in the mid-1990s. The different industry-wide organizations are then identified and their role discussed. This leads into a explanation of what is meant by operations and what trends have influenced the design of operations in the industry. The chapter concludes with an outline of the future of the industry.

DEFINING THE INDUSTRY

In order to describe, discuss and analyse the hospitality industry, it is first necessary to define the industry. This is not as simple as at first might be thought. Different sources, such as government agencies, market intelligence consultants, and other experts use different criteria for defining the industry. A good starting point is the Standard Industrial Classification, since it is the official government source of data about the industry.

Standard Industrial Classification (SIC)

The Standard Industrial Classification[2] was begun in 1948 in an attempt to provide uniform statistical records of industrial growth and activity. It defined the hotel and catering industry, under the 1968 classification, as 'Establishments (whether or not licensed for the sale of intoxicating liquors) providing meals, light refreshments, drink or accommodation'. The classification was subsequently revised in 1980. It comprises 'divisions' made up of broad groups of economic activity. Within each division, individual industries are known as 'classes', which are then subdivided into sectors or 'groups'. Groups can further be subdivided by 'activity'. Most of the hospitality industry is classified in division 6 'Services', class 66 'Hotels and Catering', and further subdivided into six groups. However some activities are included in division 9 'Other Services'. The SIC is illustrated in Table 1.1.

There are, however, some problems with the SIC approach, notably with regards to industrial catering. The classification only includes those operations undertaken by specialist catering contractors. So the turnover and employment of staff in catering units operated by business firms is measured under the main activity of the firm. For instance, petroleum or electronics companies may run their own catering operations, but this would not be included under SIC activity 6640. In addition, the classification tends to be based around the UK's approach to licensing premises, either with regards to health and safety or the sale of alcohol. Whilst this makes classification and data collection relatively easy, licensing arrangement may not be the best way to understand and analyse the industry.

Table 1.1 The Standard Industrial Classification of the hospitality industry.

Division 6		Services	
Class	Group	Activity	
66			Hotels and Catering
	661		Restaurants, snack bars, cafés and other eating places
		6611	Eating places supplying food for consumption on the premises
			a. Licensed places
			b. Unlicensed places
		6612	Take-away food shops
	662	6620	Public houses and bars
	663	6630	Night clubs and licensed clubs
	664	6640	Canteens and messes
			a. Catering contractors
			b. Other canteens and messes
	665	6650	Hotel trade
			a. Licensed premises
			b. Unlicensed premises
	667	6670	Other tourist or short-stay accommodation
			a. Camping and caravan sites
			b. Holiday camps
			c. Other tourist or short-stay accommodation not elsewhere specified
Division 9		Other services	
		9310	Catering services ancillary to higher education institutions
		9320	Catering services ancillary to schools
		9330	Catering services ancillary to educational and vocational training not elsewhere specified
		9510	Convalescent and rest homes with medical care
		9611	Social and residential homes

There is further discussion of how to define and analyse the the two main sectors of the industry – the accommodation sector and foodservice sector – later in this chapter.

Hotel and Catering Training Company (HCTC)

The HCTC was originally the Hotel and Catering Industry Training Board. It continues to engage in independent research into the industry. Its Research Report 1994 is entitled *Catering and Hospitality Industry – Key Facts and Figures*. This report illustrates the extent to which more than one source is needed in order to identify all the 'key facts'. And that these sources vary quite widely. It tends to use the SIC definitions of sectors for the 'commercial sectors' (i.e. hotels, restaurants, pubs and bars); but has to draw up its own definitions for the 'catering services sectors' (i.e. education, travel, medical, retail distribution). In identifying the size of these sectors, by number of establishments, it cites a number of different sources including the British Tourist Authority (BTA), Home Office, British Hospitality Association (BHA) and Business Monitor, before stating its own estimates of numbers. For instance, according to the BTA there are 27,712 hotels in the UK, whereas the HCTC cites 52,600. In view of the comprehensive review of sources conducted by the HCTC, most of the data about the industry cited in this chapter will be derived from their 1994 report.

THE ORIGINS AND DEVELOPMENT OF THE UK HOSPITALITY INDUSTRY

In order to understand the industry and the different sectors that make it up, it is insightful to review how the industry has developed in the UK. The impetus to the growth of hotels, and subsequently the modern hospitality industry, was provided by the railways. The profitable companies began to invest in large comfortable hotels generally located near the main railway stations, and by 1902 there were 70 major hotels owned and controlled by them. This stimulated hotel building by other companies in city centres and at seaside resorts, and the result was a transformation from relatively poor culinary standards of the old coaching inns to the highest and most sophisticated standards of cuisine. The lead was taken by D'Oyly Carte, who brought over César Ritz, and the man whom Ritz himself described as 'certainly the best chef in the world, he surpasses all the other chefs I have ever met' – Georges Escoffier. Escoffier was responsible for creating many classical dishes, perfecting the partie system and influencing greatly the organization of kitchen practice. Eating out in such establishments was, at that time, very formal. Customers were expected to wear evening dress and women were seldom seen in public restaurants. Ritz was largely responsible for breaking down this formality and grill rooms 'emerged from the desire of American tourists to avoid the dining ceremonial each night'.[3]

At the other end of the scale, two companies emerged to provide eating out of a better quality for the masses – the Aerated Bread Co. and J. Lyons. Their immediate popularity was due largely to women, who could not frequent taverns or fashionable restaurants unless escorted. Although they began as tea shops, they started to serve more substantial meals and to establish national chains of restaurants around the country. What is more significant is the fact that they were far more profitable businesses than the hotels.

The development of the motor car revitalized a sector of the hospitality industry that had declined during the railway age, namely smaller hotels and inns. Many such establishments had become public houses, selling only alcoholic beverages and neglecting the provision of food or accommodation. By 1900, the public-house sector had been considerably affected by government legislation during the nineteenth century, such as the Sale of Food and Drugs Act 1875 and numerous licensing Acts. The restriction on the number of licences issued had the direct result of influencing the brewers to invest in the retail-trade and in effect cause the start of the tied-house system. The growing influence of large brewing companies also led to a gradual transition from the old tavern and ale house into the splendid Victorian public house. None the less, standards of public-house operations were not immediately improved by the expanding brewing companies who effectively kept new entrants out and forced low-profit margins upon their tenants, as a result of which beer in particular was often adulterated or diluted. So bad was this state of affairs that Earl Grey began the Public House Trust Company in 1903, which was to become the Trust Houses hotel chain. The company bought up free houses and redeveloped the art of innkeeping by offering commission to the company's managers on the sale of food and accommodation but not on liquor sales. The motor car ensured that Trust Houses and other burgeoning hotel companies were to become very successful.

The First World War, 1914–1918, interrupted the development of the industry and severely limited food service in particular, due to the imposition of restrictions, regulations and, towards the end of the war, rationing. The greatest impact was in the field of industrial catering, which hitherto had been virtually non-existent. Feeding millions of service personnel and eventually the whole population compelled the government to consider a nation's dietary requirements. This led to the government's pressing employers to recognize the importance of adequate nutrition for the workers. By the end of the war, the number of industrial canteens had increased tenfold to nearly 1000, supplying nearly a million meals a day. It is sad to reflect that immediately after the war, industry failed to maintain these catering facilities so that it was not until the emergence of the Welfare State and the effect of another world war that industrial feeding developed more fully.

Another effect of the First World War was to raise the expectations of the population. This is not to say that *haute cuisine* was introduced to the general public. Although popular catering in the ABC and Lyons style became smarter and more hygienic, it remained basically simple fare – 'for the masses it was tea shops during the year and the landlady's cooking at the seaside on holiday'.[4] So in the 1930s a new type of catering establishment emerged in this sector. Between 1935 and 1937, nearly 100 milk bars opened up around the country and although they originally only sold milk products and ice creams, many of them moved into the mainstream of popular catering.

Despite the Depression years of the 1930s, overall the inter-war years were good ones for the hospitality industry. After rationing ended, there was a growth amongst all except the lowest social class in the popularity of eating out. Restaurant sales were boosted by the Licensing Act 1921, which allowed drinks to be served after 11 p.m. if accompanying meals. London, or at least Soho, saw the growth in Chinese and Indian restaurants, so that for the first time there was an alternative to the expensive French cuisine of top-class establishments or the British fare of the popular catering units. Slowly too, the more enlightened employers were recognizing the value of canteens and their contribution to job satisfaction and productivity. Public houses built in the period were more spacious and more comfortable than ever before, while rural inns found they were increasingly popular with cyclists and motorists. An increasing number of roadside hotels began to concentrate on providing good, well-cooked food, with a reasonably good wine list. Finally, for the first time in peacetime, the government began to concern itself with the nutritional needs of the population and the foundation of school meals was laid by the introduction in 1934 of the 'Milk in Schools Scheme'.

In many respects, the impact of the Second World War was similar to that which had ended only 20 years previously, except that business was further devastated by destruction due to bombing, as well as the disruption caused by rationing food and requisitioning premises. Thus, whilst the luxury hotel and restaurant trade declined, there was a tremendous increase in mass feeding. Professor Medlik writes[5] that 'probably the most important development of the war was the emergence of communal feeding on an unprecedented scale', while 'industrial catering developed beyond recognition'. But unlike after the First World War, the expansion in these sectors did not decline at the end of the Second World War. The election of a Labour government resulted in the development of institutional catering in schools and hospitals within the framework of the Welfare State, and the sheer number of industrial and staff canteens, some 25,000 by 1945, ensured that catering for employees would continue. From this, industrial catering contractors developed during the 1950s, such as Bateman's, Sutcliffes and Midland.

The fact that people were now being catered for at work introduced many to the eating-out experience for the first time. Furthermore, the 1950s and 1960s saw a real improvement in living standards and a narrowing of the gap between the expenditure of the

Table 1.2 Employment in the hospitality industry 1992.

Hotels	289,200
Restaurants	295,500
Pubs and bars	327,000
Clubs	138,300
Contract catering	115,700
Industrial*	262,100
Education*	247,800
Medical*	342,100
Travel*	34,800
Self-employed	165,000
Other sectors*	191,500
(includes recreation/cultural, retail distribution, and public administration)	
Total industry	2,409,000

Source: HCTC Research Report 1994, citing data from Census of Employment and Labour Force Survey.
*Data for these sectors includes 500,000 domestics (i.e. cleaning staff) and housekeepers.

richest and the poorest sections of the population. At the same time, the working week gradually became shorter with a consequent increase in leisure time and holidays. The availability of cheap mass-travel abroad has widened the horizons of most Britons and dietary trends show that we drink more milk and coffee and consume more poultry, eggs, vegetables and fruit than before 1939.

This did not mean that everyone could afford the luxury of an extensive à la carte menu served in sophisticated surroundings. Frank Berni recognized the need for the simpler meal experience in a pleasant atmosphere and developed the concept of a steak house, which filled a gap in the market between public houses and popular catering units. This latter sector has always had to keep pace with the changing tastes of the public and developments in the industry. Since the milk bars of the 1930s, there have been innumerable variations on the popular catering theme – Kardomah cafés, Golden Eggs, Wimpy and espresso coffee shops predominated in the 1960s and 1970s. The last in this long line of changing images and products is the fast-food operation. Speciality or concept restaurants too have expanded, due to the growth of our multi-racial society and membership of the EEC, so that in large cities and towns the national cuisine of many European and Far Eastern countries may be experienced. As Taylor and Bush say[6] – 'changes in the last 30 years have indeed been immense, whichever facet of catering [sic] one examines'.

SIZE AND SCALE OF THE UK HOSPITALITY INDUSTRY

As previously mentioned, the size and scale of the industry is very difficult to measure accurately due to problems of definition and data collection. Thus the figures from one source, such as the HCTC, may be quite different from those from a market research organization such as Marketpower. In order to avoid contradictory data, this section of the report mainly cites the HCTC Research Report 1994,[7] which in turn draws on a number of sources.

The industry continues to be a major employer in the economy, as illustrated in Table 1.2. The industry in the UK employs nearly 2.5 million people, representing 10 per cent of the working population. The HCTC Research Report identifies a 2 per cent decline in

Table 1.3 Establishments in the commercial sectors of the hospitality industry 1991.

Hotels	52,200
Restaurants	99,900
Pubs and bars	77,100
Clubs	16,100
Contract catering	19,200
Total	264,500

Source: HCTC Research Report 1994, citing data from Census of Employment and Labour Force Survey.

employment levels between 1991 and 1992, which is a good performance by the industry in view of the economic conditions in which it was operating. Employment in hotels and contract catering were hardest hit by the recession. Total employment in the industry can be broken down by job category, mode of employment and gender. In 1992, according to the Labour Force Survey, 17 per cent of the workforce were in management positions, 29 per cent in housekeeping and cleaning services, 28 per cent in food preparation and cooking, and 14 per cent in food and drink service. Less than 1 per cent were employed as hotel receptionists or porters. Employment in the industry tends to be part-time, with 63 per cent of those employed in this category. In general, part-time employment is greater in the not-for-profit sectors. Finally, in 1992, 72 per cent of the workforce was female, also especially in the not-for-profit sectors. However, there were some job categories that were biased heavily towards one gender. For instance, according to the Labour Force Survey, 91 per cent of housekeepers are female, whereas 100 per cent of hotel porters are male. Amongst managers, the gender balance is almost equal, except in the licensed trade, where males predominate.

It is only possible to count the number of establishments in the hospitality industry that operate in the commercial sector, as illustrated in Table 1.3. Of the 264,500 establishments, 60 per cent are owned or operated by self-employed people, especially in the hotel sector (70 per cent of hotels). Most of these establishments (87 per cent) are small, employing ten employees or less. Only in the hotel sector is there a significant proportion of establishments (6 per cent) employing more than 25 people. Between, 1984 and 1991 there has been a 5 per cent growth in the total number of hospitality establishments. But different sectors have experienced different levels of growth or decline. The number of restaurants grew by 14 per cent in this seven-year period, contract catering by 10 per cent and pubs and bars by 5 per cent. However, the number of hotels fell by nearly 9 per cent and clubs by 5 per cent.

It is estimated that nearly 4.5 billion meals are served in this country every year, and it is reckoned that over 23 million people eat out in a week. In 1990, the number of meals eaten outside the home was 3.76 meals per person per week.[8] A major issue for the hospitality industry is the proportion of consumer expenditure spent on catering and accommodation. In 1992, the total market for catering meals and accommodation was estimated to be £20 billion in the UK.[9] However, consumer spending on meals and accommodation is very sensitive to overall economic conditions. During the 1980s, there was a percentage increase in real terms spending of around 8 per cent, but an estimated decline of 3 per cent in 1991 due to the recession. In 1985 catering meals and accommodation represented 6.4 per cent of total consumer expenditure, by 1992 this was estimated to be 7.5 per cent, despite the decline of expenditure in 1991.

Table 1.4 Sales turnover in the commercial sectors* of the Hospitality Industry 1991 (£m).

Hotels/residential	6,406
Restaurants/cafés†	3,841
Fast food/take aways‡	4,264
Pubs and bars	10,447
Clubs	2,877
Contract catering	2,175
Holiday camps/caravans	1,115
Total	31,125

Source: HCTC Research Report 1994, citing data from Business Monitor SDA 28.
*Only includes establishments over VAT threshold.
†On-premises consumption only.
‡Off-premises consumption wholly or in part.

Sales turnover in the commercial sectors of the industry were over £30 billion in 1991, as illustrated in Table 1.4. Financial turnover has been increasing in some sectors much more than in others. For instance, in the six years from 1985, the fast food sector and contract catering doubled their turnover, whereas pubs and bars and hotels only increased by 50 per cent, and clubs, reflecting the decline in number of establishments, grew by only 35 per cent.

ORGANIZATIONS IN THE HOSPITALITY INDUSTRY

In considering hospitality, we can identify a large number and variety of organizations involved in the industry. The growth of such organizations is a result of the following factors:

- The structure of the industry which continues to have very many small, individually owned units, in spite of the growth of large companies.
- The industry is heterogeneous – split up into many different, identifiable sectors, each with its own specific needs.
- Geographically, the industry is widespread, with some types of operation concentrated around population centres, although this is not essential for all types.
- The industry is a very large employer and offers a wide range of job opportunities and employment categories.

The HCIMA's Reference Book 1993/94 has a UK directory totalling 223 different organizations associated with the industry in one way or another. These include trade unions (such as the GMB, Transport and General Workers Union); trade associations (for instance, English Vineyards Association, National Federation of Traders); non-industry specific professional associations (for example, the Institute of Management Consultants, Chartered Society of Designers); advisory bodies (Butter Council, Commercial Gas Centre, Royal Society of Health); research agencies (Leatherhead Food Research Association, World Travel and Tourism Environmental Research Centre); consumer bodies; government departments (Department of Employment, Department of Trade and Industry); and others (Guild of Professional Toastmasters, The British Sandwich Association, National Carpet Cleaners Association, Microwave Association).

There are broadly two types of organization: voluntary ones, for either individuals or organizations, and government and quasi-government agencies directly relating to the hospitality industry.

Voluntary Organizations for Individuals

The *Hotel, Catering and Institutional Management Association* is the professional body for the mainstream of the industry. Its membership exceeded 21,000 in 1994 and comprised fellows, members, licentiates, students and associates. The association sees its main priority as establishing recognition of the association in order to influence developments in the industry and to provide better job opportunities for its members. In this respect, it provides advisory services for members, maintains a central library, publishes a monthly magazine called *Hospitality*, and employs officers specializing in employment, careers and technical aspects. The HCIMA is also closely involved in discussions concerning catering education at all levels and runs its own full-time and part-time courses leading to association membership, which is recognized as a management qualification.

In addition to this industry-wide association for managers, there are also sector-specific management associations. These include the *National Association of Licensed House Managers*, *The University Catering Officers*, *Hospital Caterers' Association*, *Local Authority Caterers Association*, *Catering Managers' Association* and *Society of Catering and Hotel Management Consultants*.

As well as management associations, there are a number of associations for the professional groups in the hospitality workforce. These include *United Kingdom Bartenders' Guild*, *Craft Guild Of Chefs*, *Court of Sommeliers Worldwide*, and *The Federation of Bakers*.

Voluntary Organizations by Sector

The *British Hospitality Association* is a typical trade association – a 'voluntary' non-profit-making body formed by independent firms to protect and advance their common interests. Its mission is to 'take the initiative to ensure that the views of the British hospitality industry are strongly represented to the U.K. government and to policy makers in the U.K. and internationally in order to ensure its members' businesses can flourish'. To achieve this, it offers a range of services and benefits, has a strong Parliamentary lobby, discusses legislation affecting the industry with government departments, offers advice on recruitment and training of staff, and provides information services to its members through publications or from its specialists. In 1994 there were 11,000 establishments in direct membership, with another 5,000 affiliated through local hotel associations.

The *Brewers' Society*, too, is a trade association involved in sponsoring scientific research into brewing, improving trading relations, discussing with government changes in licensing law which resulted from the Monopolies Commission report, and liaising with other national and international brewing organizations. Of particular interest is the society's annual report on trends in the sale and consumption of alcoholic beverages in the UK.

Other trade associations include *International Flight Caterers Association*, *Restaurateurs Association of Great Britain*, and *Catering Equipment Manufacturers Association*.

Governmental and Quasi-governmental Agencies

The *Hotel and Catering Training Company* (HCTC) is now a non-governmental agency. It was originally set up as the Hotel and Catering Training Industry Board (HCITB) under the Industrial Training Act 1964 and intended to ensure a trained workforce, secure an improvement in the quality and efficiency of industrial training and share the cost of training more evenly among firms. It was funded by a levy of the 1500 or so largest employers, as defined by the size of their payroll. Those employers who systematically met their own training needs were exempt from the levy, while the money over was spent as specific grants to encourage training in particular areas or as key grants to the smaller, non-leviable employers. It operated mainly by training on-the-job instructors within the firms themselves, by providing regional training centres to undertake specific training of personnel and by offering advice and aid through their staff of training advisers. By 1986 nearly 20 per cent of its income was derived from commercial activities. Such activities included operating a wide range of training courses, the small business start-up programme, an extensive open-learning initiative, video and print publications, and management consultancy. In 1992, the Board was closed and the Company formed to operate as an entirely commercial agency, using former HCITB funds in order to continue a research role for the industry.

The *British Tourist Authority* is predominantly concerned with the development and promotion of tourism to Britain, whilst regional *Tourism Boards* are active encouraging British residents to holiday within the UK. Probably the greatest impact has been the opportunity that the Boards have offered to independent hoteliers and restaurateurs to publicize and advertise their establishments. In 1987 the English Tourist Board successfully introduced the Crown Registration system for hotels.

HOSPITALITY OPERATIONS

So far this chapter has looked at the hospitality industry and the sectors that make it up. But this text is also concerned with hospitality *operations*. It will focus on how organizations go about delivering their product/service to the consumer. At this point it is therefore necessary to differentiate between accommodation and foodservice, because essentially they are different kinds of operation. Johnston[10] has proposed the concept of three main types of operation – product processing operations; customer processing operations; and information processing operations. In reality most activities are a combination of all three – product, customer and information – albeit in different proportions. This concept is useful in understanding the difference between accommodation and foodservice. An accommodation operation is predominantly a customer processing operation, with very little product and information processing. Whereas a foodservice operation is a product processing operation (i.e. the meal), with a significant element of customer processing (i.e. the 'meal experience'), and limited information processing.

A simple definition of accommodation services is the provision of facilities for an overnight stay. Likewise foodservice can be simply defined as the provision of food and drink ready for consumption away from the home. This, however, fails to differentiate the foodservice industry – which provides 'meals', from the retailing industry – which provides 'food'. Medlik[11] recognized this problem and defined a catering [*sic*] establishment in these terms:

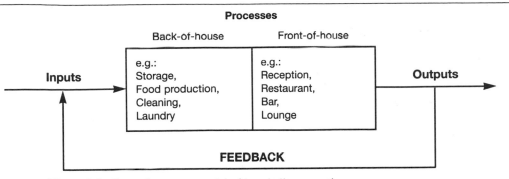

Figure 1.1 General systems model of hospitality operations.

1. The goods sold are usually consumed on the premises.
2. The buyer is able to determine the quantity of the goods purchased in a retail shop, but in a catering unit the caterer determines quantity, i.e. portion size.
3. The caterer also determines quality as in most cases the customer orders the meal without seeing it before the order is placed.
4. The caterer is a processor of materials as well as a retailer of goods.
5. In general, the caterer holds less stock and there is a shorter time between receipt of raw materials to point of sale than for most retailers.

Both these types of hospitality operation can be more easily understood if they are considered as 'systems'. Kirk[12] warns that systems theory has some shortcomings and that its terminology is not always correctly used nor its ideas properly applied. None the less, experience suggests that operations analysis is greatly helped by systems modelling or 'flow process charting'. Systems theory proposes four key elements of any system – inputs, processes, outputs and feedback. A key feature of most such systems is that they are made up of a number of processes carried out 'back-of-house', i.e. out of sight of the customer; and other processes performed 'front-of-house, i.e. with the customer's involvement. In the hospitality industry, typical back-of house processes include materials storage, food production, laundry, bedroom cleaning, and so on; whereas front-of-house operations include guest reception, restaurant service, bar operations and lounges. This can be illustrated in Figure 1.1.

If an accommodation operation is systems modelled in this way, as a *customer processing operation*, it is possible to identify a 'core system', which is based around the provision of a space in which to sleep, along with a number of sub-systems or 'ancillary services' which may or may not be offered, according to the nature of the service (i.e. hostel, hotel, hospital, etc.) Such services might include laundry, meals, drinks, business services (telephone, fax, etc.) and leisure services (fitness centres, swimming pools, etc.). This can be modelled as in Figure 1.2.

Foodservice, when modelled as a system, largely focuses on aspects of the *product processing operation*. Jones[13] proposes that there is a maximum of ten stages in the foodservice process, but that these can be combined in different ways, with some of the stages being eliminated. These alternative configurations reflect the different kinds of foodservice operation that have been devised to meet different customer needs. This is illustrated in Figure 1.3.

In modelling the complex, real world in this way, it should be made clear that these

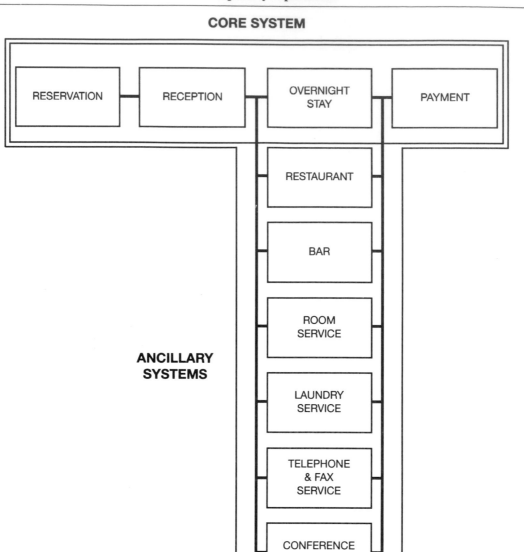

Figure 1.2 Systems model of hotel accommodation operations.

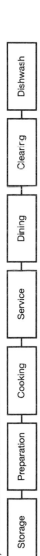
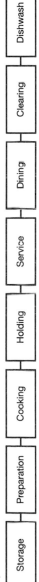
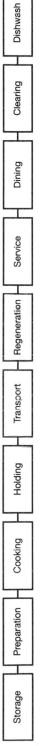

(a) Conventional à la carte restaurant

| Storage | Preparation | Cooking | Service | Dining | Clearing | Dishwash |

(b) Conventional table d'hôte restaurant

| Storage | Preparation | Cooking | Holding | Service | Dining | Clearing | Dishwash |

(c) Buffet/Sandwich bar

| Storage | Preparation | Holding | Service | Dining | Clearing | Dishwash |

(d) *Sous-vide* or cook-chill operation

| Storage | Preparation | Cooking | Holding | Transport | Regeneration | Service | Dining | Clearing | Dishwash |

(e) Call/Short order operation

| Storage | Cooking | Holding | Service | Dining | Clearing | Dishwash |

(f) Fast food

| Storage | Preparation | Cooking | Holding | Service | Dining | Clearing |

(g) Assembly-serve operation

| Storage | Regeneration | Service | Dining | Dishwash | Clearing |

(h) Japanese *hibachi* operation

| Storage | Preparation | Cooking | Dining | Clearing | Dishwash |

Figure 1.3 Systems models of foodservice operations

systems diagrams (or flow process charts) are considerable simplifications. In addition, Pickworth[14] suggests that systems can either be 'multi-faceted' i.e. serve a variety of functions, or 'dedicated' (i.e. perform a single function). A good example of a multi-faceted system is a hotel kitchen which produces food not only for the restaurant but also for floor service, banqueting and lounge service. Likewise fast food restaurants are adding take-out windows and home delivery provision to their operation. Good examples of dedicated service delivery systems would be a sandwich bar, a pub bar, or a hotel laundry. Each of these is designed to serve one purpose and one purpose only.

TRENDS IN OPERATIONS DESIGN

A fundamental principle of operations management is to reduce complexity, as this adds to costs, threatens quality, and creates inefficiency. Indeed Thompson[15] has stated that the ideal operation is one in which 'a single kind of product [is produced] at a continuous rate and as if inputs flowed continuously at a steady rate and with specified quality'. It is therefore not surprising that a clear trend in the hospitality industry has been to develop operations that reduce complexity by reducing the number of systems within one operation. In the accommodation sector this has seen the emergence of motels, budget hotels and even 'capsule hotels' in Japan. Likewise, over the last 30 years there has been a trend to move away from multi-faceted service delivery systems towards dedicated ones. In the foodservice industry, many of the recent developments in restaurant chains, cook-chill and *sous-vide* correspond with this aim.

Jones[16] has proposed that there have been three major ways in which hospitality operations have developed over the last twenty years. These three trends are production lining; decoupling; and increased customer participation.

1. *Production-line approach*. It has been suggested[17] that the total system might be looked at as a production line. Thus traditional 'craft-based' kitchen and restaurant operations can be turned into batch-process or mass-production systems. This technocratization of service can be achieved by using 'hard' technologies, such as automatic-vending machines, or 'soft' technologies, which focus on the people and systems in operation. This approach has largely been adopted by the foodservice industry. Because accommodation provision is largely a consumer processing operation, it is difficult to introduce new technology into the system.

2. *Decouple*. Chase[18] has suggested the idea of isolating the technical core of the service business so that efficiency could be improved in the non-contact part of the provision. This is most suited to the service industries he describes as 'low-contact', since the approach suggests that the technical core can then by set up to operate continuously irrespective of short-term changes in customer demand. Cook-chill and *sous-vide* food production enable such decoupling (see also Figure 1.3).

3. *Increased consumer participation*. Another trend investigated involves greater levels of consumer participation in the service experience, both in terms of self-selection and self-service. So approaches to increasing consumer participation might include family-style or self-help salad bars in restaurants, and automated check-in to budget hotels.

These three approaches may be considered as a hierarchy. The production-line approach has potentially the greatest impact on efficiency, productivity and profitability and should be considered first of all. Decoupling enables the industrialization of a part of the service delivery system, usually the technical core. Finally, if neither of these are implemented, the consumer-participation approach should be investigated, with the introduction of an element of self-service into the front-of-house operation. In foodservice, all these approaches have been applied to operating units, but they have had less impact on accommodation operations.

FUTURE OF THE HOSPITALITY INDUSTRY

In 1988 it was identified[19] that a number of factors would significantly affect the industry in the future. Many of these continue to apply in the mid-1990s.

The impact of *legislation* has been significant in the 1980s and early 1990s. Employment legislation has made it easier for employers to recruit staff, although arguably employees' conditions of service are relatively poor. The changes to licensing law have brought the UK into European practices with regards to the availability of alcoholic beverages for consumption on premises. The 'privatization' of public-sector catering dramatically altered the nature of catering in these areas, irrespective of whether it was contracted out or retained in-house. This factor will continue to be important, especially with regard to the impact of the European Union laws and regulations, resulting from the formation of the so-called single market in 1992. In the public sector, European Union legislation on procurement will have a significant impact on materials purchased by universities, local authorities and other public sector hospitality providers. The Health and Safety at Work Act 1974 was updated through a set of six new regulations in an effort to conform to a European standard. Likewise the European Council agreed the Unfair Contract Terms Directive which affects contractual relationships between hospitality providers and their customers. Finally, there was the long-awaited EC Food Hygiene Directive. Its implementation will mean a revision of UK hygiene laws and new guidelines on effective practice.

A second factor has been the growth of *health awareness* and the trend towards a more healthy diet. This has been recognized by all sectors. This was illustrated by Wimpy's introduction of their wholemeal bun, major campaigns by many local education authorities, the growth of salad bars in steak-house chains, and so on. However, the change in the British diet is far less dramatic than that in the USA, where low-calorie, low-cholesterol and low-sodium items are found on many menus. This reluctance to change may reflect the natural conservatism of the UK population, or it may be a result of the farming lobby in the British Isles, in particular the meat and milk producers, effectively damping down interest in more healthy foods. A number of agencies have responded to the influence of these vested interests. In 1987 there was a £2 million, government-sponsored campaign called 'Look after your Heart'. In 1994, the government was continuing to try to change the hearts and minds (and hence the health) of the population through yet another campaign.

A third factor is the *technological advances* made in preserving raw or semi-prepared foodstuffs, and finished, ready-for-consumption meal products. The two most innovative techniques are the irradiation of raw materials and *sous-vide* techniques for finished dishes. Meanwhile, cook-chill has been widely adopted across many sectors. Whilst

Figure 1.4 Japanese *hibachi* restaurant.
Source: Benihana, London.

technology will continue to have an impact, the type of technology in the late 1990s will be very different. Rather than large-scale production technology, the greatest impact will be from information technology; this will not be so much as a result of the introduction of new hardware but rather, through the development of new software systems. Such systems will greatly simplify reporting procedures, forecasting, inventory control, staff scheduling, energy management, and other complex information processing activities within hospitality operations. Before the year 2000, focused operations (or 'dedicated service delivery systems') such as fast food or home delivery will incorporate fully integrated software systems that largely plan and control all activities within the operation. For instance, Taco Bell in the USA have already installed throughout all their outlets such a system which they call TACO (total automation of company operations).

The role of *suppliers*, too, also developed in the late 1980s. A growing trend was the development of cash-and-carry chains aimed specifically at the foodservice market, such as Booker's 'Chef's Larder'. Wholesalers have also increased in size. By 1987 there were five wholesalers with a catering turnover of over £30 million. There is also a tendency for caterers to expect a 'one-drop' service, i.e. a supply of the full range of commodities from one supplier in order to reduce delivery frequency, ordering complexity and invoice administration. This has necessitated suppliers' investing in multi-temperature vehicles. In the 1990s the major trend is the level of supplier involvement with their customers. Suppliers will become much more proactive in working with operators in the development of their menus and products. For instance, in the flight catering sector Pourshins

PLC annually holds a menu development workshop for all the major airlines and contract flight caterers.

Finally, the industry is almost certainly likely to become very much more *competitive* in the future, as a result of the increasing size of catering firms seeking sustained growth in a relatively stable market. It has long been established that hotels, flight catering companies, and fast food operators compete on a global basis. But other sectors of the industry are also showing signs of growing internationalism. Sodexho, ARA Services, and the three major British contract catering firms are rapidly expanding outside their home markets. Theme restaurant chains, often American in origin, such as TGIFridays, Hard Rock Cafe and Benihana, illustrated in Figure 1.4, have also set up operations in major cities around the world. There is therefore no doubt that the industry has an exciting and dynamic future.

REFERENCES

1. Jones, Peter (1988) *Foodservice Operations* (2nd edition), London: Cassell, pp. 12–13.
2. CSO – Standard Industrial Classification, revised 1980.
3. Taylor, D. (1977) *Fortune, Fame and Folly*, London: IPC Business Press.
4. Ibid.
5. Medlik, R. (1978) *Profile of the Hotel and Catering Industry*, London: Heinemann.
6. Taylor, D. and Bush, D, (1974) *The Golden Age of British Hotels*, London: Northwood.
7. Hotel & Catering Training Company (1994) *Catering and Hospitality Industry – Key Facts and Figures*, London: HCTC.
8. MAFF (1991) *Household Food Consumption and Expenditure 1990*, London: IIMSO.
9. MSI (1992) *MSI Databrief: Catering: U.K.* London: Marketing Strategies for Industry (UK) Ltd.
10. Johnston, R. (1987) 'A framework for developing a quality strategy in a customer processing operation', *International Journal of Quality and Reliability Management*, Vol. 4, No. 4, pp. 37–46.
11. Medlik, R. op. cit.
12. Kirk, D. (1995) 'Hard and soft systems: a common paradigm for operations management?', *New Visions for Hospitality Operations Management Conference*, Chelmsford, November 4.
13. Jones, Peter (1990) 'Thinking about catering systems', *International Journal of Operations and Production Management*, Vol. 10, No. 8, pp. 42–52.
14. Pickworth, J.R. (1988) 'Service delivery systems in the foodservice industry', *International Journal of Hospitality Management*, Vol. 7, No. 1, pp. 43–62
15. Thompson, J.D. (1967) *Organisations in Action*, New York: McGraw-Hill.
16. Jones, Peter (1988) 'The impact of trends in service operations on foodservice delivery systems', *International Journal of Operations and Production Management*, Vol. 8, No. 7, pp. 23–30.
17. Levitt, T. (1976) 'The industrialisation of service', *Harvard Business Review*, September/October, pp. 63–74.
18. Chase, R.B. (1981) 'The customer contact approach to services: theoretical bases and practical extensions', *Operations Research*, Vol. 29, No. 4, pp. 698–706.
19. Jones, Peter (1988) *Foodservice Operations*, 2nd edition, London: Cassell, p. 23.

The Accommodation Industry

TWO

The Accommodation Sector

STEVEN GOSS-TURNER

INTRODUCTION

The demand for accommodation as part of an overall experience in hospitality has developed dramatically for those travelling, whether for leisure or business, ever since people had the desire, need and capability, to stay away from home. Such a rapid growth has been fundamentally linked to transport systems and the technological advances of the last 150 years. From the train to the car and the jet aeroplane, travel on an ever-greater scale has become possible. Add to this the increasingly complex patterns of business and trade, and the relatively enhanced wealth and disposable income of the western economies, and the equation amounts to a massive international demand for hospitality and accommodation.

That demand itself, has a tremendously varied nature and subset of components. The basic division between business and pleasure travellers may in turn be fragmented into a whole series of markets, users with differing needs, all dependent on factors such as availability, price, location and facilities. The accommodation industry began small, with inns and taverns, bed and breakfast and private hotels, and this is still a significant sector of the business. In many countries, such as the United Kingdom and France, the industry is still dominated in numerical units by small enterprises, often individually owned and operated. The British Hospitality Association calculates that in 1992 there were 35,000 hotels and accommodation outlets in the UK.[1] Yet only around 1500 of these businesses belonged to the large and predominantly international hotel chains such as Holiday Inn, Mount Charlotte Investments and Forte plc. The majority are small guest houses and privately owned hotels, with 6 to 26 letting bedrooms, at bed and breakfast rates of £10 per person per night. Contrast this type of operation and demand with a 5-star rated London establishment of perhaps 300 bedrooms with a room rate of £200 for a single room per night, breakfast not included. The accommodation aspect of the hospitality industry is as broad and all-encompassing as this, a circumstance which makes it all the more fascinating.

WHO STAYS AWAY FROM HOME AND WHY?

The types of customer served by the accommodation sector may be broadly divided into those people engaged in travelling on business or recreation, and those people not

Table 2.1 Sources of demand for hotel accommodation 1988 (%).

Purpose of visit	Worldwide	Africa and Middle East	Asia and Australasia	North America	Europe
Government officials	5.5	9.8	4.0	3.9	7.5
Business travellers	37.1	46.7	41.0	34.5	37.5
Tourists*	35.8	24.3	35.3	33.5	36.5
Conference participants	13.4	7.2	8.6	20.6	11.4
Others	8.2	12.0	11.0	7.5	7.1

Source: Horwath and Horwath International (1989) *Worldwide Hotel Industry.*
*Individual tourists and tour groups.

engaged in travel but who are staying away from home on a temporary basis, such as students in hostels and patients in hospitals. There may also be an overlap of reasons why people are staying away from home. For instance, 'some business trips involve attending a conference and are followed by a holiday'.[2] Broadly speaking, the 'travellers' are served by the commercial hotels chains, and the non-travelling customers by the not-for-profit sector.

In the commercial hotel sector, hotel guests can be divided into two main sources, 'geographically from domestic and foreign markets of origin, and, from a distribution viewpoint, direct or through intermediaries in the travel industry'.[3] This report reveals that in 1988, 36 per cent of hotel reservations were made directly by the client, 28 per cent through travel agents and tour operators, and 25 per cent through the burgeoning number of central reservations systems. This latter method has led to billions of pounds of investment by the large international chains as they try to bind their clients, both direct customers and travel agents, into making a series of reservations through one computerized reservation centre. Table 2.1 illustrates sources of demand by certain categories of individual and by continental and overall dimension. It is instructive to compare the relative percentages of business travellers, tourists and, in this study, the conference delegates. It illustrates the state of the market for different parts of the world, and indicates the forms of accommodation development that need to be developed by the international players.

It is now necessary to look at the major demand sources in a little more detail. Clearly, the more specific market sector chapters that follow will concentrate more closely on the relationship between the market segment and the accommodation provision for that segment.

Business Travellers

The purposes of business travel and the subsequent need for accommodation may be summarized as the need for company management to attend meetings, undertake sales visits, to attend conferences or conventions, to attend trade exhibitions and training or management development courses. According to the Economist Intelligence Unit,[4] 55 per cent of all such travellers stay in hotels. For the larger properties in the main cities and commercial areas, this business is crucial. It fills midweek rooms out of holiday times, it is often at a high rate and volume, and therefore highly profitable. The London-based group Edwardian Hotels claim that 64 per cent of all their business is generated from this market, and that 40 per cent of that is from the United States.[5]

What are the priorities to the business traveller in selecting a particular hotel? A major survey of business people has itemized their key decision-making factors. Location and its convenience was predictably high on the list of priorities, as well as transport schedules and the overall comfort of the accommodation, summarized as 'a business setting in comfortable surroundings.'[6] This business setting must include efficient and sufficient business facilities, the office away from home. Many respondents, from both the USA and the UK desired 'corporate and recreational facilities', meaning the most up-to-date business centre, with all required modern communications technology, and a fully equipped leisure centre, on site and readily available for relaxation periods. Other important factors were staff attitude, and the ambience and decor of the property, with a concentration on room furnishings and facilities, notably features such as direct dial telephone, desk space and lighting, and trouser presses.

Major hotel companies fully recognize both the rate and volume advantages of business travellers and are adapting accommodation to meet the growing needs of this market for which competition is so intense. One such example is the mid-sized British group Friendly Hotels. This company's research showed that senior managers preferred to conduct business meetings in their own lounge rather than in public areas. In some of their hotels in highly commercial locations, they have built suites, 'so that the lounge area can double up as a temporary office or boardroom, with fax and work desk'.[7] These suites contain many of the features required by today's business people – colour teletext TV, radio, in-room videos and/or satellite channels, phone, tea and coffee-making facilities and welcome drink, trouser press, minibar, hair dryer, and personal toiletries, with a kitchenette equipped with refrigerator and microwave. Other companies have endorsed their increasing segmentation of the business market by offering executive floors to the higher spending senior management, often termed 'Clubs', where there are dedicated executive lounges, with permanent staff to arrange all business needs and to offer special facilities such as fast check-in and check-out and immediate onward reservations to other hotels within the group. The Tower Thistle Hotel in London has recently opened just such an executive floor, known as the 'City Club', with the stated aim of being a more attractive venue for high level executives, especially 'if we could create a smaller hotel inside the hotel'.[8]

Another developing business travel opportunity emanates from the aforementioned demographic trends and the increasing number of women in senior positions. Companies are attempting to offer women a superior product and service tailored to their specific needs. The New World Victoria Hotel in Hong Kong calculated that no less than 41 per cent of its business and leisure travellers were women.[9] This is in line with figures from the US Travel Data Center, reporting that 40 per cent of all business travellers are now women. The New World Victoria has introduced a series of measures to afford greater personal security and comfort. For example, it offers to meet guests at the airport and drive them to the hotel, and has added door safety locks and extra patrolling security guards. On the comfort front, the hotel has ensured that rooms have full-length mirrors, skirt hangers in wardrobes and up-market bathroom accessories. Other hotel companies and indeed many female executives themselves prefer to receive the standard product and service, including many of the above features, rather than be singled out.

Another source of demand connected to the business world is that known as 'incentive travel'. Many firms are using travel and holidays as a motivational tool for its successful employees as rewards for excellent performance, particularly where targets have been met, notably within the sales departments. The value of this market to the accommodation industry has been estimated at $4.2 billion in Europe and $5.7 billion in North America.[10] Furthermore this business is expected to increase at perhaps 13 per cent per year until the year 2000. Much will depend on national taxation policies.

Recreational Travellers

According to the Economist Intelligence Unit, about 33 per cent of total worldwide demand for accommodation is leisure-oriented. A vast market, it is the rival of business travel in many parts of the globe, as previously illustrated by Table 2.1. Yet the tourist market has features which set it apart from the business sector. It is far more price-sensitive, or price-elastic, as tourists are paying from their own pockets, not from a company travel budget. It is also highly sensitive to economic conditions, both in the country of origin and the country of destination, and is greatly affected by political circumstances such as terrorism and civil unrest in once popular tourist locations. Individually, recreational travellers are subject to the leisure time and disposable income available, as well as basic necessities and considerations such as transportation, weather prospects, and even the status or image of a destination.

Goodall[11] discusses the factors which affect a person's choice of holiday, relating to the 'push' and 'pull' influences: 'A distinction should be made between the role of motivations which PUSH a holiday-maker into a decision and the attraction exercised by holiday images which PULL the holiday-maker towards a particular holiday and destination.' The 'push' factors include an individual's specific motivations, goals and personal preferences: in other words, their criteria for what they want to get out of a holiday. The 'pull' factors are tied up with the images of the destination and the products and services it has to offer. This will include perceptions about the level of hospitality, the quality of hotel accommodation, and other 'perceived attributes' like climate, scenery, history and culture. Accommodation and hospitality is a vital component part of this scenario, and companies and individual businesses must play a leading role in projecting the appropriate image, and becoming strongly associated with the all-important attraction element of a recreational travel location.

The accommodation industry must also be aware of the amount of time available for recreational travel their many and various potential markets may possess. There are tremendous differences across national boundaries with regard to working hours and holiday entitlements. For instance, according to research by the Union Bank of Switzerland, the average worker in a European city, such as Brussels or London, works around 1700 hours in a year, compared with over 2000 hours in the Far East. Likewise, a worker in Amsterdam on average has nearly 35 vacation days each year, whereas in Hong Kong the average is only eight.

One more source of accommodation demand connected to the individual traveller rather than the business community is that of 'personal travel'. Consultants Horwath and Horwath rate this as high as 9 per cent of worldwide demand. The reasons for this form of travel are normally concerned with visiting friends and relatives, job seeking, house hunting and regrettably unfortunate circumstances such as serious illness or funerals. This market is stable, though the trips are often unavoidable, and it is another price-elastic demand as the cost is nearly always borne by the traveller. Many accommodation outlets have constructed special rates for this type of travel, particularly the visiting friends and relatives sector, known within hotel reservations departments as the VFR rate. Christmas and New Year, and other occasions of family celebrations, are notable VFR periods, and many hoteliers believe this is an untapped source of income as it has been estimated that only 25 per cent of people visiting family or friends actually stay in hotels.

Institutional Residential Demand

As well as demand from business and leisure travellers, a very large number of people stay overnight away from home in 'institutions'. Such institutions include hospitals, prisons, residential care facilities, university, college hostels, YMCA, YWCA, and accommodation related to outward bound training courses.

THE NATURE OF THE ACCOMMODATION EXPERIENCE

In the past the need was for the simplest form of overnight accommodation, as the term 'bed and breakfast' implies. For many people, the very thought of staying away from home was an unusual and intimidating prospect. It was also seen as a luxury and a significant aspect of an individual's development and maturity. However, across all markets, especially within

Figure 2.1 Typical budget hotel bedroom (Courtyard Marriott, Leamington Spa).
Source: Marriott Hotels.

Figure 2.2 Typical mid-price hotel bedroom (Strathallan Hotel).
Source: Mount Charlotte Thistle Hotels.

the last 50 years, consumers have demanded more and more sophisticated accommodation and services. More travel, and tourist holidays overseas, has increased the expectation of hotel, hostel and even hospital users. Accommodation consisting of little other than the bed itself has been augmented by washing facilities, from washstands to hand basins to bathrooms; by comfort facilities, from bedside tables to armchairs to suites; and by entertainment facilities, from radio to television to in-house video.

All parts of the hotel industry in particular are striving to improve their amenities and invest in better products and services, from en-suite bathrooms to leisure equipment and business-oriented technology. Increasingly they are having to respond to the demands of their markets, markets which seek choice and quality as well as affordable prices. Small hotels and guest houses, often at seaside resorts, now proudly boast private bathrooms, sauna and solarium, even a swimming pool and mini-gymnasium. Hotel chains and other multi-unit organizations have attempted to reach all sectors of the accommodation market, from so-called budget hotels, to mid-priced commercially oriented properties, and to top-of-the-range exclusive and internationally renowned outlets. These are illustrated in Figures 2.1, 2.2 and 2.3.

These developments in accommodation have been triggered by the needs of the customer. The principle markets for accommodation, the leisure traveller and the business traveller, need some duplicate facilities but also some crucially differing services. The person or family on holiday needs a home from home, with furnishings and service that

Figure 2.3 Typical luxury hotel bedroom (Mottram Hall Hotel).
Source: De Vere Hotels.

enhance comfort and indulgence. The business person or conference delegate needs an office away from home, with all the administrative and technological communication resources that enhance efficiency and purpose. Everyone expects high quality and value for money.

The provision of overnight accommodation is greatly influenced by the economics of both developed and developing nations. The commercial sector is particularly susceptible to changes in the social and economic environment of its customers and markets, and these various factors need to be understood. With regard to the industry's place in the wider issue of economic development, it is useful to consider a model constructed by Kleinwort Benson Securities,[12] referred to as a structural theory of hotel business demand, and therefore assessing the relationship between an economy and the demand for accommodation by business travellers and companies. This theory identifies three phases in an economy's growth which in turn exert a varying influence on the demand for hotel accommodation.

The first phase is an economy where activity is predominantly manufacturing, and business people need hotels for overnight stays only, during trips to different areas of the country to sell and promote the products. These clients tend to be middle-ranking executives from single-unit companies and the demand is neither consistent nor particularly lucrative. Phase two is when the service industry begins to assume dominance, as in the UK of the 1980s. Companies within this sector tend to develop into multi-unit concerns, as personified by retail, banking and other consumer-based services. Such an economy boosts the demand for hotel accommodation, often directly associated with corporate gatherings such as sales meetings and training courses. Phase three shows demand stabilizing and any growth is at a much slower rate. Organizations are now developing their own corporate centres and regional networks which may reduce the need for employees to be increasingly away from home.

All accommodation businesses should also be aware of wider socioeconomic changes which in time fundamentally affect the environment and the demand for residential outlets. In particular it is important to draw attention to demographics; that is, the structure and profile of populations, and the concept of disposable income, 'the amount of money people actually have available to them to spend or invest'.[13] With regard to the former, the UK must recognize that it has an ageing population, as do most western economies, including the United States and the European Union (excepting Portugal and the Republic of Ireland). The number of people over pensionable age in the UK is projected to exceed 16 million by the year 2031, more than double the number in 1961. This equates economically to 46 people of pensionable age for every 100 of working age, also about double the 1961 figures. It is for national governments to consider the implications of these statistics regarding economic activity, social policies and taxation. For the hospitality and accommodation sector there are other potential outcomes to review.

The industry must realize the changing profile of its markets, its consumers, and indeed its workforce. The effects of lower birth-rates from the 1970s, and rapidly improving life expectancy, are having considerable longer-term impact upon the developed countries' populations. As a result, there is an ever-larger group of the population in the age band from 25 years to 44 years. People in this bracket are often young professionals, middle and senior managers at the height of their business careers. They are often two-income families, using hotels and travel for pleasure as well as business, 'broadening personal experience'. They tend to be relatively affluent, status conscious and particularly aware of brand names, a situation not lost on many of today's market leaders.[14] Population changes and changing work patterns are also contributing to more and more women in the workforce, many at senior management levels as more women return from maternity leave or delay starting a family until well into their thirties.

The ageing population is most notable at the age of 45 years and beyond, an age band often now termed by marketing managers as the third age. Apart from living longer, older people are generally healthier than previous generations, and more active, and many now have the time and the disposable income to commit more expenditure on leisure. Further, this age group tends to want more comfortable, full-service accommodation facilities. Statistics have also revealed that they are more likely to stay at home for holidays, whereas the 25-to-44-age-band members are most likely to go abroad.[15] Other demographically influenced factors to be considered are the steady, ever-present demand for the family holiday, the increasing number of single female business travellers, and the larger number of people desiring and being able to afford short breaks and activity holidays.

The *Social Trends* report of 1994 also clearly indicates that disposable income is generally increasing within the UK. It reports that disposable income per capita is now 80 per cent higher than in 1971. Its analysis of household expenditure shows not only significant rises in spending on catering specifically, but that income and time devoted to leisure, recreation and entertainment have soared. In 1966, 7 per cent of the UK population took two or more holidays. In 1992 that figure had risen to 24 per cent, and in the same year, expenditure on leisure represented 17 per cent of the household budget.

SIZE AND SCOPE OF THE ACCOMMODATION SECTOR

The increase in demand for leisure and business accommodation has been international, with a resultant development in competition, especially for the multi-unit, global organizations. It is these companies that have become the innovators and developers of the essential facets of the hospitality experience. Many of these firms have emanated from the United States, the United Kingdom and France. Kleinwort Benson Securities illustrated this fact graphically in their Fifth Annual Review of stock market quoted companies in the hotel industry.[16] Around 83 per cent of the quoted hotel rooms in the world are controlled from these countries. Examples of such organizations are the Marriott Corporation from the USA, Forte Hotels from the UK, and Accor from France. In all these cases, such companies have been national first and international second. 'The most common pattern has been for hotel chains to evolve and expand towards national coverage within their home country before attempting international expansion.'

This fast international development in hospitality accommodation has led to a range of types of organization and business formats, from wholly owned businesses to franchises, to joint ventures and firms specializing in management contracts. As a result we have an increasingly complex and inter-linked industry, with many brand names and business concepts. Few members of the public know that Hilton International is owned by Ladbroke, the British leisure and betting shop firm, or that Holiday Inn is part of Bass, the UK brewing giant. Individually owned properties join together in marketing consortia, and yet seem to be part of international groups such as Best Western or Logis of Great Britain. The Heathrow Marriott Hotel is actually owned by Scotts Hotels of Canada, but Marriott hold the franchise and hence the brand name.

A form of hospitality conglomerate has developed, epitomized by the USA-based Hospitality Franchise Systems (HFS), the largest hotel chain in the world in 1993, with 384,442 rooms worldwide. Yet within HFS there are many autonomous groups with well-known names, with accommodation targeted at different markets, such as Ramada, Howard Johnson Motels, and Days Inns. Accor, the French hospitality leader, had nine brand names at the last count, including Novotel, Sofitel, Ibis and Formule 1. Table 2.2 shows the size and international scale of the accommodation business today. The hospitality experience has indeed come a long way from 'bed and breakfast'.

Another recent factor is the greater participation of hotel companies and investors from the Far East and Third World nations as their governments recognize the enormous value and potential of international tourism and business travel. Accommodation as part of the wider hospitality experience is a clear function of economic growth. 'The range of goods used by the hotel industry is vast and covers most of the manufacturing base of an economy, from building materials to the full range of furniture and fittings. Moreover, hotels also use the full range of professional services from advertising agents to merchant banks.'

Yet the hospitality accommodation experience is about much more than economics, global representation and sophisticated products and services. Above all it is about the

Table 2.2   Top 15 hotel chains, 1993.

Rank	Hotel chain	No. of rooms
1.	Hospitality Franchise Systems	384,442
2.	Holiday Inn World Wide	340,881
3.	Best Western International	272.743
4.	Accor	250,319
5.	Choice Hotels International	229,784
6.	Marriott International	173,048
7.	ITT Sheraton Corp.	129,714
8.	Hilton Hotels Corp.	94,924
9.	Forte	78,691
10.	Promus Cos.	78,309
11.	Hyatt Hotels/Hyatt International	76,057
12.	Carlson/Radisson/Colony	75,986
13.	Club Méditerranée SA	65,128
14.	New World/Renaissance Hotels	55,591
15.	Hilton International	52,930

human element of service, and the fulfilment of the specific needs of the customer. Indeed, as hotels in a particular market segment become more physically similar, as their facilities become standardized and predictable, so the aspects of service and quality become the competitive edge between hotels and companies. Businesses now recognize and give full strategic attention to the components of such service and quality. They are properly concerned with human resource management, with providing their employees with better training and work conditions, with understanding their customers' needs more carefully and responding effectively to them. President of the American chain Four Seasons Hotels, Isadore Sharp, summarizes it as follows: 'Until the late 1980's, most hospitality companies saw service as peripheral. Now, competition is driving service to the top of the corporate agenda'.[17]

It is also important to place the accommodation industry as a prime element of the overall tourism industry. For this purpose a tourist may be considered to be a traveller for pleasure, or on business, or visiting friends and relatives. 'People travel for a variety of reasons, to visit friends and relatives, to conduct business, or simply for a holiday'.[18] The scale and contribution of the tourism industry cannot be stressed enough in the economies of the world today. As an invisible export, acquiring large sums of foreign currency from overseas visitors, it outstrips the major UK exports of petroleum, financial institutions, civil aviation, sea transport and consultancy firms. In 1992 there were 18.1 million overseas visitors to the UK, up 9 per cent on the 1991 figure, whilst they spent £7.6 billion, up 6 per cent on the previous year.[19] Domestic tourists within the UK added a further spend of over £13.9 billion in 1990. The Annual Report of the British Hospitality Association for 1993 estimates that spending on tourism that is attributable purely to accommodation is 31 per cent, not including an additional 5 per cent as part of package trips. This compares with 25 per cent of tourism spending attributed to eating and drinking and 15 per cent on shopping and entertainment.

The actual number of hotel businesses in the UK is difficult to assess. It is dependent on the definition utilized. Residential accommodation may cover hotels, motels, holiday camps and holiday centres, guest houses, inns and boarding houses and hostels. UK data for 1991 shows 14,382 hotels registered for Value Added Tax (VAT) and 2006 holiday

Table 2.3 Analysis of UK hotels by turnover (£).

Turnover (£000)	Number	Percentage of total
24– 49	3,786	26.3
50– 99	3,261	22.7
100–249	3,639	25.3
250–499	1,875	13.0
500–999	1,035	7.2
1000–4999	658	4.6
5000+	128	0.9
Total	14,382	100.0

Source: Business Monitor PA1003, 1991/Key Note.
Note: Figures are for legal units, excluding those which are below the VAT registration threshold.

camps[20]. The total number of hotels and other residential accommodation seems nearer to 35,000. The British Tourist Board comes to a figure of 27,400, offering over 920,000 bed spaces. With the number of bed spaces (i.e. a double bed equals two spaces), certainly around 1 million in the UK, the scale of the hospitality industry's accommodation provision is enormous.

The number of businesses rose steadily in the 1980s, and VAT-registered hotels' turnover leapt from £2.75 billion in 1981 to £6.34 billion in 1990. Net capital expenditure, further displaying the importance of the industry in injecting prosperity into an economy, rose from £198 million in 1981 to £1.23 billion in 1990.[21] As mentioned earlier, this UK national industry, as with many other European countries, is still primarily based on smaller businesses. This is illustrated in Table 2.3. The majority of VAT registered hotels, therefore the relatively larger ones, had turnovers in 1991 below £500,000. Indeed the single most occupied band was a turnover between £24,000 and £49,000. Such revenue is derived from four operating departments within the hotel. In 1992/93 this was estimated[22] to be 54 per cent from room sales, 37 per cent from food and beverage, 4 per cent from telephone, and 5 per cent from laundry/leisure. Since this rooms revenue resulted from an average occupancy of 62 per cent, there remains tremendous potential for growth in the post-recession mid-1990s.

However in order to understand a hotel's operation it is necessary to understand not only its level of turnover, but also its operating costs. A report in the *Caterer and Hotelkeeper* in 1993,[23] in conjunction with Pannell Kerr Forster Associates gives a detailed breakdown of the UK hotel revenues and expenditure in the financial year 1992/93 by reproducing a profit and loss account for the UK hotels sector as if it were a single company. This is illustrated in Table 2.4. Comparison with the previous year clearly shows how the recession reduced turnover, and how the industry responded by cutting costs dramatically so as to achieve a higher level of operating profit on the lower sales figure.

Whilst the recession of the early 1990s took its toll on employment within the hotel and catering sector, longer-term trends still highlight a gradual increase, with forecasts for considerable skill shortages if and when the economic upturn arrives. The trend has been one of recession redundancies followed by a slow improvement. Department of Employment statistics show that in 1980 there were 241,700 people employed in the hotel sector alone, and that this rose by 17.2 per cent to 283,200 in 1990. In 1991, when the economic downturn really pinched, this figure dropped to 260,000. It is significant that

Table 2.4 A 'profit and loss account' for the UK hotels sector.

	1992/93		1991/92	
	(£m)	per cent	(£m)	per cent
Turnover	12,303.6	100	12,587.7	100
Wage costs	3,953.2	32	4,262.4	34
F & B costs	2,586.0	21	2,819.5	22
Other purchases	2,717.2	22	2,844.8	23
Operating profits	3,047.2	25	2,661.0	21

Source: Tarpey, D. and Walsh, D. (1993) 'Quality, service and rising costs', *Caterer and Hotelkeeper*, 12 August.

approximately 60 per cent of the workforce is made up of women, of whom 32 per cent are part-timers. Indeed around 44 per cent of all hotel workers are part-timers. Wages assume tremendous importance in such a labour-intensive industry and payroll is on average 32 per cent of turnover in UK hotels.

ACCOMMODATION OPERATING SYSTEMS

In Chapter 1, it was identified that a hotel was an operation made up of a set of 'core' operating systems, augmented by a number of 'ancillary' operating systems relating to the size and grade of provision. The core operating systems of any accommodation provision relate to reservations, reception, housekeeping, and billing. Each of these systems or departments of the operation will be briefly introduced. Subsequent chapters that look at each sector of the accommodation industry will explore these departments in more detail, as well as discuss the additional operating systems found in some kinds of provision.

Reservations

Most accommodation operations have a reservations system of some kind. This is largely because the operation has fixed capacity, that is to say there is a fixed number of bed spaces. In order to ensure the most efficient use of these spaces, and the most profitable use in the commercial sector, advance bookings enable occupancy to be maximized. Reservations can either be computerized or charted manually on well-established formats, often referred to as density charts. The overall aim of the department is to maximize occupancy at the best possible average room rate. Reservations may also be the centre for guest history information and guest correspondence.

Reception

Although accommodation operators prefer to take advance reservations, in many cases customers can also arrive on the day without an advance booking. Whether they have a reservation or not, all customers need to be 'received', a function performed by the reception staff, and known as the check-in procedure. Reception is a key method of giving information to guests throughout the stay, a customer care role sometimes augmented by the concierge department in larger hotels. Concierge is a point of information and also of many guest services in the larger city-centre hotels, providing the guest with theatre booking facilities and other travel and entertainment arrangements.

Housekeeping

The main back-of-house department linked to accommodation, housekeeping has an over-all responsibility for maintaining standards of cleanliness and the presentation of the principal accommodation product, the guest's bedroom. Staff and departmental systems are concerned with the servicing of bedrooms, bathrooms and corridors, including the replenishment of linen, arranging guests' laundry needs, and the checking of rooms for faults, maintenance requirements and safety. The liaison and communication between housekeeping and reception is clearly crucial in ensuring maximization of guest satisfaction during the stay, and room occupancy, ensuring there is complete agreement on the readiness of rooms to be sold and occupied by incoming guests.

Billing

At the end of the stay, all guests have to check out of their rooms and settle their accounts with the hotel. For individual clients, this will normally entail asking reception or cashiers (in larger properties) for their final account or bill. Payment is then made by a method normally previously agreed, and most often by cheque, credit card or charge card. In commercial properties, many firms have special accounts with the hotel and the guest merely has to check the particulars of the bill and sign the document. Payment is then handled directly between the firm's and hotel's accounts department. The summation of the daily totals of bills paid and accounts settled becomes the hotel's daily banking summary, the sales turnover attributable to a particular day's business.

CONCLUSION

From this introductory review of the sources of accommodation demand, it can readily be understood that awareness of the markets available is essential to the manager of a successful accommodation business. More than that, it is necessary to recognize the users and their differing needs, and their changing needs, as trends and socioeconomic factors alter and influence. Demand patterns change, market characteristics change, the needs and tastes of consumers change and competition increases. The hospitality manager must keep fully up to date with this turbulent and ever-changing market place, and be familiar with the principles of market segmentation.

Awareness must lead to action, and the successful businesses respond quickly and effectively, not waiting for the competition to take an unassailable lead. Already European and American companies are reacting to the demographic trends, developing new accommodation products with features particularly relevant to the older guest and the disabled. Accor have for some years been planning a new brand of Mediterranean coastal properties with full medical facilities and qualified staff,[24] and even in provincial France one can come across small hotels describing themselves as suitable for the 'troisième age'. Companies are also reacting to topical issues and concerns within their markets. In the United States a number of major hotels have started recycling and energy conservation programmes, partly to save money and partly to promote a better image, to attract the sections of the market that are increasingly environmentally conscious[25]. Hilton International has introduced a customer care programme directed at its increasing Japanese market segment, providing its guests with '*Wa No Kutsurogi*' service — meaning, 'comfort and service the Japanese way'. Part of this programme is a guarantee of Japanese-speaking staff and hotel literature translated into Japanese[26].

In recent years the drive to know your market segments better and respond to their wants has led many hotel chains towards branding their hotel products. We mentioned earlier the experience of Accor in France and Hospitality Franchise Systems in the United States. Through proper product branding, firms aim to win brand-loyalty from consumers who desire consistency in the quality and provision of goods and services. A recent example from the UK is the switch from Holiday Inn to Marriott branding by Scotts Hotels. Since Holiday Inn is now controlled by a British company, Scotts felt that the Marriott name would attract more US customers, a plan which seems to be working.

This differentiation of a group's hotel products began in the USA with organizations like Quality Inns, developing alternative products at different standards and different prices to suit different markets. This form of branding must be complemented by a sophisticated central reservations system, with the consequential ability to refer clients from one outlet to another, making immediate bookings, whether direct or through a travel agent. The loyalty factor can then be consolidated by repeat business recognition schemes, loyalty clubs which offer the customer ever-increasing benefits and privileges. Hilton introduced its 'Honours' programme in 1987 and in one year the membership was up to 1 million. It has even begun a 'Gold Passport Club' for frequent users and, for the most special deals and privileges, there is a special club for its 1000 top customers[27]. Clearly, Hilton believes in looking after and keeping hold of its top income-generating clients. Small, individually owned businesses and global hotel chains alike know that they must identify their markets, and provide the type of residential facilities at the level of price and quality desired. This approach will give their operators the upperhand in the increasingly competitive industry of hospitality accommodation.

REFERENCES

1. British Hospitality Association (1993) *Annual Report*.
2. Economist Intelligence Unit (1991) *Competitive Strategies for the International Hotel Industry*, Report No. 1180, March.
3. Ibid.
4. Ibid.
5. Editorial (1993) 'London hotels are recovering', *Business Travel News*, 22 November, p. 22.
6. Editorial (1993) News Item, *Time Magazine*, June, p. 16.
7. Ruggia, J. (1992) 'In progress', *Hotels and Motels Magazine*, May, p. 19.
8. D'Ambrosio, R. (1993) 'Key upgrade by Mount Charlotte Thistle', *Business Travel News*, 5 April, p. 43.
9. Knipp, S. (1993) 'Hong Kong aid 1997', *Hotels and Motels Magazine*, November, pp. 27—31.
10. Green Belfield Smith (1990) *European Incentive Travel Survey*, Green Belfield Smith.
11. Goodall, B. (1991) 'Understanding holiday choice', in Cooper, C.P. (ed.) *Tourism, Recreation and Hospitality Management*, Vol. 3, London: Belhaven Press.
12. Kleinwort Benson Securities (1991) *Quoted Hotel Companies: The World Markets 5th Annual Review*, Kleinwort Benson Securities.
13. Central Statistics Office (1994) *Social Trends*, Her Majesty's Stationery Office.
14. Economist Intelligence Unit op. cit.

15. Central Statistics Office op. cit.
16. Kleinwort Benson Securities op. cit.
17. Editorial (1992) 'Welcome to the club', *The Travel Agent*, 3 May, p. 48.
18. Key Note Report (1991) *Tourism in the United Kingdom*, Key Note Publications Ltd.
19. Editorial (1992) op. cit.
20. Key Note Report op. cit.
21. Central Statistics Office op. cit.
22. Kleinwort Benson Securities op. cit.
23. Tarpey, D. and Walsh, D. (1993) 'Quality, service and rising costs', *Caterer and Hotelkeeper*, 12 August, pp. 6–8.
24. Barham, K. and Rassam, C. (1989) *Shaping the Corporate Future*, Unwin Hyman Ltd.
25. Editorial (1992) 'Hotels recycle', *New York Times*, 8 August, p. 18.
26. Editorial (1992) 'In progress', *Business Travel News*, 4 May, p. 19.
27. Editorial (1993) 'Honour thy customer', *Direct Marketings*, May, p. 20.

THREE

Business and Conference Hotels

STEVEN GOSS-TURNER

INTRODUCTION

The last century has clearly witnessed the most unprecedented development of trade and industry, from national to international boundaries, from the western economies to the Far East. Driven by technological advances and a consumer-based society, economies have become more complex and volatile, and have moved from a purely manufacturing base to more mixed economies, often service-industry dominated. As a result the business community has assumed a vital role in society, and service industries such as the hotel sector have become crucial elements in the provision of necessary services to enable businesses to operate effectively.

The first period of rapidly increased business-oriented travel came in the 1920s and 1930s between the world wars. Companies began to grow, often from their original location; they began to distribute goods and to travel to inform consumers about their products; and they began to be conscious of selling and promoting. The advent of better forms of transport facilitated this new approach. This period has been described by Medlik as one of 'rapid development of transport, by car, motor coach, and by air, bringing new custom to hotels, which had to adapt themselves to the increasing restlessness of holiday makers, and to the increased volume of business travel'.[1] Since the Second World War, the importance of business travel to the hotel industry has very often superseded the significance of recreation travellers. Hotel companies, developing into ever-larger chains and groups, have primarily targeted business locations for new sites and properties. These locations have varied from commercial and market towns, to the major cities and conurbations, from business parks and industrial estates, to roadside and airport sites. In May 1994, the hotel group Swallow, based in the north-east of England, reported that 85 per cent of all bookings to its 35 hotels were from guests travelling on business or attending meetings and conferences.[2]

This level of hotel revenue from the business community is all the more significant when one considers that such trade is often at a high average room rate, high food and beverage spend, and at a much greater margin of profit than that obtainable from the leisure and holiday market. Across all industrial sectors, firms have become much larger organizations in the last 30 years, conglomerates covering the globe, with the subsequent need for national and international travel, for high-quality accommodation and services, and for impressive venues for important meetings and conferences. These needs provide the hotel industry with an outstanding opportunity, and the multi-national hotel chains are in a hugely competitive battle to win the custom of business travellers. Indeed, as we shall explore in this chapter, the entire travel industry is forming alliances and joint ventures in order to exploit more effectively the relentless growth in worldwide business activity. When one considers that the computer giant IBM has an annual travel and accommodation budget for its United Kingdom division alone of £15 million, one can understand the strategic significance of business customers to airlines, to travel firms, and to hotel companies alike.[3]

HOTEL DEVELOPMENT AND LOCATION

The location of business and conference hotels has been determined by the level of economic activity, by the characteristics and the needs of the demand from business. Centres of commerce like London provided an early impetus for hotel development, but so did the growth of manufacturing industry and the railways. Stations became prime sites for business hotels, some with direct walkways from platform to hotel reception. Indeed one of the most prestigious companies earlier this century was British Transport Hotels, actually owned by British Rail. Industrial towns throughout Britain were also key locations, as business people began to meet clients, hold sales meetings and negotiate with suppliers. The 'commercial traveller' entered the vocabulary and hotels began to advertise themselves with this new market in mind. Hotel groups still target business towns today, and the marketing manager of Mount Charlotte's Thistle brand has stated that 'we plan to have a Thistle hotel in every industrial city in England by the end of 1995'.[4]

More recently the motor car has become the principal means of travel for business executives, as sales of company car fleets blossomed and motorways and dual carriageways afforded fast and convenient routes. The 1960s saw the advent of hotels located primarily for the road user, such as the original Post Houses of the then Trust Houses Ltd, and the introduction from America of the concept of the motel, the motor hotel. To this day, hotel and catering companies seek sites near to the major roads and motorways, attracting the business traveller with time-saving location, ample car parking, accommodation, food and drink under one roof.

Locations have also changed with the changing pattern and structure of industry. The shift towards service companies and technological firms, and the decline of heavy industry and manufacturing, has meant that new criteria have entered the location decision process. Many of the new firms in electronics and consumer services relocated to new towns and business parks, away from the high rentals of city centres and away from traffic congestion and parking difficulties. Such firms also sought the new pools of labour in the developing urban areas. The development of corridors of electronics-based industry, as in the Thames Valley, also developed new centres of commerce in towns like Reading and Bracknell in Berkshire. Naturally, hotel chains followed the demand. The French company Campanile in 1992 planned a development of 12 new hotels near to business centres as diverse and geographically spread as Dartford in Kent, Wrexham in North Wales and Washington in Tyneside. 'Campanile positions its hotels on main roads near cities to capture business travellers and tourists as do Forte Travelodge and Whitbread's Travel Inn',[5] reported a director of the company.

We have already noted how the hotel accommodation industry has followed the major forms of transport of the day, from railways to roads, and more recently how the sudden development of air travel has influenced location of hotel businesses. The aeroplane has changed the pattern of international trade and travel out of all recognition. Since the 1950s in particular, travelling by aircraft for both holidays and business has become an integral part of the modern industrialized society. As a result airports have become prime centres for hotel development, and a drive around Heathrow or Gatwick Airport is a drive past a cordon of hotels representing almost every international hotel chain. Airports attract business people for travel, for meetings and conferences, and as the road systems to airports have improved, so they become points of convergence and convenience, whether or not the airport itself is to be used. As a result, airport hotels have become a hybrid of business and conference centres, with the additional market of airline crews and airline passengers also on their doorstep. The American-based group Choice Hotels recently opened its European flagship property at the Charles de Gaulle airport in Paris, including extensive conference facilities and fast shuttle services to and from the airport.[6] According to one report, one-fifth of all the major hotels built in 1990 were airport hotels.[7]

This latter example of international development highlights a key trend in the location decisions of major hospitality companies: to seek out the centres of commerce throughout the world and be represented. Already the recently liberated countries of Eastern Europe are attracting interest, with companies like Forte and Marriott entering Poland for example. The rapidly developing markets of the Far East are clearly going to be high on the agenda for expansion. One reason for such worldwide development is the fact that many hotel chains feel they have saturated the business market in their home countries. 'The history of the UK hotel industry in the eighties was the history of expanding hotel chains which grew to capture more than one third of all hotel rooms in the country. Now expansion is on a global basis', was how consultant Paul Slattery introduced the International Hotel Groups Directory[8] of 1991.

Before leaving the subject of location, a recent trend regarding the venues for meetings and conferences must be established. As businesses have reviewed their style and manner of conducting in-company meetings, training courses and seminars, so many have chosen to return to the peace and tranquillity of the countryside. Country house hotels have found some new and lucrative business as a result, and have found the need to create or upgrade their facilities for smaller gatherings of senior executives. Such hotels can provide a calm and relaxing ambience in which business people can focus their minds on decisions affecting the future of their company. Such locations may also provide the leisure element which many conference organizers now feel is a significant aspect. Hotels with golf courses are an example of this trend, where leisure centres are as important as the conference room technology. Scottish hunting lodges, historic castles and stately homes such as Lucknam Park are some of the venues now utilized by the business community.[9] In East Sussex for example, the 3-red-star Netherfield Place Hotel may often sell all its 14 bedrooms to a single company mid-week, providing the perfect environment for a relaxed meeting. This mid-week business is clearly greatly complementary to the weekend country house trade, especially out of the holiday season. Netherfield Place has had to upgrade its business-oriented technology, as so many business people now need support systems for their lap-top computers. It can also provide business executives with recreational pursuits, including archery, clay-pigeon shooting, and nearby golf. A leisure centre and swimming pool is on the agenda for the future.

SIZE AND SCALE OF THE SECTOR

The significance of business travellers to hotels is clearly illustrated by the UK Tourism statistics of 1990. These figures show that 66 per cent of business travellers use hotels, compared with only 18 per cent of recreational travellers. This importance is further endorsed by the analysis of overseas visitors to the UK in the same year. The average stay of business travellers was shorter, 5.7 days on average, whereas the holiday tourist averaged 9.9 days, but the business traveller spent £88.80 per day and £506.30 per visit, whilst the holiday traveller spent only £41.40 per day and £410.20 per visit.[10] The Economist Intelligence Unit summarizes the UK hotel industry as being, 'twice as dependent on the business market for room revenue, as on the holiday market'.[11] Its estimates for 1989 were that business travellers accounted for 18.7 million room nights compared to 9.4 million room nights attributable to holiday-makers, and that 25 per cent of that business demand comes from overseas.

The larger international chains have thus become more and more dependent on this enormous market. Key Note[12] identify that about 'two-thirds of most leading hotels' occupancy rates is accounted for by the business and conference market', and that Hilton Hotels, owned by the British company Ladbroke plc, has reported that 70 per cent of its revenue comes from business travellers. This international revenue from business is still concentrated on the USA and European trading areas, though Japan and the fast-developing economies of the Far East, such as Singapore, Malaysia and Korea are beginning to be greatly influential. However, it is important to note the recent comments of the head of the Carlson Travel Company in Europe, Geoffrey Marshall: '50% of the world's business travel originates from the U.S.A. – about 25% from Europe'.[13]

For hotels to maximize their revenues and profits they need to be in a mutually beneficial arrangement with the key players in this large business and conference sector. In particular, there needs to be a nurturing of key accounts – the multi-national corporations such as IBM mentioned earlier. Such firms have professional travel managers or buyers who contract specific travel agents to obtain the best possible deal on the travel and hotel elements of their executives' business trips. IBM (UK) Ltd, has contracted the Thomas Cook agency to work with specific hotel chains in getting the best rate available for its 2000 employees who regularly travel on business, some 35,000 bed nights in 1993, at an average room rate of £54.[14] These figures dramatically illustrate the size and scale of the business, conference and airport-based sector of the hotel accommodation business. It is now a truly global industry with a complex scenario of hotel chains, travel agents, travel suppliers, travel buyers and conference organizers, increasingly linked by the modern technology of central reservation systems.

These central reservation systems (CRS) have done much to augment the scale of the international business market. Originally developed by the world's major airlines, they have become the focus of all computerization of the travel industry. Hotel chains and international consortia of hotels are aware that they must be a part of such systems, that their own bookings networks must be linked to one of the major CRS, such as Sabre or Galileo. Only then can they be involved in a system which attracts business travel buyers, because they can book the air flight, the hotel accommodation, the car hire and any other travel-related service required in one transaction. Swallow Hotels has reported that in the year following linkage with the Sabre and Galileo CRS, it secured £500,000 of extra business revenue. The Holiday Inn chain, owned by the British brewing firm, Bass, links to

Sabre, Galileo and Amadeus systems through its own Holidex reservations network. Via 24 Holiday Inn international reservation offices, it is interfaced with 60 Holidex terminals within company head offices for direct input, and over 240,000 airline terminals around the world.[15] This system handles more than 70,000 reservations daily and over 30 million bookings annually.

MARKETS SERVED

When reviewing the sources of demand for hotel accommodation in Chapter 2, it was established that across the worldwide hotel industry, business travellers account for 37.1 per cent of demand, conference delegates 13.4 per cent and government officials 5.5 per cent, a business-oriented market of at least 56 per cent of total accommodation demand.[16] The profile of this market and the needs of the market is subject to rapid change. World trade is increasingly international and competitive, and today's business people need the services and products that a modern technological environment demands. However, the market can be segmented into a number of different levels and during the recent recession in Europe company travel budgets were often cut drastically and business trip expenses reduced. As a result a good deal of price and product differentiation has taken place, and the large chains like Accor and Forte have branded their hotel divisions to be attractive to a range of users and budgets. In the UK, Forte Hotels introduced a clear branding and pricing strategy, with a one price per room approach. At the budget end of the market, a business traveller could stay in a Travelodge at £29.95 per room, or a Post House at £39.95, or a Crest at £49.95 and so on through to its Grand and Exclusive collections of hotels, with service and facilities appropriate to each price level.

A good example of a hotel which caters for the business and conference market is the Heathrow Marriott Hotel, a 4-star, 350-bedroom property, franchised to the American chain Marriott Corporation by the owning company, Scotts Hotels of Canada. The hotel is one of 20 major properties at Heathrow, which between them offer more than 5000 beds every night. It is situated a few miles from the airport, next to the M4 motorway near Windsor and Slough. As a result it is a business and conference hotel as well as an airport hotel. The hotel has to assure appropriate service and product quality to a variety of markets, from business clients, to conference delegates and organizers, to air crews, to airline passengers (both in-bound and out-bound), and to a leisure market as well, the hotel being convenient for the historic tourist town of Windsor. The overall market must be considered transient, 43 per cent of guests staying only one night. The methods of bookings vary from 38 per cent booking direct, 34 per cent through a travel agent and 18 per cent through the Marriott central reservation system. There is also a reservation desk at the airport for incoming travellers, particularly Americans who recognize the brand name of Marriott as a familiar symbol of quality. The hotel operates within Marriott's 'Honoured Guest Award Programme' a frequent-user club giving benefits and privileges to regular customers. This is also attracting more of the USA market, as the company has more than 500 hotels in the United States.

The Business Market

The business traveller market is recognized as having particular needs, and bedrooms are being upgraded to provide better work areas and dataports – that is, facilities for lap-top computers to be hooked up. There is also an executive lounge with an area for meetings, a business secretarial service and complimentary refreshments. A basic but important feature for a hotel near a motorway is ample parking, which is free, and being near Heathrow there is a courtesy coach service to and from each airport terminal, also free of charge. Fast check-in and check-out is another crucial service. Business hotels offer a variety of room rates. At the Marriott, there are special corporate rates for company bookings, including a travel agent corporate rate for reservations through firms such as Thomas Cook and American Express Business Travel. Such bookings are subject to a travel agents' commission of 8 per cent. There is also a local privileged rate for those companies in the area which use the hotel regularly.

The Conference Market

The conference market is crucial to a hotel in such a position as the Heathrow Marriott, near to the many firms of the Thames Valley, near to the airport and to a confluence of motorways from all directions. The conference market is divided into those on a day-delegate rate, including room hire, lunch and refreshments, and a 24-hour rate to additionally include breakfast, dinner and accommodation. The latter is excellent business for the hotel, and ensures good take-up of the food and beverage outlets. Training courses have proved a particularly useful source of demand in an area where firms constantly need to update their employees on changing technology, service and production systems, and on management techniques and practices. There are two distinct types of training course delegate, from the course that is held totally within the hotel to the use of the hotel for residential purposes only, as many firms now have their own well-equipped training centres.

Conference organizers, like the previously mentioned company travel buyers, are the important people for hotels to satisfy in this sector of the market. All arrangements must be checked in great detail, and the hotel must deliver the promise and ensure that the conference goes smoothly. Particular issues are transport arrangements, including car parking and transfers, timing of the catering to be in line with the programme of the conference, and excellent communication between all the hotel departments concerned, from reception to the conference and banqueting office to the food and beverage team. Message handling is often a problem for all business people when away from their offices, and hotels must ensure this issue is dealt with efficiently. Leisure clubs and indoor swimming pools are an important attraction to conference delegates and business travellers alike, as they take time to unwind and keep fit at the end of a long day.

The Airport Market

Airport hotels also cater for a number of different sections of the airport and airline users market. Accommodating the air crews from various airlines is a regular and lucrative market. Pilots and cabin crew staff need regular stopovers in a nearby hotel between flights. The Heathrow Marriott has a contract with two international airlines, reserving a number of rooms every night. The airline agrees a room rate with the hotel, and often gives the staff a daily amount of money to be spent on hotel services, known as a 'per diem'. Air crew business has some special needs, with the emphasis on basics like efficient laundry service for uniforms, ironing facilities, leisure and health and beauty salons, as well as good transport to and from the terminal buildings, and in some cases their own lounges and recreation areas. They may even require black-out curtains in their bedrooms so that they may sleep during daylight hours between flights. Also, the hotel must be geared to check-in and check-out at all times of the day or night, dependent on flight times. Another airport-connected business which calls for fast flexibility is that of delayed flights. Bad weather, technical difficulties or terrorism scares can all lead to airlines needing to accommodate large numbers of people at short notice. Airport hotels normally build up cooperative relationships with certain airlines, with an agreed rate for food and accommodation. There needs to be a pool of nearby and willing staff to organize meals and rooms – often at short notice – for what may be hundreds of customers.

The final airport-related market is that of in-bound and out-bound passengers. Passengers arriving at airports often require immediate hotel accommodation, particularly after long-haul flights, or such a stay may be part of the original package. Many hotel companies form agreements with airlines and offer special inclusive rates for these independent travellers. Due to its American links, the Heathrow Marriott has partnerships with airlines such as Delta, TWA, and American Airlines. Here is another reason for being interfaced with the airlines' CRS booking networks. Airport hotels also try to tap the out-bound market, where passengers need to be in the area of the airport the day before the flight. Indeed, many airport hotels have developed 'Take-off/Touch-down' packages to include free car parking at the hotel for the duration of the trip, and of course there is the courtesy coach to take clients to and from the airport terminal.

With a market profile so business-oriented as the above indicates, there remain particular challenges for maximizing occupancy at business, conference and airport hotels like the Heathrow Marriott. There are predictable troughs in the trading pattern which need to be tackled. Holiday times, particularly when schools are also out of term-time, mean that a lot of business people are away on holiday as well, not travelling on business or attending conferences. As a result there can be some worrying weeks at Christmas, Easter and in August, when alternative strategies need to be adopted in order to fill the hotel bedrooms. Furthermore the age profile of many of the travelling business people means that they are precisely the age-group that have young families to take on holiday. Weekends can also be a problem, as all business clientele check out on a Friday morning to return home. This is when the leisure facilities could be utilized by weekend-break customers, whilst the function rooms could be promoted as the venues for local wedding receptions.

THE PRODUCT OFFERING

Business travellers now need more in their hotel bedrooms than comfortable beds and well-lit desk areas at which to work. Today's business market needs business systems and technology at hand in the hotel, such as the fast communication systems of today like fax machines and electronic mail. The refurbished Athenaeum Hotel & Apartments in London highlights in its brochure the features that many executives now look for in a hotel bedroom:

- CD and video in every room with free video and CD library service
- Two-line telephone.
- Voice mail.
- Fax and modem facilities.

Figure 3.1 Hotel conference facillitics (Swallow Hotel, Sunderland).
Source: Swallow Hotels.

- 110/240-volt converters.
- Full air-conditioning.
- Power showers.
- Personal room safes.
- Full valet service.
- 24-hour room service.
- Bedside controls for lighting and air-conditioning.

Whilst location, price and levels of service and quality remain essential factors, it is features like those above that are now being demanded by the top end of the market.

The products offered by this sector of the hotel industry are becoming more and more sophisticated, as hotels try to keep pace with technology changes in the office and in the area of communications. However, such businesses must not forget the basics of service and quality, and with this in mind, many of the business hotel chains are embarking on product branding to ensure consistency. This form of branding includes setting standard specifications, consistent quality and consistent marketing.[17] Many large organizations are implementing Total Quality Management (TQM) programmes in order to be absolutely clear on the specifications of service and product standards. The conference market has been particularly targeted by hotel chains as an area where consistency must be achieved. A wide range of different types of meeting room are available, as illustrated

Figure 3.2   Hotel meeting-room facilities (Swallow Hotel, Waltham Abbey).
Source: Swallow Hotels.

in Figures 3.1 and 3.2. Marriott has drawn up a seven-point 'no-risk meeting plan' feature to ensure success. This includes cost quotations, meetings with management, a guarantee of meal breaks and refreshment breaks being served on time, even a complimentary pager for conference organizers. Hotel groups are agreeing standards for conference table settings, from notepaper to pens and name cards, all with the group's logo and consistent print-style. There will also be a standard range of conference equipment available from flip charts to video-monitors and, for international venues, simultaneous translation facilities.

ORGANIZATION

The successful operation of any hotel requires the effective coordination of a number of individuals and departments. Business and conference hotels need that coordination to be both effective and efficient, fast yet smooth. The business person is often under pressure and needs to work quickly, and though courtesy is always necessary, so is speed of response. The management of an organization needs to be clear as to the needs of their clients, and have systems and procedures which ensure their satisfaction.

In a recent survey of business and conference hotel users, communication between

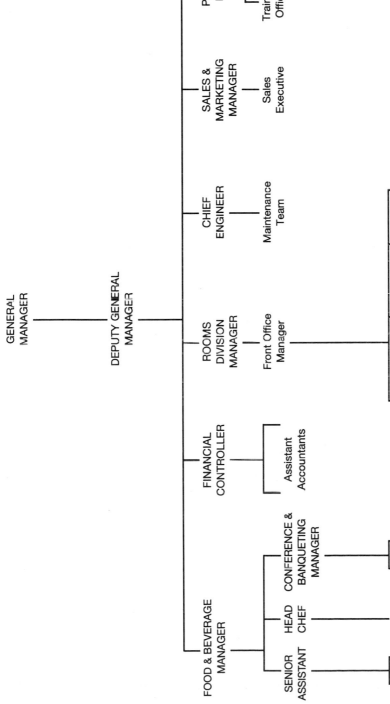

Figure 3.3a Organization chart of a 1980s hotel.

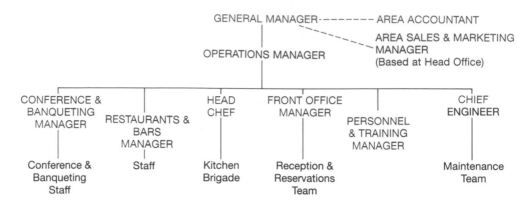

Figure 3.3b Organization chart of a 1990s hotel.

management and the key departments came out as the most crucial factor.[18] A successful conference, for example, is the culmination of many different people's commitment to the task. Though many are involved, the end result must appear as an effortless realization of the demands of the conference organizer.' Without a shadow of a doubt the most critical factor for any hotel/conference venue is to get their act together in terms of communication between management, marketing and front of house', said one organizer.

Increasingly, business and conference hotel operators are effective forms of service organization. Heskett defines such successful service firms as those that 'have a targeted market; well-defined service concept; a focused operating strategy; and a well designed service delivery system'.[19] We have already seen how hotel companies are going about achieving three out of these four factors. At the service delivery system level, i.e. operations, hotels are being radically transformed. Integration and communication are the aims of such an approach, and all must be wrapped in an appropriate management style and structure. Organizations are becoming less hierarchical with reduced layers of supervisors and managers. The empowerment of hotel employees which results will only be successful if those empowered are given the training and the motivation to enable them to grasp new responsibility and authority for the betterment of the guest experience. The most expensive reservations system in the world will be an asset in obtaining customers for a business hotel, but it is the service and the staff that will keep those customers, not only for the unit but for the whole group.

The extent to which hotel organization is being transformed is illustrated in Figures 3.3a and 3.3b, which show the typical organization structure of a business and conference hotel in the late 1980s compared with one in the 1990s. The striking differences in levels and hierarchy of management is an example of the delayering of organizations and the move towards empowering departmental managers and their teams of employees. The General Manager is more concerned with business planning and the future, whilst liaising closely with more specialist company personnel in the areas of finance and sales and marketing. The Operations Manager deals with the day-to-day running of the business, coordinating the work and communication between the departmental managers, ensuring that important business and conference clients receive fast and high-quality service, and that they are not subjected to the slow workings of a hierarchical bureaucracy. The emphasis is to be near to the customer not to be an unseen administrator hidden away in back offices. The simplicity of the organization chart depicting a more recent structure (Figure 3.3b), is in itself symbolic of the speed with which action may be instigated compared with the tortuous networks of reporting relationships seen in the first example.

CURRENT ISSUES AND FUTURE TRENDS

The development of CRS and global booking networks is undoubtedly still going to be a key issue for the future of business and conference hotels. It means that only the largest hotel chains and consortia can possibly consider the capital outlay involved. It is going to be increasingly difficult for the independent hotel to compete with the financial power of these multi-national organizations. Such organizations are spending even more money on advertizing themselves direct to the travel trade as well as direct to the customers. Alliances are being formed all the time, such as Radisson's move into Europe via marketing and reservations links with Edwardian Hotels of London and SAS Hotels of Scandinavia. Hotel companies are joining forces with the travel firms themselves, as in 1992 when Forte Hotels signed a five-year international marketing deal with American Express.[20] This joint programme included the promotion of Forte Hotels in American Express magazines, and the encouragement by hotel staff for guests to pay by the American Express charge card.

Paradoxically, technology could also be a threat to some conference hotels as videoconferencing becomes a reality. There is the possibility that business people will need to travel less and attend less meetings and conventions if more communication can take place via satellite television from one continent to another. Certainly modern dedicated conference centres will provide tremendous competition to hotel facilities in the major commercial centres. A recent example from Germany is of a conference centre in Kalsruhe with the capability of accommodating up to 16,000 delegates in all, in rooms suitable for gatherings of between ten and 5000 people, with simultaneous translations into nine languages, plus television cable connections and a video-conferencing studio.[21]

Traditional hotels may also find the competition hotting up from all-suite hotels, principally developed in the USA, but now often featuring meeting rooms and conference facilities. The Boston-based Guest Quarters Chain has properties with up to 250 suites plus meetings facilities for around 75 delegates. These suites include one or two bedrooms, separate lounge, full kitchen and bar, and a grocery delivery service if guests do not wish to use the in-house restaurant.

Trends and issues to be addressed on rather more mundane but nevertheless important revenue sources concern food and beverage sales and telephone revenue. Many hotels are reporting lower bar spends and generally healthier lifestyles associated with lighter lunches and breakfasts. Furthermore, the advent of mobile phones and car phones, plus charge cards, has greatly reduced the telephone revenue. One London hotel reported that sales had reduced from £4 per guest per night to £3, a significant sum over the whole year. It has recently been estimated that telephone revenue counts for about 4 per cent of total turnover across the UK hotel sector.[22] This is evidently a trend with serious implications for the industry.

CONCLUSION

The importance of the business traveller and the conference delegate has been established. The major international hotel groups will continue to covet this market sector, and will expect hotel management to respond effectively to the needs of these particular customers. The environment of fast-moving change requires management to keep in the closest touch with the market. Sir Rocco Forte, the Chairman and Chief Executive of Forte plc, believes that 'market conditions are more difficult to predict and competitors more numerous,' and that unit managers need to perceive 'a wider dimension to their role'.[23] This approach demands that operations managers are aware of the business world at large, in their local, national and international community. Above all, it requires managers to monitor the changing needs of their customers, the companies and the travel buyers, the conference organizers and the travel agents, the airlines and the airport managers.

However, hotel management must never lose sight of the day-to-day operation within their business. The business market demands high levels of quality, and in a highly competitive situation there is choice available in abundance. Service must be guaranteed and requirements fulfilled. The business traveller of today needs flexibility of options, not rigidity of routines in the way hotels are run. The implications for the quality and training of personnel are clear. Major companies like the Marriott Corporation are aggressively advertising the caring, flexible approach adopted by and instilled into its front-line employees. A recent campaign highlighted instances of exceptional customer service by specific members of its staff in some of its international business hotels, proclaiming how the company empowers its employees to use initiative in ensuring customer satisfaction. The business traveller may well require the information and communication technology of the moment, but he or she also needs to experience the real meaning of hospitality.

REFERENCES

1. Medlik, S. (1981) *Profile of the Hotel and Catering Industry* (2nd edition), London: William Heinemann Ltd.
2. Anon. (1994) 'News roundup', *Travel Weekly*, 11 May.
3. Craymer, J. (1994) 'Computer commuters', *Business Travel World*, pp. 20–2.
4. D'Ambrosio, R. (1993) 'Key upgrade by Mount Charlotte Thistle', *Business Travel News*, 5 April, p. 43.
5. Anon. (1992) News Item, *Travel Trade Gazette*, 9 April.
6. Anon. (1992) News Item, *Travel Trade Gazette-Europa*, 1 October, p. 12.
7. Key Note (1991) *Hotels*, Key Note Publications Ltd.
8. Slattery, P. (1991) *International Hotels Directory*, Huddersfield Polytechnic, p. 5.
9. Butler, D. (1992) 'Picking the spot' *Management Today*, January, pp. 61–2.
10. Key Note op. cit.
11. Economist Intelligence Unit (1991) *Competitive Strategies for the International Hotel Industry*, Report No. 1180, March.
12. Key Note op. cit.
13. Editorial (1993) 'Business travel section', *Sunday Times*, 21 November.
14. Craymer, J. op. cit., pp. 20–2.
15. Teare, R. and Olsen, M. (1992) *International Hospitality Management – Corporate Strategy in Practice*, London: Pitman Publishing.
16. Anon. (1989) *Worldwide Hotel Industry*, New York: Horwath and Horwath International.
17. Economist Intelligence Unit op. cit.
18. Knight, J. (1994) 'Star attractions', *Business Travel World*, July, pp. 34–5.
19. Heskett, J.L. (1986) *Managing in the Service Economy*, Boston: Harvard Business School Press.

20. Anon. (1992) 'Amex and Forte enter into marketing tie-up', *Travel Trade Gazette*, p. 23.
21. Knight, J. op. cit., pp. 34–5.
22. Tarpey, D. and Walsh, D. (1993) 'Hospitality GB – the annual report', *Caterer and Hotel-keeper*, 12 August, p. 8.
23. Teare, R. and Ingram, H. (1993) *Strategic Management*, London: Cassell.

FOUR

Resort Hotels

ANGELA ROPER

INTRODUCTION

At first sight the terms in this chapter may appear confusing and perhaps overlap with the section on small hotels and guest houses. This is because traditionally resort hotels have been known in the British market as those hotels located in seaside 'resorts' such as Blackpool, Brighton and Scarborough. Such towns have been dominated by small, independently owned and operated hotels. But this chapter focuses on a different set of accommodation types. Since the Second World War the term 'resort' in this country has taken on a new, American, meaning. To be a resort, a property must be in its own spacious grounds and offer a central basic theme activity, such as a championship golf course, with a wide range of supporting activities (anything from water sports to hunting), and be exclusive. As distinct from conventional hotels, resort hotels are positioned as destinations in their own right. In other words, there is no need for guests to go anywhere outside of the resort itself; it is completely self-contained.

There are two main types of resort hotel categories in the UK. Firstly, there are *country resort hotels* which are hotels located outside main towns or in the country with extensive leisure facilities. Although also enjoying peaceful, rural settings, country resort hotels with their extensive leisure and recreational facilities and profit motivation have a different emphasis compared to traditional country house hotels. They are operated on a large scale, often having 100 hotel rooms or more, and are either converted existing hotels/mansions or purpose-built properties. They are commercially driven, which has meant that they have had to appeal to a wide client base – business, conference and local markets – as well as to the leisure market which is also served by more traditional country house hotels. And they have responded positively to increased leisure time by adding extensive leisure and recreational activities to their properties.

Secondly, there are those *holiday villages and holiday centres* where the operators, such as Butlin's and Holiday Club Pontin's, have ploughed heavy investment into the development and up-grading of facilities and accommodation. If using an international definition of 'resort' hotels, these resorts would still not be 'exclusive' enough despite this investment. However, in terms of the UK marketplace their impact is still significant and as they share the other characteristics of resort hotels they are included here. The policy of these resort hotel operators is to provide a range of accommodation – apartments, villas, chalets and so on – as well as full-service hotel rooms, and in this respect they appear very similar to some resort properties abroad.

Figure 4.1 Typical resort property.
Source: Kirtons Hotel and Country Club.

This chapter therefore seeks to focus on resort hotels in the UK defined as country resort hotels, and modern style holiday villages and holiday centres.

SIZE AND NATURE OF THE SECTOR

Country Resort Hotels

It is difficult to gauge accurately the entire market size of this type of resort property. However, the number of corporate hotels is more easy to estimate, as the majority are operated by hotel companies in the UK. In 1991 there were approximately sixty corporate hotels operated by seven major companies – Country Club Hotels, De Vere Hotels, Jarvis Hotels, Mount Charlotte Thistle, Queens Moat, Stakis Hotels and Voyager Hotels. In terms of ownership, the subsidiaries of several brewery groups are important. The Country House Hotel Group owned by Whitbread plc is the main chain in Europe in this sector with 11 hotels and 1215 rooms in UK and Germany. All its hotels provide extensive indoor and outdoor leisure facilities. De Vere Hotels, part of the Greenalls Group, operates several country resort hotels with a golf and leisure orientation, including the world-famous Belfry Hotel. Guinness plc is the owner of the 236 room Gleneagles Hotel in Scotland, which is rated as one of the top resorts worldwide. Overseas operators have also taken a foothold in running commercial country resort hotels. One of the best examples is the Turnberry Hotel, owned by Nitto Kogyo.

Holiday Villages and Centres

The holiday village and centre market was estimated to be worth £465 million in 1993. The main operators in the UK are identified in Table 4.1. These may be classified into two groupings.[1] Firstly, there are long-established holiday centre operators in the UK such as Haven, Warner and Butlins, all owned by the Rank Organisation. Secondly, there is the newer entrant, Center Parcs. The latter was originally a Netherlands-based company but

Table 4.1   Major operators of holiday village and centre resorts in Britain.

	Number of resorts	Number of beds
Butlins	5	38,927
Center Parcs*	3	8,750
Haven	41	62,000
Holiday Club Pontins	22	34,000
Warner	11	n/a
Total	82	143,677

Source: Mintel Publications (1994).
*Author's estimates.

was acquired in 1989 by Scottish and Newcastle PLC, which already had some experience in this market as the owner of Holiday Club Pontins. Center Parcs, with only 6 per cent of beds, provides a level and standard of facilities similar to country resort hotels, especially compared with the other holiday centre operators. Based on this operator's success (with occupancy rates never lower than 98 per cent) another new entrant, Lakewoods, is developing a similar-style village in Humberside. This is a joint venture company bringing leisure operator Granada Leisure and builder John Laing together.

Both sectors of the resort hotel market sector in the UK are dominated by hotel and leisure companies. This matches trends worldwide. The results of a survey of 16 worldwide resort areas[2] showed that large hotel chains such as Hilton, Sheraton and Marriott commanded aggregate market shares of 70 per cent of total available rooms. Although there are still no resorts operated by these hotel chains in the UK, groups such as Sheraton have begun to look more seriously at the prospect of managing resort hotels in this country. Club Med is the largest European resort operator, with resort hotels in over one hundred destinations worldwide, whereas the most publicized resort in Europe has been Euro-Disney, located outside Paris, which operates 5211 rooms in six hotels.

THE RESORT HOTEL MARKET AND CUSTOMERS

Both types of resort hotel are more dependent on leisure customers than conventional hotels. In addition, although the core market for revamped holiday centres used to be the C2D socioeconomic groups, this is changing in line with new competitors (such as Center Parcs) and with country resort hotels, both of which are marketed as relatively up-market resorts to the middle and upper classes. Therefore, resort hotels now tend to be positioned as 'country clubs' offering peace and relaxation as opposed to excitement and entertainment (which traditional holiday centres used to provide) and target more up-market families with their high standards of service and accommodation.

Increased leisure time, the growth of the short-break market estimated to be worth £32.5 million in 1993,[3] the increased demand for mid-week breaks from the 60-plus market, and a greater interest in sport, health and fitness activities have all contributed to the new popularity of holiday centres in the UK and have moved them away from the traditional base of providing holidays for price-conscious families. Operators like Butlins and Pontins have been expanding their seasons and coming up with new brands in a bid to encourage a more diverse and up-market clientele. For example, Holiday Club Pontins has divided its holiday centres into four categories:

- Family favourites – nine centres targeted at the value-for-money family holiday market.
- Chalet hotels – premium accommodation in 3- and 4-star chalets.
- Reserved for Adults – centres aimed at customers over 50 years old.
- Coast 'n Countryside – centres that provide a base for touring holidays.

In terms of market segmentation, Center Parcs regards the overall holiday experience as the company's main attraction and therefore targets young families, young retired people and peer groups (such as squash or golf clubs), all in the ABC1 social groups. It does provide some meeting rooms and associated facilities in order to target businesses for conferences and training seminars. However, in reality the company has found it very difficult to mix markets in its Centers; for instance, business users and all-male sports groups are not easily integrated into a predominantly family, holiday environment. Its typical customer therefore remains ABC1 leisure seekers who holiday mainly as a family unit. Interestingly, up to 50 per cent of this core market are repeat customers (a very high level compared to conventional hotels). In the summer months more long holidays are sold, whilst during the rest of the year short breaks of up to four nights are more popular.

In comparison, country resort hotels target more diverse customer groups. Their extensive facilities allow them to avoid seasonal trading troughs by matching the availability of accommodation to specific, different market needs and also enable them to target local markets (a market actively avoided by holiday centre operators). They are geared more to the weekend, short break and overnight business markets than the long holiday market, their average stay being usually no longer than two nights. Although their guests appear to be similar in terms of demographics to hotel guests generally (usually between 35 and 54 years of age) they show a stronger bias than other hotels towards more affluent groups. They are also often popular with overseas tourists, in particular those from Japan and the USA. An example of a Country Club Hotel Group hotel is Dalmahoy Hotel Country Club Resort, near Edinburgh. Its target markets are the Edinburgh area for membership and golf; the UK for conferences and short breaks; and Scandinavia, Germany and Japan for recreation holidays or breaks during business trips in the UK.

Whilst business tourism, in the form of conferences and overnight stays, contributes approximately half of country resort hotels custom, an important additional form of revenue to these hotels is from their sports and leisure facilities. For example, annual membership of their golf and leisure clubs often contributes an additional 20 per cent of revenue. This can optimize hotel occupancy by adding up to 20 per cent to room occupancy levels. In addition, local membership means that they are able to replicate demand to other centres for overnight stays. Sports tourism is therefore as important to these resort hotels as business tourism. It is also a growing and lucrative market, for example, spending on golf tourism (holidays where golf forms the main part of the experience) by Europeans is estimated to be £1270 million per year[4] with an average spend of £224 per golfer. Country resort hotels such as Gleneagles in Scotland and Hanbury Manor in England have more recently become popular as incentive travel destinations. Incentive travel is used by all kinds of employers to reward their managers/employees for high levels of performance in the workplace. Incentive planners are attracted by the ambience, exclusivity, up-market image and the flexibility offered by the extensive grounds and facilities in these country resort hotels.

LOCATION

It will be obvious by now that one of the most important factors affecting the location of resort hotels is the requirement for extensive land. For instance, a golf course, which is an intricate part of a country resort hotel, is estimated to take between 120 and 175 acres of land (and of course several resort hotels comprise more than just one course). The Wentworth Golf and Country Club in Surrey is located in over 700 acres of land. Due to the high cost of land in the UK and the planning problems associated with such large developments as resort hotels, the growth of this sector has certainly been compounded. Many schemes have also fallen foul of conservation worries, a problem characteristic to resorts worldwide due to their requirements for beautiful, natural settings as well as the need to artificially landscape facilities such as golf courses and accommodation units (in the case of holiday centres). Having said this, Center Parcs develops only 7 per cent of a total site of 400 acres.

However, resort hotels are not always unwelcome additions to rural areas. They require not only a large population (anything between 5—8 million people) within a certain catchment area (often no further than a two-hour drive away) in terms of customers, but also a local labour pool. The Sherwood Forest Holiday Village (a Center Parc) employs hundreds of people on site, the majority of which come from the surrounding area, and it employs far more people indirectly through the use of local suppliers and firms. For all resort hotels, accessibility is also very important. Country resort hotels, due to their reliance on both business and leisure tourism, require locations that are near to commercial centres. Also, if they are targeting overseas markets they will need to be close to an airport or a railway station. The ideal location characteristics for a Country Club Hotel Group property are as follows:

- a total site of at least 130 acres, to include one golf course as a minimum (sometimes an existing course and clubhouse, with fine impressive, extensive grounds, may be deemed suitable);
- a large town/city within 20 miles (a good commercial centre), with a population of at least 200,000;
- a nearby airport or railway;
- close to a community that has some attraction to overseas markets;
- close to local markets for golf, entertainment and conferences;
- fast and easy access.

In England, Center Parcs' hotels are within close proximity to major cities such as London, Southampton, Birmingham and Derby. A further important location decision criteria for the group, throughout Europe, has been its targeting of countries with a very changeable climate, its 14 Centers are therefore located in the Netherlands, Belgium, France and the UK.

Therefore, although traditionally holiday centres have been located in seaside locations, new holiday village operators and country resort hotels have quite different location criteria.

PRODUCT OFFERING

Many conventional hotels have added leisure centres; however, these bear little resemblance to resort hotels. Whilst standard 4- and 5-star hotels in the UK have added on a few of these amenities, resort hotels are designed entirely around their extensive recreation and leisure facilities. They are year-round centres/clubs/villages where innovative and extensive indoor and outdoor facilities form an integral part of the resort. A country resort hotel such as Hanbury Manor, in Hertfordshire, offers the following products and services:

- 200 acres of parkland.
- 18-hole golf course designed by Jack Nicklaus II.
- Tennis courts.
- Putting greens.
- Croquet lawn.
- Jogging trail.
- Walled garden.
- 36 acres of *pinetum*.
- Clay shooting.
- Archery.
- Hot air ballooning.
- Horse riding.
- Fishing.
- Three restaurants.
- 96 five-star bedrooms.
- Cocktail bar.
- Swimming pool/spa.
- Health and beauty facilities (such as aromatherapy, massage, steam rooms, sunbed, sauna, facials, body treatments, hairdressing, etc.).
- Fitness studio.
- Dance studio.
- Gymnasium.
- Crèche.
- Squash courts.
- Conference facilities for between ten and a hundred people.

Besides offering the use of these facilities, Hanbury Manor also provides services such as professional coaching, lifestyle evaluations and tailor-made fitness plans. This example demonstrates that resort hotels provide a 'complete experience', not just the use of facilities.

It is these facilities which have helped develop the reputation of this hotel, and many other resort hotels in the UK, as an up-market golf and leisure-oriented hotel. Added to these facilities, the fact that such hotels often have a higher number of rooms than conventional hotels means that they can attract conferences and corporate entertainment events at premium rates. The sports and leisure orientation of resort hotels is therefore a key differentiating feature over conventional hotels, so much so that a company such as Country Club Hotel Group has become the largest operator of golf courses in the UK. In addition to resident customers who play the courses, the company has enrolled over 6000 members into its golf clubs and 16,000 members into its leisure clubs.

To keep pace with rising consumer expectations, all holiday centres are investing in better-quality accommodation, restaurant facilities and general comfort. Butlins for example, has undergone a £43 million accommodation upgrade which includes the introduction of new 3-star standard County bedrooms in hotels or Suites at Holiday World. Centres now also provide a choice of self-catering or full-board catering, a trend that reflects transatlantic resort influences. Guests can choose from a range of cafés, bars, and restaurants offering everything from a quick snack to a full meal. The provision of self-catering facilities has been the reason why holiday centre operators have often not been included in the 'hotel company' category. However, an operator such as Center Parcs provides extremely high-quality self-catering accommodation and the option to hire fully serviced villas, or even hotel rooms at the Elvedon Forest Holiday Centre in Suffolk. Each villa is relatively secluded from neighbouring villas and is supplied with an open fireplace, central heating and colour TV connected to a video-film network. Villa rental prices are not fully inclusive of all facilities, however – they only include access to the swimming facilities.

The Center Parc concept has more selling features than just high standards of accommodation. Perhaps its main 'unique' selling point is the central complex; this provides a sub-tropical atmosphere (it is covered by a transparent sliding all-weather dome) with shops, restaurants, terraces, sports facilities (Jardin des Sports) and the pool complex. The pool area comprises a sub-tropical dome (kept at a constant 30 degrees centigrade) with artificial wave pool and waterslide, bubble bath, hot whirlpools, children's pools, solaria, saunas and outside heated pool. There are over ten different types of restaurants and bars on site, ranging from Le Caprice, where average spend per head is £30, to the value-for-money Country Pancakes and American Family Restaurant.

Whereas other holiday centre companies have invested substantially in new product development there have been few major alterations to the Center Parcs product since it was first introduced into the UK in 1987. The newest Parc, the Forest of Longleat Holiday Village in Wiltshire, which cost an estimated £85 million to construct, has just been designed using even higher-quality products than the previous two sites in order that less investment will be required in the future.

ORGANIZATION AND STAFFING

The prominence of sports, leisure and recreational facilities in all types of resort hotels means that their organizational structures and corresponding staffing requirements are quite different from traditional hotels and holiday centres. Studying the contribution of different operating departments reiterates this point. Non-room turnover at De Vere's golf hotels is estimated to be 62.5 per cent of total hotel turnover,[5] compared with 50 per cent in conventional hotels in the UK; this incorporates not only restaurant and bar revenue but a high level of revenue from green fees and pro shops. Meanwhile, Center Parcs earn up to 60 per cent from villa rental, 25 per cent from catering, 15 per cent from shops and nearly 10 per cent from other recreational activities. As a result of product development, the company is likely to increase its average spend per customer whilst on site, so that in the future the contribution from non-villa rental sources will be higher. These statistics have obvious effects on the organization and management of resort hotels, and also mean that break-even points are harder to figure out due to the complexity of the operations.

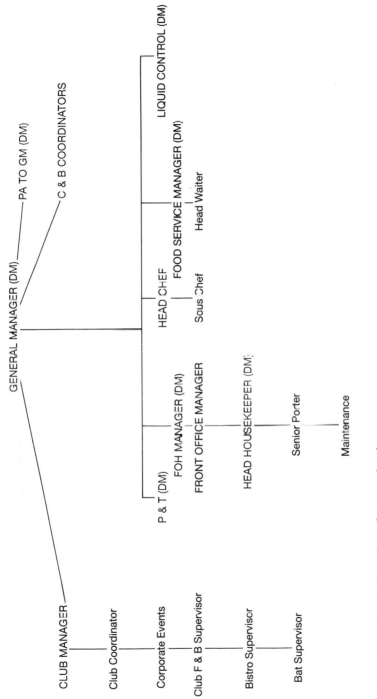

Figure 4.2 Organization chart of a resort hotel.

A hotel executive may know little about the different operational demands of the sports and leisure areas, therefore an experienced leisure/recreation manager has an important role to play in resort hotels, as illustrated in Figure 4.2. Golf, in particular, because it has its own etiquette and set of specific rules, needs professionals/experts managing the facility. They will have a better appreciation of customer needs and the confidence to know that what is being offered meets with expectations. Safety, of course, is another important operational aspect which must be managed correctly, and is made more complex by the addition of guests involved in recreational and sporting activities.

Successful resorts also tend to achieve higher occupancy and higher sales per room than other categories of hotels. Whereas average occupancy achieved by English hotels in 1993 was 47 per cent, De Vere's golf hotels achieved 67 per cent, whilst their room yields were some 11 per cent higher than other UK hotels.[6] However, corporate country resort hotels are probably the most expensive hotels to operate. They average a higher number of employees per room (due to their high service levels), and thus their payrolls are much higher than for other kinds of hotels.

Holiday centres, in terms of the number of staff employed, are large establishments. Center Parcs, for example, employs over 800 people in total, over a quarter of whom work in its catering outlets. In addition, occupancy rates of 98–100 per cent all year round mean that productivity is paramount. Butlins, Pontins and Warners are also reporting high percentage occupancy rates, in the 70s, as a result of their far more flexible and relaxed style and their more sophisticated packages. Over Christmas Butlins Holiday Worlds sometimes cater for over 62,000 guests. Just like other service sectors, customer care is an important aspect of staff training. Warner's operate a 'Quality Through People' customer-care training programme and Center Parcs has, as one of its goals, an approach to guest service that is second to none.

STANDARD OPERATING PROCEDURES

Once again, extensive leisure amenities, the scale of operations and the holiday 'experience' (offered particularly by holiday centres and villages) make some of the operating procedures for these hotels distinct. The economics of leisure and sports facilities are similar to those of a hotel. The purpose is to maximize yield through full utilization of capacity. For accommodation this means that all rooms/villas are occupied to their optimum capacity, while for sports like golf, all courses are fully booked by complete foursomes spaced at proper ten-minute intervals with the maximum number of playable hours.

Excepting changes in the weather for outside activities and the different popularity of certain sports, systems can be installed in order to maximize facility use and manage the capacity of these amenities. Corporate country resort hotels, for example, operate different 'use' categories such as 'peak' and 'off-peak' membership, and computerized booking systems for sports facilities are used by all types of resort hotels.

An important operational task in the large-capacity holiday centres is the management of large peaks in demand, due to their less varied demand and specified arrival and departure dates. For example, at certain meal times when all restaurants and snack bars are busy (on arrival days demand is exceptionally high), procedures that assist in managing these trading peaks include the use of queuing systems or, in some instances, bookable facilities. Services such as laundry are also often best contracted out in order to help with the huge demand for linen on changeover days. The prepayment of short breaks or long holidays also reduces the front-of-house operation (and relieves the need for a major cashiering function) on arrival and departure days. Center Parcs, for instance, requests that for bookings taken more than eight weeks in advance a deposit is paid within ten days of receiving booking confirmation and that the total cost is received in the period before the start of the holiday. For bookings within eight weeks of the holiday the whole cost is payable immediately. The reservations function of this company is therefore very important and it is also likely that, compared to conventional hotels in this country, substantial interest may be earned on these pre-stay payments, particularly as the Parcs can be up to 60 per cent booked two months prior to arrival.

Many non-accommodation facilities in resort hotels, such as retail outlets, bars and restaurants, utilize computerized point-of-sale equipment in order to monitor the use of these facilities and as a feedback system for recognizing demand trends. These information systems are particularly significant given the importance of these additional sources of revenue.

Country resort hotels tend to use the conventional mix of hotel distribution channels. However, business and conference houses, incentive planners and sales representatives overseas are particularly important sources of business given their characteristics of demand. Meanwhile, many holiday centres are keen to work with the travel trade; they all operate efficient booking systems and commission structures. Their long and short holiday breaks are easy packages to sell through this route and there is the possibility for agents to earn extra commission by selling add-on items such as rail travel to and from the holiday centre. However, in reality Holiday Club Pontins gains less than 30 per cent of its bookings through the travel trade and Center Parcs operates through direct selling only – in other words, its holidays are not available through travel agents.

CURRENT ISSUES AND FUTURE TRENDS

So far resort hotels have been responding to meet changing customer expectations and aspirations and the tastes of an increasingly affluent, more widely travelled leisure consumer. In the future, it is likely that UK leisure trends will follow the pattern in the United States. The market will then be driven by affluent and active middle-aged and early-retired consumers. Resort hotels, particularly corporate country hotels because of their quality of accommodation provision and high service levels, will be the best placed to benefit from this expected growth in active leisure demand, as conventional hotels do not have enough of the facilities necessary to meet this emerging demand.

The sector will continue to be constrained in terms of new supply, however, due to the sizeable land requirements and inclement weather in this country. In addition, all resort operators will have to take more note of the environmental impact of their operations. Center Parcs has led the field so far environmentally – in 1990 it won the English Tourist Board's inaugural award for Green Tourism.

The key market for the future will be the short break market, rather than the long holiday market. Holiday centres in particular should continue to target ABC1 families with children under 14 years of age, a group of consumers set to increase (by 1996 it is estimated that there will be 100,000 more under-fives and 280,000 more 5–14 year olds in the population).

Following overseas trends again, there is the potential for UK resort hotels to become more mixed developments. In other words, a hotel, villas, condominiums and homes for time-share could all be developed on the same site. The real estate opportunity could therefore be exploited to the advantage of those resort operators who own their own properties, extending their expertise into different accommodation forms. An example of an existing type of mixed resort in Europe is the Hyatt La Manga Club Resort in Spain. This has recently been upgraded in order to attract business year-round and to put it on a competitive footing with top-ranked destination resorts worldwide. The resort is set in 1400 acres and comprises a 192-room 5-star hotel, 72 apartments (ranging from studios to extensive villas in their own grounds), three 18-hole championship golf courses, an 18-court tennis centre with gymnasium and spa, a beach club for water sports, a soccer field, crown green bowling and equestrian centre, and a range of different types of restaurants. Interestingly, this is owned by a British company, Peninsula & Oriental Steam Navigation Co., although the group appears to have no plans at the moment to replicate this type of resort in its home country. This could, however, assuming investment was available, be the future type of resort development in the UK, given the success of present operators and the ever-increasing demand for relaxation and leisure.

REFERENCES

1. Mintel Publications Ltd (1994) *British on Holiday at Home*, London: Leisure Intelligence, Vol. 1, pp. 1—26.
2. Angelo, R.M. and Vladimir, A.N. (1994) *Hospitality Today: An Introduction*, East Lansing, MI: Educational Institute of the American Hotel and Motel Association, p. 125.
3. Mintel Publications Ltd op. cit.
4. Hegarty, C. (1993) *European Golfer Spending*, London: Golf Research Group.
5. Kleinwort Benson Research (1994) *Quoted Hotel Companies: The World Markets*, London: Kleinwort Benson Securities.
6. Ibid.

FIVE

Budget Hotels

KEITH JOHNSON AND WARWICK CLIFTON

INTRODUCTION

In contrast to most traditional forms of accommodation provision, budget hotels are a relatively new phenomenon within the UK. Up until they emerged, in the mid-to-late 1980s, budget accommodation in Britain was dominated by guest houses, inns, farmhouses and other forms of bed and breakfast provision. Consequently, budget hotels had to compete with a vast, and diverse, range of pre-existing, low cost accommodation in order to establish themselves and penetrate the marketplace. Where such competition was largely absent, as in the USA for example, budget hotels were able to capture the market more easily and, therefore, develop earlier and consolidate more rapidly. For this reason the motel has been a significant feature of the US accommodation industry for a much greater period than its British counterpart.

Given this historical background, it could be argued that the budget hotel is not a particularly innovative concept. Within the British context it could be seen as simply a repackaging of low-cost accommodation in such a way as to be defined as a hotel. Consequently, a new product is created by systematically stripping out many of the features of conventional, full-service hotels in order to create a lower service offering. This can then be provided at an appropriate tariff to the existing market for low-cost accommodation.

On the other hand, the rapid growth of budget hotels and the high occupancy levels that they typically achieve have been interpreted by some as evidence that a new market has been created. It is argued that a significant slice of budget hotel customers have never previously patronized other forms of low-cost accommodation. Viewed in this way, budget hotels can claim to be highly innovative, since both a new product and a new market have been established. The extent to which budget hotels constitute an innovative feature within UK accommodation provision will be explored in the remainder of this chapter.

DEFINITION

In order to understand the nature and operational characteristics of budget hotels it is necessary to define the product/service combination at the outset. Unfortunately, there is a lack of definitional consensus amongst both academics and industrialists alike. This leads to confusion as to which hotels are budget hotels and what are the requirements to become one. Through common usage the term has come to imply that rooms are offered at lower tariffs than industry norms and with facilities and services that do not match the usual provision found in traditional hotels. However, the lower tariff rates and service provision are not the only factors which differentiate budget hotels. Indeed, as these hotels have developed they have diversified and this adds to the definitional confusion. As Roper and Carmouche[1] point out, budget hotels should not be regarded as a homogeneous sector of the hotel industry as there is substantial segmentation within this type of provision.

Projection 2000 offers a basic but useful starting point. 'Budget hotels offer 2/3 star accommodation at 1/2 star tariffs. Mainly located on major roads, they are designed with 'no-frills' convenience as a priority ... The budget hotel has two principal differences when compared with a standard hotel or guest house: price and location.'[2] The key features identified here are those of lower tariff, reduced facilities and locational characteristics.

The reductionist approach to facilities and services used by budget hotels has called into question the appropriateness of the term 'hotel' when describing that which is left. Conventional hotel guide/classification schemes had difficulty in embracing budget hotels given their level of product/service offering. However, both the AA and RAC have acknowledged the importance of budget hotels and have altered their classification schemes in ways so as to capture them.

As the AA states:

> In 1987, the AA introduced a new category of hotel called 'Lodge'. This was necessary to meet the rapid expansion of this type of property throughout Britain. Lodges generally provide a high standard of accommodation with a wide range of facilities required by the business and leisure user, but often provide none of the traditional hotel 'services' expected, and the catering operation is usually housed in an adjacent block. Lodge accommodation usually means two star standard but for the above reasons, does not qualify for a star rating.'[3]

It would seem that any attempt to define budget hotels using only the tangible features of tariff, facility levels and location will be limiting. So much so that the word hotel has to be eliminated and replaced by the term 'lodge'.

The English Tourist Board (ETB) seeks to widen the definition by seeing budget hotels not only in terms of their facilities but also in terms of what these facilities might mean for customers.[4] It stresses that such hotels provide a highly standardized and branded product, with simple front-of-house and back-of-house operations, offering a standard national room charge (excluding breakfast) with minimal public/common facilities and no discounts. The RAC provides a similar insight: 'Lodges are designed to provide inexpensive overnight accommodation for the traveller. They are usually located on major road networks or on the outskirts of urban areas. Food service is usually provided by adjacent motorway or roadside restaurants.'[5] Despite using the term 'Lodge', the interesting features highlighted here are the use of the reference to the market as 'the traveller' and its general concurrence with the definitional characteristics offered by the ETB.

The English Tourist Board has followed the lead of the AA by recognizing budget hotels in their classification schemes by again using a lodge classification. This has been introduced to 'acknowledge the purpose-built bedroom accommodation that is springing up along our major roads and motor ways'.

In summary, the main features that these three major classification schemes have identified as being pertinent to the budget hotel concept are as follows:

- lower tariffs than industry norm;
- 2/3-star standard of accommodation;
- limited facilities and services;
- aimed at the transient market;
- located on major road networks or in secondary urban locations (retail parks);
- catering is usually provided by an adjacent food operation;
- purpose-built in terms of location and design;
- standardized operational procedures and charges nationwide;
- branded network of hotels.

It is a compound of these features that will be utilized as a definition of budget hotels for the remainder of this chapter. They are generally good-quality, value-for-money bedrooms designed and marketed in such a way as to appeal to the travelling public.

GROWTH OF THE SECTOR

Forte (then Trusthouse Forte) initially fuelled the penetration of the budget hotel in the UK with the introduction of their first Travelodge in 1985. As with other sectors of the UK hotel industry, the prosperous years of the late 1980s facilitated rapid growth in provision. However, whilst 3-, 4-, and 5-star hotels suffered at the hands of economic recession and the Gulf War at the turn of the decade, the budget sector flourished with demand increasing and outpacing the supply. Conditions of economic stringency seemed to have less impact on the budget sector. Indeed, the economic necessity of 'trading down' from high tariff hotels could have actually benefited budget hotels. However, this point should not be overemphasized since the building of new budget bedroom blocks did slow during the difficult 1990 93 trading period. The size of the sector and its importance, the major brands and their number of units is illustrated in Table 5.1.

Whitbread and Forte have emerged as market leaders with the Travel Inn and Travelodge brands respectively. Both of these groups have successfully completed a degree of synergy between these new brands and their previous line of business. Forte were in an ideal position to capitalize on this new market opportunity with their well established roadside catering operations of Little Chef and Happy Eater. Obviously, they already possessed the skills required to run hotels due to their portfolio of traditional units. Whitbread, like a number of other brewery-related companies such as Greenalls, already had a portfolio of appropriately located, low-cost accommodation in the form of their public house estate. Purpose-built bedroom blocks, adjacent to the public house and/or roadside restaurant were used to improve accommodation facilities and provide the standardization required of a brand.

The Granada group also saw the potential of adding budget hotels to their existing motorway service area operations. In a similar way the portfolio of Friendly Hotels was already targeted towards value for money accommodation for the business and leisure traveller. Consequently, the entry of all these domestic operators into the budget hotel sector was perceived as synergistic to their existing businesses.

The remainder of the UK budget hotel sector is made up of North American and French motel concepts which have been 'imported' into the UK. These imported brands

Table 5.1 Major operators of budget hotels in UK.

Brand	Hotel group	Number of budget hotels	Number of budget hotel rooms	Tariff (£)
Travelodge	Forte	92	3798	33.50
Travel Inn	Whitbread	59	2518	33.50
Granada Lodge	Granada Group	21	944	34.95
Campanile	Société de Louvre	15	913	35.75
Premier Lodge	Greenalls Group	23	834	39.50
Garden Court	Holiday Inn	5	576	44.50–79.00
Courtyard	Marriott	4	448	61.00
StopInns	Friendly Hotels	5	303	34.75
Formule 1	Accor	3	208	19.00
Sleep Inn	Choice	1	102	39.50

Source: Projection 2000.

do not have the advantage of synergy with existing units. They are sometimes handicapped, for expansion, by the lack of suitable development sites. This problem is not as acute for a domestic operator with an existing chain of underdeveloped roadside sites/units. However, the greater maturity of both the French and US motel markets gives these overseas brands more exposure to the operational learning/experience curve than their UK-based counterparts.

The majority of the budget hotel brands mentioned above are operated in an owner-operator capacity by the hotel group owning the brand. However, due to the highly standardized nature of the product and the strength of the brands involved, franchising is likely to become a dominant feature of the budget hotel sector. In the USA, franchising of budget hotel concepts is big business with franchisees continuously being sought by franchisers. It is likely, that with the involvement of foreign hotel groups (Accor, Choice, etc.) that franchise agreements will become as common in the UK as they are in their home countries. For example, approximately 75 per cent of all Campanile hotels are operated on a franchise basis.

THE BUDGET HOTEL CUSTOMER

It could be argued that the economic recession of the early 1990s could not have come at a better time for the budget hotel operators. With the standard of accommodation on offer at the lower tariff rates, the budget hotels were in a perfect position to capitalize on trends in business and consumer travel expenditure cutbacks. It has been accepted that the budget hotel has two main target markets through which to maximise its profit potential. The first and core market is the business traveller. It has been estimated that this target market represents around 60 per cent of all bedroom sales in the budget sector, and dominates the Monday to Thursday market. These transient business travellers are thought to be junior managers in large corporations on £50 per night expense accounts who would rather utilize the high standards of the budget hotel than use a local independent hotel or guest house with which they have no guarantee of standards. This business user has been joined, since the recent economic recession, by a large number of middle managers who have been forced to 'trade down' from traditional full-service hotels due to cuts in what is seen as unnecessary expenditure. The second target market is the leisure user. The average consumer now travels more frequently, further away from home and more independently than ever before. This trend, in conjunction with the increasing number of families who take short-break holidays within the UK, has led to more demand for affordable, quality accommodation in convenient locations. Room pricing is attractive to the family market with rates charged per room, not per person. This is also ideal for visitors who do not intend to physically stay in their hotel for the total duration of their visit. These are consumers who are not looking at the hotel as a venue at which to spend their time, but as a functional place in which to rest, eat and drink. This new provision has, therefore, encouraged a demand from customers hitherto not users of traditional hotels. These could be guests who decide to stop at a budget hotel to break a journey overnight instead of travelling straight through, or those who utilize the simple and straightforward convenience of the accommodation instead of stopping with friends or relatives when visiting. The budget hotel and its different culture and atmosphere from traditional hotels has, to some extent, diminished the class structure of the hotel system due to its informal, impersonal and simple mode of operation. The budget hotel is not a home or exclusive club of any one set of users, it is simply a place of rest which holds no barriers against usage. Due to its lack of public areas it holds no informal dress codes and can therefore be considered to have 'classless' appeal. This enables a wide variety of potential users to be targeted.

Budget hotel users appear to be attracted by the fact that they can pay for the combination of facilities that they want to use. Paying full price for full service makes little sense if you have neither the time, nor the inclination, to use the services provided. Slight alterations to the product/service offering can therefore appeal to a particular group of users and segment them for particular targeting. Segmentation of budget hotels has occurred in order to target certain user groups more specifically.

It is expected that foreign visitors will take an increasingly important role in income generation for the budget sector in the future. The French for example are more accustomed to the philosophy and culture of the budget concept and are likely to be a prime market in the south of England as the Channel Tunnel begins operation.

In summary, a number of different types of budget hotel customer have been identified. These include:

- business users down-trading from hotels with higher service levels;
- business users trading up from bed and breakfast style accommodation to standardized accommodation facilities;
- transient UK leisure users who are attracted by low tariffs – particularly for family occupancy;
- overseas leisure users already familiar with the budget hotel concept within their home market;
- first time/new users attracted by 'value for money', i.e. the ability to pay only for those facilities which they actually use.

The future for the budget hotel market looks rosy. The supply has segmented and niched remarkably early in its UK life cycle, possible due to the experience of operators in other countries (France and the USA). It is likely that the customer markets will continue to segment in response to their needs for particular combinations of product/service offerings.

Figure 5.1 The development of public house sites by breweries is evident in this example. This roadside public house has been developed to offer budget accommodation in the form of an adjacent bedroom block and with restaurant facilities being provided with the original 'shell'. The budget hotel concept in these sites is reinforced by the roadside presence of strong branding in the form of signage.
Source: Premier House

LOCATIONAL CHARACTERISTICS AND SITE CHOICE CRITERIA

As stated above, site location is of similar importance to price in the marketing mix for budget hotels. The correct location is the key to the success of a budget hotel. It must be situated in a place with easy access. Adequate car parking space is important. Land and planning permission must be available at the right price. These criteria therefore limit the choice of sites available to potential developers and operators. Budget accommodation cannot be provided, economically, on premium-priced land. For example, city-centre locations are off-limits due to the price of land, therefore budget hotels are forced into out-of-town 'secondary' urban locations on main trunk roads. This fits in well with recent building developments in the form of retail and leisure parks in out-of-town locations, and many new retail and leisure developments include planning for a budget hotel. Motorway service areas also make attractive sites.

Campanile insist that 'further growth in this sector will depend on finding the right sites in the right locations'.[6] The importance of national coverage and the creation of a nationally recognized brand has already been indicated, and is necessary if a critical mass is to be reached. Problems have arisen to some extent in achieving such a national coverage due to high land prices and poor availability of suitable sites in some regions. The South-East has been particularly difficult for the budget hotel developers who cannot afford the land prices demanded due to the necessity to maintain low room tariffs. So despite having considerable market potential, with the operation of the Channel Tunnel, future growth in the South-East cannot be guaranteed. It is those budget hotel developers that already possessed suitable sites that have been able to develop at the greatest rate, as

Figure 5.2 The diversification and segmentation of the budget hotel sector is demonstrated in the above photograph. This new-build unit at Milton Keynes typifies how the budget hotel concept is being tailored and 'built' upon to create a differentiated product. In this instance the building has developed from a bedroom 'block' of a standardized nature, to one of character to suit the demands of the environment, whilst still retaining the previolusly identified key features of a budget hotel.
Source: Premier House

illustrated in Figure 5.1. Forte's roadside presence through their catering operations allowed them instant access to ideal locations for accommodation expansion. Forte believe that they still possess some prime sites for development, but it is logical to assume that the first sites to be developed would be those with the most potential and that it is only the less-favoured sites which are left to be developed. Consequently, their rate of expansion will be restricted by financial expediency. It can be argued, however, that it would be advisable to develop as many sites as necessary to create a full national network of budget accommodation provision, even if some of the sites may not be as profitable as some of the others. A full national network of budget accommodation controlled by a central reservation system would allow for total loyalty from travellers wherever they go.

There are basically two types of site – existing roadside properties with scope for expansion and redevelopment, or greenfield sites. Existing properties by the roadside are often public houses owned by breweries. The property is developed by the addition of an adjacent bedroom block, often with restaurant facilities being provided in the original 'shell'. For budget hotel concepts on this kind of site their roadside presence is reinforced by strong branding in the form of signage. This is required because each of the original buildings is unique. Roadside diners, such as Little Chef and Happy Eater, may also be adapted in this way. Alternatively, budget hotels can be developed on greenfield sites as 'new builds'. In this case, the property itself is tailored and built to create a differentiated product. This kind of budget hotel development is illustrated in Figure 5.2.

The financial situation with regard to site purchase and development through to

Table 5.2 Site purchase and development costs.

COSTS		
(i)	Cost of land purchase	
	Land acquisition, 1 acre	350,000
	Plus legal fees @ 4 per cent	14,000
	Agent's fees @ 1 per cent	3,500
	Total land purchase costs	367,500
(ii)	Costs of construction	
	29 rooms @ £25,000 per room plus associated fees:	725,000
	Structural engineer @ 3 per cent	21,750
	Quantity surveyor @ 3 per cent	21,750
	Total construction costs	768,500
	Total costs	1,136,000
ASSET VALUATION OF THE COMPLETED UNIT:		
29 rooms @ £33 per night =		£957
		365 ×
Total income p.a.		£349,305
Target rate of occupancy @ 75%		
Target income p.a.		£261,979

payback is shown in Table 5.2. The stated cost per room varies from brand to brand from £20,000 to £45,000. Consequently, the potential profitability of the budget hotel concept is clear and explains why there are so many hotel groups currently seeking new locations in the UK. With one budget hotel operator quoting operating costs of around £5.00 per room night including laundry and staffing it appears that net profit opportunities are potentially great in both the short- and long-term. Not only do these sites represent a good return on capital employed, but it is also highly probable that the investment value of a completed unit would far outweigh the costs required to construct it. For example, the above hypothetical budget hotel would result in an overall value of around £2 million.

THE BUDGET HOTEL PRODUCT/SERVICE OFFERING

The main features which distinguish the budget hotel have already been identified. This section will outline in detail what it is that makes up the operation of a budget hotel and what the tangible components of the accommodation provision are. The AA identifies that Lodges must meet the minimum standards for 2 stars with the following exceptions:

- porterage need not be available;
- foyer or reception area seating to be available although its existence may be limited;
- writing facilities are optional;
- a bar is not required;
- light refreshment and breakfast facilities in neighbouring restaurant (where available) will be acceptable;
- room service is not required;
- telephone need not be provided in-room;

- 100 per cent en-suite facilities are required.

This demonstrates that the budget concept places less emphasis on traditional hotel services and offers customers a different atmosphere and product. Roper and Carmouche[7] argue that the budget concept is a utilitarian purchase owing to the limited product offering and that the customers' motivation to purchase is related to convenience and occasion. This leads to a parallel being drawn to the fast food industry where the emphasis is on the tangible product and less on the service (in the traditional restaurant sense). The product is 'trustworthy', reliable and standardized to allow for customer expectations to be met irrespective of which unit they visit.

It is the design of the accommodation provision that holds the key to the success of the operation. A strict set of standard operating procedures is made possible by regulating the design of the bedrooms and reducing the consumer/staff interaction. Campanile state that since their bedroom blocks are prefabricated and since every room is built to the same specification then any two Campaniles are identical. This is seen as a strength: 'If people like the product they will keep coming back, knowing what they are going to get and how much it will cost.'[8]

It is this concentration on the product design and operation at all budget levels that makes the budget brands suitable for franchise. The budget hotel is designed to maximize revenue earning potential, whilst maintaining low build and maintenance costs. The design then, is crucial to the profitability of the budget concept. Revenue is small in comparison to traditional hotels, therefore costs have to be more keenly controlled. The maximization of revenue-earning space is achieved through the design of budget hotels with few if any public areas, standard room layout allowing for easy maintenance and economies of scale to be gained from suppliers. Public utility areas in a 102-bedroom Sleep Inn are limited in size and these are low-service level, with cafeteria-style food and drink provision and vending machines. The 'budget hotel' does not, however, conform to these rules at all times. Even though the market is far from saturated, competitive rivalry is already showing in the sense that niche sub-segments of the sector are already emerging. These niche brands are competing in this value-for-money market by offering more value-added features or by 'stripping down' further to an even more utilitarian product in order to offer an even lower tariff. This sub-segmentation and niching was seen in Table 5.1 which demonstrates where some of the major brands fall in terms of price and product offering.

Formule 1, a French brand, has gone for the basic product with automated payment, room allocation and entry to the hotel. No staff/consumer interaction is necessary at all. Four rooms share a bathroom and toilet (which are self-cleaning) and only a pre-packed continental breakfast is available as refreshment. The rooms are very modern in design with metal and plastic finishes being preferred to wood and traditional bedroom designs. The Formule 1 brand has been remarkably successful in France, but is yet to achieve anything spectacular in the UK. The first unit opened in Doncaster in 1991 and is still only achieving occupancy rates of around 40 per cent, at a price of £19.00 per room. The Travelodge and Travel Inn brands appear in the middle of the market. They dominate, with over 60 per cent of the budget bed stock between them. This domination at mid-level budget is probably what has encouraged other operators to look for alternative methods of creating a differential advantage for themselves. Forte and Whitbread enjoy the benefits of being market leaders with a national network of accommodation provision and

> **Welcome to the Premiere Lodge Operations Manual, which has been written to help you achieve the highest level of standards, customer service and efficiency. Applying all the principles in this manual will not only ensure your customer's satisfaction but will guarantee that the same level of service is experienced wherever our customers stay throughout the Premiere Estate.**

Figure 5.3   Extract from a budget hotel operations manual.

centralized reservation services. This enables the advantages of critical mass to be accrued and results in average occupancy rates in excess of 80 per cent. All of these brands at this level provide an en-suite bathroom and toilet, with remote-control colour TV. Most have double beds and a bed settee. Whitbread's Travel Inn may have a slight advantage over its main rival Travelodge, due to its catering provision.

Whitbread, like Greenalls and other brewers, have realized that there are market opportunities within the budget sector by re-establishing the 'coaching Inn' concept. Their philosophy in the building of budget bedroom blocks adjacent to public houses or restaurants is that the majority of travellers would prefer to eat and drink in a 'pub' or restaurant than in a cafeteria (as with Travelodges being adjacent to Little Chefs or Happy Eaters). 'Business travellers do not want to be cooped up in their rooms all evening, after a quick steak and chips. Beefeater are comfortable pubs, where they can chat over a couple of pints, just as they might in their local'.[9]

Greenall's Premier Lodges have gone one stage further in the budget stakes by providing satellite TV in each room with a direct dial telephone. The trend in this 'one-upmanship' may prematurely kill off the budget sector. If all the competitors follow suit in this bid to add value to their products the resulting 'facilities drift' could end up providing just another 3-star product. For example, already at the opposite end of the spectrum to Formule 1 is Holiday Inn's Garden Court, which offers all the facilities of a 3-star hotel including conference and meeting facilities but without the traditional services. However, 'facilities drift' could occur in both directions, thus polarizing the market. Moving from the middle ground of budget provision is not without its dangers however. Holiday Inn is questioning the Garden Court concept as being too elaborate for the market place. A downward move to the Holiday Inn Express brand, as the main vehicle for expansion, has been announced. However, the no-frills Formule 1 concept has only been operating at occupancy levels of approximately 40 per cent in the UK.

MANAGEMENT AND STAFFING IMPLICATIONS

Where the accommodation has been built adjacent to an existing catering operation, it is likely that the same management (frequently a couple) will run both the food and accommodation operations. However, managing a budget hotel differs somewhat from a traditional small hotel. The reception area (if there is one) may not be manned constantly. Little direct supervision is required except for cleaning and maintenance. The cleaning may be contracted out to another company and therefore the staff involved in running the accommodation side of the operation are minimal. The standard procedures for each brand allow for little of the management's individuality to influence the accommodation provision; this is controlled by head office and a manager's main role is that of cost and quality standards control. An example of these controls is illustrated in Figure 5.3, which is an extract from a budget hotel operations manual.

Marketing is controlled most often by head office, with high proportions of bookings coming via central reservations services. Skill requirements are therefore reduced from the traditional hotel provision, with emphasis on retailing and property management rather than interpersonal skills.

THE FUTURE OF BUDGET HOTELS

It is likely that the market for budget accommodation will continue to grow at a steady rate for the remainder of this century. Some reports have indicated that the market may be saturated by the mid-1990s. This looks unlikely with growth having faltered in the early 1990s, development is now progressing at speed. All the main players are announcing plans for expansion and new players are entering or are expecting to enter the UK market in the near future. For example, Travelodge planned for a total of 113 units with 4467 bedrooms at the end of 1994.[10] Despite this growth, and a tariff increase, average occupancy continues to rise and is currently in the low 80s per cent range. A shake-out of the brands is occurring on an ongoing basis, with Holiday Inns' Garden Court looking unlikely to expand any further and may be replaced with Holiday Inn Express. Climat De France had an unfortunately short trading period in the UK. Its owned and operated unit opened near to Manchester on a retail park, but quickly went into liquidation, possibly indicating the importance of a critical mass to enable expensive advertising and central reservations systems to be put into practice. It would seem likely that the market will niche further with the brewers becoming increasingly involved. The budget hotel/brewer connection opportunity is demonstrated by Holiday Inn Express who have stated an intention to utilize existing public house sites as the food and beverage partners to this new budget brand. With their Holiday Inn attachment, it would seem that Bass Public Houses would be the front-running candidates. The competition at the lower level of the budget sector could depend upon the success of franchising policies by the brand owners and the uptake by franchisees in the UK. It is unlikely that within the next ten years the UK will reach the saturation point that the USA has reached. Budget hotels are here to stay and prosper for the next ten years at least in their current format. Technological advancements may enable further improvements to be made to increase convenience. Future locations are likely to include further development of motorway service areas and airport locations. Sites like the NEC could be developed if the land prices are favourable. There is also the possibility of budget hotels being built close to hospitals as 'patient hotels'. Budget hotels have carved themselves a suitable niche within the accommodation provision currently available elsewhere in the market.

REFERENCES

1. Roper, A. and Carmouche, R. (1989) 'Budget hotels – a case of mistaken identity?', *International Journal of Contemporary Hospitality Management*, Vol. 1, No. 1, pp. 25–31.
2. Projection 2000, Budget Hotels, 1991.
3. Automobile Association (1994) *AA Hotel Services*.

4. English Tourist Board (1994) *Sure Signs Guide*.
5. Royal Automobile Club (1994) *Guide to R.A.C. Hotel Services*.
6. Day, C. (1992) 'More guests stay in budgets', *Estates Gazette*, 23 May, pp. 36–9.
7. Roper, A. and Carmouche, R. op. cit.
8. Day, C. op. cit.
9. Gordon, R. (1992) 'Battle of the budgets', *Caterer and Hotelkeeper*, 17 September, pp. 55–6.
10. Baker, J. (1994) 'Expanding budgets', *Hospitality*, December, pp. 17–19.

SIX

Guest Houses and Small Hotels

ALISON MORRISON

INTRODUCTION

This sector of the industry can be said to present the 'human face of hospitality'. As far as the accommodation sector is concerned, the majority of operating units (around 70 per cent) have less than 25 bedrooms. And many of these are operated by the owner or owners of the property. It is therefore a classic entrepreneurial business that relies heavily on the enthusiasm and expertise of many thousands of people.

In this chapter an understanding of the nature and characteristics of the guest house and small hotel sector within the UK is developed and the commercial pressures and priorities facing operators within this sector are identified. The markets in which guest houses and small hotels operate are described. Organizational structure and functional activity of operations in this sector are explored. Finally, current issues and future trends are highlighted.

DEFINITION OF THE TYPE OF OPERATION

The small, independently owned guest house and hotel continues to dominate the accommodation sector in the UK, Europe and internationally. Definition of their activities is included in SIC 66 Hotels and Other Residential Establishments, along with motels, holiday camps, boarding houses, hostels and other similar establishments, providing furnished accommodation with food and service for a monetary fee. In general, the classification is governed by the Fire Precautions (Hotels & Boarding Houses) Order (1972) which covers premises sleeping more than six persons (three bedrooms), including both guests and staff. Further, attempts to define what represents a 'hotel' have been numerous. In some cases, these are legal definitions as in the Development of Tourism Act 1969. In others they are academic definitions, as for instance those by Burkart and Medlik[1] and Medlik.[2] Such definitions tend to be very broad due to the diversity of physical facilities, geographic location, markets served, and manner of business operation. However, they agree that a hotel broadcasts the fact that it is in business to provide accommodation, food, drink and other facilities in return for monetary charge.

There is however a legal difference between a guest house and a hotel. The Hotel Proprietor Act (1956) states '[a hotel is] an establishment held out by the proprietor as offering food, drink and, if so required, sleeping accommodation, without special contract, to any traveller presenting himself who appears willing and ready to pay a reasonable sum for the service provided and who is in a fit state to be received'. Unlike a hotel, a guest house has no legal obligation to receive *all* persons who arrive at the door, and has the right to be selective.

Guest houses also differ in that they tend to have the character of an extended family, welcoming guests into the household in a very person-to-person manner. Finally, the English Tourist Board defines a guest house as 'an establishment, licensed or unlicensed, which provides accommodation, meals and sometimes other services for residents only'. Thus, in the UK, a guest house is variously described as a private hotel, a guest house, bed and breakfast, or a boarding house. Indeed, owners often use the terms interchangeably to suit the specific guide book, or market segment, in which they wish to be represented. They tend to be smaller than hotels (four to nine rooms), with more limited facilities for residents.

For the purposes of this chapter, guest houses and small hotels are therefore defined as follows. In terms of physical facilities, service capacity, number of employees and market share they represent small scale accommodation providers, in comparison to the largest units of operation in the UK. The businesses are financed by one individual or small-group, directly managed by its owner, or part owner, in a personalized manner and not through the medium of a formalized management structure.

It can then be seen that compared to a Travelodge owned by the large Forte corporation, guest hotels and small hotels welcome a much smaller number of customers. The owner manages and operates the property himself, on a daily basis, and does not employ managers to do the job for him. The business is not part of a chain of similar establishments, it is privately owned and operates as an independent business. As such, the owner is totally responsible for making all business decisions.

SIZE AND NATURE OF THE SECTOR

There are limited and often inconsistent sources of statistical information relating to the guest house and small hotel sector in the UK. This is due in part to:

- the absence of universally accepted organizational definitions;
- the fact that many operate below the VAT registration threshold level;
- many are not registered with officialdom as they offer fewer than three rooms for let;
- lack of government policy for compulsory registration;
- seasonal and intermittent patterns of operations;
- active avoidance by operators aiming to avoid bureaucratic, legal and fiscal scrutiny;
- general inconsistencies in the manner in which they are counted.

As a result, accurate information regarding supply is difficult to obtain and when it does exist that on the smaller properties is often missing.[3] For instance, in presenting the number of hotels per UK geographic region the HCTC[4] excludes establishments owned and managed by self-employed people – that is to say the very types of businesses which are the focus of this chapter. Furthermore, in calculating UK hotel stock Harrison & Johnson[5] took the HCTC base of 52,200 units, discarded units which are guest houses, other non-hotel establishments and those having less than the required number of bedrooms, to

Table 6.1 Number of hotels and guesthouses by UK region (1994).

	Northern Ireland	Scotland	England	Wales	Total
Hotels	123	2,876	17,200	1,794	21,993
Guest houses	140	1,442	9,874	3,325	14,781
Total	263	4,318	27,074	5,119	36,774

Source: National Tourist Boards.

arrive at an estimate of approximately 19,000 hotels. This leaves 33,200 accommodation units in the UK in limbo, many of which may fall into the guest house and small hotel sectors. Drawing on available information from the national tourist boards, which readily admit that the statistics are anything but comprehensive, Table 6.1 gives an indication of the numbers of hotels and guest houses in Britain. However, it still does not identify the number which could be classified as 'small'.

Despite these problems, a vast amount of information about these accommodation providers can be found in the printed media. The national tourist boards (NTBs) produce official 'Where to Stay' guides to hotels and guest houses, which are revised annually. In addition, there is a wide range of other directories organized and published by, for example:

- motoring associations (e.g. AA, RAC);
- good food guides (e.g. Egon Ronay, Taste of Scotland/Wales);
- consumer associations (e.g. Which Hotel, Good Hotel);
- professional associations (e.g. BHA Hotels & Restaurants of Britain);
- other (e.g. Signpost, Best Loved Hotels, Ashley Courtney).

Each of these different organizations uses their own grading and classification schemes to assess and monitor overall quality. For instance, since 1986, the Scottish Tourist Board has systematically inspected hotels and guest houses, defining the standards that visitors expect, and helping owners and operators meet those standards. In a two-tier scheme, hotels and guest houses throughout Scotland are graded for quality and classified for their facilities. The scheme covers over 3300 serviced accommodation establishments, which represents 38,000 bedrooms in Scotland.

The high proportion of small businesses in the accommodation sector has been traditionally explained by a number of factors. There is *relative ease of entry* into the sector. The capital investment required is lower than in many other industries, specialist knowledge and qualifications are desirable, but not a prerequisite, and there is no compulsion to join trade or professional associations or similar organizations which have codes of practice such as consumer protection schemes.[6] *Market demand* is highly segmented, many of which segments do not lend themselves to satisfaction by standardized corporate properties. As a result, this diversity of demand is often best satisfied by a wide range of small establishments offering a wide variety of locations, quality ranges, physical facilities, and special interests/activities to niche markets. *Consumer satisfaction* is achieved through the close identification of the providers with their guests. The nature of accommodation provision is such that the small establishments may be better suited to respond quickly to customer needs and expectations in a highly personalized, flexible environment. As such they are well positioned to provide specialist services which have the potential to add quality, variety and authenticity to the products offered to the tourists. The small, often family, business can be *economically viable* in a limited, specialized or local marketplace, where there is often not enough profit for large businesses with their high overhead costs. As such Kleinwort Benson describes this sector of the hotel industry as the equivalent of the 'corner shop'.[7] It occupies a niche, is convenient for the local market, is usually run by local people offering a limited product range, but nevertheless enjoys strong customer loyalty.

However, these mainly positive factors have to be located within the realities of the 1990s. The following points highlight the continuing domination of the smaller business and its significant role as an employer. Regrettably, this is tempered by the fact that their viability is threatened by operating only a small number of rooms, mainly at low market levels, resulting in relatively low turnover and profit-earning potential. As such, for many, guest house and small hotel operation represents high risk businesses. *Ownership* is highly entrepreneurial. Kleinwort Benson[8] estimates that hotel room stock, which is not owned by the large groups, accounts for around 66 per cent in 1994. This represents a 15 per cent decrease from 1987, and 25 per cent since 1936. In 1994, the HCTC estimated that 70 per cent of all firms in the hotel and catering industry were operated as sole proprietor or partnership and were frequently family run. There are 165,000 persons *self-employed* in the hotel and catering industry, which represents 12 per cent of total employment in the sector. Small businesses having ten or fewer employees accounted for 87 per cent of hotels in 1991.[9] Properties in this sector are *small in size*. Using one hotel establishment as a unit of measurement, estimates of the percentage of hotel stock which falls into the 'small' category (50 rooms or less) vary between 65 per cent and 75 per cent.[10, 11] While the average number of rooms in a small independently owned hotel is 15, compared with 89 in group-owned properties in the UK, in Wales, for example, 60 per cent of hotels have less than ten rooms, and guest houses have approximately three letting rooms. They also tend to operate at a relatively low *market level*. 75 per cent of all UK hotels operate at the 2-star/unclassified market level, compared to around 18 per cent of corporate-owned hotels, and achieve an average annual room occupancy of 45 per cent to 55 per cent. This grouping accounts for around 78 per cent of the small accommodation providers. This results in relatively *low turnover and profit earnings*. The sector has the highest number of low turnover companies of any industry in the economy. More than 90 per cent have a financial turnover of less than £250,000.[12] Moreover, the independent hotel delivers a trading profit per room seven times less than the corporate hotel,[13] reflecting a general lack of the economies of scale enjoyed by the larger groups. All of these factors contribute to the high level of *business risk* associated with small hotel operations. During the 1990–93 recession many small businesses were trading at levels which were below their critical break-even point, bringing about a dangerous situation of banks and creditors deciding to foreclose on business. At the time the National Westminster Bank commented that 'it was an unfortunate fact of life'. While this situation has eased, the relatively high capital and operations costs, in combination with a small number of rooms, make start-up and operation of the small property higher risk than other types of accommodation provision.

MARKETS SERVED

The main demand occurs during April to September inclusive, concentrated on July to

September, which accounts for 60 per cent of overseas visitors and 40 per cent of UK trips. However, while the pattern of trade remains highly seasonal, the spread is not as severe as in previous decades, in part due to the fact that these sectors are now seen as ideal vehicles for the robust short break and shoulder season market. Furthermore, the nature of the product encourages a high level of core repeat business (50 per cent) while passing trade from touring customers with no forward reservations accounts for about 50 per cent of bookings.

The profile of typical customers is made of two main markets, the domestic and the overseas. The domestic market is dominated by the leisure, secondary or short-break holiday guest using guest houses and small hotels for short stays of four to seven nights mainly during April to September. The majority travel by private car, average party size is four, drawn mainly from ABC1 socioeconomic groups, and are aged 35 plus. Approximately 80 to 90 per cent of accommodation arrangements are made independent of travel agents or tour operators, with guests booking directly with the individual operators. While 5 to 10 per cent of customers purchase inclusive packages, with the remainder booking through Tourist Information Centres and travel agents, generally, of all persons taking domestic breaks of at least four nights duration, 10 per cent use guest houses while 20 per cent use small hotels.

The overseas market is also dominated by the leisure guest with over 33 per cent of overseas visitors on their main holiday, 20 per cent on an additional holiday, and 13 per cent visiting friends and relatives. The average length of stay in the small hotels and guest houses tends to be two to three nights. Around 80 per cent of guests belong to AB socioeconomic groups, tend not to be accompanied with children, and are aged between 25 and 54, with the 25–34 age group alone accounting for 33 per cent of all visitors. Approximately 77 per cent make independent accommodation arrangements, with only 23 per cent booking through travel agents. Generally, of all overseas tourists 32 per cent use small hotels and 31 per cent use guest house accommodation provision, given that quality expectations are satisfied.

Market segmentation is becoming an increasingly vital issue in the hotel trade,[14] and no more so than to the guest house and small hotel sectors. Standard market segmentation approaches based on socioeconomic, lifestyle, interests and geographic factors are as applicable and as implementable to the guest house and small hotel sector as to the large corporate groups. The range of variables which can be used include age-group, lifestyle, interests/activities, mode of travel, vacation type, season of travel, length of stay, average spend, method of reservation, newspaper readership and purpose of visit.

From these variables, guest house and small hotel operators can develop the profile of the specific market segment they wish to target. In particular, the locations are well positioned to exploit the growing demand for environmentally sound, outdoor pursuits, special interest courses, and itinerary planning for car tours. This can best be achieved through linking with other accommodation providers, activity/interest specialists, and transport companies. In this way clearly defined and priced, attractive packages can be developed and communicated to core and specialist markets.

As the majority of guest house and small hotel reservations come direct from the guest, Travel Agents account for only around 15 to 20 per cent of reservations, exposure in guides and directories represents a key method to target specific segments. Furthermore, it has been found that the more individual the property, the more likely that a directory will be used as an information source on which to base purchase decisions, as such astute

Table 6.2 Reservation sources of information.

Automobile Association	Royal Automobile Club
Ackerman	Good Food Guide
Johansens	Michelin
Les Routiers	Ashley Courtney
Egon Ronay	Good Hotel Guide
Signpost	Which Hotel

entries are vital to small hotels and guest houses. Other than those produced by the national tourist boards, a selection of the guides and directories most favoured by the UK guest houses and hotels are listed in Table 6.2.

There are six priority segments for the guest house and small sectors:

1. UK short-break promoted directly to the customer, by-passing the travel trade.
2. USA/Canada independent travellers reached through direct mail, press coverage, consumer advertising, carefully selected wholesalers, retailers and BTA/NTB press departments.
3. Special interest and activity (e.g. golfing, craft course, walking, bird watching).
4. European holidaymakers travelling independently and, to a lesser extent, travel operators. This segment is best targeted through retail travel agents which tailor itineraries to customers' specifications (e.g. 'Go As You Please' car touring types of programmes).
5. Families are a durable segment which need nurturing by devoting more effort to providing children's menus, meal times, baby-sitting services, entertainment and activities, and appropriate pricing policies.
6. Visiting friends and relatives will be recommended to use a local guest house or small hotel of sound, established reputation and reasonable price as a substitute to staying with friends and relatives.

However, it should be emphasized that guest houses and small hotels are continually struggling to attract these priority segments, as they lose market share to the hotel groups. This is due to corporate groups having the capacity to advertise nationally, and their capability of offering overall greater quality, consistency and value for money, ease of purchase through central reservation services, as well as a full range of locations and invariably a wider range of facilities than the small operators. Thus, the day of the totally independent small business is history if they want to stay in business. In the 1990s the way forward is through linking into marketing consortia which can cost-effectively reach these segments through combining resources, offering a full range of locations, and often a central reservation service. This strategy is more fully discussed under the heading 'Current issues and future trends' later in this chapter.

LOCATION

The majority of existing guest houses and small hotels can be found in secondary and tertiary locations, reflecting historic travel patterns of both domestic and overseas consumers (e.g. seaside resorts, country coaching inns). As a result they are generally smaller, lower market level, serving mature or declining markets, suffer from a high degree of seasonality and general demand fluctuations, and produce lower trading profits. For this grouping of accommodation providers Conrad Hilton's much quoted three success factors for hotels of 'location, location, and location' have a different interpretation. There are very few guest houses and small hotels that are sited in prime locations. Most are well hidden, up long driveways, in the back of towns and remote scenic areas. However, perhaps their location is in fact a major strength, as the charming names adopted by the guest houses in particular reflect their attractive location (e.g. Hill Top, Beach Dunes, Riverside, Wood End). This combination of name and location characteristic which is typical of many of the small accommodation properties can be illustrated with a quote from one small hotel's brochure: 'Poised above Tobermory Bay, in the Sound of Mull, the Western Isles Hotel combines friendly hospitality with breathtaking views over an ever-changing vista of mountain and sea.'

When selecting a location for a guest house or small hotel, decisions are influenced by a mix of personal and business factors. Personal factors would include the likes of: get on well with the locals; can pursue my hobby/sport; enjoyed the area during previous holidays; and pleasant environment for the children to grow up in. While business factors focus on: demand actual/potential; tourist attractions in the area; proximity of competition; capital investment requirements; length of season; profit-earning capacity; potential for future growth or diversification; eligibility for public sector financial grants; and projected return on investment. However, frequently the personal factors override the business, which may bode ill for a sound commercial future.

PRODUCT OFFERING

Guest houses and small hotels are found in all grades of properties from de luxe, to unclassified. In tourist areas, particularly seaside resorts, such properties are often clustered together, with whole streets turned over to visitor accommodation. This is illustrated in Figure 6.1. In rural areas, the former use of the building is often obvious by its name, which will often include words such as mill, farm, manor, castle, parsonage, old school, almshouse and vicarage. For instance, Contin House is a former Church of Scotland manse built in 1774. It is now a traditional Highland Lodge, tastefully refurbished to achieve a very high standard of accommodation whilst retaining the homeliness of a private house. The house is situation in its own garden, surrounded by pasture land, on a peaceful island in the River Blackwater.

The majority of owners are genuinely interested in their guests and pride themselves on the warmth of welcome and quality of service. Furthermore, hosts are usually local people with a good knowledge of the area so they can advise on all tourist information requirements. The viability of the sector has strengthened as domestic and overseas visitors have become bored of the bland, standardized sameness of many of the corporate-group-owned hotels. As a result they are seeking out a more personalized, individualistic environment offering a specialized product – often a style of living to which the guest would like to become accustomed!

Hopefully this trend will continue, provided the small operators can deliver increasingly high standards in the physical product and service elements to match customer expectations. However, this may be a problem as many operators are in a situation where they cannot afford to put off refurbishment programmes, but cannot afford to finance them on present levels of revenue. The realities are simple, profit margins are low and

Figure 6.1 Typical small hotels (Eastbourne seafront).
Source: Adrian Carpenter.

cash flow cannot support additional borrowings required when such improvements are unlikely to yield substantial revenue growth. In certain circumstances, funds from public sources, and government assistance, are generally available to alleviate the burden of refurbishment. For instance, the Wales Tourist Board is encouraging guest house improvements in resorts through allocation of Section 4 funds to assist in upgrading. However, there seems to be an inbred reluctance among small operators to get involved with such public sector schemes, perhaps because it is feared that involvement may result in red tape or threaten individuality.

The ideal components of the core product, that is, the guest house or small hotel in the 1990s, consist of:

- a warm welcome;
- comfortable facilities;
- attractive location;
- satisfaction of perceptions of value for money;
- pride in preparing and serving good-quality local produce;
- 'caring' represented by the owner taking a personal interest in guests;
- efficient, friendly staff mirroring the attitude of 'mine host', tailoring customer service to each individual guest's needs.

- availability of special interest and activities programme;
- easy to purchase, attractive packages of all the components needed for a tourism experience.

Perhaps the most critical of these components to the success of the operation is the human, caring element – mine host and the staff. Take that out and the unique selling proposition disappears, the heart of the operation has been extracted. With all the components in place, the owner has a clearly focused, differentiated market proposition, a specialist product with which to strengthen market appeal in niche markets and prosper.

ORGANIZATION AND OPERATIONS

There is a timeless quality to the organization of guest houses and small hotels, with traditional hospitality values and personal objectives mixing with commercial imperatives. As a result business organization frequently reflects the historic way of doing business, rather than any revolutionary, modern management system. In order to better understand factors which influence business organizations two issues need to be discussed: degree of income dependency and 'amateur' status.

Firstly, three main levels of income dependency on the business can be identified, each of which will result in differing attitudes and motivations towards organization and staffing. Firstly, the hotelier or guest house owner may run the unit as their primary source of income. They are therefore likely to be heavily reliant on overdraft facilities and loan capital. Secondly, the business may be a secondary source of income, while the owners carry on their 'real' professions. Finally owners may be in the 'comfort zone': the property has been purchased outright, and the owners seek only to achieve a 'comfort level' in terms of level of income generation to sustain desired lifestyle.

A second issue is the 'amateur' status of guest house and small hotel operators, which has historically been a characteristic of these sectors. Operations are often started by an individual with enthusiasm for the social aspect of the business, but with only very basic knowledge of business practice and operations. Many have been 'in business' before as opposed to 'running their own accommodation business' and have no idea of the reality. Indeed, Boer[15] commented that the supply of unskilled entrepreneurs to the hotel industry continues seemingly unabated.

As a result of these two factors owners bring different levels of commitment and abilities to the business organization. Frequently, motivations are highly lifestyle-driven, rather than commercial, which often results in operations operating below optimum. In addition, outdated management mentalities and general management weaknesses are common. Such business flaws were masked during the more buoyant 1980s, but the 1990s are being less tolerant of the inexperienced amateur. This prediction is as relevant now as it was in 1947 when Moncrieff advised that 'For too many people, the idea of running a small hotel has a curious fascination. Hotel-keeping is a serious business in which there is little room for optimistic, inexperienced amateurs. Only by being shrewd and careful can a modest income be earned.'[16]

No matter what the size of the accommodation unit, marketing, housekeeping, maintenance, food and beverage, and human resources all need to be professionally planned, managed and controlled, profits maximized and accurate records maintained. What is different in the small operations is that it is the owner alone who has to cope with these

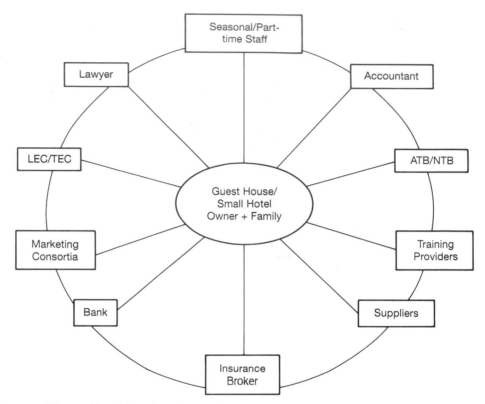

Figure 6.2 Hub and spoke organization for the small operation.

tasks, without a team of subordinates to delegate to. It is the ability to successfully juggle these roles, a strong engaging personality, combined with excellent service, which will influence the success of the operation. The following quotation sums up the complexity of the small operation and is very apt relative to the specific nature of the accommodation sector: 'it takes a lot to become an entrepreneur. It demands the dedication to work long hours, and to persuade others to work long hours, at a kaleidoscope of tasks, ranging from immediate response to operational emergency, through to cool appraisal of planning and development for the future.'[17]

In order to cope effectively with this 'kaleidoscope of tasks', the operator employs a team of experts to give the benefit of their specialist knowledge and advice. Managing a small business can be a lonely affair; unlike the large corporate groups there are no superiors, or a head office, to ask for specialist advice. Thus, this team of professionals is a substitute for the more formal support network of a large firm, with the organizational structure being one of 'hub and spoke'. This is illustrated in Figure 6.2. Within the operation the organizational structure is simple, reflecting more the image of an extended family rather than any hierarchical configuration. Family members are looked to first as a source of convenient and economic labour. From that core of 'staff', employees will be kept to the minimum number required to cope with the differing seasonal demands. Hotels in remote, out of town, locations may find it difficult to attract and retain good-quality staff, and generally need to provide staff accommodation.

Training is generally done 'on the job', but operators are currently being encouraged to increase the training provision for their employees through, for example, the Welcome Host programme. This is designed to improve the standards of service and hospitality provided to tourists and was launched in the UK by the Wales Tourist Board in 1992 and the Scottish Tourist Board in 1993. In most areas TEC/LECs are providing a subsidy to reduce the price payable by participants to encourage the use of Welcome Host training providers.

It would be easy to theorize about the range of standard operating procedures such small operations should have in place, in terms of induction packs, customer-care procedures, purchasing specifications, etc. But the reality is that, in the main, no such formalized procedures exist. The owner/manager is so directly involved in the day-to-day operation that he/she knows intuitively what needs to be done in the best interests of the business. There is no need to document every step. It is implicit, rather than explicit. For the owner and staff the procedures are just all part of the daily routine to be followed. Thus, while a 600-page standard operating procedure manual is appropriate to the massive McDonald's corporation, it is not as relevant to the smaller operation. However, standard forms are frequently in use for the likes of booking charts, forward booking forms, guest registrations, staff records and general accounting functions. For those establishments which employ a significant number of persons, a standard induction pack may have been developed to cover standard house procedures of customer care, phone answering, taking of reservations, personal presentation, and general conduct.

CURRENT ISSUES AND FUTURE TRENDS

In 1989 it was predicted[18] that the small accommodation operator had a future. In 1994 there is less certainty about this. However, in the late 1990s it is still hoped that the need for wide geographic coverage, the relative ease of entry into the sector, coupled with customers who increasingly search out more differentiated products, will ensure their continuity. So long as the small business operator continues to offer a professional, unique, highly personalized, quality product.

For those tough guest houses and small hotels which have survived the recession, now is the time to plan, to stand back from today's pressures and take a strategic view of the future. However, one of the problems which is faced within this sector is the uphill struggle to persuade owners of the need and value of thinking strategically. This has never been more important, as the dominant competition – the corporate groups – has access to all the tactics available to the independent owner but in addition has many more opportunities and resources denied the small operator. As such, the smaller operators have little hope of changing the rules of the competitive game.

For the future, two strategies appropriate to the small accommodation sector have emerged in this chapter. At first glance they may seem to be in conflict: product differentiation and cooperative networks. The first urges the operator to be unique, specialized, a loner, while the second recommends that he/she becomes a team player. However, together these two strands of strategy can present a winning combination.

Product Differentiation

In current hotel product marketing there is seldom reference to a 'common' hotel product, but more to a specific type of hotel (e.g. fishing, golfing, country house, non-smoking). Thus, for the 1990s the guest house or small hotel needs to consider the possibility of transforming an 'all-purpose' operation into a more differentiated product, capitalizing on its unique selling points of the personalized environment, cherishing the customer, and customizing the product offering to their individual needs. In doing this the operators are developing niches in which corporate groups have no particular interest or advantage. Thus, the small operator is offering a specialized product, with a distinctive image, serving the needs of a targeted market niche.

Cooperative Networks

The trend in the tourist industry as a whole is towards greater integration through cooperative networks which bring together all components of the tourism product (i.e. airlines, car hire, accommodation, credit card companies, special activity programmes). Such cooperative networks enable the packaging and effective distribution of a compound tourism product, of which the guest houses and small hotels are part. As a result, in the 1990s astute small accommodation management is becoming more that of a 'team sport'. Operators are developing cooperative networks to assist them with professional advice and support, centralized marketing, access to central reservations systems (CRS) and global markets, financial services, and access to public sector funding and information. This can be seen mainly in the form of marketing consortia such as Consort, Best Western, Pride of Britain. Indeed, with respect to CRS involvement, Go and Welch[19] state that: 'From the standpoint of the smaller operator it is hard to see how overall independence of action can be maintained, without becoming less visible to the public and sales agents, consequently losing market share.'

CONCLUSION

It is obvious that guest house and small hotel ownership and operation brings with it tremendous, stimulating 'highs' and just as extreme, depressing 'lows'. It is agreed that it is exciting, challenging, and very hard work with the future filled with many uncertainties. Survival will depend upon well-balanced management expertise, marketing muscle, traditional values of hospitality, value for money, high quality, investment in staff training and, importantly, a revival of the 'entrepreneurial spirit'.[20] At a more basic level, successful operation is dependent on steely determination and a toughness which is intolerant of amateurism. Guest houses and small hotels may not be perfect in every aspect of their operation; however, they represent the human face of hospitality within the UK accommodation sector as a whole. Without them the hospitality industry would be bereaved and much less vibrant.

REFERENCES

1. Burkart, A. and Medlik, S. (1981) *Tourism Past, Present and Future*, London: Heinemann.
2. Medlik, S. (1994) *The Business of Hotels*, Oxford: Butterworth Heinemann.
3. Hughes, H. (1992) *Economics for the Hotel and Catering Industry*, London: Hutchinson.
4. Hotel & Catering Training Company (1994) *Catering and Hospitality Industry: Key Facts and Figures*, London: HCTC.

5. Harrison, L. and Johnson, K. (1992) *UK Hotel Groups Directory*, Hotel and Catering Research Centre, University of Huddersfield, London: Cassell.
6. Boer, A. (1992) 'The banking sector and small firm failure in the UK hotel and catering industry', in *International Journal of Contemporary Hospitality Management*, Vol. 4, No. 2, pp. 13–16.
7. Kleinwort Benson Securities (1994) *Quoted Hotel Companies: The World Markets 1994*, 8th Annual Review, London.
8. Ibid.
9. Hotel & Catering Training Company, op. cit.
10. ICC (1991) *Business Ratio Report: An Industry Sector Analysis: Hotels*, Middlesex: ICC Business Ratios Ltd.
11. Key Note Report (1991) *A Market Sector Overview: Hotels*, Middlesex: Key Note.
12. Boer, A. op. cit.
13. Kleinwort Benson Securities (1992) *Quoted Hotel Companies: The European Markets*, 6th Annual Review, London.
14. Go, F. and Welch, P. (1991) *Competitive Strategies for the International Hotel Industry*, London: The Economic Intelligence Unit.
15. Boer, A. op. cit.
16. Moncrieff, M. (1947) *The Small Hotel*, London: Blandford Press.
17. Milne, T. and Thompson, M. (1988) *Patterns of Successful Business Start-up*, Stirling: Stirling University.
18. Witt, S. and Mouthino, L. (1989) *Tourism Marketing Handbook*, London: Prentice-Hall.
19. Go, F. and Welch, P. op. cit.
20. Horwath & Horwath (1994) *Business Review*, No. 13, Spring, London.

SEVEN

Hospital Hotel Services and Residential Care

JUDITH BROWN

INTRODUCTION

Hotel services within hospitals and care homes are the same kind of services that a hotel provides for its guests. These services consist of food and beverage provision, domestic services, portering, laundry and transport. This chapter will concentrate on accommodation provision, often referred to as 'domestic services' in the health care sector, as food and beverage service is discussed in Chapter 16. It will demonstrate the importance of hotel services to the patients and staff of a hospital or the residents of a care home. It outlines the operation of the domestic service within hospitals and shows how these services are changing radically in the context of the UK's national health service (NHS).

Domestic services are amongst the most important services provided in a hospital and constitute a major part of the hotel services department of all hospitals. The service has three main objectives, the most important being to control the spread of infection through the effective cleaning of all areas within a hospital. Secondly, the hospital building and its contents must be kept in the optimum condition and this is accomplished through the careful scheduling of regular cleaning and maintenance using the correct equipment and materials. The third objective of this department is to provide a bright and cheerful atmosphere for staff and patients. This cheerful environment comes not just from the physical surroundings of the hospital, which of necessity are often fairly utilitarian, but also from the attitude and manner of the staff. Domestic staff, like all hospital employees, have a role in the care of patients and it is from this role that many staff acquire high levels of job satisfaction. The domestic services staff often feel the same sense of pride as the medical staff when patients go home after successful treatment.

NATURE AND SCALE OF PROVISION

There are some 475 National Health Services Trusts in the UK at present. Most of these control between one and five hospitals. The Trusts are responsible for the management of all the services within the hospitals. Around 200 hospitals continue to be managed by District Health Authorities or Family Health Service Authorities. These remaining hospitals in the UK will probably acquire Trust status within the next few years. The size and nature of hospitals varies from units of around 20 beds up to more than 500 beds. The size and complexity of the hotel services department varies accordingly, smaller hospitals may employ two or three domestic staff, with larger units employing over 100 staff in the domestic services department. Very small hospitals are often managed by a nearby larger unit.

Since the early 1980s all hospitals have been obliged to participate in compulsory competitive tendering which has included putting their domestic services out to tender. This has encouraged hospital domestic services management to carefully review the work carried out to ensure it is done as effectively as possible, as well as giving value for money. All hospitals must ask outside companies to submit tenders for the catering, domestic and other services every 3–5 years. Most of the in-house services submit tenders and in a lot of cases the contracts are given to these (called direct service or direct labour organizations), but many are also given to contract companies. Most hospital domestic services have now been through this tendering process. It is therefore important that any domestic service gives value for money and an effective service for the customer, either patient or hospital staff.

In addition to NHS provision, there is also the commercial health sector. People who prefer private medical care pay for the facilities and service similar to those in a 3- or 4-star hotel. Medical insurance often covers the cost of this. There are an estimated 230 independent (private) hospitals, often run by specialist health care companies. Most NHS hospitals also have a small number of private rooms run along similar lines.

In addition to hospitals, there are also a large number of care homes throughout the UK with more than 140,000 residents in total.[1] Such homes concentrate on providing long-term residential accommodation for people unable to care for themselves – in particular the elderly and the physically handicapped. One study[2] in Yorkshire identified that on average there were typically between 14 to 41 residents, of whom 88 per cent were women. Their ages ranged from 65 to 101, with an average age of 86 years. The average length of stay was 3.5 years. These homes provide a range of services from simple residential accommodation without any nursing support through to 24-hour medical supervision.

During the 1980s, there was a significant shift in the nature of such provision. In 1981 the main providers of such facilities were local authorities with nearly 3000 such homes, the private sector with around 2000, and the voluntary sector with approximately 1000 homes.[3] By 1991, whilst local authority and voluntary provision had remained almost static, the private sector provision had increased by 450 per cent to nearly 9000 homes. Herne[4] identifies four main reasons for the growth of residential accommodation for the elderly. Firstly, a lower birth-rate results in fewer children to share responsibility for an elderly parent. Secondly, the increased divorce rate reduces contacts within families. Thirdly, greater geographical mobility amongst the workforce may leave elderly people with no relatives living nearby. And fourthly, the increase in the proportion of women taking full-time employment results in there being fewer at home to provide care. In addition, the reforms to the NHS and policies on 'Care in the Community' have greatly reduced its provision of long-stay beds.

DEMAND FOR HOSPITAL AND CARE HOME SERVICES

The 'users' of a hospital include the patients, salaried or volunteer staff, and visitors, who may be either visiting patients or visiting staff as part of their jobs, such as delivery people or sales representatives. A typical large general hospital may have 20 wards with around 25 in-patients in each ward, 100-plus out-patient visits per day, around 200 medical and paramedical staff, more than 200 support staff, and 500-plus visitors per day.

The patients can be considered the customers of the hospital. Most people, at some time in their lives attend a hospital, either as out-patients, day patients or staying in hospital for one or more nights. They may be confined to bed or may be physically fit enough to be up and around. There are few long-stay patients in hospitals nowadays but for these slightly different provision is often made. The length of a patient's stay in hospital tends to be as short as possible.

In most hospitals the patients are outnumbered by the medical, paramedical and other staff. Staff within hospitals, often work on a shift basis to give 24-hour cover. Volunteers may provide services such as hospital radio, libraries, etc. as well as reception services. These have to be catered for according to the hospital's customs. The great variety of staff in hospitals and their varying requirements for living and working accommodation means that the domestic service must be flexible. Living accommodation is often provided for at least some of the medical and paramedical staff, particularly junior doctors and nurses in nurses' homes and doctors' residences. For every patient in hospital there is usually at least one visitor each day. Some of these visitors are able to stay overnight (usually the parents of young patients), and so accommodation is provided for them.

Accommodation provision in the care home sector, especially with regards to elderly residents, provides particularly complex challenges. Elderly people may originally enter a home because of one main reason. Either they have social problems resulting from bereavement, loneliness or lack of family support; or they are mentally or physically frail. As they grow older, additional problems may arise simply as a result of ageing or the degenerative nature of their condition. The most common combination of conditions might be dementia, arthritis, and failing eyesight or hearing or both. As a result of this, care home managers face five major challenges in caring for their very vulnerable clients.[5] Firstly, the 'elderly' are not one single group but many disparate groups from different generations, ethnic backgrounds, and social origins. Secondly, there is evidence to show that elderly people in residential care are afraid to complain for fear of retribution. Thirdly, elderly people are resistant to change and like set routines. Fourthly, many require special diets as part of the treatment for their medical conditions, such as diabetes, or just for general health reasons, such as overweight. And finally, residents may require help with normal functions such as eating or going to the toilet.

THE HOTEL SERVICES PRODUCT OFFERING

Accommodation for patients in hospitals is usually in wards of between two and 30 beds, although in some hospitals single rooms are provided as well as the wards. Day rooms are often provided and in some hospitals a separate dining area is located on the wards. Single rooms are provided with private bathrooms for private patients, usually with a higher standard of furniture and furnishings. Also provided in hospitals are out-patient and day-care facilities; operating theatres, laboratories and consulting rooms; and a variety of areas for physiotherapy and other specialisms. A greater emphasis is being placed on day visits to hospital and shorter stays than in the past, meaning that out-patient areas are expanding and patient bed numbers are reducing. Some hospitals have specialist facilities such as burns units or labour wards, depending on the type of hospital.

The aim of domestic services within a hospital is to provide a specialized cleaning service of the appropriate standard for all these areas within the constraints of the budget. As a general rule an allowance of around three hours per bed per week is allocated to cleaning in hospitals. Unlike many other establishments within the hospitality industry, the aesthetic appearance of these areas within a hospital is not of prime importance, although in private rooms or in private hospitals a standard of appearance similar to that in a 3- or 4-star hotel is normally found. In public sector hospitals, the surfaces, furniture and fittings are purchased with a very strict budget in mind, both for the initial purchase and for their cleaning and maintenance. Surfaces and furniture are expected to be durable as wear and tear is heavy and replacement may only be possible on a very infrequent basis; hence, for example, metal-framed beds and heavy-duty vinyl floors are selected for many areas.

Because of the high hygiene requirements of many areas within a hospital, surfaces which are easy to keep to these high standards are usually present. Surfaces are chosen according to the areas for which they will be used; for example smooth floorings may be selected for ward areas, theatres and treatment rooms because they provide limited scope for microbial growth. In contrast in day rooms and offices the comfort of the user may be considered to be more important and floors may be carpeted and walls papered. However, many hospitals, as in the private health care sector, now want to make their patients' stay as pleasant as possible, thus more consideration is being given to the choice of surfaces and furniture which create a pleasant environment. Carpet and furniture manufacturers are providing items which are practical from the hospital point of view. These specially designed items are usually stain resistant and easy to keep clean, but also warm, comfortable and attractive.

Fire resistance is an important consideration in hospitals, so inherently fire-resistant wall and floor coverings are normally in place. Textile items such as curtains are purchased with fire-resistant finishes which have to last for up to around 60 washes.

ORGANIZATION AND STAFFING

Staffing accounts for around 90 per cent of the total cost of the domestic service in hospitals. The staff are employed either by a contract cleaning company such as Mediclean or by an in-house domestic service department. Both of these operate on a contract basis to provide the cleaning service. The organization and reporting system of domestic services varies slightly depending on whether the service is contracted out or not. This is illustrated in Figures 7.1a and 7.1b.

The Domestic Services Manager (or Assistant Hotel Services Manager) is responsible to the Hotel Services Manager for the management of all aspects of the domestic service. Usually they will have a number of years' experience, often having previously held a post as Assistant Domestic Services Manager and will usually hold a management qualification in the field of Hospitality Management. In private hospitals this post is usually called Housekeeper, although as they are normally fairly small units the job is often combined with that of the supervisor. The Domestic Services Manager in hospitals is also responsible for controlling the budget given to the department and must allocate money to cover the costs of all the staff equipment and materials used to clean the hospital. The Domestic Services Manager is also responsible for the recruitment of all the staff within the department (although this may be delegated to the Assistant Domestic Services Manager) and for the organization of training of staff. The operative staff (ward maids, domestics,

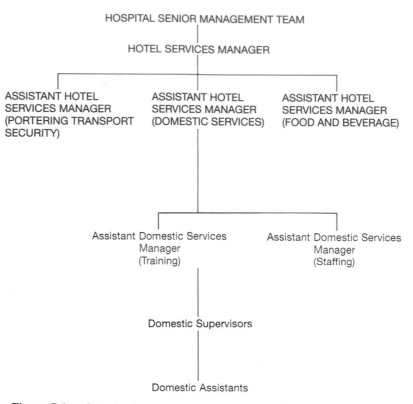

Figure 7.1a Organization chart for in-house domestic services.

etc.) are usually trained by the supervisors; however, induction and issues such as health and safety or fire prevention are often organized and carried out by the Domestic Services Manager or assistant. The Domestic Services Manager is responsible for maintaining the quality of the cleaning service and has to ensure that the standards agreed for each within the unit are adhered to. This involves installing quality-control mechanisms and in-depth liaison with the Infection Control Committee and the senior hospital management. In hospitals where a contract cleaning company is used, the Domestic Services Manager is responsible for liaison with the cleaning company and for ensuring that standards are maintained by them.

In larger hospitals usually one or more Assistant Domestic Services Managers are employed. They are often people with a hospitality management qualification and one or two years' management experience. The Assistant carries out the more routine tasks delegated by the Domestic Services Manager, such as recruitment, induction and training of operative staff, the distribution of cleaning supplies and ensuring quality-control procedures are carried out effectively. Often Assistant Domestic Services Managers are given a specialized function within the department such as training or quality control.

Where a contract cleaning company is employed their work is monitored by Monitoring Officers who are responsible for ensuring that standards of cleaning are maintained throughout the hospital. This is done by spot checking a number of areas each day and reporting back if standards fall below a pre-agreed acceptable level.

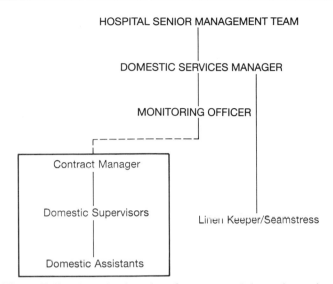

Figure 7.1b Organization chart for contracted domestic services.

Supervisors are responsible for ensuring that required standards of cleaning are met through the day-to-day management of staff in their specific area of the hospital. Usually the supervisor is responsible for a team of cleaners or for a specific area within the hospital, whether it be a ward or a department. Supervisors are responsible for the cleaning of the area, and, in wards, often for the service of meals and drinks. They are generally responsible for ensuring that the staff work the correct hours according to their contracts and are punctual and efficient. They are responsible too for their appearance, attitude and hygiene. Training of new staff and re-training of existing staff is an important aspect of their jobs. They are responsible for ensuring that the correct cleaning and food supplies are available in their work area, as well as liaising with the nursing staff to ensure the cleaning is carried out with the least disruption of other services. The supervisor is also concerned with the control, distribution and cleanliness of equipment and materials used in the area. Supervisors in some hospitals will be responsible for the distribution of the correct quantity of linen to the wards. Most supervisors undertake some cleaning duties along with the domestics. They may also undertake some tasks which are traditionally nursing duties, such as making beds and providing hot drinks. The department for which the supervisor carries out these duties has to transfer money to pay for these services to the Domestic Services Budget. The supervisors are responsible for reporting complaints, criticisms and compliments to the Domestic Services Manager so that appropriate action can be taken.

Domestics are mostly part time, and carry out cleaning duties according to the needs of the department. Cleaning methods are tightly prescribed in hospitals and the domestics will receive at least a two or three days training when they commence employment. Most work is carried out during the day, particularly in the morning. In areas which are used only during the day (e.g. out-patient wards, operating theatres, etc.) cleaning is carried out at night when they are empty. Normally two or more domestics work together in quiet areas especially at night. As many areas in a hospital are busy 24 hours a day the domestics must work around the other users of the area. In particular they must try not to interrupt the work of doctors and other medical staff and try to fit in with the routine of the other hospital staff in the area. The domestic is sometimes the only link a patient has with normal daily life, and patients may confide their fears and sometimes their symptoms to that person rather than to the nurses or doctors. It is up to the domestic to pass on the information if it appears to be important. In many hospitals the domestic staff are responsible for the service of food and drinks to the patients, although in some hospitals this task has been assumed by the nursing staff so that they have more social contact with the patients. The domestic staff are often also responsible for washing up after each patient meal.

Many hospitals have a linen room and employ linen assistants and sometimes seamstresses. They are responsible for receipt, checking, repair, marking, storing and distribution of clean linen. Seamstresses will make items such as curtains, although in many hospitals all items are bought in ready-made. They are also responsible for the provision of certain of the staff uniforms as well as for any mending.

Supervisors, domestic and linen room staff may be employed by a contract company rather than by the hospital. A contract manager is usually employed by the contract company to ensures that the work is being carried out effectively and to the correct standard.

DOMESTIC SERVICES OPERATION

Because there are very tight financial and quality controls in place in hospitals, the organization and planning of the cleaning service is carried out with a great deal of attention to detail. In order that this planning can be carried out satisfactorily, the Domestic Services Manager will draw up a very detailed description of all the areas which have to be cleaned, along with a detailed list of their contents. This is normally done by walking around the building in a logical way, listing each area and its contents on a pro-forma. This is often a plan of the building. The information collected in this way is updated regularly. Times for the cleaning of each item in each area are usually available and these are allocated to each of the areas. When the times are totalled a cleaning time for each area is available. This is illustrated in Figure 7.2.

In order to decide what the staffing requirement is for the areas, extra time is then added to this to allow time for staff to have breaks or to rest. From this the number of staff needed to clean an area can be calculated, depending on the hours they are expected to work. Most of the domestic staff in hospitals are part-time workers, working varying lengths of shifts, depending on the areas in which they work and the hours of cover needed. Staffing can be worked out on a day-to-day basis depending on the work that has to be done, related to factors such as the number of patients in a ward and any changes in occupancy. Longer-term staffing decisions can also be made based on the figures achieved in this way, such as Christmas and Easter holiday cover.

When the number of staff has been calculated, the number of supervisors can be assessed depending on the areas to be covered, the number of staff and the hours of coverage needed. Usually one ward or number of areas close together will need one supervisor who works full time, but this will relate to the shape and size of the buildings. Staff rotas (telling staff the hours they are expected to work) and timetables (telling staff what they have to do during the hours they are at work) can be worked out from this information. These procedures can ensure that a cleaning service is provided at the minimum cost to the hospital.

Patient Care Duties
Ward Standard Hours Summary

Date – 15.05.94

Hospital No 1   Hospital Name: St Mary's
Ward No 6   Ward Name: Top Floor   Number of Occupied Beds – 14
Task Type: Weekly

Code	Task Description	Unit of Measure	No of units	Weekly Freq.	Secs/ Occ.	Total Secs	Total Hrs
100	Dust bed	bed	22	1	66.48	66.48	1.11
106	Dust bed curtain rail	bed	22	1	3.97	3.97	0.07
108	Change locker bag	bed	14	14	3.00	41.99	0.70
109	Move ward bed	bed	14	1	10.17	10.17	0.17

Figure 7.2   Extract from ward cleaning hours summary.

In many hospitals the linen is dealt with by the nursing staff and in others by the domestic staff. Various systems are used for the collection and distribution at ward level. Linen is divided into three categories before being sent to the laundry. Soiled linen which is not infectious is bagged and sent to the laundry according to hospital practice. Linen which has been in contact with blood, faeces, vomit or urine is called fouled linen. It is bagged separately, usually into a plastic bag, and the top tied securely. Special category linen has been in contact with any of a number of serious infectious diseases such as hepatitis or typhoid. This is bagged and the top tied with water-soluble alginate thread. The bags are placed directly into the washing machine to reduce human contact with the infected linen. Domestic staff are often responsible for stocking the ward linen cupboard regularly.

Because hospitals have to work to certain guidelines and standards in order to prevent the spread of infection, any decisions about cleaning must relate to the standards of hygiene required for the area. Three standards are commonly adhered to in hospitals. A reasonable, non-clinical standard of appearance and cleanliness is provided in areas such as waiting rooms, day-care facilities and offices. In areas such as wards, treatment rooms etc. a clinical standard must be maintained meaning that all surfaces must be kept clean and free from infection. High-risk areas such as operating theatres and isolation units are areas which must be kept to a very high standard of cleanliness in order to prevent the risk of infection. Staff are usually required to wear special protective clothing including hair and shoe coverings in these areas.

Hygiene standards are monitored in most hospitals by the Infection Control Committee, who take samples from surfaces in different areas on a regular basis to check that microbial growth is within safe limits for the area. The results of these tests are reported to the domestic services team and they are obliged to act on them. The Environmental Health Officer visits once every six months to ensure that hygiene policies are adhered to.

In order to maintain the very strict standards of hygiene, hospitals have very tight quality-control measures. The supervisor, Assistant Domestic Services Manager or the Monitoring Officer check the work of the domestics regularly. Checking is done with the help of checklists, or in many hospitals with a computerized monitoring system similar to the hand-held computerized stock control equipment used in supermarkets. All areas are checked frequently, but no routine of checking is established. Each area is divided in a number of sections, each section is checked and failures to achieve the required standard are noted. A failure rate of more than 5 per cent is considered unsatisfactory and action is taken either with the domestic staff and supervisors or with the contract company.

In order to implement the high standards of work required, all staff in the department are given fairly extensive training. Domestics are usually given around three days' training by their supervisors in the day-to-day work required of them, whereas training in such issues as health and safety and fire procedures is carried out by the Domestic Services Manager or the assistant. Training of the supervisors and managers is usually a combination of on-the-job and off-the-job training carried out over the first few weeks or months of employment

Because of the rigid quality-control mechanisms in place in hospitals, the types of cleaning equipment and materials to be used have to be carefully selected, although similar selection procedures to hotels are usually followed. The variety of items is minimized so that staff are less likely to be confused about what equipment and materials to use in a specific area. However, in order to control the spread of infection, colour-coded cloths and other items are used. For example, all items used in ward areas may be green, whereas items to be used in toilet areas may be red. Generally in most areas neutral synthetic detergents are used. In baths, showers and toilets, sanitizers are used. Traditionally in hospitals, disinfectant and bleach were used a great deal; however, today their use is minimal except in areas where there is a serious risk of infection. Vacuum cleaners used in hospitals are usually purchased with very high levels of filtration, usually around 99 per cent to minimize the possibility of microbial spread. Usually floor maintenance machines (polishers) have vacuum skirts to avoid the spread of dust when they are used for polishing or buffing. Many hospitals also have procedures for dealing with complaints and compliments made by the hospital patients. This means that staff are encouraged to maintain high standards of work as well as customer care skills.

CURRENT ISSUES AND FUTURE TRENDS

This is an area which is undergoing a great deal of change and will continue to do so. The use of contract cleaning companies will become more common as it means that the responsibility for cleaning can be lifted from the hospital management to experts in the field with minimal overseeing by the hospital staff.

Domestic staff are taking over more of the non-nursing duties, such as bed-making and service of meals, from nursing staff on the wards to allow them more time to use their nursing skills. The hotel services department charges the other departments for the use of their staff. Allied to this, awareness that cleaning is a skilled job very different from household cleaning in the home is growing; consequently the standards of training and supervision are becoming higher and more respect is given to jobs within the domestic services department. In order to give more credence to the training given to hospital domestic staff awards such as Investors in People are being sought by many hospitals.

Also many staff in this area are being encouraged to achieve National Vocational Qualifications.

There is at present a policy within the health care sector to provide a more acceptable and positive experience for people attending hospitals. Complaints mechanisms have been set up in many hospitals and they are gradually adopting more of the service skills used in the hotel industry, so more customer care training will be needed by domestic staff. Standards of facilities are improving and are also gradually becoming similar to those provided in hotels. Also, more attention will be paid to the selection of surfaces, furniture and fittings so that they are easily and cheaply cleaned as well as looking good. This will affect the methods and frequencies of cleaning used by the domestic staff. Improved quality standards are being reflected in the fact that some Hospital Domestic Services are acquiring BS 5750, the British Standard for Quality Systems.

Domestic services departments within hospitals will be expected to be more financially accountable than ever before, as budgets allocated will be tighter and any other department in the hospital will be expected to pay for the domestic services used.

Hospitals have been aware for many years of the psychological effects on patients of their stay in hospital, particularly if it is a long stay. Patients often feel worthless and that they are missing their normal daily life. The domestic services department has to have a greater part to play in making the patients feel welcome and valued. In some hospitals, patients who are physically not too unwell help out with some of the cleaning duties for the staff, which gives them an occupation which is preferable to long hours of sitting in bed.

REFERENCES

1. Department of Health Social Services, Local Authority Statistics (1992) *Residential Accommodation for Elderly People and Younger Physically Handicapped People*, London: HMSO.
2. Herne, S. (1994) 'Catering for institutionalized elderly people: the care home's dilemma', *British Food Journal*, Vol. 96, No. 9, pp. 3–9.
3. Department of Health Social Services op. cit.
4. Herne, S. op. cit.
5. Ibid.

EIGHT

Hostels and Halls of Residence

MICHAEL DEAKIN

INTRODUCTION

Hostels are houses or halls of residence for groups who have specific needs – typically students, young workers, tourists and organized parties. The majority of hostels came into existence in response to a demand for safe, affordable, long-term accommodation. Education establishments, universities, public schools and private colleges have had a long history of associated accommodation provision and many children of the middle and upper classes were 'sent away' to be educated. Then in the late 1800s, large numbers of young people moved away from their homes for the first time to find work. They too required secure and respectable accommodation that ideally gave them access to social and leisure activities with people of their own age and interests. Hence the development of YMCAs and YWCAs (Young Men's/Women's Christian Associations).

One exception to the traditional demand for long-stay hostel accommodation is the Youth Hostel movement. It became a fashion, between the First and Second World Wars, that young workers and student groups left the towns to walk and cycle around the countryside. There was in fact very little alternative, apart from the traditional British seaside resort holiday, as this period predated the charter flights to Spain and other popular destinations. Before 1950 foreign travel was considered unusual and not for the masses. Youth Hostels were common in Germany in the early 1900s and provided inexpensive overnight lodging for one or two nights. The idea spread rapidly throughout the rest of Europe and in 1932 the International Federation of Youth Hostels was formed. In 1980 the International Federation of Youth hotels had 50 national members.

To some, the term 'hostel' has become synonymous with poor-quality, short-term accommodation. It is thought of as provided by charities, such as the Salvation Army, for the very poor or homeless in society. In this context it is used as a derogatory term signifying the occupants' failure to take care of themselves and implying a residence giving the very minimum of comfort and security for little or no monetary return. For these reasons this type of hostel is not considered part of the commercial letting industry. Although this type of accommodation plays an important role in society, it is still just one very small element of the total hostel provision. As we shall see in this chapter, much hostel accommodation is of a very high standard indeed.

DEMAND FOR HOSTEL ACCOMMODATION

The management of accommodation and the experience of the hostel product certainly differs according to the needs of the user groups. The majority of commercially let hostel accommodation is provided for the younger members of society. College halls of residence, youth hostels, the YMCA, YWCA, school study centres and the like all exist predominantly to serve the needs of youth. Security, affordability, a functional living environment and easy access to leisure activities are equally important to each user group.

Young Workers

CACI Acorn profile projections show that there are many more young workers in society than ever before, and the young working society in general is much more mobile and willing to move away from home to take up a job. Young people between the ages of 15 and 29 years are estimated to make up 20 per cent of the total population of the United Kingdom and most seek work in their late teens or early twenties. With such a mobile population, it is reasonable to assume that not all young workers will be able to find permanent suitable accommodation immediately, and not everybody likes the privacy or isolation given by private rented housing. Therefore for young workers in their first or second jobs, hostels can provide a residential place, either as a long-term home base until the occupant moves on or as a short-term solution until more suitable alternatives can be found.

Students

It is in the interest of universities and colleges to provide hostels or residences, as it keeps the students close to the lecture rooms and libraries and involves them in college activities. This is especially true of institutions built on 'greenfield sites' away from existing population centres, such as Keele and Warwick. Some universities can only guarantee a student place in a hostel for the first year of study. Student populations engaged in the higher education sector have been seen to increase consistently over the last 20 years and most universities and colleges have been unable to keep pace with the demand for rooms.

When choosing a place at university, students express a preference for those educational establishments that can offer a place in halls of residence. Usually it is the students' first time away from home and a room in college implies that they don't have to worry about maintaining their accommodation or preparing their own food or remembering to pay the household bills.

Tourists

In Europe as a whole, 2 per cent of all holidays taken by young adults are spent in youth hostel accommodation.[1] The tradition of youth hostelling is not quite so established in the United Kingdom but there are 240 YHA hostels in England and Wales and 300,000 active members.[2] The YHA is a registered charity and membership is essential for anyone wishing to stay in one of its hostels. The YHA by far the biggest provider of this type of accommodation and the only obvious competition is the small guest house sector of the industry. However, many of the hostels are located away from centres of population and form the backbone of walking and trekking holidays in remote locations, as illustrated in Figure 8.1.

Figure 8.1 Typical youth hostel.
Source: Adrian Carpenter.

Conference and Activity Breaks

Higher education institutions in the UK are largely state-funded through the Funding Councils. However, universities, as autonomous self-governing bodies, will seek to increase their total income as this will enable them to provide improved facilities. Since halls of residence or student hostels are used for an average academic year of 36 weeks duration in each year, the time they are left empty represents an under-utilized asset that can be used for conferences and a variety of other letting purposes and therefore commercial activities.

The British Universities Conference & Exhibition Venues organization, the British Universities Accommodation Consortium Ltd (BUAC), represents 67 universities and colleges, all of which offer a wide range of accommodation to conference organizers, part-time students, holidaymakers on activity breaks and individuals looking for budget accommodation.[3] Higher education colleges are represented in the same marketplace by HEAC, the Higher Education Accommodation Consortium. There is no doubt that this type of venue has advantages for a wide range of potential user groups. Facilities usually include a considerable amount of purpose-built accommodation in an academic environment. Most educational establishments have more than 500 single-study bedrooms available for letting and some five times this amount. The range of associated facilities is impressive and can include lecture rooms, language laboratories, computer workshops, television and film studios, exhibition areas, sports and recreation facilities and libraries.

Occupancy patterns tend to be short term, the letting periods are limited by the needs of the full-time student body who come and reclaim their rooms as each new term begins. However, in most cases, conference and activity-break organizers need only a few days or at most a couple of weeks to complete their programme of events. The unpretentious nature of the study bedrooms and the functional nature of the catering facilities is offset by the vast scale and capacity of the venues. University bursars and caterers are used to dealing with large numbers of young adults throughout the year, and residential events of a thousand delegates in the middle of the summer vacation does not confront them with problems they have not met before.

Organized School Activity Workshops

Organizers of schools parties use hostels to provide budget accommodation in support of school activities. Residential visits to youth hostels, activity centres, and nature study centres support the work of pupils studying elements of the National Curriculum. Complete hostels can be booked to ensure that school parties do not disturb other residents and centres will plan the itinerary of the visit to ensure maximum benefit is gained.

THE HOSTEL PRODUCT

Hostels are clearly not hotels. They do not provide the same level or range of service and they do not consider the people who use them as guests. Nor is hostel accommodation a by-product of another overriding activity. Hostels therefore cannot be compared or considered in the same way as accommodation provided by the hospital service or the prison service. The motivation to use hotel accommodation is created by the user for either short-term or longer-term living space and to give the user access to leisure or work. The level of intervention, by hostel management, in the living activities of the residents is much less than most serviced accommodation as hostels become the home of the user, if only for a very short time. The management of hostels is, therefore, less intrusive and less sophisticated than in a hotel or guest house; in some cases the relationship becomes more related to that of landlord and tenant than of hotelier and guest. It is therefore not unreasonable to expect people who use hostels to provide much more in the way of goods needed for day-to-day living.

The range of facilities provided by hostels and the associated intensity of service is reflected in the prices charged, but the significant advantage of hostel accommodation over the commercial alternatives is that they all provide the resident with an increased level of security and to some extent safety through supervision.

A typical study bedroom in a university hall of residence has to fulfil two basic needs of the student, firstly to act as a home bedroom where the student lives, and secondly as a place where the student can work at his/her studies. It is equipped with a single bed, wardrobe, wash hand basin, bookcase, coffee table, desk and desk chair and an easy chair; soft furnishings are kept to a minimum in order to reduce maintenance. Bathrooms, shower rooms, and toilets are usually shared but some of the newer halls have en-suite facilities, as illustrated in Figure 8.2. If a hall of residence does not include its own

Figure 8.2 Typical hostel bedroom (New Hall, University of St Andrews hall of residence).
Source: University of St Andrews.

dining facilities it is likely that self-catering kitchens will be provided between several rooms and most rooms have access to small food preparation areas to make hot drinks and reheat pre-prepared food items.

YHA hostels, on the other hand, are constantly upgrading their facilities but most bedrooms are still dormitory style, sleeping from 4 to 12 people. It is increasingly common, however, to find hostels that have twin rooms on offer and smaller dormitories that can be used as family rooms. In keeping with the youth hostelling culture, bedding is restricted to a laundered linen sleeping bag although pillows and duvets are provided. Youth Hostels provide evening meals and breakfast in communal dining rooms and the food is usually pre-plated for convenience of service; hostel residents are asked to help clean up afterwards, again in keeping with the hostelling culture. The times of access to hostels is somewhat restricted, visitors are not allowed into YHA hostels after 10.30 p.m. and lights are turned off in the dormitories at 11.30 p.m. Residents are not encouraged to get up too early in the mornings either; most hostels are 'closed' until 7.00 a.m. It used to be that entry to a YHA could only be gained if the young travellers had made their journey under their own efforts, walking, cycling or by canoe. These days many hostels have car parks and do not mind if residents have used the bus to get there.

The YMCA movement came into being in 1844. It was the inspiration of George Williams, a devout Christian who felt there was a need for secure hostels for young working men. Not all YMCAs have accommodation but their guidebook lists 74 hostels in towns and cities in England and Wales with a total of 6049 rooms available for letting.[4] From its earliest beginnings religious belief has not been a barrier to entry into a YMCA hostel and hostel managers admit both young men and young women. Single rooms are available on either a bed and breakfast basis or as self-catering bed-sitting rooms. Most residents stay for extended periods of up to two years or more; most residential hostels have extensive leisure and sporting facilities and some have limited restaurant facilities.

Founded in 1855, the Prayer Union and the General Female Training Institute came together as the YWCA to develop residential accommodation and a forum for common interest and debate. It operates 60 hostels in England and Wales, many of which have long waiting lists. It has no connection with the YMCA movement and is centrally managed from its Oxford head office. It offers hostel accommodation aimed at young people between the ages of 16 and 25. The YWCA does not insist that residents are Christian or female although the organization still has a strong religious foundation.

MARKETING

The demand for hostel accommodation is dependent on the extent of the booking period, on the pricing strategies and on the membership practices adopted by the hostel management. Little external marketing is carried out by hostel operators where residents stay for long periods of time and particularly where prices are consistent with, or marginally below, the value of commercial letting policy.

Long-term Residential Lets

Halls of residence in the university sector and young workers' hostel places are always in demand and waiting lists are not uncommon. In these environments internal marketing is carried out to maintain an atmosphere of understanding between residents and the hostel management. It would be easy to assume that because the hostel residents regard the rooms as their temporary homes that they, as a client group, become a captive audience. Common marketing strategies include direct mail to residents' rooms, keeping residents informed of changes in routine, improvements to the administration of their accommodation, and activities in which they can join. Notice boards and posters involve residents in the activities of the hostels and at the very least keeps them informed of what's going on. By far the most effective marketing is carried by personal contact and word of mouth; in common with most closed communities, students' opinions are formed by the people they talk to and hall wardens are a major source of information.

Short-term Residential Hostels

Where Hostels rely exclusively on short-stay residents, such as in a youth hostel, it makes sense to encourage users to become hostel members. This identifies people who have used the hostels in the past and hopefully will use them again in the future. The membership fee fulfils two roles for an organization. Firstly, it helps to maintain cash flows throughout the year regardless of the occupancy levels of the hostels. Secondly, it provides the organization with a database of names and addresses to which it can directly market itself knowing that these are the people who know and like the organization and can be encouraged to re-buy.

Membership magazines, accommodation guides, newsletters, promotional offers are all typically used as ways of affecting buyer behaviour and encouraging repeat business.

OPERATION OF HOSTEL ACCOMMODATION

Just as the marketing of a hostel varies according to whether it has long-stay lets (as in the case of a student hall of residence), or short-stay lets (as in a youth hostel), so also does the operation of these facilities.

Halls of Residence

A typical university may have between five and 20 halls of residence accommodating between 200 and 2000 students. The halls of residence themselves are likely to be located on campus if the university is one of the newer universities built during the 1960s and 1970s, or on sites spread throughout the area if an older university. They typically consist mainly of single study bedrooms and usually are big enough to justify their own catering facilities. Perhaps 20 per cent of all such accommodation will be self-catering. In addition, some halls of residence may have twin-bedded accommodation. This style of room is only let in term time on a single-sex occupancy basis and they are not popular with the majority of students who value periods of privacy and quiet study time.

The Accommodation Services Department would coordinate various student contracts in the halls, as well room renting and leasing schemes in the private sector, which supplement the total stock of rooms available to students. Rooms are allocated to incoming students at the beginning of each year. New students are asked to complete letting contracts, which specify the payment of fees and the rules of the college in terms of both their behaviour and their understanding of their responsibilities as residents. Students entering college for the first time, students from outside the immediate locality of the college, and overseas students are usually given priority. Allocation is based, where possible, on students' personal needs. For instance, smaller halls may be set aside for occupancy by mature students, or even students with young children, so that additional facilities such as a crèche and a self-service laundry may also be provided.

The head of Accommodation Services would typically report directly to the college principal for all issues that may arise from the management of the halls. Each of the halls is likely to have a warden who is given some responsibility for general student conduct, and to act as the first point of contact in a crisis or emergency. Wardens are usually drawn from the amongst the university's staff or student body and live in an apartment or room in the hall for which they are responsible. If students, wardens are usually either final-year students or postgraduates. They are given some compensation in rent as payment for their services.

Within the Accommodation Services team, support will be provided to the wardens both in terms of dealing with the residents and dealing with the hall of residence. Should a warden have a problem with a resident, a 'student services manager' is usually available to provide advice. Ultimately, if problems continue, the conditions outlined in the student contract will be enforced and students will be asked to leave the halls if their behaviour warrants it. Likewise, if an emergency occurs at any time of the day, the Estates Manager is likely to have a service engineer available to deal with the problem. In addition there will be emergency contractors from the gas, electricity and water utilities.

As well as student services, estates, and wardens, the accommodation service is also likely to include cleaning services managers with responsibility for day-to-day cleaning and maintenance of the halls. Supervisors may work throughout the day and can help the cleaning services manager with planned maintenance, the planning of redecoration and replacement of furnishings such as carpets and curtains. They also ensure that the halls have adequate supplies of cleaning materials and that cleaning equipment is regularly serviced and in good working order. Typically, cleaning staff work for a limited period of the day, with most cleaners being employed for three hours each morning. Students are expected to make their own beds and provide their own bed linen and towels; they are asked to keep their rooms generally tidy. Cleaners will only ensure the cleaning of floors, flat surfaces, sinks and bathroom equipment. Student rooms are cleaned once every two weeks, although most rooms are inspected every two days for student safety. Daily cleaning is provided for all shared areas such as bathrooms, toilets, kitchens and corridors. Jobs are assigned to cleaners who individually will be responsible for a block of rooms and its service areas; supervisors inspect the work to ensure that tasks have been carried out correctly. Cleaning service managers may on occasions organize a group of staff to carry out jobs that require a team effort such as carpet shampooing, window cleaning or intensive cleaning of a lobby or public area.

The Accommodation Services Manager is likely to coordinate the department through regular contact with staff. These meetings serve a particular purpose at the end of each academic term as they allow for the halls to be organized for the residential conferences booked by the Conference Office, or equivalent. This office has the responsibility of maximizing the use of the vacated halls of residence and academic facilities. Costs associated with the university's physical assets, its campus and buildings, still continue to be accumulated regardless of occupancy levels in the halls. Any income and profit that can be earned during the holiday periods helps to offset these costs and provides money for further investment.

Universities promote themselves as exhibition and conference venues in various ways – such as tourist information literature, direct mail to prospective clients, and through advertising material produced by a consortium of universities. Typically bookings are taken centrally by the conference office staff and this is communicated to the Accommodation Services Manager in the form of a request for accommodation. Similar requests are sent to the college caterers and campus managers who control access to the lecture rooms and sports facilities. In essence the facilities of the college, including all the hostel accommodation, become available for the use of the conference office.

The role of the cleaning services department changes with the type of room occupant. When rooms in the halls are let to conference delegates, they have to be fully serviced daily, beds are changed daily with linen provided by the cleaning services department, along with towels, soap and other accessories. This increased level of service inevitably means a change in staff working patterns and longer working hours; the housekeeping role becomes much closer to that expected by a hotel guest as the intensity of the service is increased. None the less, colleges and universities, with thousands of student rooms, still have remarkably few staff in relation to the numbers of room occupants.

Hostels

The informal culture of the hostel movement is reflected in the informality of its organization. The YHA, YMCA and other similar types of hostel operator rely on small teams of people who maintain the standards of the organization according to their rules and operating methods. Organization charts appear very flat in this style of hostel, with one or two people being responsible for the practical operation and management, with a mixture of full-time, part-time, casual, or as in some cases, volunteer staff providing the labour force. In a bigger hostel the scale of the operation demands a more formalized structure as the management task increases.

CURRENT ISSUES AND FUTURE TRENDS

Hostel accommodation provision forms only a small part of the accommodation industry. Its origins are rooted in responses to very precise needs. It is worth noting that organizations with clearly targeted user groups or market segments are successful in attracting high occupancy levels. The demand for hostel accommodation is not diminishing and most organizations are opening new hostels or refurbishing old ones as funds allow. The YHA opened its newest youth hostel in Manchester in January 1995. It has a loyal independent and family membership from both the United Kingdom and Europe. Hostels are frequently very busy and have found a new market segment in school groups, who occupy hostel accommodation outside the traditional holiday periods. YHA hostels are moving closer towards the standards of facilities and service expected by holidaymakers who traditionally would have used guest houses or small hotels.

With regard to universities and colleges, it is difficult to envisage a time when all students will be guaranteed a place in halls of residence. Whether or not student attendance at university declines, student accommodation is a key factor in attracting students to any one particular institution. The student hostel is part of the total package offered by educational establishments and can directly contribute to students' ability to study. The competitive nature of this sector will encourage redevelopment and new-build projects which will provide flexible accommodation for alternative uses outside the traditional term times.

REFERENCES

1. British Tourist Authority (1994) *British National Travel Survey 1993-94*, London: BTA.
2. YHA (1995) *Accommodation Guide (England & Wales)*, Youth Hostels Association.
3. BUAC (1995) *The Choice is Nationwide*, British Universities Accommodation Consortium Ltd.
4. YMCA (1995) *Y.M.C.A. Guidebook*, YMCA.

PART B

The Foodservice Industry

NINE

The Foodservice Sector

PETER JONES

INTRODUCTION

The author and broadcaster Derek Cooper wrote in 1964:

> I have the utmost sympathy for caterers who are trying hard to do a self-respecting job in the face of almost universal indifference ... There is, alas, no reason for optimism on the eating front. For the minority prepared to pay for the privilege, there will always be a small number of good restaurants. The majority of us will continue to put up uncomplainingly, perhaps even with a sort of masochistic pleasure, with this kind of bad food and bad service.[1]

Thus Cooper puts the blame, if blame there must be, for poor standards of catering in Britain fairly and squarely on the consumer. He argues that if the consumer refused to accept food and service that was inadequate, then the caterer would have to improve those standards or go out of business. But he was writing in the 1960s. Do the British public still have such low expectations? How has the industry responded to consumer needs?

This chapter examines the nature of foodservice provision from a consumer perspective. It discusses the foodservice consumer and the reasons they may have for eating out. It looks at and analyses what has been described as the 'meal experience'. It then goes on to give an overview of the size and scale of this sector in the UK, before looking in more detail at the operating systems used in the industry. All the major systems and technologies are explained, including both back-of-house systems such as call order and cook-chill, as well as front-of-house service systems such as table service and self-service. It concludes that the industry in the 1990s is very different from that of the 1960s, not least because the British customer has at last stopped being indifferent to poor food and lousy service.

WHO EATS OUT AND WHY?

Obviously there are many different types of customer – male and female, young and old, single people and families, rich and poor. It is essential that foodservice operators are aware which of these customers their operation will attract. It may attract all of them, although this is unlikely. Most people have preconceived ideas about the suitability of certain foodservice establishments for certain types of customers. For the purpose of economic analysis and research, the population in Britain has been broken down into 'socioeconomic groups'. Basically it is the subdivision of the population into groups with broadly similar incomes, occupations, education levels and resources. This has been used as one of identifying distinct market segments. More recently, this kind of demographic segmentation has been replaced by a more sophisticated analysis based around so-called 'life-style groups' based on psychographics.

The implications of such segments are many, since research has shown that 'expectations, values, usage and attitudes are likely to vary between groups. Members of different groups are likely to give different priorities to certain needs, and the upper socioeconomic groupings are likely to be able to satisfy certain needs more easily than others'.[2] Thus to answer the question, 'What factors contribute to the customer's enjoyment of a meal?' is by no means easy. For each type of customer, with each type of need to be satisfied, there is an operation that will be satisfactory. All we can do is look at those factors that contribute to the meal experience in some way or another and draw some general conclusions about how they affect the customer.

Probably everybody in the UK has 'eaten out' at some time in their life. As we have seen in Chapter 1, there are many different sectors of that industry, each catering for very different consumer needs. Essentially, however, there are some sectors of the industry that cater for people who have no choice but to eat there – hospitals, institutions, prisons, and so on – that have a captive market; and those restaurants, cafés and cafeterias where the consumer chooses to eat. In some cases, this choice is very restricted, on a train for instance, or in a staff dining-room; but in most cases, the choice is vast. If people decide to eat out, then it follows that they have decided on this course of action in preference to some other. In this respect, the foodservice operator is competing with alternative experiences that might attract consumers' hard-earned disposable income, and these may be far removed from any gastronomic delights. The consumer may choose to go to the theatre, to play squash, to visit the races, and so on. So let us look a little more closely at why a person chooses to eat out instead of indulging in some other pleasurable activity.

Graham Campbell-Smith[3] listed a total of 43 different reasons why people may choose to eat out. It is really no surprise then that there is such a rich diversity of eating-out establishments available to the public. However, six basic reasons have been identified as to why people eat away from home:[4]

- *Convenience.* This factor includes all those people who are away from home for some reason – shoppers, commercial travellers, commuters – who are physically unable to return home at normal meal times. It would also include people who do not have the time to eat at home and eat out in conjunction with some other leisure activity.
- *Variety.* Just as people do not go to see the same film every week, people are stimulated by trying new foods or drinks in different restaurants. Also, people who live in circumstances where meal experiences are limited, such as in hostels at universities or colleges or in poorly equipped bed-sits, may choose to eat out for this reason.
- *Labour.* The desire to have someone else prepare, cook, serve and wash up a meal most certainly influences some people's decision to eat out. Or for medical and other reasons domestic help may be required and may not be available. The

popularity of fish and chip shops is a long-standing example of this, as is the recent growth in take-aways and fast-food operations.

- *Status*. Both for personal and business reasons people may choose to impress their guests by taking them out to a fashionable and/or expensive restaurant. In many parts of the world, the business lunch is an accepted way of sealing successful business transactions, while in the USA, the executive even has a working breakfast. On the personal level, eating out may be partly attributable to conforming with the social pattern of the neighbourhood.
- *Culture/tradition*. Eating can be described as 'a part of our cultural heritage, and a manifestation of kinship'. In Britain, celebrations of special events such as anniversaries and birthdays are often associated with eating out, although not to the same extent as the Belgians and French under such circumstances.
- *Impulse*. This is rather like saying that sometimes people have no particular reason for eating out, they do so on the spur of the moment, so that it is a catch-all for any circumstances that have not been included previously. But there is no doubt that in certain businesses, notably retailing, impulse-buying is very significant and that it contributes to sales in the foodservice industry too.

A more recent study by the American National Restaurant Association in 1989, identified five main reasons for eating out in the USA and can be summarized[5] as:

- *Doing the easy thing*. This is a simple replacement of eating at home with eating out to save time and effort.
- *Having a fun time*. This sees eating out as a reward or a treat, usually in celebration.
- *Having a nice meal*. This decision is based on eating out for the pleasure of doing so.
- *Making sure everyone has something to eat*. This relates to providing a convenient way of feeding family members each operating on different schedules.
- *Satisfying a craving*. This is the most impulsive reason for eating out. It is especially important in the take-away and home delivery markets.

Whether there are five or six or more reasons for eating out, the important point that is being made is that *many people do not eat out just for the food*. It is all too easy for the professional to believe that because the food is the most visible product of a restaurant and is what the customer most obviously pays for, that it is the be-all and end-all of successful foodservice. As we have seen, however, customers may be eating not to satisfy hunger at all (although in most cases they will be) but to satisfy other needs like social contact, status and curiosity.

FACTORS IN THE MEAL EXPERIENCE

The following discussion of the meal experience was originally developed by Jones in 1988.[6]

Food

Although people do eat for reasons other than simply to satisfy their hunger, food is still the heart of the experience. But because everybody in the western world eats every day, everybody is an expert about the subject. People know what they like and expect to be served it. For many years the most popular meal in the UK has been prawn cocktail, steak, chips and peas followed by ice cream. However, the recent growth in healthy eating has seen a decline in the popularity of red meat and an increase in fish and chicken consumption. From the operator's point of view, it is extremely unlikely that we can change the consumers' preconceived ideas about food. The customer has partly chosen the restaurant on the basis of what type of food is served and will select from the menu those dishes that are most appealing. The palate is a delicate instrument that should be cared for and educated; all the various sensory impressions or sensations such as odour, taste, texture and variety complete the gastronomic experience throughout life. The successful foodservice operator is the one who ensures that the appearance, aroma, taste, texture and temperature are all just as the customer expects them to be.

- *Appearance.* The expression 'looks good enough to eat' has not become a cliché by chance. Food has to look good on the plate – a factor that all the major foodservice firms are aware of. They spend a great deal of time and effort in ensuring that their units sell a product that looks good.
- *Aroma*. The second thing that will affect customers' reaction to the food, even before they eat it, is the smell. Dining out in an Indian restaurant or buying fish and chips would not be the same without distinctiveness of aroma. Some operators even exploit this factor by ensuring that the ventilation leads out on to the street in order to attract customers, and although this may be very effective for fresh bread shops and doughnut houses, not all cooking smells are desirable. While eating food, much of the sensation is derived from the olfactory centre of the nasal cavity, without which most of what we eat and drink would lack its subtlety. In drinking a vintage wine or a good brandy, much of the enjoyment is derived from its 'nose', and the same can be said of other gastronomic experiences.
- *Taste.* The taste buds of the tongue are only able to detect four basic flavours – sweet, sour, salt and bitter. It is the many variations of these four that combine to create the unique flavour of a particular food. For the consumer, the combination of flavours is quite important and can be used to good effect in various dishes: sweet and sour pork, lamb with mint sauce, and so on. It is also relevant to the sequence of dishes since sweet items are generally left until the end of a meal lest they upset the palate.
- *Texture.* There are many textures of food – rough or smooth, hard or soft, fluid or solid, dry or moist, and tough or tender. The consistency and shape properties of food are experienced by pressure and movement receptors in the mouth. It is these that signal our dislike of food that is rubbery, slimy or tough, and a customer's choice of a rare, medium or well-done steak is partly derived from the influence of texture upon the palate.
- *Temperature.* Customers enjoy the variety that temperature can add to a meal – a piping-hot stew followed by ice cream for instance. Wealthy Victorians ate a sorbet in the middle of their long banquets in order to refresh their jaded palates as the citrus-based ice was refreshing. But temperature not only provides variety, but affects flavour too. The sweetness of a dish is accentuated when served hot, while the saltiness of a soup is reduced at a high temperature.

Service

Customers are not familiar with nor care for the problems of providing service. They are only concerned that the service is of the standard that they expect. If they are in a hurry then they will go to fast-food outlets that will provide a speedy meal; if they are out to impress, they will go to a sophisticated restaurant providing *guéridon* service. There are many differing styles of service, each tailored to meet the particular needs of a certain type of clientele.

Social groups AB do spend more than any other group (40 per cent of their expenditure on eating out) in restaurants, hotels and steak bars where 'service' is provided, whereas groups DE spend 30 per cent of their expenditure in cafeterias, pubs and cafés. This of course reflects the cost and value for money as much as an attitude towards service, but there is no doubt that consumers who are not used to full silver service or *guéridon* work feel uncomfortable in those situations where it is provided. Campbell-Smith argued,[7] 'At the lowest level of socioeconomic grouping, there is probably no need to have more than four or five types of eating establishment, from a general café to a fish and chip shop, hamburger bar, bacon-and-egg speciality restaurant and possibly a simple snack and sandwich bar.' This rather condescending 1960s attitude seems very dated now.

The expectations of the British public are much higher with regard to the range of restaurants now available, the variety of product range, and the improved standards reflected in fast-food and roadside catering, compared with the popular catering outlets and transport cafés that Campbell-Smith was familiar with. There does appear to be a trend for customers to complain more than in the past. This is not necessarily because they have more to complain about, but they are becoming less reluctant to do so. This is particularly true amongst male customers in the AB category and over-45 age group. And it is slow and poor service that is most frequently complained about. Nearly one in four customers in the Gallup Survey of 1986 had cause to complain about this.

Cleanliness and Hygiene

In the USA, the preoccupation with hygiene is more developed than in Britain, and, along with the influx of US-style operations, some of their ideas about cleanliness have been introduced. As we shall see, disposables, which are probably the most hygienic means of serving food, are becoming more acceptable, and we shall probably see other ideas, such as cellophane-wrapped cutlery, crockery and so forth, assuring us of their pristine state, on tables in restaurants in Britain quite soon. The power of advertising and the media to influence people is also making consumers more and more aware of personal hygiene and hygiene in the home which is bound to affect attitudes to eating out. Already there is a growing movement towards the banning of cigarette smoking in public places, and many places, including cinemas, canteens and public transport, have segregated areas for smokers and non-smokers.

Whether justified or not, Britain does not have a very good reputation for cleanliness. Tourists from abroad find our streets, parks, buses and public buildings dirty and litter-strewn in comparison with their own countries, and this attitude is extended towards our hotels and restaurants. The archetypal British eating establishment had encrusted sauce bottles on a not very clean table, with waitresses having a quiet cigarette in the corner. Hopefully, this image is fading, if not gone forever. The caterer is aware that cleanliness and hygiene are selling points and that the regulations laid down are only a minimum standard to be met. In 1986, dirtiness and poor hygiene were relatively low on the list of complaints consumers had about the industry.

Essentially there are three areas of concern for the foodservice operator: staff, equipment and environment.

- *Staff*. Customers will not expect staff to wear a uniform, although most foodservice operations do encourage staff to wear a uniform as part of their overall image (fast-food outlets are a good example of this). But staff will be expected to be smart and clean. People tend to ascribe cleanliness to particular aspects of appearance – clothes, which they expect to be well-pressed and stain free; hair, which should be clean and looked after well; nails, which should be clean and manicured; and body odour, which should be non-existent (i.e. neither sweaty nor overly perfumed).
- *Equipment*. Customers will notice if equipment is not clean since much of it is literally put under their very noses. All table appointments, cutlery, crockery, and so forth, must be clean and polished and not defective in any way (for instance, cups chipped, plates cracked or forks bent).
- *The environment or room itself*. Because most restaurants and foodservice outlets have direct access onto the street and have a great deal of human traffic in and out of them they collect a lot of dirt and dust. The operator must ensure that floor and wall surfaces are cleaned regularly and fittings such as pictures and prints and lights are dusted properly.

At this point one might reasonably presume that the next factor that influences the customer's enjoyment of a meal will be that indefinable factor – atmosphere. Ask anyone why they go to a particular restaurant and they will probably say one of the three things – they like the food; it is good value for money; or they like the 'atmosphere'. But, if you ask someone to explain what 'atmosphere' is, they are not usually able to define what they mean. They may say that they like the surroundings, the music played there, the other customers or some other aspect of the operation, but usually they will not be very clear about it. This is because so many of the factors that contribute towards creating an atmosphere are received by the customer on a subconscious level. So rather than talk about atmosphere in vague terms, we will look at these factors in some detail.

Decor

'In the year since redesigning its Notting Hill outlet, Wimpy International has trebled its turnover there. And at the THF Cavendish Hotel, a redesign has improved bar turnover by 50 per cent.'[8] So good interior design is obviously important to an establishment's success. But to analyse what is good and what is not so good is very difficult. Newell (1965)[9] wrote: 'Atmosphere is ethereal, evasive and indeterminate. The response of an individual to atmosphere is personal and ... the individual's reaction to any combination of the factors [which influence atmosphere] can only be determined or controlled by rudimentary principles.' The problem lies in the essential paradox that customers need to feel 'at home' in their surroundings, without feeling that they are at home. Thus the decor of a restaurant must be different without undermining the sense of security of customers; it should provoke feelings of pleasure and relaxation rather than tension and anxiety. The decor must also play an integral part in the whole surroundings: if customers are paying a lot for a meal then they will expect plush surroundings, whereas if customers want a quick, cheap meal then they will expect functional rather than decorative decor.

Lighting

The lighting in a foodservice operation is determined in conjunction with the decor. In the same way that colours can affect moods, brightness or dimness can too. Generally, bright light will promote a sense of warmth and sociability, whereas dim lighting will have the reverse effect. Thus restaurants that aim to attract couples will have dim lighting that will make the partner appear to be more attractive and increase the sense of relaxation, whereas restaurants catering for groups of people will be bright to aid sociability. Lighting can also have the effect of distorting true colours – for instance, butchers have used a particular light bulb to enhance the redness of raw meat, while the effect of ultraviolet light on white is well known. The foodservice operators must ensure that the lighting does not have an adverse effect upon the appearance of the food, decor and customers. Lighting should also reflect the time of day, so that at lunchtime it is more acceptable to eat in a bright environment than at dinner. Finally, lighting in conjunction with turnover can help to establish a fast turnover of customer by creating a brisk atmosphere.

Air conditioning

In the USA, with its far greater extremes of heat and cold, air conditioning is found everywhere. This is not the case in Britain and generally the problems of heating and ventilation are dealt with separately. Restaurants are busy places, or should be, with customers coming in and going out and waiting staff to-ing and fro-ing, so that it is very difficult to maintain a constant temperature. Similarly, the proximity of the kitchen must give rise to cooking smells that may stimulate the appetite but can just as easily be off-putting. There are two aspects to heating the establishment – actual and psychological. Both the illumination and the colour scheme can affect the customer's sensation of warmth, and other factors have a similar effect. For instance, a convected air curtain over the entrance gives an immediate sensation of warmth for people coming in off the street in winter, or of coolness in summer. Similarly, an obvious radiant source of heat like a coal fire also creates a feeling of warmth, even if its contribution to the actual room temperature is minimal. It can also have the undesired effect of making people feel too hot – customers have even been known to ask to be moved to another table because they are too hot from fake gas-fired 'coal' fires that give off no heat. As far as the actual temperature is concerned, the most pleasurable temperature for people sitting down is around 18°C. This will be affected by the number of people in the room since sitting ten customers in a room will produce about as much heat as a one-kilowatt fire. In this respect, heating that is controlled by a thermostat is desirable: if not, a small thermometer placed in the room will give the caterer an indication of the room temperature. Customers will also strongly object to sitting in a draught. The source of most draughts is doorways or windows. Screens near the service doors and entrance should help to eliminate draughts and, likewise, windows should be checked and possibly double glazed, particularly those with an easterly or northerly aspect. At the same time, it is desirable that the air in the room be circulating and moving to remove unwanted smells and to help maintain the ambient temperature. This must be done in a controlled way, using fans or extractors. In the kitchen, too, extractor fans must be properly sited and maintained correctly to minimize cooking smells in the restaurant itself. Finally, there is growing concern about smoking in public places. More and more outlets are providing no-smoking areas in parts of their operation.

Furnishing

The functional design of restaurant furniture reflects greatly upon customers' enjoyment of meals and the length of time they will spend in the establishment. It will also affect the number of covers that can be accommodated in the food service area and thereby influence customers' sense of security and intimacy. This same factor will also affect the profitability of the enterprise, so that a great deal of research has gone into the design of tables and chairs, to the extent that the Council for Industrial Design set up an Advisory Committee on Hotels and Restaurants that has made recommendations concerning restaurant furniture.

Consumers, of course, are not concerned with this detailed analysis; their only concern is comfort and well-being. Thus, if customers are in parties of four or six, they will prefer to sit at a round table, which enhances personal contact and conversation, rather than at a rectangular table, which from the caterer's point of view will increase the seating capacity. Likewise, it was found in popular catering units that fitted booth-seating, where there were places for four people, couples preferred to sit next to each other since it was difficult to talk to each other when facing each other across the table without addressing the people on either side. This meant that the seats had to be made sufficiently long and wide to allow people to turn inwards without discomfort. Customers, too, are fussy about where they sit in a restaurant. Many people, for instance, will insist on sitting so that they are facing into the room, partly so that they have something other than a wall to look at and partly because they feel more secure with a wall behind them. Finally, according to research by the Council for Industrial Design, women seem to have different sitting habits to men. Men prefer to slump back or lean on their elbows in a relaxed position, whereas women can sit upright for longer periods without suffering the same amount of fatigue as men. Obviously it is impracticable to have two sorts of chairs, but if a restaurant wishes to encourage people to linger over their meal, it must provide chairs with arms.

Acoustics

Restaurants are noisy places, or they would be if care was not taken to reduce the level of noise. In fact, reducing the level of noise of movement and bustle is the first step taken by restaurateurs who want to upgrade their premises. The most important point to note with regard to levels of acceptable noise is that age group rather than social class is the determining factor, young people being able and willing to accept much higher levels.

There are three contributory factors to noise in a restaurant (apart from outside or extraneous noise that presumably could be avoided if necessary).

- *Voices*. Customers need to communicate with each other and with the staff. Therefore the general level of noise should not exceed that which makes ordinary conversation impossible. Obviously, the more people in the room, the more noise there is, but as one can hardly request customers to talk more quietly, the caterer must reduce the general level of noise by reducing the input from the two other factors.

- *Operational*. Eating and serving food can be a fairly noisy business. Apart from the noise derived from serving food, there is also noise caused by movement. Some floor surfaces are much noisier than others – for instance, tiling as opposed to carpeting. But in addition, the decor can contribute. Carpeting and curtains can reduce noise, while a textile wall fabric made in France called '*mur de silence*' was credited, in one report,[10] with reducing noise from an adjacent room by up to 90 per cent. The same report states that if 'premises are carpeted, the electricity heating bill can be reduced by 12 per cent, according to research conducted in Japan'. The main factor contributing to this saving is pile height, irrespective of whether the carpet is wool, nylon, polyester or acrylic.

- *Music*. Most experts agree that music has a direct and strong effect on the customer's mood. It is used in many different environments – on Waterloo station or in supermarkets to speed up the flow of people, in factories and workshops as 'music while you work', and extensively as background music in hotels and restaurants. It can achieve many things for caterers so long as they are aware of one essential point – that background music is forced upon the customer whether they like it or not, and if they do not like it then the restaurant loses customers. Otherwise, music may be used to create an environment of bustle until the restaurant fills up and then be turned down to allow for conversation. It can reinforce the particular image of the restaurant by playing appropriate music: rock music in the Hard Rock Café, and chamber music in the Ritz. It has even been suggested that music can be used to overcome customers' prevailing moods of depression on a wet, rainy day by playing bright and cheerful tunes. Newell[11] proposes the following points to consider: no vocals because people listen to vocals; no 'top ten' because they are fashions and become dated too quickly; a balance of light pop, film themes, musicals and any music that will have lasting popularity; and not mass-produced but carefully considered for the particular style of restaurant.

Size and Shape of the Room

This factor will certainly affect the atmosphere of the eating environment by creating feelings of intimacy or spaciousness. As we have seen, the operation can affect people's reactions to the room by careful use of colour, patterns and lighting. Unless the restaurant is purpose built, operators may have to resort to employing the skills of the interior designer to modify establishments where the ceiling is too high or too low, the room is too narrow, too small or whatever. Many high-street sites, for instance, are designed with shops in mind and therefore tend to be long and narrow (the wider the frontage onto the street, the greater the expense of buying or renting the site) which is why so many catering units in such sites have mirrors along one wall, in order to create an illusion of width.

Clientele

This factor is one over which the operator only has limited control. Most certainly, however, customers' enjoyment of the meal will be affected by the other customers in the room. In general terms they will feel at home and reassured if the other customers are of a similar age, wearing similar clothes and behaving in a similar way. Whereas they will be upset if others are behaving too loudly (or too quietly), or if they are casually dressed when they are formal and vice versa. In most instances, however, the restaurant will reflect the socioeconomic and age group that will be attracted to it, as outlined above. A person who dines at the Savoy will expect to eat in formal, reserved surroundings with others of middle age and thick wallets, and someone eating in a Happy Eater will expect to see children.

The only control that operators have over clientele is that of refusing to serve customers, which so long as the restaurant is not an inn as defined under the Hotel Proprietors Act 1956, they are perfectly entitled to do. It was the practice in years gone by to refuse customers on the basis of their dress, and some places still insist that male customers must wear a tie, although this practice appears to have died out.

Price

The idea of service providing value for money has been mentioned, but consideration has not yet been given to the impact that price has upon the customer's enjoyment of a meal. In the economic climate of the 1990s, many people would argue that this factor is the most important consideration in the mind of a potential customer. What is certain is that, in the foodservice industry, pricing has tended in the past to take little account of its effect upon customers. The traditional cost-plus method has recently been seen to be a poor policy in a consumer-oriented business, since it means that more expensive items such as steak, lobster, and so on, are priced higher still by adding a fixed percentage. This has led to suggestions that a fixed amount rather than a percentage should be added to all items, so that, irrespective of cost, all dishes on a menu would have, for example, £1 added to the cost.

THE FOODSERVICE SECTOR DEFINED

In order to discuss the foodservice industry in some depth, it is first necessary to define the industry. However, to the best of my knowledge nobody has yet attempted to do so in the UK, primarily because foodservice is seen as a part of the hotel and catering industry as a whole. This assumption was perfectly reasonable 40 years ago or so, when with a few exceptions, the main establishments serving meals were hotels, liners and inns. However, since 1945, the entire complexion of hotelkeeping and catering has changed with the development of institutional and industrial catering, the growth of the 'popular' sector and in recent years, the boom in fast food. Thus there is now a very real need to separate the provision of accommodation from the provision of food and drink in order to appraise and evaluate the foodservice industry in its own right.

In effect, this textbook has already defined the foodservice by the way it is organized. The second half of this text has nine chapters, each of which is devoted to a specific sector. In some cases these sectors match sectors as defined by the Standard Industrial Clas-

Table 9.1 Sectors of the foodservice industry.

Sector	SIC classification	Differentiating factor
Restaurants	part of 6611	'the quintessential foodservice outlet'
Hotel foodservice	6650	'for people staying away from home'
Motorway & roadside	part of 6611	'foodservice for the motorist'
Licensed trade	6620 & 6630	'food for people out for a drink'
Fast food & take-aways	6612 & part of 6611	'meal package for people in a hurry'
Employee feeding	6640	'for people at their place of work'
Welfare catering	9310, 9320 & 9330	'for people unable to feed themselves'
Travel catering	none	'for people on the move'
Outside & social catering	none	'service where it was never intended'

sification, in other cases they discuss and analyse foodservice provision outside of the SIC, as illustrated in Table 9.1. The underlying principle for classifying the industry into these sectors is the focus this text has on *operations*. If this text were only concerned with the size and scale of the industry, then the SIC would be the best way to organize the text. However, this text focuses on customers' needs and how the industry responds operationally to these needs. Varying customer needs results in a different set of priorities of factors in the meal experience. These alternative sets of priorities have led to the development of specific kinds of operation to serve each of these markets. For instance, fast food grew up to satisfy the need for a high value, quick-service meal item. The sectoral classification is also consistent with the original text *Foodservice Operations*, where the issue was discussed.

> This division is not arbitrary but an attempt to examine particular aspects of food service, and in many respects it is a classification that many caterers would accept as being identifiable in the industry ... The diversity of the industry means that there are some operations which cannot be easily classified ... [such as] takeaways and vending. At the same time, the distinction between one sector and another is blurred when the same firm operates in more than one sector ... [the] industry's classification is meant to illustrate the *essential* feature of providing food and drink under particular circumstances. Each chapter has a subtitle ... [which] attempts to put into a single sentence the features or problems of that sector which differentiate it from any other.[12]

These differentiating factors are identified in Table 9.1.

In Chapter 1, key statistics relating to the hospitality industry as a whole were identified. In this part of the book, each chapter on a sector of the foodservice industry will also identify key operating statistics in terms of the size and scale of each sector. It is therefore unnecessary to duplicate this information here. None the less there are some key facts, based on this author's estimates derived from a composite of a number of sources, that need to be emphasized. The foodservice industry employs approximately 1.83 million people, compared with around 0.6 million workers engaged in the provision of accommodation services. Of these around 70 per cent will be part-time employees. These employees work in over 200,000 commercial outlets and at least 40,000 non-commercial operations (education, health, public sector, etc.). The average size of a foodservice operation is therefore very small. This is largely because about 150,000 pubs, hotels, and restaurants are owner-operated. Two sectors dominate – 30,000 outlets are fish and chip shops, take-aways, and sandwich bars, whilst there are nearly 80,000 pubs. The financial turnover of the industry in 1993 was at least £20 billion. Arguably the largest single catering operation in the UK is the National Health Service, which spends over £450 million each year.

FOODSERVICE OPERATING SYSTEMS

In Chapter 1, the foodservice industry was identified as being made up of a sector with a number of different operating systems (see Figure 1.3). Although traditionally, meals were both prepared and served in the same premises this is not necessarily the case today. It is therefore important to consider back-of-house operations and front-of-house operations separately.

Back-of-House Operating Systems

In 1981, four basic food production systems were identified.[13] These four types are still a valid way of thinking about the foodservice industry. Their relationship to the systems models presented in Figure 1.3 is explained below.

- *Conventional or traditional.* The customer's food is prepared on the same site as it is to be eaten, using mainly raw or semi-prepared products, such as pre-portioned meat, frozen vegetables and so on. This system is to be found typically in the hotel and restaurant sectors of the industry. There are three main sub-systems. The à la carte system (see also Figure 1.3a) depends on the customer ordering the food prior to cooking or finishing, so that dishes are cooked or prepared to order. Clearly, the type of food items and method of cooking are restricted by the necessity to serve the customer within a reasonable time span. The second sub-system is the table d'hôte system (Figure 1.3b), which involves much greater preparation of dishes in advance. This enables the chef to prepare entrée dishes such as stews and braized meat items, which require longer cooking times. Thirdly, there is call order operation (Figure 1.3e), which is similar to the à la carte operation but largely reliant on prepared foodstuffs purchased from suppliers.
- *Commissary.* This system has food prepared in a central kitchen, using conventional methods; service, however, takes place on several different sites. This system may be used in the industrial or institutional sector and is of particular significance in outside catering. Increasingly, commissaries are using ready-prepared food systems (see below).
- *Ready-prepared system.* This is the food system whereby foods are prepared to be served at a later time, either on the same site or in several different locations. It is the system adopted by in-flight airline caterers, but may also be used in the industrial or institutional sectors. There are three main technologies available for retaining the quality of the ready-prepared dishes. These are cook-freeze, cook-chill and *sous-vide* or vacuum-packing (Figure 1.3d). Foods are usually prepared in bulk and then either held in bulk by chilling or freezing, or held in portions by chilling, freezing or vacuum-packing.
- *Assembly serve.* In this instance foods are purchased pre-prepared from the food-processing industry and reconstituted on the premises. Such foods are typically frozen or of the boil-in-the-bag type. This system is successfully used in the fast

Table 9.2 Typical operations manual (fast food).

1 Introduction
    Background to the company
    Organization chart

2 Finance
    Cash and turnover summary
    Weekly stock and usage sheet
    VAT
    Weekly finance reports
    Payroll

3 Products
    Delivery
    Storage
    Ordering
    Recipes
    Food preparation
    Method
    Presentation, holding and serving of each menu
    Packaging
    Portion control
    Stock control
    Menu storage, relating to different times of the day

4 Equipment
    Specifications
    Operation
    Cleaning
    Maintenance

5 Marketing
    Advertising
    Public relations
    Point-of-sale/display material

6 Job descriptions
    Managers
    Supervisors
    Crew members

7 Training

8 Staff
    Recruitment
    Selection
    Engagement
    National Insurance Contributions
    PAYE
    Absence from work
    Holidays
    Discipline, warnings and dismissal procedures
    Food hygiene and safety policy

9 Standard forms
    Standard letters
    Job application form
    Medical questionnaire
    Staff engagement form
    Contracts of employment
    Disciplinary procedure

Source: Acheson and Wicking (1992).[14]

food industry (Figure 1.3f), although almost any other sector of the industry could adopt such a system (Figure 1.3c and 1.3g).

This analysis is implicitly based on the development of food-production systems over the last 40 years and although certain sectors of the industry can quite clearly be identified with one particular system, there is no reason why this should be so. It is clear that economic restraints and technological advances have resulted in *all* sectors of the industry moving away from the more conventional systems towards less labour-intensive systems. There is no reason to suppose that hotels and restaurants might not adopt assembly-serve production methods. Indeed, if such methods were sophisticated enough, the customer would be quite unaware of how the food had been prepared, for the establishment could continue to *serve* the food in their traditional manner.

Front-of-house Operating Systems

Lillicrap (1971)[15] identified nine styles or types of service including *guéridon*, full silver, plate/silver, plate, family, counter (or cafeteria), snack bar, French, and Russian. Of these, the last two – French and Russian styles – are hardly used at all in the industry today; likewise, cafeteria service developed during the 1970s with several variations designed to increase throughput such as free-flow, scramble and carousel systems. In addition, there are also buffet service, tray systems, trolley service and automatic vending. Subsequently, further systems analysis has been carried out[16] and five types of front-of-house service style have been identified.

- *Table service*. This is service to customers sitting at a laid cover. It includes silver service, family service and plate service.
- *Assisted service*. This is any combination of table service and self-service. For instance, many restaurants have incorporated self-help salad bars into their operation.
- *Self-service*. Customers select food and drink items from either a single counter or several counters, often using a tray, and pay at a till point. Alternative configurations of counters are known as 'free-flow', 'scramble', echelon and carousel.
- *Single point service*. Customers are served at a single point, and food may be consumed on the premises or taken away. This includes take-aways, kiosks, vending, food courts and bars.
- *Specialized or in situ*. This refers largely to the service of food and drink to customers in places not primarily designed for foodservice consumption. It includes tray serve systems, such as in hospitals or on airlines, trolley service, home delivery, drive-ins, and hotel floor service.

Whatever back-of-house and front-of-house system is adopted, the operational activity will centre on the effective and efficient delivery of the meal experience. The range and scope of such activities can be exemplified by considering the typical operations manual of a foodservice outlet. The manual for a fast food restaurant is illustrated in Table 9.2.

CONCLUSION

The foodservice industry has probably experienced a greater level of innovation than the accommodation industry. This has largely centred around the production of meals rather than their service. Such advances, whether they are process redesign or new technologies, have enabled meals to be produced more quickly and in larger quantities at lower unit cost. This, in combination with trends in consumer expectations, has led to significant improvements in the quality of provision throughout the industry. Whereas in the 1970s, consumer experts such as Egon Ronay could rightly criticize whole sectors of the industry, such as motorway service areas, schools and hospitals, in the 1990s all sectors of the industry now perform to high standards of provision.

REFERENCES

1. Cooper, D. (1964) *The Bad Food Guide*, London: Routledge and Kegan Paul.
2. Cannon, T. (1980) *Basic Marketing*, Eastbourne: Holt, Rinehart & Winston.
3. Campbell-Smith, G. (1967) *Marketing the Meal Experience*, Guildford: University of Surrey.
4. Jones, P. (1988) *Foodservice Operations* (2nd edition), London: Cassell, p. 148.
5. Goldman, K. (1993) 'Concept selection for independent restaurants', *Cornell H.R.A. Quarterly*, pp. 59–72.
6. Jones, P. op. cit.
7. Campbell-Smith, G. op. cit.
8. Hempel, S., in *Caterer and Hotelkeeper*, 8 February 1979.
9. Newell, M. (1965) *Mood and Atmosphere in Restaurants*, London: Barrie & Rockcliff.
10. Anon. (1979) *Catering and Hotel Management*, January.
11. Newell, M. op. cit.
12. Jones, P. op. cit.
13. Ibid.
14. Acheson, D. and Wicking, N. (1992) 'Fast-food franchising and finance', in S. Ball (ed.), *Fast Food Operations and Their Management*, Cheltenham: Stanley Thornes.
15. Lillicrap, D. (1971) *Food and Beverage Service*, London: Edward Arnold.
16. Lillicrap, D. and Cousins, J. (1990) *Food and Beverage Service* (3rd edition), London: Hodder and Stoughton.

TEN

Restaurants

PETER JONES

INTRODUCTION

In many respects the difficulty in analysing this sector lies in the origin of restaurants. As Derek Taylor points out, before the Second World War 'the most common route for restaurateurs was to acquire a following when acting as a head waiter elsewhere and then to set up their own shingle'.[1] The famous Quaglinos restaurant was established in just this way. Thus restaurants tend to be owned and operated by individuals and individualists. There is no neat formula for opening and operating a successful establishment. That is not to say that some firms have attempted to do so, which has led to the development of the popular catering market. Such chains of restaurants depend for their success on mass appeal, so that two broad groups of restaurant can be identified, namely popular catering units, now known as quick service restaurants in the USA, and 'speciality' restaurants.

The restaurant sector has also been significantly influenced by ideas developed in the USA This does not refer only to the introduction of US 'cuisine' (hamburgers, fried chicken or exotic ice creams), but to the significant influence over the last 20 years of US ideas and techniques on the British foodservice operations; for example, fast-food techniques have revolutionized the traditional British fish and chip shop. The extent of this American influence is great. For instance, the development of the popular restaurant sector of the industry was significantly influenced by three British operations based on US ideas – Kentucky Pancake Houses, Wimpy Bars and Golden Egg restaurants; the nationwide chains of roadside restaurants (notably Little Chef and Happy Eater) were developed from a US prototype; the fastest growing sector of the industry, fast food, is based firmly on US practices; and coffee shops and grill rooms in hotels originated in the USA.

The impact of American ideas has continued on into the 1990s. Home delivery is a development from the take-away, but instead of customers having to visit the shop in person, all they need to do is telephone their order and the meal will be delivered to their home. Drive-ins have been slow to develop in the UK partly due to its different climate and car size, despite the fact that Rank opened the first roadside 'drive-up' fast-food facility on the A1 near Darlington in 1981. Convenience stores provide self-serve food and drink facilities in a retail outlet. And food courts operate several catering concepts in one location, sharing the seating capacity. They are found at air and rail terminals, such as Euston and Gatwick, and in shopping malls, such as the Newcastle Metro Centre.

RESTAURANTS DEFINED

There is no easy way to identify this sector. A restaurant can be defined as an 'establishment where refreshments or meals may be obtained', but many different types of establishment may be included in this definition: snack bars, cafés, speciality restaurants, popular restaurants, pubs, and so on. In the previous chapter, this sector was identified as 'the quintessential foodservice operation'. The key point is that this is the sector where customers of choice go to have a complete meal experience. There are various ways in which a classification of restaurants may be made.

The Spectrum

This analysis,[2] carried out in the USA, assumes that there are three most important variables – menu, service style and price. It originated to define restaurant categories in hybrid markets, so that in theory there should be room for at least one of each type of restaurant, since they each appeal to a different market segment. Eleven types of restaurant are defined:

- take-away;
- snack stand;
- limited menu, low price, self-service;
- limited menu, low/moderate price, self-service;
- limited menu, moderate price, service;
- full menu, low/moderate price, service;
- full menu, low/moderate price, self-service;
- full menu, moderate price, service;
- full menu, moderate/high price, service;
- luxury menu, high price, continental (*guéridon*) service;
- social caterer.

The major problem with this classification is that although it could be applied to the UK, as yet no data have been compiled here on this basis. In an early study in the USA the Spectrum study yielded some interesting information. Over 55 per cent of sales were in operations with a full menu, so that fast-food restaurants in the USA (like McDonald's) are tending to extend their menus to provide greater appeal. Second, over 60 per cent of sales are made in operations that provide service as opposed to self-service. This slightly contradicts the third point, that nearly 70 per cent of the market is through low- or moderately low-priced outlets.

A Restaurant Typology

This approach to restaurant classifiction[3] attempts to analyse restaurant types using completely different criteria, namely the sophistication of the system and the system's innovativeness. The classification is shown in Figure 10.1.

Expanded Restaurant Typology

This classification[4] was also developed in the USA in 1992. It explicitly recognizes that the growth and significance of multi-unit restaurant chains has altered for ever the

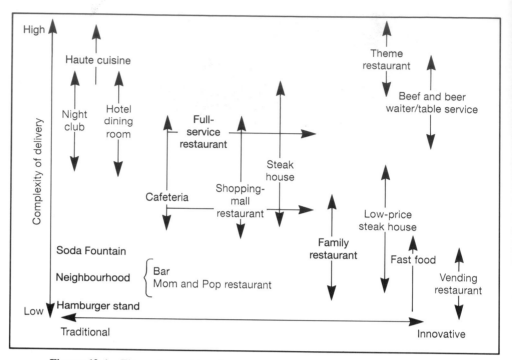

Figure 10.1   The restaurant typology.
Source: Powers, T.F. (1985) 'A restaurant typology', *Cornell HRA Quarterly*, June.

structure and make-up of this sector. It proposes five types of restaurant, each of which has distinctive menu characteristics and operational features. These are:

- quick service, offering low price, speed, and consistency;
- midscale restaurants, based around menu choice, value and comfort;
- moderate upscale, delivering ambience, flexibility and a 'fashion statement';
- upscale outlets which deliver an experience, style and ambience;
- business dining, based on location, price and value.

Each of these five types of chain has distinctive menu characteristics, strategic focus, and operational imperatives. Of these five, three can be identified as matching UK styles of restaurant quite closely.

Restaurant chains such as Garfunkels, Beefeater, Pizza Hut, and Harvester share many of the characteristics of the midscale restaurant. There is a fairly broad menu appeal, with large portions, and commodity items; the focus is on standard operating procedures, building traffic volumes and pricing points; and operational success is based around the size of the facility, cost controls and the execution of process standards. The moderate upscale concept is exemplified in the UK by TGIFridays, restaurants operated by My Kinda Town, and some pizza/pasta chains. Here the menu is trendy and fashionable, based on a limited inventory with some cross-utilization; the focus is on energy and service, with some innovation; and keys to success are 'theatrics', good staff, and strong concept/decor. Finally, the upscale restaurant in the UK is largely not chain operated but

Figure 10.2 Typical midscale restaurant (The Crab and Dragon).
Source: The Pelican Group plc.

Figure 10.3   Typical moderate upscale restaurant (TGIFridays).
Source: TGIFridays plc.

represented by the high-profile restaurateurs or owner/chefs operating just one or two restaurants, such as Prue Leith, Gary Rhodes and Tony Worrel-Thompson. This style of restaurant has a menu which is complex, highly presented and customized; the strategic focus is on price to screen out 'unwanted' custom, high product differentiation and a quality image; the key to success is largely based on the individual skill and expertise of the restaurateur. The differences between these styles of restaurant are illustrated in Figures 10.2, 10.3 and 10.4.

Concept Categories

The American National Restaurant Association has developed, in conjunction with CREST, the idea of 'concept groups'.[5] This further develops three of the five types of restaurant mentioned in the extended typology. The quick service segment is subdivided, mainly on the basis of core product, into 'concept groups' of chicken, donut, Mexican, pizza, and so on. Midscale restaurants are made up seven concept groups – cafeteria, casual-dining, family-style, hotel, steakhouse, speciality (seafood, ethnic), and varied menu. Finally, the upscale segment has concepts described as casual-dining, high check (high priced), moderate check (moderately priced), hotel, speciality and varied menu.

On the basis of the above classifications, this chapter is concerned with those restaurants which operate as stand-alone outlets, offering mainly full menus, in the midscale and upscale segments. Thus take-aways, fast food (or quick service outlets), hotel restau-

Figure 10.4 Typical upscale restaurant (Quaglino's).
Source: Conran Restaurants Ltd.

rants, and roadside/motorway diners are specifically excluded, and each of these is dealt with in subsequent chapters.

DEVELOPMENT OF THE RESTAURANT SECTOR

The restaurant industry in the UK has developed over the last seventy years in five distinct stages.

1930 to 1955: Depression and War

Prior to the 1930s, restaurants in the UK were limited to either local taverns or 'coaching house', or large hotels where customers were expected to wear evening dress and the atmosphere was very formal. The situation was much the same in the USA, where for the average family in small cities and towns dining out was an occasion. The working man's restaurant and boarding house were strictly 'meat and potatoes'.[6] During the 1930s, however, the Aerated Bread Co. (ABC) and J. Lyons opened tea shops in urban centres throughout the UK. These quickly developed the service of more substantial meals and became the first national chains of restaurants. In 1931, Frank and Aldo Berni also opened their first restaurant which was to turn after the Second World War into the first chain of steakhouse restaurants.

The Second World War was to have a major impact on the development of the UK restaurant industry. Whereas in the USA the industry continued to innovate and develop, in the UK business almost ceased altogether. Firstly, the bombing of major cities literally knocked down restaurant premises, as well as, not surprisingly, deterring customers from eating out! By May 1945, nearly 24,000 hotels and pubs had been destroyed or damaged by bombs and fires.[7] Secondly, there were major food shortages during the war that led to food rationing that continued for some years after the end of the conflict. Indeed the Meals in Establishments Order of 1942 imposed restrictions on the number of courses to be served, introduced a maximum price for a meal, and prohibited consumption of meals in public after midnight in London and 11.00 p.m. elsewhere. This decline in the restaurant industry was matched by tremendous growth in the industrial foodservice sector. Factories were encouraged to provide meals for the workers and schools were enabled to provide a two-course hot meal at reasonable prices. So although the number of establishments increased by 30 per cent between 1941 and 1946, and the number of meals served almost doubled during the same period,[8] this growth was due to industrial, institutional and military catering.

1955 to 1970: 'Never had it so good'

From 1950 onwards the restaurant industry began to make up lost ground, but only very slowly. Consumers were not free to eat as much as they could afford until the end of rationing in 1954. And the emphasis was on dining at home. So between 1954 and 1967, during which time Harold Macmillan, the British Prime Minister, coined the phrase 'you've never had it so good', there was only modest growth in demand for restaurant meals.[9] Thus the average rate of growth in expenditure on food by caterers and restaurateurs was only 2 per cent per annum during the 1960s. At the same time, spending on food by households was almost static, indicating people were eating out slightly more. One of the first major studies on eating out habits in the UK was undertaken in 1965, sponsored by Smethurst Foods. This National Catering Inquiry showed that 40 per cent of people surveyed ate away from home daily at their workplace or nearby, whereas only 25 per cent of people had a meal for social reasons at least once a week. The main reason for not eating out socially was given as the cost. But the same study also reported that 'some married couples admitted to being stumped for conversation when alone at table' and that a large number of people avoided upmarket restaurants due to 'snooty waiters and flamboyant, incomprehensible menus'.[10]

During this period the only major mid-market restaurant chain to develop was Berni Inns, largely through converting public houses into steakhouse restaurants. In the mass market, the Wimpy, Golden Egg and Kardomah restaurant chains developed, but, unlike in the USA where this style of restaurant had developed as fast food, these chains offered table service. The British also remained very conservative in their eating habits. The traditional meal of roast meat with potatoes and two vegetables, followed by a sponge pudding was very much the norm. The 'carvery'-style restaurant was developed on this tradition by Lyons who opened their first 'carvery' in the 1960s.

The relatively slow development of the restaurant industry up to 1970 was probably due to a number of factors. Firstly, the foodservice industry as a whole was dominated by the licensed trade. There were over 70,000 public houses in the UK, a high proportion of which were owned by the big six brewers – Bass Charrington, Allied, Whitbread, Watney Mann, Scottish and Newcastle, and Courage. In the 1950s and 1960s, these companies regarded pubs as retail outlets for selling their product – beer. There was also a unique form of franchising public houses in the UK, known as the tied-house system. In effect, the brewers leased their property to the pub 'landlord' at peppercorn rents. In return the brewer had exclusive rights of supply to those licensed premises. Landlords of tied-houses received little or no training in catering and were not encouraged to develop the food side of their business. A second factor that held back restaurant development was related to the dominance of public houses. Licensing law in the UK prohibited young people from using pubs. Under-14s were not allowed in at all, and under-18s were not allowed to purchase or consume alcohol. As the 'local' was often the centre of social life outside the home, there was no tradition of eating out as a family in the UK. Finally, commercial television – ITV – only began in 1958 so that national advertising of restaurants was not possible until the 1960s. Even then the BBC continued to capture a high proportion of viewers and ITV advertising was dominated by fast-moving consumer goods.

However, the range of opportunities for eating out was extended during the 1960s in two ways. The first roadside diner was opened by Trust Houses as a Little Chef in 1963. Originally based on a US concept, the diner was quickly developed to reflect British expectations. The menu was very similar to that found in restaurant chains located in high streets and the service style was table service. The second development was related to ethnic cuisine, both Indian and Chinese. Restaurants offering both these menu styles grew up from the historic association of the UK with Hong Kong, Singapore, India and Pakistan. Many people of these former colonies had rights of citizenship and immigrated into the UK during the 1950s and 1960s. Such immigration was often associated with political and social upheaval in their home countries. For instance, many Asian immigrants arrived from Uganda during and after the dictatorship of Idi Amin. Their culture encouraged entrepreneurship and their experience led to them opening restaurants, usually in high-street locations. By 1970 there 'were about 4,000 Chinese restaurants' in the UK[11] and a growing number of Indian restaurants. Over half the people surveyed in the National Catering Inquiry of 1965 had experienced this style of cuisine.

The 1970s: Signs of Competition and Innovation

The restaurant industry grew significantly during the 1970s largely due to the overall growth in consumer expenditure. In 1974 the Trends in Catering survey was commissioned by the Hotels and Catering Economic Development Committee. In 1975, this showed that 4600 million meals a year were consumed away from home, with an expenditure of £2000 million (excluding alcohol). This was the equivalent of two meals a week for the average Briton and represented 4 per cent of total consumer spending.

The 1970s was a period during which new chains emerged to compete in a number of market segments. The Happy Eater chain was founded to compete head-to-head with Little Chef in the roadside dining sector. New steakhouse chains, such as Beefeater, Angus Steak House and Chef & Brewer developed to compete with Berni Inns. Steakhouse restaurants originated in the licensed trade sector of the catering industry. Their origins and continued success are based on a menu centred around steak which requires a limited amount of kitchen equipment (i.e. grill and deep-fat fryer), and hence capital investment; little technical expertise for the preparation, cooking and service of steak-based meals; popularity of the meal item; pre-portioning of the product from the supplier; relative ease of storage and reasonable shelf-life; and little or no wastage. This type of restaurant served plated meals with a table d'hôte menu, comprising three starters, usually soup, prawn cocktail and one other; rump, sirloin or fillet steak grilled to order; ice cream or cheese board; followed by coffee or a selection from a range of speciality coffees. The price of the meal is based on the cost of the main item, and since to attract custom pricing is competitive, strict portion control is employed. Most operators specify exactly the presentation of each of the dishes on the menu and support this with illustrations of how each dish should be presented on the plate.

In 1974 the first McDonald's restaurant was opened in Greenwich, a south London suburb. In 1976 Peter Morton opened the London Hard Rock Café, Bob Payton opened the Chicago Pizza Pie factory, and Roger Myers and Karen Jones opened Peppermint Park and Coconut Grove in 1979. These were signs that the restaurant industry was about change dramatically during the 1980s.

The 1980s: A Rapidly Maturing Industry

In a 1980 survey[12] of 680 establishments of all types, the commercial operation of speciality restaurants was investigated. Restaurants identified as selling French or Italian cuisine were the smallest of all restaurant types surveyed – 43 per cent served less than 50 covers per day and only 7 per cent recorded over 200 covers on average per day. This was a reflection on the average amount spent per head of £7.50 exclusive of VAT and service, which is considerably higher than the average for other sectors. 'Ethnic' restaurants (which include Indian and Chinese cuisine) had an average spend of around £3 per head, but a correspondingly higher turnover with 70 per cent of them having a turnover of 50 covers or more per day. There was also a significant difference in policy with regard to take-away food sales. Only 15 per cent of French and Italian restaurants had some take-away trade, and this only accounted for approximately 10 per cent of their sales. For 'ethnic' restaurants, however, take-away sales were important – 'over a quarter of Chinese and Indian restaurants got between 20 and 50 per cent of their business from takeaway meal purchases'. It seems that many operators recognize that a change in service style, towards more self-service and take-away operations, is one of the most significant developments in the industry.

Although nearly 90 per cent of restaurants were independently owned and managed, the performance of these single units and the approach of their owners was very different from that of chain restaurants. In the mid-1980s the average turnover of an independent restaurant was £115,000 compared with £270,000 in a chain unit.[13] This reflects the size of the units: independent units averaging less than 60 seats, chain units around 80. The independent restaurateur also tends to open longer hours to achieve this level of turnover. In comparison, in 1986 a typical managed public house had an annual turnover of £210,000, of which 20 per cent derived from food sales.[14]

This was reflected in the way in which the large brewers operating such chains organize and manage these outlets. Nearly all of them developed separate divisions for such restaurants with an operations director whose background is in catering rather than the licensed trade. In 1986, Bass operated Toby Restaurants, Grand Metropolitan Berni Inns, and Allied-Lyons had the Vittle Inns chain and New England Restaurant Group. Such divisionalization, the increasing sophistication of the customer, and the much greater levels of competition have led the chains into broadening the product range on offer and diversifying out of the steak-based concept.

Until the opening of the first McDonalds in Britain in 1974, most UK restaurant chains operated table or plate service or, in small snack-bar units, counter service. These high-street restaurants found it increasingly difficult to continue this style of service for several reasons. A very large increase in high-street rents and rates necessitated maximizing the seating capacity of restaurants. Table service does not necessarily have higher staffing costs than a comparable fast-food operation but the staffing cost per unit sale is lower due to the higher turnover of fast-food restaurants. Customers' tastes have changed and effective marketing by the new operators has forced the traditional popular catering units to rethink their policies.

There was also a significant shift in taste away from red meat towards more healthy eating. This had a major impact on the steakhouse chains. Berni diversified out of steak into a number of branded concepts, but eventually Grand Metropolitan sold 150 of their 208 outlets to Whitbread who absorbed them into their Beefeater chain. The 1980s also saw the emergence of family-style restaurants such as Harvesters and TGIFridays. The first UK-based TGIFridays was opened by Whitbread in March 1986. There was also significant growth of restaurants based around pasta and/or pizza. Between 1984 and 1986, the number of UK pizza restaurants increased from 110 to 450. For instance, Whitbread expanded its Pizza Hut chain from 20 to 75 units, claiming that sales had responded outstandingly to television advertising.[15]

1990s Onwards: Growing Sophistication and Competition

The development of theme restaurants towards the end of the 1980s was of major significance within the UK. It marked a major and permanent change in how the British think about eating out. Right up until the mid-1980s, most restaurants were seen as a substitute for eating at home. Such substitution was either necessary, convenient or in order to celebrate a special occasion. But eating out was still not perceived as a 'leisure experience'. Unlike the French who are said to 'live to eat', the British continued to 'eat to live'. With the growth of theme restaurants the British have decided that eating out is fun, that it is a leisure activity, and that it is more than just the consumption of food. As Thomas says in defining a theme restaurant, it is 'largely a destination ... [with] an intangible, overall ambiance and theatre which takes you somewhere other than where you are'.[16]

SIZE AND SCALE OF THE RESTAURANT SECTOR

In 1993 there were just over 17,000 'restaurants, cafes, and snack bars selling food for consumption on the premises'.[17] This number of outlets has remained more or less unchanged since 1988, whereas between 1982 and 1988 there was a growth of nearly 45 per cent. These estimates are likely to be below the total figure as it excludes those outlets operating below the VAT threshold. Of these restaurants, only 2 per cent generate sales of over £1 million per year. The majority, around 70 per cent, have an annual

Table 10.1   Major operators of chain restaurants 1993.

Operator/trading name	Ownership/franchiser	Number of outlets
Little Chef	Forte	350
Pizza Hut	Whitbread/Pepsico	293
Beefeater	Whitbread	280
Wimpy	Wimpy International	230
Perfect Pizza	Scott's Hospitality	241
Toby Restaurants	Bass	200
Big Steak Pubs	Allied-Lyons	170

Sources: Key Note 1994/Company Reports/Trade Press.

turnover of £50,000 to £249,000. The total turnover of the restaurant sector (excluding fast food) in 1993 was estimated at £4.540 million. Growth is greatly influenced by economic circumstances, so was erratic over the previous three years. Whereas the fast-food sector increased at around 5.5 per cent per annum from 1990 onwards, the restaurant sector experienced growth of nearly 14 per cent in 1990/91, but a decline of 2 per cent in 1991/92.[18] The sector employed an estimated 307,600 workers in 1993, of which 58 per cent were part-time.

'The U.K. restaurant sector is highly fragmented, with a large number of independent businesses operating locally and few national chains.'[19] Of the ten largest chain operations, three are fast-food operations (McDonald's, KFC, BurgerKing); one is a roadside dining chain (Little Chef); one has both fast-food outlets and table service restaurants (Wimpy); and four are restaurant chains, three based around steak (Beefeater, Toby Restaurants, Big Steak Pubs) and one around pizza (Pizza Hut). The main restaurant chains are illustrated in Table 10.1 (fast-food chains are shown in Table 14.3). The top five brands dominate their sectors: McDonald's has 40 per cent of sales in the burger segment, KFC easily dominates chicken-based operations, Pizza Hut has 35 per cent of the pizza restaurant market, Beefeater one-third of the steakhouse sales, and Little Chef has three times as many outlets as any other brand.

UNDERSTANDING THE RESTAURANT CUSTOMER

If the restaurant sector is made up of a number of different types of restaurant, it follows that each of these is directed towards market segments. For instance, Muller and Woods propose that each of their types of restaurant has distinctive 'customer decision attributes'. The midscale restaurant offers value, comfort, table and counter service, with an appropriate menu mix and choice. In using a moderate upscale restaurant the customer is making a 'fashion statement' and seeking ambience. The upscale restaurant customer is very much into the full meal experience, with a great deal of style, ambience and service, whilst the business dining customer wants an easy purchase decision, value, and an accessible location.

Such segmentation has to be placed in the UK context, however. Even in 1993 only 46 per cent of those surveyed ate out at lunchtime and 60 per cent in the evening,[20] and the average amount spent on meals outside the home in 1992 was a measly £1.72.[21] Even amongst those who do eat out, the frequency of restaurant visits is low – only just over 8 per cent of average consumers visit a restaurant more than once a month.[22] The five types of restaurant most frequently visited are 'English', Chinese, Indian, Italian and pizza-style outlets, which between them have nearly 70 per cent of the market.

LOCATION OF RESTAURANTS

The diverse types of operation and wide range of market segments served make it difficult to be precise about the criteria for selecting a restaurant site. In addition, UK legislation and planning restrictions on the development and use of business premises for catering purposes often mean that foodservice operators have a limited choice as to where to locate their outlets, especially in towns and cities. There are therefore two ways in which an operator can go about selecting a site for a restaurant. The first way is to identify a location and develop the right kind of restaurant for that site; the second way is to define the restaurant concept and then seek a location with the appropriate market demographics. The first approach is usually adopted by independent restaurateurs operating single units, whereas the latter is the approach adopted by chains.

Goldman[23] compares and contrasts these two approaches, as follows:

- *The preselected location approach.* The first step is to carry out an analysis of the secondary data available with respect to the chosen location. This is followed by a primary market study which reviews the competition and establishes the needs and wants of people in the area. Both this primary and secondary data enables the specification of life-cycle categories and trends, from which it is possible to draw up a specification of market segments. These segments are usually defined by age, income, family structure. From this a customer profile is drawn up, which then enables a restaurant concept to be defined.
- *The preselected concept approach.* In many respects this is the reverse process. The operator starts with a well-defined concept, identifies the customer profile, defines the segmentation, collects secondary data on several potential areas, carries out primary research on likely suitable locations, and then selects the most appropriate market area.

Whichever of these two approaches is adopted the operator needs data on a number of key characteristics in order to determine the suitability of the location in general, and the specific site for the restaurant. Location selection criteria include factors such as population density, population mix, economic characteristics, geographic features, employment characteristics, and levels of competition. Site selection criteria include traffic flow, visibility, access, utilities, and traffic patterns. In the USA Melaniphy[24] suggests that there are as many as twelve different types of site on which restaurants may be developed. The structure of the US industry, economic profile, geographic features, and other factors may mean that not all these apply to the UK. Types of restaurant site that are typical of the UK include city or town centres (so-called 'high street' locations), retail or shopping centres, adjacent to or within leisure or tourist attractions, commercial areas, residential areas, or out-of-town sites.

OPERATIONAL FEATURES

In 1981, Jones wrote: 'In view of the wide diversity [in the restaurant industry], no clear service style can clearly be identified'.[25] Since then, Cousins and Lillicrap have redefined styles of foodservice[26] (see p. 120), so that it is now possible to say that the predominant style of service in restaurants is 'service at a laid cover'. Within this category food is served in a number of ways.

Plate Service

This style of service has the food item plated then individually served to each customer. In the 1980s, this was typical of the 'pub grub' segment of the market. With the growth of bistros, family restaurants and in particular *nouvelle cuisine* and other styles of gastronomic cooking, this style of service has also been adopted in midscale and upscale operations. Plate service is particularly suitable for this as it enables the chef to present the food artistically.

Family Service

This style is ideal for use in restaurants serving Far Eastern cuisine. Eastern eating habits differ from the European concept of eating a sequence of courses, including a principal dish or main course. In India, for instance, food is traditionally served on a large tray or that containing different dishes and accompaniments, and people help themselves to small amounts from one dish at a time, although there is no hard-and-fast rule for the order in which food should be eaten. Likewise, in China every bowl, from a wide selection, is available to all diners and they serve themselves from each dish with chopsticks. Thus, in opening restaurants in Britain, Indian and Chinese restaurateurs have adapted their service style to meet western demands in a similar way to their adaptation of their cuisine to western tastes. Family service is the service of food in dishes, from which customers are expected to help themselves as the dishes are placed on the table. Apart from maintaining links with tradition, the style of service requires fewer staff than silver or *guéridon* service would require, and also less training in service skills is necessary. The key element to the success of such operations is ensuring that the temperature of the food is maintained. This means that the kitchen must serve very hot food into heated dishes, customers must be supplied with hot plates, and that the dishes are kept hot by lamps or hotplates placed on the table. The restaurateur may also find that disposable table linen is preferable, as in serving themselves the customers may not be as efficient as a waiter and spillages often occur.

Silver Service

This used to be the 'standard' style of service found in restaurants and hotels. Food is presented on 'flats' (serving trays) or in dishes to the customer and then served by the waiting staff onto the plate. Silver service originated because food is traditionally served on silver flats to enhance the appearance and maintain the temperature of the food and it provides the customer with a degree of 'service'. It is becoming outdated because the economic necessity of using stainless steel instead of silver has removed one of the main attractions of *'silver service'*. If food can be presented attractively on the plate from the kitchen then the need for service equipment, dishes and flats is reduced, along with capital investment and operating costs. Also, silver-service waiting staff require a level of skill and consequent training that simpler food service methods eliminate.

Guéridon

This style of service was developed during the Edwardian era and is symptomatic of the Edwardian's gastronomic indulgence. A *guéridon* is a table or trolley placed beside the customer's table at which the waiter prepares, fillets, carves and sometimes cooks the dishes to be served. This style of service is flamboyant and emphasizes the personal attention and service that a customer receives. It is also associated with menu dishes that are of the highest quality, and are very expensive, being based on classical French cuisine. For this reason, *guéridon* service is restricted to restaurants catering for a market that is prepared to pay the high prices that must be charged to cover operating costs. High costs are due to several factors – the service is labour-intensive requiring a *chef de rang* and *commis de rang* to serve an average 10 to 12 customers; staff must be trained extensively and paid a salary commensurate with their high level of technical skill; fewer customers can be seated in a restaurant operating *guéridon* service than in other styles of service due to the need for space to move trolleys around the room; and this style of service requires relatively greater capital expenditure in equipment than do other styles of service which, due to the expectation of clientele, is usually in silver plate.

This emphasis on defining a restaurant as an operation producing meals should not overshadow the fact that it is estimated that only 62 per cent of total sales in the sector derive from food sales, with a further 32 per cent from alcoholic drinks.[27] This compares with 30 per cent and 65 per cent respectively in the licensed trade.[28]

FUTURE TRENDS

Many types of business, including restaurants, may be franchised, but the foodservice market is particularly suited to this form of operation. A franchise has been defined as a form of licensing under which an individual or company joins in partnership with an experienced organization for their mutual benefit. Such an agreement can be seen to extend advantages both to the franchiser (the organization granting the franchise) and the franchisee (the person buying the franchise). The number of franchise operations in Britain is changing all the time, particularly with the development of fast food, but restaurants that are franchise operations include TGIFridays, Pizza Hut and Pizza Express. A major trend in the latter half of the 1990s is the likely extension of new franchised brands such as Pierre Victoire, a chain originating in Scotland despite its French brand name; Cafe Flo; and Bella Pasta.

Health is also likely to play a major factor in planning menus. Burger and fried chicken sales have come under pressure and most restaurants have developed vegetarian alternatives and introduced more salads onto their menus. The diversification of the mainstream restaurant industry into more healthy menu items has actually led to a decline in the number and popularity of vegetarian restaurants. For instance, the Cranks restaurant chain nearly ceased trading in the early 1990s.

In addition to the major brands, there will be a growth in the number of middle-sized chains with 30 to 50 outlets, each with their own niche market. Many of these will be variations on the 'theme restaurant', offering a less formal atmosphere, consistent product, lively ambience, and affordable prices. For instance, Bright Reasons restaurants operated 160 pizza and pasta restaurants in the UK in 1994, with three major brands. City Centre Restaurants also operate a number of different brands including Deep Pan

Pizza (99 outlets), Garfunkels (35 outlets) Cafe Uno, and Biguns. Harry Ramsden's fish and chip restaurants had nine restaurants in 1993, with a further five planned to open in 1994. The Pelican group had 28 outlets at the beginning of 1994 operating a number of branded restaurants, including Café Rouge, Café Pelican and Yankee Doodle. Likewise, a new family restaurant concept was launched in 1993 called Heroes of Sport Restaurants, with athlete Steve Cram as a major shareholder.

Finally, in addition to the well-established ethnic restaurants, new-style cuisines have and will continue to become more widespread. This includes Thai, Indonesian, Japanese, Vietnamese, Lebanese, Caribbean and Cypriot styles of cooking. This is because the British holiday-maker has now travelled further than the Mediterranean resorts to more exotic locations and because there has been an increase in the number of British citizens originating from these locations.

CONCLUSION

Restaurants in some form or another have a very long history, and there is no doubt that they will continue to serve food and drink for many more years. Despite the growth of fast-food outlets and take-away restaurants, people enjoy dining out, and restaurants satisfy this demand, whether they are unique or part of large chains. Furthermore, it appears to be the latent ambition of many people in the catering industry to run their own restaurant business. This sector, perhaps more than any other, offers the opportunity to individuals to fulfil this ambition. A restaurant requires less investment than a hotel, it is smaller in scale than many other types of operation and has greater status attached to it than public houses or outside catering. In many respects it fulfils the criteria of a business suitable for any budding entrepreneur. However, at the same time, it must be recognized that a restaurant is a risky business venture. Although there are examples of staggeringly successful restaurateurs, such as Bob Payton of My Kinda Town, there are equally many unsuccessful restaurateurs. The main reason for this is that apart from being proficient and expert caterers, restaurateurs must also understand the market in which they operate. The restaurateur is selling a non-essential product – it is a luxury item – and must compete with other products for the customers' hard-earned disposable income.

The sector is made up of a number of different restaurant 'products' each of which is at a different stage of their life cycle. Ethnic restaurants, especially Indian and Chinese outlets, are at the mature stage. The number of outlets has remained largely unchanged since the 1970s and the menu and concept is equally predictable. Steakhouse restaurants are also at the mature stage, if not in decline, due to more health-conscious consumers. Family restaurants have grown rapidly in the 1980s and are now reaching maturity, with consequent 'thinning out' of major brands. Theme restaurants continue to develop and are still at the growth stage of their life cycle. But the most significant fact about the UK restaurant industry is the attitude the British customer now has towards eating out. Until the emergence and growth of theme restaurants in the late 1980s, people dined out to *eat*, often because it was convenient, sometimes in order to celebrate. Nowadays however, more and more people are treating the eating out experience as a leisure activity in its own right. Restaurant dining is not a substitute for eating at home, it is one of a range of leisure pursuits to be enjoyed. This more than anything will continue to transform the restaurant sector in years to come.

REFERENCES

1. Taylor, D. (1977) *Fortune, Fame and Folly*, London: IPC Business Press.
2. Spectrum.
3. Powers, T.F. (1985) 'A restaurant typology', *Cornell HRA Quarterly*, June, pp. 33–45.
4. Muller, C.C. and Woods, R.H. (1994) 'An expanded restaurant typology', *Cornell HRA Quarterly*, June, pp. 27–37.
5. Goldman, K. (1993) 'Concept selection for independent restaurants', *Cornell HRA Quarterly*, December, pp. 59–72.
6. Taylor, D. op. cit.
7. Tarpey, D. (1993) 'Looking back at 1943', *Caterer and Hotelkeeper*, 4 March, pp. 40–4.
8. Ibid.
9. O'Connor, J. (1993) 'A review of dining out patterns in Britain', *International Journal of Contemporary Hospitality Management*, Vol. 5, No. 5, pp. 3–9.
10. Tarpey, D. (1993) 'Looking back at 1968', *Caterer and Hotelkeeper*, 4 February, pp. 30–4.
11. O'Connor, J. op. cit.
12. Gallup Survey (1980) *Caterer and Hotelkeeper*, 19 June.
13. Jones, P. (1988) *Foodservice Operations* (2nd edition), London: Cassell.
14. Key Note (1994) *The Restaurant Industry*, London: Key Note Publications, p. 25.
15. Thomas, K.-M. (1994) 'Themed Restaurants: Their Emergence, Future and Position in the Marketplace', Unpublished thesis, University of Brighton.
16. Ibid.
17. Key Note op. cit.
18. Ibid., p. 21.
19. Ibid., p. 3.
20. BRMB International (1994) *Target Group Index (TGI) Survey*.
21. National Food Survey.
22. BRMB International op. cit.
23. Goldman, K. op. cit.
24. Melaniphy, J.C. (1992) *Restaurant and Fast Food Site Selection*, New York: John Wiley.
25. Jones, P. op. cit.
26. Cousins, J. and Lillicrap, D. (1990) *Food and Beverage Service*, 3rd edition, London: Hodder and Stoughton.
27. Marketing Strategies for Industry (1992) *MSI Databrief: Catering: U.K.*, London: MSI.
28. Key Note op. cit.

ELEVEN

Foodservice in Hotels

PETER JONES

INTRODUCTION

Good cooking was brought to Britain by the great chefs and hoteliers who came from the Continent to work in the grand hotels of Britain in the 1880s and 1890s. For a long time the only place where one could eat in style was in a hotel, and during their heyday these hotel restaurants were very successful, although not necessarily very profitable. Hotel restaurants were usually the loss leader designed to entice the clients to book bedrooms. Restaurants acted as positive attractions and in assessing profit and loss many genuine costs were ignored or forgotten in hotels. But with the increase in the growth of restaurants, the narrowing of the gap between rich and poor and the increase in travel for business rather than for pleasure, hotels have increasingly become a facility for accommodation rather than for dining in. By the 1960s, the image of many hotel restaurants was old-fashioned and uninspiring, and the early 1970s saw a conscious effort by hoteliers to improve this image, typified by Trusthouse Forte's development of La Fontaine and La Piazza restaurants in the Grosvenor House Hotel in London. Hoteliers attempting to expand their market and attract new custom have to create a new image. As Bruce Whitehall wrote about many hotels' attempts to promote weekend food sales: 'an establishment which is full of expense account businessmen throughout the week may have difficulty in projecting the informality and liveliness increasingly appropriate to the British Sunday'.[1]

Things remained little changed during the 1980s, until the recession hit in the early 1990s. As a result of this, there has been a quiet revolution in terms of how foodservice is carried out in hotels. It is a 'quiet revolution' because many hotels are not able to transform their provision due to constraints such as their star rating. Hence some provision, notably lounge service, room service, bars and banqueting have changed very little. The major change has been in terms of restaurant provision and breakfast service. In the mid-1990s two alternative strategies are being pursued. Either hotels, in keeping with the strong brand image of the hotel, are branding their restaurant provision, or they are creating unique restaurants to compete with independent theme restaurants.

THE HOTEL FOODSERVICE SECTOR

It is extremely difficult to establish the number of foodservice outlets that exist within UK hotels. In Chapter 2, we identified that it is even difficult to establish the number of

Monday Morning

This is typically the quietest morning. People are checking out of the hotel after their leisure break or having travelled down the night before preparing for an important early-Monday morning meeting. During the rest of the week we get plenty of our business residents using the Traders restaurant for breakfast.

Monday Lunchtime

We are getting into the heart of the week's business. We have business customers – anything from middle managers to managing directors. We also get some leisure customers who are here for a few days' break. But the bulk of our customers are business people. They are effectively adopting the hotel as their home while they are with us. We need to remember this and treat them well. It can be stressful for business people, especially if they spend a lot of time on the road. The hotel and Traders become a kind of haven.

During the day

During the day the business customer is looking for efficiency from us. They may be meeting colleagues or customers. We need to be friendly to them but to remember that they are conducting their business and want to appear professional. This means we need to be professional to them (they can take advantage of our meeting rooms and facilities if they need to). However, it is important not to be afraid to approach business people and offer them more to eat or drink. The knack is in getting the timing and style right.

The kind of business conducted in the lounge is varied. You get people doing business reviews. You get reps calling in to see people. You get recruitment agencies holding informal screening interviews in the lobby. The meetings are usually one-to-one. These meetings continue all day.

In Traders near leisure and tourist destinations you get people using the Traders lounge for afternoon tea and cakes before doing more sight-seeing. These people stay during the week and are usually retired professional people – very much the traditional Posthouse customer.

At lunchtime we also get day conference guests. We get conferences taking place drawing people from a 50-mile radius. They usually have food laid on as part of the conference but some do use the Traders restaurant. We also get older guests coming in for a meal.

Early evening during the week

Early evening we get some families with young children coming in for a meal. These are local people from different backgrounds. We also get some people popping in on their way back from work in local offices for a quick meal and a drink. Between 7.30 and 8.00 we get business people who have checked in, showered and want something to eat and a couple of drinks. We also get people having a few drinks with us after their conference. Later in the evening we get younger couples coming in to eat and some families with older children in their teens.

Friday afternoon

This marks a real change. The business people generally check out and people coming for weekends away check in. The demands on and of Traders change dramatically.

The Weekend

At the weekend we get families staying with us for a break. We also get people staying overnight because they have a family function to go to, like a wedding. Over the weekend you see a lot more children in Traders. It is very important to make families and their children feel welcome. In the past children in licensed premises have been treated as second class citizens. We need to reverse this and help the parents to relax. We don't want the parents to feel embarrassed and hide away in their rooms and not spend money with us.

We get all kinds of families who are attracted by the excellent value we offer. We also get couples for romantic weekends away and older couples too.

On Saturday afternoon we get people popping in to watch a cricket or football match on our sports TV channel. They usually have a few drinks with us while the match is on.

The service needs to be flexible enough to reflect these different markets.

Figure 11.1 A week in the life of a Traders Restaurant (Posthouse Hotels).

hotels in the UK let alone how many restaurants and bars they may have. In 1993, it was estimated that there were 13,310 hotels in the UK most of which would at least serve breakfast to their customers.[2] Approximately 28 per cent of the sales turnover of these businesses derives from the sale of meals and refreshment, and a further 18 per cent from the sale of alcoholic drinks.[3] In 1992, this was estimated to be £1.5 billion in food sales[4] and £1 billion in alcoholic drink sales.

The main market served by hotel foodservice operations is, of course, the hotel guest. Hence the market segments using these outlets reflect the nature of markets attracted to the hotel property, as discussed in the chapters in Part A of this text. However, hotels also serve non-residents, competing directly with the restaurant sector. They also provide banqueting facilities for both residents and non-residents. Provision can therefore be divided into four main areas:[5] restaurants (which account for 68 per cent of hotel catering sales), banqueting (20 per cent), room service (8 per cent), and bar/lounge service (4 per cent). However, this breakdown of a hotel's catering sales-mix needs to be treated with some caution. Firstly, there can be wide variation between different types of hotel. Obviously budget hotels have hardly any foodservice provision, whereas business and resort properties may have extensive conference and banqueting facilities. Secondly, even within the same segment, hotel provision varies, often due to the original design of the property. For instance, the Churchill and Cumberland are 4-star London hotels within 100 metres of each other. The former has a restaurant, carvery, coffee shop and Japanese-style restaurant, whilst the latter has one restaurant. Thirdly, the sales mix can vary from year to year. During the period 1990 to 1993 there was a marked decline in demand for banqueting due to the recession; banqueting gradually began to pick up again in 1994.

The nature of hotel foodservice can be be fully understood by reading the extract shown in Figure 11.1 from the operations manual of Traders Restaurant, the concept currently in place in all Forte's Posthouse Hotels.

FOODSERVICE OPERATIONS IN HOTELS

In order to adapt to the changes in demand for foodservice, increases in the tourist market and the need to improve profitability, hotel operators have had to examine critically all aspects of their operations. The foodservice manager in a hotel must therefore have a very clear idea of what each aspect of the operation is attempting to achieve and which customers' needs the unit is serving. This will ensure that the essential operational features of the coffee shop or floor service, for example, are recognized and maintained. After all, a hotel does not need to have three or four different types of restaurant if all its clients' needs are the same.

Restaurants

Hotel restaurants vary widely in terms of size and service style. A unique feature of hotel foodservice provision is breakfast meal service. Unlike in the USA where chain restaurants and fast-food operators have developed the breakfast market, in the UK breakfast is almost only eaten away from the home when staying in hotels. Until the 1990s, there were basically three types of restaurant found in hotels – the coffee shop, the carvery and the silver-service restaurant.

Plate-service restaurants

Typically, plate service is found in the coffee shop – an American concept introduced into hotels during the 1960s. The operation is usually open from early morning until late at night, serving breakfast, morning coffee, lunch, afternoon tea and supper. In some cases there are different menus from each of these meal periods but more often than not one menu is in use throughout the day. The service style is table service or plate service, with all dishes portioned and plated in the kitchen. The coffee shop concept developed for a number of reasons. Firstly, it reduced the operating costs of conventional silver-service restaurants by introducing plate service, which increases the number of customers served per member of staff by up to 60 per cent, eliminating the capital investment in service equipment and reducing the floor space per customer by up to one-third. Secondly, it provides a meal and beverage facility that serves throughout the working day to guests travelling from abroad who may arrive from different time zones and require full meals at unusual times. Thirdly, it modernized the image of hotel restaurants by introducing a more contemporary and relaxed atmosphere, and meeting the growing demand for snack meals rather than traditional three- or four-course meals. And finally it met the growing demands of the American tourist market and the youth market.

Carvery

A carvery-style operation is not a new idea – restaurants were operated in this way in the early part of this century. The basic concept is that roast joints form the basis of the menu. These are carved in the room and customers serve themselves from the carvery counter, selecting whichever meat and vegetables or salad they choose. The name 'Carvery' is in fact the registered brand-name of restaurants operated in this way by the J. Lyons organization, and other firms have had to find other names to describe their operations, such as 'The Chef's Table'. The typical carvery menu comprises a three-course table d'hôte menu, with a selection of five or six starters, three of four roast meats and possibly one or two alternative main courses and a selection of sweets. Waiting staff take the customer's order and are responsible for serving the first and third course, and coffee if required, while the customer is served at the carvery counter by a *trancheur* or 'carver', who is usually dressed in chef's whites. The counter may be a straight line or bow-shaped and consists of boards for carving, hot cupboards or overhead heat lamps and *bains-marie* for vegetables. Sauces and accompaniments may either be served at the table by waiting staff or customers may help themselves at the carvery counter. The advantages of this style of operation are that the presentation and carving of meats and food items in the restaurant is a promotional tool and enhances sales; customers are allowed to select as much as they wish for an all-inclusive price that promotes a sense of value for money; the menu requires a smaller kitchen area and fewer kitchen staff to prepare the dishes, as little or no cooking to order is done during the service period; and since there is an element of self-service, fewer waiting staff are required for a carvery than in a traditionally organized restaurant. For the carvery supervisor or manager, there are specific potential problem areas. The policy of allowing the customers to help themselves to as much as they wish makes control and pricing very difficult. Many such operations have abandoned this policy by either stating on the menu the portion size or using portable carving trolleys with the *trancheur* serving customers at the table, rather like *guéridon* service. Since joints are pre-cooked, close control of the appearance and palatability must be exercised, and unused meats must be reused in *rechauffé* dishes or in cold meat salads to reduce waste.

In the 1980s, the carvery at the Regent Palace Hotel in London was typical of many carvery operations, and certainly of those operated by Trusthouse Fort hotels since there was a standard menu throughout the group. Thus at the Regent Palace, since all their food-stuffs are purchased through Trusthouse Forte Supplies, the joints that they serve on their carvery will be of the same specification and quality as those served elsewhere. However, the catering manager selects and serves the choice of vegetables and salads that accompany the roast, and also determines the items to be found on the sweet trolley. The unit operated on about 55 per cent gross profit. This was lower than the average gross profit percentage for the hotel of about 65 per cent, but was accounted for by the carvery's policy of allowing customers to help themselves to as much as they like. The unit was open every day from 12.00 to 2.30 p.m. and from 5.15 to 9.00 p.m. This is not typical but reflects the type of customer that the carvery attracts: at lunchtime, trade is fairly regular and is predominantly business people, whereas in the evening, custom is derived from residents, pre-theatre diners and business people, and it is particularly busy at weekends. There were 112 covers in total, operated by eight waiting staff with their own stations, each serving 14 covers. In view of the set price for the meal, nearly every customer spends approximately the same. In an average week the unit served over 1600 covers.

Silver service restaurants

This style of service is based around the service of food with a spoon and fork (or other appropriate service gear) from dishes or flats by waiting staff at the customer's table. This style of service was very common in the archetypal hotel restaurant of the 1960s and 1970s. Such a restaurant would typically offer an à la carte menu of individually priced dishes, based on classical French cuisine, along with a set price table d'hôte menu. Tables would be laid with linen clothes, silver cutlery, and crystal glassware. In many respects, especially in 4- and 5-star hotels, these operations had remained unchanged for a hundred years. Unlike carveries and coffee shops, these restaurants would be open only for lunch and dinner, and often they were staffed by men only.

There are hotels that continue to operate one or more of these three types of restaurant. This is largely because hotel general managers and head chefs with a Swiss hotel school training are extremely reluctant to overturn the tradition of the 'hotel restaurant' based around classical cuisine, especially in London, and there has been a very low return on capital investment from hotel foodservice. However, a new style of hotel restaurant provision is emerging in the 1990s which is not based around the restaurant/carvery/coffee shop profile. In essence, the aim is to look at restaurant provision as a profit centre for the hotel and market it as a restaurant in its own right. This means that hotels are copying trends in the restaurant sector of the industry. Hotels can follow two strategies to achieve this and implement this strategy in two different ways. One strategy is to create a standard brand, just as the hotel is branded; the alternative is to create a unique restaurant modelled on current fashions and trends in that sector. To implement either of these alternatives, the hotel company can do so itself; or it can go into some kind of joint venture with another partner to do it for them.

In some respect the standardized coffee shop operation (described above) is a precursor

Welcome to your Traders Restaurant!

We hope you'll enjoy it to the full and if there's any dish you'd like and you can't see it on our menu, ask your waiter and we'll try our best to help you!

See Blackboard for today's specials

We offer great value to youngsters!

Children aged 5-12 can enjoy a child's size portion of the dishes marked on the main menu for half the marked price, or alternatively can choose from Marvin's Menu

APPETISERS (HALF PRICE AVAILABLE)

GARLIC PRAWN SIZZLER £5.25
Prawns sizzling in garlic butter with garlic bread on the side.

HALF MELON £3.15
Light and refreshing.

CAJUN SPICED MUSHROOMS £2.95
Deep fried mushrooms, accompanied by Creole Dip.

LUXURY PRAWN COCKTAIL £3.95
Prawns served on a leaf salad with Thousand Island dressing

MUSSELS £5.95
Irish mussels in butter and a blend of herbs.

SEAFOOD POT £4.65
A pot of prawns, calamares, cockles and mussels in a spicy sauce of tomatoes, chillies, bacon and olives with a hint of garlic. Served with garlic bread.

FRENCH ONION SOUP £2.15
A classic soup topped with a toasted cheese crouton.

HICKORY SMOKED WINGS £2.95
Chicken slow smoked over hickory chips, served with your choice of sour cream or barbecue sauce.

CHICKEN LIVER PATÉ £3.25
Served with hot toast and rich Cumberland sauce.

TRADERS BASKET £3.65
Chicken in a crispy coating with sesame seeds and prawn crackers, accompanied by a wholegrain mustard sauce, served in a basket.

JALEPENO PEPPERS £4.50
Jalepeno peppers filled with cream cheese coated in breadcrumbs and deep fried. Served with our red pepper and chilli jelly.

FRESH ASPARAGUS TORTELLINI £3.25
Served with a four cheese sauce topped with grated cheese and chopped parsley.

CRAB CLAWS £4.95
Crab claw tips stir fried with prawns, carrot, peppers and mushrooms with Sweet and Sour Sauce on a bed of crisp Chinese vermicelli.

SHARING APPETISERS

THE WESTERN £6.95 FOR 2
Loaded potato skins, Cajun spiced mushrooms, ribs coated in barbecue sauce, Mexican tortilla chips and fried onion rings together with spicy Creole sauce and sour cream and chive dip.

THE ORIENTAL £7.25 FOR 2
Chicken satay, spring rolls, hickory smoked wings and prawn crackers, with chilli and peanut sauce for dipping.

CHICKEN COMBO £6.95 FOR 2
Barbecued wings, southern fried chicken pieces, wings of fire, crispy chicken strips coated in sesame seeds with noodles. Served with 2 dips, sour cream and chive and a creamy hollandaise sauce with wholegrain mustard.

ITALIAN DISHES

LASAGNE VERDI £7.25
Layers of lasagne verdi with a bolognese sauce of prime minced beef topped with cheese in a creamy sauce, served with a mixed salad.

FRESH TORTELLINI WITH FOUR CHEESE SAUCE £7.55
Fresh tortellini filled with smoked ham topped with a rich four cheese sauce and served with a mixed salad.

FRESH TORTELLINI WITH NAPOLETANA SAUCE £7.55
Fresh tortellini filled with Italian cheese and basil topped with Napoletana sauce and served with a mixed salad.

THE ORIGINAL PIZZA £7.95
An enormous 12" home baked pizza topped with tomato, mozzarella and cheddar cheese, prosciutto, black olives, chopped onion and sprinkled with pizza spices, served with a mixed salad.

PIZZA PICCANTE £7.95
A 12" home baked pizza topped with tomato, mozzarella and cheddar cheese, diced red and green peppers, slices of pepperoni and fresh green chillies, sprinkled with pizza spices and served with a mixed salad.

BRITISH CLASSICS (HALF PRICE AVAILABLE)

All British Classics served with a selection of vegetables and Parisienne potatoes

PRIME MINI BEEF JOINT £12.95
Your own prime 12oz British roast beef joint served on a skillet with Yorkshire puddings, horseradish sauce and gravy.

PRIME MINI LAMB JOINT £12.95
Your own prime 18oz British lamb mini joint served on its own skillet accompanied by roast sugar onions, gravy and mint sauce.

WHOLE ROAST CHICKEN £10.50
Your own chicken a minimum of 16oz - oven roasted and coated with honey to give a crisp, sweet coating. Served on its own skillet with bread sauce, sage and onion stuffing and gravy.

SIZZLING DISHES

SEVEN SPICED BEEF £9.25
Strips of stir-fried beef served sizzling, together with onions, peppers, sour cream and chives and buttered new potatoes.

SIZZLING DUCK BREAST £10.50
Slices of breast of duck served sizzling on a skillet together with an orange sauce and potato bake

CAJUN DISHES
Dusted with Cajun spices, seared and brought to your table sizzling on a skillet. Served with our original curly fries.

BLACKENED SIRLOIN £10.25
BLACKENED CHICKEN £9.25

FAJITAS

How to eat Fajitas
1. Load your Mexican pancake with salad, sauces and sizzling chicken / beef and vegetables.
2. Fold it on one side and roll.
3. Pick it up and enjoy!

SIZZLING CHICKEN FAJITAS £9.25
Strips of Cajun chicken with Mexican pancakes, served with salsa, red, green and jalopeno peppers plus guacamole, sour cream and chives and salad.

SIZZLING COMBO FAJITAS £9.55
Strips of prime beef with Cajun chicken and Mexican pancakes, served with salsa, red, green and jalopeno peppers, plus guacamole, sour cream and chives and salad

ORIENTAL DISHES

Served with naan bread £1.35

All Oriental dishes are served with mango chutney, lime pickle, natural yoghurt, poppadums and Basmati pilau rice.

BALTI TANDOORI CHICKEN TIKKA MASALA £9.50
Grilled chicken tikka cooked in a cream sauce with herbs and spices, served in a traditional balti and sprinkled with fresh coriander.

BALTI CHICKEN JALFREZZI £9.50
Chicken cooked in butter and cumin seeds together with ginger and a special blend of spices and then mixed with tomatoes and green peppers. This medium / hot dish is served in a traditional balti and sprinkled with fresh coriander.

BALTI LAMB KORMA £9.50
A mild dish of diced lamb in a coconut sauce with garlic masala, kashmir and chillies coarsely cut, served in a traditional balti pan with fresh coriander.

TANDOORI MIXED GRILL £9.95
A mixture of shish kebab, tandoori, prime chunks of chicken tikka with red and green peppers and onion. Served sizzling on a skillet.

FISH

TRADITIONAL FISH AND CHIPS £7.75
A large traditional in-house battered fish*, deep fried and served with traditional chips, mushy peas and bread and butter.
*Cod or haddock - subject to availability.

SWEET AND SOUR CRAB AND PRAWNS £9.50
Stir Fried Crab claw tips with prawns, carrot, peppers and mushrooms with sweet and sour sauce on a bed of crisp Chinese vermicelli.

CHARGRILLED SALMON £9.50
Salmon chargrilled just right and served with a butter sauce and potato bake.

BUTTERFLY PRAWNS £8.95
Prawns coated in breadcrumbs, served with traditional chips, tartare sauce and fresh lemon.

Figure 11.2 Hotel restaurant menu.
Source: Posthouse Hotels.

of the idea of a restaurant chain created within a hotel chain. Since 1993 the Posthouse chain of hotels has had the Traders concept (discussed in Figure 11.1). The thinking behind this concept is to encourage hotel guests to stay in the hotel, as well as to attract local people to use it. The menu has a wide range of dishes in order to appeal to as many people as possible, as is illustrated in Figure 11.2.

The alternative strategy is to incorporate an existing restaurant brand into the hotel. For instance, the Hilton group has two Chinese restaurants franchized by the Zen chain and two Japanese outlets franchised by Hirolo in four of its hotels.[6] Likewise, the tropical brasserie theme of Trader Vic's, a Polynesian-style restaurant/bar operation, has been incorporated into 21 hotels worldwide. The UK restaurant chain My Kinda Town is expanding overseas by adopting this strategy. The SAS hotel in Brussels has a Henry J. Bean franchise within it, with a franchise fee of around 7 per cent of turnover. Sometimes the restaurant chain is part of the same group as the hotel in which it is incorporated. For instance, Forte's Excelsior Hotel at Heathrow has a Wheeler's restaurant.

The alternative to branding is to create a unique restaurant aimed at attracting anyone seeking to eat out. For instance, Hilton have opened an American-themed diner called Ike's at their hotel in Croydon. Operated by the hotel, it has its own budget and sales targets. The same is true of the Pavilion restaurant at the Grosvenor House Hotel. This 130-seater restaurant has a 'bright, informal, non-hotel image'. It serves around 2500 customers with an average spend of £21. The Churchill Hotel has also developed its own restaurant concept with a distinctive decor, ambience and menu.

The alternative to creating your own unique restaurant in the hotel is to get a restaurateur to do it for you. An example of this is Nico at Ninety, the joint venture between Nico Ladenis, the established chef-patron, and Forte's Grosvenor House Hotel on London's Park Lane.[7] This restaurant is more up-market than the Pavilion and Ladenis has complete freeedom to operate the restaurant as he wishes. He has negotiated a five-year lease for the space within the hotel, although Forte funded the refurbishment costs of £250,000. Other examples include Marco Pierre White at the Hyde Park Hotel and Peter Kromberg at the Inter-Continental.

Lounge Service

This type of service is now only provided in 4- and 5-star hotels or in those hotels where there is no coffee shop. The main food and beverage items served in the lounge are morning coffee and afternoon tea, as illustrated in Figure 11.3. These are served in the lounge, partly for guests' comfort and partly because the traditional hotel restaurant needs to be cleaned and prepared between each meal service. Lounge service also provides for the service of alcoholic drinks to residents at times when the hotel's bar must close to comply with the licensing law. None the less, lounge service is labour-intensive and demand is erratic, which accounts for its decline. It is common for a member of the restaurant staff to be rostered on lounge duties.

Room Service

Room service must be provided in those hotels wishing to attain a 4- or 5-star rating, but like lounge service, room service is expensive to operate and demand is uncertain. Most hotels have replaced some room-service facilities with vending machines, such as in-

Figure 11.3 Hotel afternoon tea service.
Source: Consort Hotels.

room cocktail bars or soft-drinks vending machines and shoe-cleaning facilities in corridors. To comply with the licensing law that only residents and their bona fide guests may
purchase alcoholic drinks throughout the 24 hours of a day, they must be sited in the
guest's room or designed only to operate for residents (i.e. by use of a special key). For
those hotels that continue to provide traditional room service, breakfast is the meal that
most guests choose to eat in their rooms. To simplify the service, hotels have encouraged
the trend towards continental breakfasts, either by making continental breakfasts inclusive
in the room tariff and charging extra for a full English breakfast or by making the latter
only available in the hotel's restaurant or coffee shop.

There are two basic systems for providing service in a guest's room: the floor-pantry
system and centralized floor service.

In the *floor-pantry system,* floor service staff are based on each floor or on every second or third floor and operate from a service pantry. The pantry is stocked with the
goods and equipment necessary to provide beverages and snack-type meals for those
rooms that the pantry has to service. Any dishes or drinks unavailable in the pantry are
collected from the main kitchens or dispense bar as required. The main advantages of this
system are twofold. Staff should be able to respond quickly to a request since they are
located close to the rooms. Secondly, a customer who uses room service a great deal can

achieve some rapport with the server responsible and feel a greater sense of well-being from the personal attention. There are, however, several disadvantages with the system. Demand is erratic, peaking at breakfast time and in the early and late evening, so that extra staff must be employed at peak periods. Secondly, a hotel with ten floors may employ five room-service staff, one for every two floors. If several guests on the same floor require service, one server is rushed and provides poor service, while others are doing nothing. Thirdly, a server stationed in a floor pantry at times of slack demand feels isolated and lacks job satisfaction. Fourthly, control of materials, foodstuffs and beverages is made more difficult by having several points and stock-taking also takes longer. Finally, ordering by guests is made difficult. Either they telephone the floor pantry directly, in which case they may be unable to place an order if the waiter is busy, or they telephone the switchboard or reception to order, from where it is relayed to the floor waiter, which is time-consuming and places extra strain on telephonists and receptionists. Because of these drawbacks this approach to floor service is rarely found, except if a hotel has a so-called executive or concierge floor.

To overcome most of those problems identified above, many hotels operate a *central floor service*, from which all floor service staff operate. As each order is telephoned into room service, the staff serve the orders in turn, irrespective of the floor the orders come from. This type of service is possible using high-speed lifts. The advantages of a centralized system are that fewer staff are required to provide a comprehensive service, especially during off-peak periods; control is made easier since the central point is usually located close to the main kitchen; equipment stock levels are lower, since it is not necessary to equip individual floor pantries with beverage-making facilities, etc.; valuable and expensive floor space is saved on each floor that may be better used for revenue making; the room-service telephone is staffed 24 hours a day by a member of the team; job satisfaction is enhanced by working as a member of a team and by sharing out the workload equitably between the servers.

One of the criteria for achieving 4- and 5-star status is that the hotel must provide 24-hour room service. Up to the 1970s, it was common for a guest to be able to order anything from the hotel's extensive à la carte menu to be served in the room. During the 1980s most hotels reduced the scope of this provision as only a small proportion of certain dishes were ever ordered. Floor-service menus were devised to include the most popular items from the à la carte menu, plus some snack items from the hotel's coffee shop. In the 1990s, this provision has been further modified so that there is often a breakfast menu, a lunch/dinner menu available from late morning up till about midnight, and an all-night menu with considerably fewer menu items. Typical dishes on room service menus are 'standards', such as grilled steak, American-style hamburger, club sandwich and Caeser salad.

Demand for room service can vary quite widely according to the market profile of the hotel. For instance, the Churchill Hotel accommodates a large number of guests from the Middle East who make extensive use of room service, especially during the night. Changes to foodservice provision in other parts of the hotel have also affected room service. It was the case that guests were encouraged to take breakfast in their rooms because silver-served breakfast meant that restaurants were crowded and slow. With the switch to buffet-style self-service breakfast, hotels now discourage room service, as compared with breakfast buffets, room service is slow and uneconomic.

Banqueting

Banquets, conferences, wedding receptions and dinner dances are an important source of revenue for most hotels. But it would be a mistake to believe that the hotel sector exclusively carries out function catering – outside caterers, banqueting houses, institutional and industrial caterers are other types of foodservice business involved in the 'banquet' trade. Functions vary in size from small private parties for 10 or 12 people up to large affairs for 1000 or 1200 people; they may be family celebrations, social events or business functions; the meal may be lunch, dinner or wedding breakfast; and the dishes may range from only canapés, as at a cocktail party, up to those to be found in a six- or seven-course menu. This diversity means that each function is different and must be approached individually, taking especial note of the function organizer's particular requirements. To enable the foodservice manager to do this, details of each function are usually entered on a function form or banqueting memorandum. Function forms have a number of advantages. A well-planned form ensures that the caterer discusses all the essential points with the function organizer. It may be used as a contract between caterer and organizer. It can be circulated to all relevant departments of the hotel or establishment so that all staff are informed about the function.

The staffing of the banqueting department of a hotel will depend on many factors: the size of the banqueting rooms, time of year, popularity of the hotel, availability of staff, management philosophy, and so on. Broadly speaking, a distinction can be made between hotels that have a banqueting manager and full-time staff and hotels that do not. Obviously the larger and more popular the banqueting facilities, the greater the likelihood that full-time personnel will be employed.

In organizing the banqueting operation in a hotel, pre-planned menus are often devised. These have both advantages and disadvantages. Pre-designed menus should ensure that the principles of good menu planning are adhered to. Function organizers with little catering experience may select dishes that they themselves like, without considering the impact that these dishes may have upon the meal as a whole. Secondly, menus that are planned in advance enable the banqueting manager to quote a price to the customer immediately, since they are pre-costed. The cost of a menu determined by the customer has to be calculated from scratch. Menus can be designed that accommodate the availability of both kitchen equipment and service equipment, without placing unnecessary strain upon the stocks of plates, cutlery, pans, etc. The quality of food served is likely to be higher if the kitchen staff are preparing dishes that they are familiar with and have prepared often. The dangers of pre-planned menus are that they may not be flexible enough to cater for the wide range of customer demand. They may be too stereotyped and lacking in originality. They may be unresponsive to changes in the conditions of supply of goods and commodities, especially fresh meat, fish and vegetables. They may reduce job satisfaction due to staff having to prepare and serve the same dishes repetitively. It is therefore wise for banquet menus to be changed every two or three months, and both banquet and kitchen personnel should be involved in their compilation.

The second element of planning is applied to seating and table plans for functions. In most cases all the possible seating arrangements of a particular function room will be well-established from constant use. The two main table arrangements for functions are formal (top table with sprigs), and informal (rows of round tables, as illustrated in Figure 11.4).

Figure 11.4 Hotel banqueting suite.
Source: Hilton Hotel, London.

The third element of planning is ensuring that the proper number of staff are available and fully briefed before the start of the function, especially if they are casual staff. The briefing should include details such as the location of guest and staff toilets, the table or station each waiter is to serve, the menu and details of each dish, the order of service, who to see if a guest requests something unexpected, and so on.

Different service styles are adopted because of the diversity of functions. Broadly speaking these service styles are silver service, family service, plate service, and buffet service, listed here in decreasing order of staffing requirements. The first three of these service styles are discussed above, whilst buffet service is explained below. The choice of which particular style of service to use will depend upon how much the customer is prepared to pay; the availability and expertise of the service staff; the size of the function room in relation to the number of guests to be served; the nature of the menu items selected; and the time of year, since cold dishes rather than hot tend to be served from buffets and are therefore more appropriate for the summer months.

A buffet can be defined as a refreshment bar, and the original style of buffet for a hotel or restaurant was a counter stocked with cold drinks, beers, wine, hot beverages, tobacco, pastries, cakes, sandwiches and ice cream. Today, of course, such a buffet is more likely to be found at a railway station than in a hotel or restaurant. Buffet service in the modern restaurant refers to the presentation of a wide selection of dishes on a buffet table or counter

Figure 11.5 Typical hotel buffet (Piccadilly Hotel).
Source: Jarvis Hotel.

from which customers help themselves, as illustrated in Figure 11.5. It is a style of service particularly suitable for banquet catering or catering for guests staying on demi-pension or full-board terms, since the all-inclusive price can be calculated to allow the guests the freedom to select their own meals. The type of dishes served tend to be salad items, although there is no reason why hot dishes cannot be served. If they are, however, equipment such as plate warmers and hot-plates must be made available to keep the food hot and more service staff will be needed to help the guest with the service.

The main advantage to the operator of adopting this style of foodservice is that it greatly reduces the number of staff required for the meal service, while a neatly laid-out buffet presents the food in an attractive and spectacular way. It is not a service style that is appropriate for formal occasions. Important points to consider in operating a buffet are as follows. In order to accommodate the food for a large number, the buffet table may need to be quite long, in which case it may be advisable either to have two separate service points or to split the buffet in two identical sections so that guests may start at either end of the table. Dishes and flats must be replenished as soon as they are empty and where necessary redressed to maintain an attractive presentation. Staff must be available behind the buffet to advise the guests and help with their selection. Thought must be given to presenting the dishes on the buffet in a colourful and appetizing manner. There must be an adequate supply of plates and service equipment, and finally the buffet table should not be placed near to a radiator or in direct sunlight.

There are, however, problems with buffet service that must be recognized and dealt with. Wastage may occur if the quantities of each dish are not estimated accurately in advance. This is made difficult by the variety of dishes presented, so that predicting accurately which dishes will prove most popular is made more difficult. The type of food suitable for buffet service is perishable, and the method of presentation at normal room temperatures will tend to hasten the rate of spoilage. Suitable buffet dishes tend to be highly priced: cold joints of meat, dressings relying on oil, and so on. In addition, to present the food as attractively as possible, the decoration of the dishes will increase both food and labour cost. The preparation of a good buffet is a skilled job, making difficult demands upon the expertise of the kitchen staff; and furthermore, by placing a buffet in a room the seating capacity is reduced, and thus revenue is potentially lost also.

FOODSERVICE ORGANIZATION IN HOTELS

The internal organization of food service in a hotel will depend upon the size, style and turnover of the unit, which as we have seen can vary quite widely from one hotel to another. It will also be greatly influenced by the management policy of the hotel company's directors. In a small hotel, the director may well also be the manager and the management structure may be relatively simple. In effect, control and direction is in the hands of one person, with supervising staff reporting directly to that person. In much larger hotels the management structure is very much more complex and various grades of manager and supervisors can be identified. Within such a hierarchy, the role of food and beverage managers varies widely, and often he or she will have two distinct functions.

In many hotels, the manager will be responsible for carrying out, rather than instigating, policies with regard to the provision of food and drink. This will cover all aspects of food service – monitoring suppliers and foodstuffs received, monitoring standards of cuisine and service, staffing the restaurants and bars, promoting food and drink sales, liaising with the customers themselves, appraizing costs and turnover and, most importantly, ensuring that a satisfactory gross profit margin is maintained. In this respect, a food and beverage manager is no different from managers in other sectors of the catering industry.

As a member of the management team, the food and beverage manager will be placed on call usually during a day or evening shift, to be responsible for all the activities of the hotel's operations. In addition to routine duty management tasks such as checking security, supervizing staff and so on, the duty manager is expected to deal with any ordinary events such as staff absences, guest complaints, and so on.

Thus, a food and beverage manager in a hotel needs knowledge and skills of hotel-keeping in addition to those of catering. At the same time, within the larger hotels he or she is supported by specialist staff such as personnel and training managers, controllers and sales personnel whom other sectors of the industry do not employ, at least within the unit. The food and beverage manager in a hotel is very much a part of the management team within the hotel; in popular, industrial and institutional catering, the manager is usually in sole charge of the unit.

CURRENT ISSUES AND FUTURE TRENDS

In 1994, the major trends in hotel foodservice in the USA[8] were more conceptualized and casualized dining rooms; standardizing menus and three-meal coffee shops; cutting wine prices; competitive prepackaged, all-inclusive banquet meals; and more healthful menu items. All of these can also be applied to the UK hotel foodservice scene. The top two challenges were to 'help restaurant managers develop an entrepreneurial style that customers have come to expect at independent restaurants', and 'to create marketing and promotional programs to drive sales'. As we have seen, hotel operators have adopted four different approaches to this entrepreneurial challenge based around branding and/or joint ventures. With regards to marketing and promotion, three UK trends emerge. Firstly, hotels no longer just think of their guests as their market. They are segmenting their foodservice offering into different markets with promotions aimed at each. So a hotel located in a business area may target office workers and business people at lunchtimes through local advertising and promotions. Many hotels have successfully developed Sunday lunchtime trade by promoting family lunches or 'brunch' aimed at local householders. Secondly, there is an increase in 'loyalty dining cards'. These are credit cards that entitle the holder to a discount related to how frequently the customer uses the outlet. Hilton, Hyatt and Intercontinental hotel chains have all introduced this concept for their guests. Finally, hotel foodservice managers are working closely with suppliers, especially wine and spirits suppliers, to carry out in-house promotions.

A further major trend is conceptualizing the accommodation provision as separate to the foodservice provision, and hence operating them separately, sometimes by different companies. The leasing of restaurant space to high-profile restaurateurs has been referred to above, along with the incorporation of restaurant brands into hotel properties. One future trend may the contracting out of the entire foodservice provision. Already, the 4-star Bailey's Hotel in London has contracted out its restaurant, banqueting and room service to The Restaurant Partnership.[9]

CONCLUSION

The foodservice manager in a hotel has a wide range of service styles and operations to deal with. Each of them has its special problem and the manager must be familiar with all the different needs and requirements. Each of the main areas will have a different clientele. In the restaurants, the customers will either be residents or non-residents. For many years, the residential diner was regarded as the cornerstone of hotel restaurants. Today, however, the hotel cannot rely upon residents to provide them with the turnover required to operate a successful restaurant. Thus the hotel's restaurant must compete, in its own right, with other foodservice operations found locally. Thus, the larger hotels have a selection of restaurants to compete with the variety of restaurants found in any main street – an up-market, speciality restaurant, a coffee shop or fast food operation, a grill-room or steakhouse-style restaurant, and so on. Furthermore, to enhance this competitive stance, these restaurants have a strong base and are marketed with the aim of attracting customers who are non-residential.

The room-service customer has a different need. Any guests who require refreshment do so for reasons of thirst or hunger that need to be satisfied quickly and/or discreetly and their expectations are that the service will be prompt and as good as they might get in the hotel's bar or restaurant. Finally, the guest at a function or banquet is there because it is a special occasion, be it a social event or business meeting. Therefore, the essential qualities of a good banquet are a smooth running, efficient service, care to keep to the arranged schedule and food that is as good as that a customer in the hotel's restaurant might receive.

REFERENCES

1. Whitehall, B., quoted in Jones, P. (1981) *Foodservice Operations*, Eastbourne: Holt, Rinehart & Winston, p. 160.
2. Key Note (1994) *The Restaurant Industry*, Hampton, Middlesex: Key Note Publications.
3. Ibid.
4. Mintel (1992) *Britain Eating Out*, London: Mintel Drink Intelligence Report.
5. Ibid.
6. Edwards, M. (1993) 'Playing the name game', *Caterer and Hotelkeeper*, 4 February, pp. 36–8.
7. Harmer, J. (1994) 'Calling in the experts', *Caterer and Hotelkeeper*, 7 July, pp. 60–2.
8. Weinstock, J. (1994) 'New hotel strategy: offer more for less', *Restaurants & Institutions*, 15 July, pp. 68–72.
9. Harmer, J. op. cit.

TWELVE

Motorway and Roadside Restaurants

PETER JONES

INTRODUCTION

Roadside dining is not a new idea. The original coaching inns were established in order to serve customers travelling the length and breadth of Britain by road. Just as the railway was significant in the development of hotels, the motorcar has played a major role in the development of the foodservice industry. In the 1950s, the number of cars increased by over 200 per cent, and by nearly 140 per cent in the 1960s. By 1992 there were 20 million vehicles on the road, nearly 16 times more car traffic than 50 years earlier. The impact of this growth on the foodservice industry was first felt in the 1960s. Prior to the emergence of restaurant chains, roadside catering was either provided by pubs and hotels, or the archetypal transport café. But in 1959 Forte opened the first Little Chef. This was based on American-style roadside diners originally and was little more than a hamburger and hot dog stand. Quite quickly these units were developed into table service restaurants.

One year later in 1960 the first motorway service area (MSA) was built on the M1 at Newport Pagnell, as illustrated in Figure 12.1. At this time it had 20,000 vehicles per day passing by; in 1990 it was over 120,000 vehicles per day. The first MSAs were fairly rudimentary, consisting of little more than a petrol filling station, toilets, and a cafeteria. Since the original legislation that enabled these requires operators to pay annual rents that increased with turnover, there was little incentive to invest. An editorial in the *Daily Mirror* in the late 1970s stated that 'British Rail catering, on the way up, passed motorway cafes, on the way down, some time ago', and certainly during that time motorway catering faced a great deal of criticism.[1] In fact in 1978, the situation was so serious that the government set up the Prior Commission to look into the whole question of motorway service areas. The report stated that the service areas provide many things including petrol, breakdown/repair facilities, toilets, retail shopping, catering in a wide variety of units and even overnight accommodation, but that the legislation that had originally set them up was too detailed and complex. Therefore revised conditions were established and operators were granted 50-year leases. Thereafter provision had to guarantee 24-hour parking, petrol, toilets and some form of catering.

In the 1990s two main sectors remain distinct – motorway service catering and roadside restaurants – and each of these will be looked at separately. Current trends and future developments in motorway and roadside catering will be considered at the end of the chapter.

MOTORWAY SERVICES

It is possible to specify motorway service areas clearly, as all sites in England are currently owned and controlled by the Department of Transport. However, in August 1992, in the first major change since 1978, the UK government announced changes in policy, towards deregulation. These changes include reduction in the minimum interval between MSAs and hence an increase in the number of possible sites; privatization of site ownership, largely by enabling the existing leaseholders to purchase their sites; relaxation of control over site development, by enabling private sector developers to apply directly to local authorities; and some modifications to the restrictions placed on operators with regards to minimum levels of service. These restrictions now require a minimum number of parking spaces in relation to the existing and projected traffic flows past the site, disabled access, 24-hour petrol, and a minimum level of catering. During the consultation between the DoT, MSA operators, motoring organizations, local authorities and other interested parties, it had been proposed to allow the sale of alcohol at MSAs and the development of large retail stores and leisure complexes. These proposals were rejected. MSAs exist solely for the convenience and use of the travelling public – motorists, coach passengers, and commercial drivers.[2] There is also the growth of accommodation provision at MSAs. Such budget hotels have already been discussed in Chapter 5.

Size of the Sector

Only 1 per cent of all public roads in Great Britain are motorways. There are just over 3000 kilometres of such highways. However, per kilometre, motorways carry very much more traffic than other roads. During the 1980s this type of road had 20 per cent growth, compared with only 2 per cent on principal and trunk roads. By 1992 there were 56 MSAs in Great Britain, of which 47 were in England, five in Scotland and four in Wales. The sector had an estimated sales turnover of £287 million, which represents about 55 per cent of the total roadside market.[3] This share has remained more or less the same throughout the 1980s and 1990s. In 1991 it was estimated that 200 million people used MSAs, of whom 140 million made a purchase in the restaurant. The sector employs around 8000 staff, of whom the majority are catering staff. The market is dominated by four main operators[4] – Granada (18 MSAs), Forte with the Welcome Break brand (17 MSAs), Roadchef (9) and Bright Reasons' Pavilion brand (8) – who operate 92 per cent of all MSAs. These operators may also operate MSA-style units on principal and trunk roads. For instance, there are a further seven Welcome Breaks on other major roads in the UK.

Markets Served

It is quite clear that MSAs serve the motorist when sales are analysed. Out of more than an estimated £820 million total sales turnover, £540 million is derived from petrol sales. Catering represents just over half of the remainder, with retail shops a third. The average customer spends £1.14 in the MSA restaurant.[5] The early 1990s have seen a great deal of market research by the major operators in order to understand more closely customers' needs. Such research is a result of the government's move towards deregulation, the

entrance of Bright Reasons into the market with their purchase of Rank's motorway service areas, and the development of branding. Granada research[6] showed that its typical
customer (75 per cent of the sample) was male, aged 25 to 44. In view of the fairly basic
needs that MSAs satisfy, this largely reflects the pattern of motorway usage. So although
MSAs are used by ABC1 socioeconomic groups predominantly, this reflects their levels
of car ownership, mobility and affluence.[7] But MSA usage varies quite widely throughout
the year. For instance, on Saturdays throughout the soccer season large numbers of fans
use the motorway network to get to and from matches. Likewise, bank holidays and seasonal holiday periods may cause significant increases in usage, as in the case of MSAs in
the north of England at the beginning of Glasgow's traditional holiday fortnight in July.

Location

It was the Department of Transport (DoT) that decided on the location of MSAs. Until
1992 it had a policy to provide sites about every 40 kilometres. Sites were acquired by
compulsory order and then leased at peppercorn rents to operators prepared to develop
the sites. Deregulation in 1992 revised this to enable more frequent services, within 25
kilometres of each other.[8] But in view of the current size of the MSA network, this in
effect means that new MSAs are likely to be built around the M25 or on new sections of
motorway. Such development costs vary between £10-30 million depending on the size of
the site and extent of the facilities. These high costs have tended to prevent new entrants
investing in this market. Adjacent sites are usually leased to different operators in order
to increase competition. Forte owns some adjacent sites because it purchased the Welcome Break chain in 1985 whilst already operating some sites of its own.

Style of Operation

A fairly typical MSA, serving one side of the carriageway, would have parking for 200
cars, 20 coaches and 50 HGVs; a petrol filling station and associated retail shop; a
restaurant for up to 300 customers; a general shop; toilets and showers for men, women
and disabled persons; and probably a fast food-outlet as well. Other facilities may include
telephones, amusement arcades, baby changing rooms, bank ATMs, picnic areas, specialist retail outlets such as bookshops and gift shops, children's outdoor play areas, business centres and tourist information centres. From the foodservice perspective the most
distinctive feature is the large-scale cafeteria provision which is almost unique to this sector. However, a significant recent trend has been the building of fast food and other
branded foodservice outlets on MSA sites. This is particularly the case with the provision
of fast-food, take-away provision. Thus Granada have their own Burger Express brand
now being replaced after entering into a franchise agreement with BurgerKing; Forte have
Kentucky Fried Chicken take-aways on some MSAs and an agreement with McDonald's[9]
to open two outlets on the M3 and M1 in 1995; and Roadchef opened their first Wimpy
counter service operation on the A1M in 1994. Forte have also located their Little Chef
and Happy Eater outlets (see later in this chapter) on some MSAs, whilst Granada have
an agreement to operate AJs restaurants on some of their non-motorway sites. But the
heart of the operation remains the self-service cafeteria. These too are branded – Forte
has both Julie's Pantry and Granary; Granada's brand is Country Kitchen; Bright Reasons is named Oasis; and Roadchef has Orchards.

Figure 12.1   Typical motorway service area.
Source: Hunting Aerofilms Ltd.

ROADSIDE DINING

The development of roadside dining, and especially the branded chains, is a story of new entrants growing rapidly, only to be taken over by the major players in the market. From its conception in 1959, Little Chef has dominated the marketplace. In 1973, a second chain, Happy Eater was set up and grew to rival this dominance. Then in 1986, Little Chef (with 270 units) and Happy Eater (with 85) merged when Forte bought Imperial Hotels, although they continue to be marketed as separate brands. At this time new companies entered the market with the intention of developing a chain of roadside restaurants. Kelly's Kitchens were created, owned by Bass, and then sold to Forte when 17 outlets had been built, to be converted into Little Chefs. AJ's Family Restaurants was set up by the former director of Happy Eater and has developed 30 outlets from Yorkshire down to Hampshire. These three brands now have 90 per cent of the non-motorway roadside dining market in terms of the number of outlets.

Definition and Size of the Sector

This sector of the UK foodservice industry is defined by its dominant brands. When we talk about roadside dining in the UK, what we are referring to is Little Chef, Happy

Eater and AJ's Restaurants. They are this sector. In many respects it is a remarkable story. The hospitality industry during this century has seen a number of new concepts develop in the UK – fast food, budget hotels, food courts, family restaurants, and so on. But none of these concepts have come to dominate their segment completely or entirely to replace the provision that was there beforehand. So although hamburger chains have impacted on fish and chip shops, there are still a large number of independently owned and operated fish and chip shops in the UK. But by the roadside, the traditional, independently owned 'transport cafe' has become almost extinct. There is now one of these branded restaurants for every 100 kilometres of the UK's principal and trunk roads. This success is one of the first examples in the UK of effective branding in the foodservice industry. The consistent standard of provision by roadside diners was so superior that market share was quickly established and maintained. There were over 500 roadside restaurants in the UK in 1992, of which over 80 per cent were in England. The sector had an estimated sales turnover of £238 million, which represents about 45 per cent of the total roadside market.[10]

Markets Served

Just as on motorways, the average customer reflects the profile of the motoring public. Ironically, the very feature that led to the concept's success – branding – has apparently failed to establish any major differences between the brands in the minds of most customers. One market survey[11] indicates that less than 30 per cent of respondents had any brand loyalty in 1991 and this has probably been true for many years. A survey conducted by Happy Eater in the 1970s, before its take-over by Forte, showed that the principal reason people stopped at these outlets was to use the toilet facilities, not to have a beverage, snack or meal. Customers therefore tend to stop when they need to, rather than drive on to the next outlet out of brand preference. It is also the case that although the brands try to differentiate themselves, there are major similarities in the nature of provision. So although Happy Eater is aimed more at the leisure traveller with the family, and Little Chef more towards the business traveller, location rather than segmentation is the key factor in attracting custom.

Location

The cost of developing a site ranges from £250,000 up to £500,000. This kind of investment therefore requires the application of careful site selection criteria. Until the late 1980s, most developments were on greenfield sites. In the last ten years, such sites have become more difficult to find and the emphasis has switched to locating diners at petrol filling stations. In effect, small-scale MSAs are being developed. The involvement of petrol companies and motor traders in roadside catering development reflects a trend: more and more new sites will tend to be located on petrol station sites. There are three main reasons for this. First, food and drink is not the only reason compelling motorists to stop. Research has shown that in order of importance they stop to use toilet facilities, because of tiredness, to eat or drink, to buy petrol and to let the traffic clear. Second, petrol stations have both spare land for development and existing access off and on to roads, which makes planning applications easier. Finally, motor traders are facing stiff

Figure 12.2   Typical roadside diner.
Source: AJ's Restaurant.

competition for tyre and exhaust sales due to the growth of specialist retailers/fitters, so they are seeking new ways to generate income and utilize space.

The single most important criterion for selecting a site is obviously the number of people likely to stop at the facility. However, simply counting the traffic flow is inadequate. Whilst traffic flow gives an indication of the total potential market, it does not indicate what proportion of these may use the facility. The potential usage is determined by other factors such as the location of other roadside facilities, ease of access to the site, and length of journey being undertaken. For instance, one operator opened two sites almost simultaneously. The site in Humberside had an extremely high traffic count, whilst the other in Norfolk a low count. But because many of the passers-by in Humberside were travelling probably less than two miles from their home to work or shopping, whilst those in Norfolk were travelling at least 20 miles from one town to another, the latter operation was more successful.

Style of Operation

The typical roadside diner comprises a table-service restaurant with seating for between 90 and 120 customers, a call order kitchen, toilet facilities, a small retail space often by the cash desk, and car parking for up to 50 vehicles. AJ's further developed the Little Chef/Happy Eater concept by adding a self-serve salad bar in the restaurant and a take-out counter. A distinctive feature is the unit's exterior and signage aimed at attracting the attention of passing motorists, as illustrated in Figure 12.2.

The menu offering provides a wide range of items, drawing on a range of origins in

MAIN COURSES

STARTERS & SOUPS

GARLIC BREAD 90p ORANGE JUICE 90p

HONEYDEW MELON   95p
Slice of Fresh Melon with Ground Ginger

18 BOWL OF PIPING HOT SOUP   £1.40

Cream of Tomato   Minestrone
Hearty Oxtail   Rich Mulligatawny
Celery   Cream of Chicken
Served with Roll and Butter
Your server will advise you of today's choices

19 PRAWN COCKTAIL   £2.25
Served complete with Brown Bread

20 DIPPERS DELIGHT (Serves 2)   £3.95
Chicken Nuggets, Garlic Mushrooms, Scampi
and Battered Onion Rings with a Choice of Dip

21 DEEP FRIED MUSHROOMS   £2.05
Garlic Mushrooms, deep fried with a Choice of Dip

22 SEAFOOD DIP   £2.25
Scampi pieces with Tartare Dip

25. Gammon Steak

30. Farmhouse Grill

BAKES & GRILLS
SERVED WITH EITHER, SALAD, RICE, CHIPPED, NEW OR JACKET POTATO

24 ROAST CHICKEN   £5.50
Half an Oven Roasted Chicken served with Garden Peas
and Sweetcorn with a Rich Gravy

25 GAMMON STEAK   £5.30
Griddled Prime Gammon served with a Pineapple
Ring and Garden Peas

26 SIRLOIN STEAK   £6.95
Tender Sirloin Steak served with Mushrooms,
Onion Rings and Garden Peas

27 BEEF STEW & DUMPLINGS   £4.95
A traditional tasty alternative

28 LIVER AND BACON   £4.45
Griddled Liver and Bacon served with Onion Rings,
Tomatoes, Garden Peas and Gravy

29 LASAGNE   £4.75
Traditional Italian Pasta served with Garden Peas

30 FARMHOUSE GRILL   £4.60
Griddled Egg, Bacon, Tomatoes, Sausage, Hamburger
served with Garden Peas and Mushrooms

31 PORK SCHNITZEL   £4.95
Tender Crumbed Pork served with Tomatoes,
Garden Peas and Button Mushrooms

BURGERS
4oz LEAN BEEF SERVED WITH COLESLAW AND RELISHES
AND CHOICE OF SALAD OR CHIPPED POTATOES

33 BACONBURGER   £4.15
Topped with Bacon and Grated Cheese

34 PINEBURGER   £3.45
Open Burger with Pineapple and Coleslaw

35 EGGBURGER   £3.35
Crowned with a Griddled Egg

36 CHILLIBURGER   £3.45
Hot and Spicy Vegetable Chilli

37 AJ's "MAJORBURGER"   £4.50
6oz Lean Beef served with any two of the following:

a COTTAGE CHEESE   e GRIDDLED BACON
b GRIDDLED EGG   f VEGETABLE CHILLI
c CHEDDAR CHEESE   g MUSHROOMS
d TOMATO   h PINEAPPLE

38 CHICKENBURGER   £3.35
Tender Chicken in Batter

FISH
SERVED WITH EITHER: SALAD, RICE, CHIPPED, NEW OR JACKET POTATO

39 FILLET OF PLAICE   £4.55
Breaded and deep-fried, served with Garden Peas, Lemon
and Tartare Sauce

40 FILLET OF HADDOCK   £4.55
Crispy battered and deep-fried, served with
Garden Peas and Lemon

41 SCAMPI PLATTER   £5.75
Golden Crumbed Scampi pieces served with
Garden Peas, Lemon and Tartare Sauce

40. Fillet of Haddock

39. Fillet of Plaice

SENIOR'S CHOICE
(60 and over)
Purchase a "Senior's Choice" card
for just £1.00
Present it when placing your order
at any **AJ's Restaurant** and a
20% menu price reduction will be made on
all you can eat and drink.

For the widest choice of food and drink on the roadside

Figure 12.3 Roadside diner menu.
Source: AJ's Restaurant.

order to appeal to all market segments. An example of a roadside diner menu is shown in Figure 12.3.

Current Issues and Future Trends

The development of non-motorway 'service areas', the location of roadside restaurant brands on MSAs, and the development of budget hotels mean that the issues that face both motorway and non-motorway provision are increasingly the same and future trends will reflect this. Changing consumer tastes, that are affecting all sectors of the foodservice industry, are also impacting on this sector.[12] The switch to healthy food choice and towards snacking or 'grazing' rather than main meals, has resulted in menu redesign and a gradual decline in average spend. The major trend up to the 1990s has been to extend the product range to provide a 'one-stop shop' for all the needs the motorist may have. Sales have therefore grown from the purchase of additional items. Having reached the limit of what can be made available, the future trend will be to focus on increasing the frequency of purchase. Thus in redesigning nine of Granada's MSAs, an effort has been made to 'get the salesman, who's using [the car park and toilets] ... into the service area to use the facilities'[13] and once inside design has paid attention to encouraging impulse purchases. But there is still scope to grow. The research quoted earlier showed that only one in ten people of the sample had eaten in this kind of operation in the previous month. There remains huge market potential in this sector.

REFERENCES

1. Jones, P. (1988) *Foodservice Operations* (2nd edition), London: Cassell.
2. Headland Research (1993) *Catering for the Motorist*, London: Headland Research.
3. Mintel (1992) 'Roadside catering', in *Leisure Intelligence Report*, Volume 2, London: Mintel Publications.
4. Headland Research op. cit.
5. Mintel op. cit.
6. Tarpey, D. (1994) 'Food in the fast lane', *Caterer and Hotelkeeper*, 3 November, pp. 68–9.
7. Mintel op. cit.
8. Tarpey, D. op. cit.
9. Anon. (1994) 'Big Macs make debut on U.K. motorways', *Caterer and Hotelkeeper*, 6 October, p. 9.
10. Mintel op. cit.
11. Ibid.
12. Webster, J. (1994) 'Truckers take a break', *Caterer and Hotelkeeper*, 29 September, pp. 60–1.
13. Wilson, P. (1993) 'The perfect pitstop', *Interiors*, July, pp. 4–6.

THIRTEEN

Licensed Trade Foodservice

HADYN INGRAM

INTRODUCTION

Hospitality can be defined as the 'friendly and generous reception and entertainment of guests and strangers'[1]. This definition is consistent with hospitality's origins in the inns and taverns of Britain and the warm welcome for which they are still famous. This sector of the wider hospitality industry is still of economic and social importance, but is experiencing major change. Iain Sproat MP, the Undersecretary of State for Tourism, suggests that 'the British pub provides a unique attraction for visitors to this country'.[2] Research commissioned by the Brewers Society in 1992 indicates that British pubs are popular with tourists. One American visitor remarked 'I like them. I don't understand them – but I like them'.[3]

This confusion is perhaps not surprising as the British system of bar ownership and operation has evolved over time to become like no other in the world. This chapter will explain how this historical development affects the present structure of the trade and how licensed operations are managed. It will also outline the current size and scale of the sector and key features of operations. Finally, the future will be considered – how licensed foodservice might be affected by current trends and the way in which pubs may evolve to meet those changes.

DEFINITION

Historically, licensed premises were called alehouses, taverns or inns. Alehouses tended to sell only beer; taverns have become what is now commonly called a 'public house' or pub; and inns provided accommodation as well as food and beverages. Today public houses and bars are licensed for the *'sale of drinks for consumption generally on the premises'* as defined by the Standard Industrial Classification (1992), but they also dominate the eating-out market through bar meals and the provision of more formal restaurant services. The licensed trade includes public houses, clubs, wine bars, and any bar where alcoholic drink and often food is offered for sale. Each requires a different type of licence in order to be able to sell alcoholic beverages which can stipulate the range of drinks that may be sold and the opening hours of the operation. Such premises, and the food and drink sold, represent an important part of British social life as well as contributing considerable sums to the national economy through the tax which is paid on alcohol. In 1992, £8.5 billion was paid by alcoholic drinks consumers in excise and VAT to the Treasury.[4]

DEVELOPMENT OF THE LICENSED TRADE

The British public house has its origins in the Saxon inns and taverns which brewed beer and served food for villagers and travellers. As settlements grew in size and number, the pubs became communal meeting places for social interaction. The Industrial Revolution increased urban prosperity so that consumption of beer, particularly by thirsty factory workers, grew steadily. The Ale-house Act of 1828 repealed and codified the many statutes then in existence and formed the basis of subsequent liquor licensing. In 1830, licences were issued to beerhouses in an attempt to reduce the consumption of spirits, but, in fact, more drunkenness ensued because beer became more readily available. By the following year more than 30,000 new beer shops were opened and this process continued to bring the total in existence to 50,000 by the middle of the century.[5] By 1869 these 'beerhouses' had proliferated to such an extent that the British government felt the need to monitor their operation because of the crime and disorder associated with heavy drinking. Since then, both public house premises and their managers need to be licensed by local magistrates who have discretionary powers to restrict or revoke licences in the public interest. These licensing laws were further adapted during the First World World War, when it was felt necessary to reduce the opening hours of licensed premises so as to concentrate the efforts of workers, especially in munitions factories, upon essential war work. Licensing regulations remained unchanged until 1988, when pubs were allowed to extend permitted opening hours in line with those of continental Europe.

Ownership patterns have also evolved in a uniquely British way. Until the nineteenth century, all public houses were independently owned. The brewers, numbering far more than they do today, sought to increase loans made to publicans in return for the exclusive right to sell the brewer's beers in the pubs. By the end of the nineteenth century, with the stagnation of beer sales and tightening of licensing controls, the competitive forces increased. These informal loan arrangements were turned into outright acquisitions to prevent outlets falling into the hands of competitors. This process is called vertical integration and it meant that brewers could either run their pubs themselves by employing managers or by selecting tenants who were 'tied' to sell their beers in exchange for a rental fee.

From the 1950s many mergers and acquisitions gave rise to a concentration of large numbers of tied outlets within a small number of large brewing companies, and, in economic terms, this is called an oligopoly. Since the 1960s many felt that this oligopolistic arrangement was acting against the public interest in reducing consumer choice and artificially raising prices. The Monopolies and Mergers Commission (MMC) report of 1989 – the twenty-third investigation into the licensed trade since 1966 – reported that a complex monopoly existed in brewing. The result of this report was the Beer Orders of 1990 by which licensees were permitted to purchase draught cask-conditioned beer from a 'guest' brewer. From 1992, brewers' control of tied outlets was limited to 2000 per company.

Table 13.1   Product mix of public houses 1982–1992 (%).

	1982	1988	1990	1992
Alcoholic drink	77	74	69	65
Food	16	20	25	29
Cigarettes/tobacco	3	2	2	2
Accommodation	1	1	1	1
Other	3	3	3	3

Sources: Key Note Report (1993).

SIZE AND SCALE OF THE SECTOR

In Great Britain 68,989 bars generated sales in 1992 of £11.8 billion.[6] From 1991 to 1993 over 2000 public houses have ceased trading and it is predicted[7] up to 10,000 more may close by the year 2000. The sector employed over 322,000 people along with about 50,000 self-employed persons in 1992. There are over twice as many females as males employed in the public house trade, reflecting the part-time nature of much bar work. An estimated 86 per cent of pubs serve food (around 58,000 outlets).[8] While alcohol is still the mainstay of the public house's income, it is representing an increasingly smaller proportion. Food income, however, has almost doubled in the decade from 1982 and, by 1996, is forecast to represent more that one-third of public house turnover. This is illustrated in Table 13.1.

Despite or perhaps because of these changes, the public house remains the most visited leisure venue, with around 70 per cent of the population paying at least one visit during the year.[9] The typical public house drinker is likely to be male, aged 25 to 49, and in the C2 social class,[10] but this pattern is likely to change as the number of younger people in the total population diminishes. A 1992 survey revealed that the public house is by far the most popular place to eat out at lunchtime, with 3.4 million lunches served daily, although more than twice as many visit in the evening than at lunchtime.[11] The consumer perception was that public house food offered good value for money, but that drinks were sometimes seen as expensive compared to the price paid at supermarkets. This is due, in part, to the control over wholesale prices which is exerted by major breweries, with liquor prices to the 'tied' trade far exceeding 'free' trade levels. With the advent of the Single Market in 1993, restrictive personal allowances for the import of duty-paid alcohol were abolished. This meant that travellers returning from the Continent could bring back unlimited amounts of alcohol for personal use, and current estimates suggest that this traffic represents around 12 per cent of the take-home trade.

Food being available is the second most popular reason for choosing a pub, the first being that it is the 'local' and within walking distance.[12] The availability of food is of particular importance to women, people over 45 years of age, and those in the AB socioeconomic group (i.e. the most affluent) and the E grouping (comprising a large number of retired people). There are no significant variations in the pattern of pub visiting throughout the UK.

CURRENT STRUCTURE OF THE LICENSED TRADE

Since the MMC report of 1989, the licensed trade has been divided into three clear sectors: independent, regional and national public houses.

Independent Sector

The free houses (free of brewery tie and often run by sole proprietors) and independent chains accounted for more than 40 per cent of total pub trade sales in 1993 and now represent the biggest sector both in terms of outlets and sales. This phenomenon has occurred partly because national breweries have had to dispose of pubs above the statutory limit, and also because entrepreneurial operators have been quick to seize unique opportunities to break into the market. Within the independent sector, more than one-third are directly managed by multiple chains with the other two-thirds being offered as tenancies or assignable leases. Managed houses usually are more profitable as they are better sited and have been more proactive in developing catering. One independent multiple operator with an innovative approach is JD Wetherspoon of London. Tim Martin established this company in 1979 and drew upon his legal training to convert prime high street sites into profitable managed free houses; these numbered 77 in 1994. Wetherspoon's offer branded catering in one standard menu in all their managed outlets.

Regional Sector

Regional breweries operate on traditional lines, being often family-owned and brewing beer for consumption in their tenanted and managed houses. This traditional approach is also reflected in their promotion of cask-conditioned ale which is championed by the Campaign for Real Ale (CAMRA) consumer pressure group. Regional brewers like Greene King are trying to build up a niche market for quality cask beers which develop a local identity. At present, the even split between lager and ale is beginning to tilt back in favour of cask ale, and some regionals believe that an ageing population will increase sales for their core product.

National sector

Since 1992, some national brewers have responded by re-focusing upon a single primary activity. Courage, for instance, has concentrated upon brewing, while Grand Metropolitan has recognized its brand-retailing strengths. In 1994 only four national companies both brewed beer and owned pubs, as illustrated in Table 13.2. National brewers have recognized that beer-reliant pubs may not survive, and they are refurbishing their managed estate in order to increase branded catering. The total number of national sector tenancies have been reduced by 50 per cent since 1989 because of the need to conform to the Beer Orders, and those remaining tenancies have been replaced with longer commercial leases. Andrew Palmer, Editor of *The Publican*, believes that tenants who lack the skill and funds to develop catering may be placed 'in the most vulnerable sector of the entire trade'.[13]

Table 13.2 Major operators of licensed premises.

	Managed	Tenanted/Leasehold
Allied-Lyons	2400	1800
Bass	2670	1250
Scottish and Newcastle	1750	1000
Whitbread	1600	2300

Source: Author's estimates.

CURRENT OPERATION OF LICENSED PREMISES

It is difficult to describe an 'average' licensed unit. They range from old to new, in a variety of architectural styles and interior decorations. Despite changes in the total number of outlets, their ownership and the development of pub brands, customers are still most likely to use the pub nearest to their home most often.[14] Like many hospitality operations, licensed trade units are focused upon operational matters such as preparing the premises and product for the arrival of the customer. For licensed premises, opening hours are those prescribed by law, and so the operation of supplying food and drink must revolve around those hours. In all licensed operations, whether independently or brewery owned, the manager holds the justice's licence and is responsible for everything which happens on the premises, although a licence may be held jointly by two persons. The nature of the trading hours of public houses often demands that the manager and staff live on the premises. Traditionally, public houses have been run by married couples, with the husband being responsible for liquor ordering and service, while the wife dealt with the cooking and cleaning. In many operations, this is still the case, particularly in small country properties, but in larger operations, the licensee, male or female, takes on a more executive than operational role. In the past, working behind a bar has been regarded as a temporary, low-skill and low-paid job, but recent calls for increased professionalism by organizations such as the British Institute of Innkeepers have encouraged greater staff training with the aim of improving product quality and reducing staff turnover.

Faced with rapid changes which have challenged its traditional stability, coupled with the most prolonged recession in 50 years, its future is unsure. In the face of this hostile environment, public house operators have switched focus from drink to food which has shown real growth of 50 per cent between 1988 and 1992.[15] Free houses (without brewery ties) and managed houses have been particularly proactive in developing catering with tenants and leaseholders concentrating more on 'wet' sales. Around 20 per cent of pubs serve food all day, 50 per cent do so at lunch time and in the evening, and 20 per cent serve at lunchtime only.[16] The type of meals served is related to the style of the operation. It was estimated in 1991 that 8 per cent of sales were cold food only, 63 per cent was both hot and cold food served over a food counter, and 29 per cent of sales were 'restaurant sales'.

This has developed following 'two broad patterns'[17] – snack meals and restaurant meals. Snack meals are consumed while having a drink in the bar area. They range from sandwiches up to hot, plated meals. Typically food is displayed in glass-fronted cabinets and plated by counter staff according to customers' requirements. Customers may serve themselves from this counter, or if an order has to be placed, be given a ticket to be

Figure 13.1   Typical pub foodservice.
Source: Adrian Carpenter.

served when the meal item has been prepared. In this style of operation, the tables are
'pub-style' and not laid up for meals. Often customers collect their own cutlery and
accompaniments from a service point. This may mean that the furniture is not ideal for
eating a meal, as tables are smaller and lower than those found in restaurants. This is
illustrated in Figure 13.1.

Restaurant meals in licensed premises are provided in an area exclusively set aside for
the service of meals. Of the 29 per cent of food sales served in pub restaurants, just under
half is served in restaurants 'within' the pub, and just over half in restaurants attached to
but separate from the pub itself.[18] Tables are laid up in advance, customers order from a
menu and items are prepared and served to order. Therefore the distinction between what
is a pub and a restaurant becomes indistinct. Perhaps the relative floor area of dining area
to bar may be used as a guide so that where the restaurant is less than 50 per cent of the
total floor area the operation may be considered to be a pub; an alternative (or augmen-
tative) guide to this could be if 'wet' sales (i.e. sales from drinks), are greater than sales
from food.

Larger public house operators have recognized the value of branded restaurants which
offer a recognizable concept and standardized product offering.[19] They have developed
from 'steakhouses' into popular restaurants serving a wide range of food. The menu of

❑ **STARTERS**

GARLIC BREAD	£1.25
CHEESY TOPPED	£1.75
PRAWN COCKTAIL with Granary Bread	£2.95
HOMEMADE SOUP with French Bread	£1.95
KING PRAWNS in Filo Pastry with Dip and Salad Garnish	£2.95
HOMEMADE PATÉ and Toast	£2.50
GARLIC MUSHROOMS & French Bread	£2.50

❑ **SANDWICHES** (Lunchtime Only)

Choice of Granary or White Bread

HOMECOOKED HAM	£2.25
ROAST BEEF	£2.50
TASTY CHEDDAR	£1.75
PRAWNS IN SAUCE	£2.95
PRAWNS & CHEESE	£3.50

❑ **PLOUGHMAN'S LUNCHES** (Lunchtime Only)

HOMECOOKED HAM	£4.00
STILTON	£4.00
CUMBERLAND SAUSAGE	£4.00
TASTY CHEDDAR	£3.50

❑ **FILLED JACKET POTATO** (Lunchtime Only)

All served with crispy salad and a choice of two fillings £3.95

HAM, CHEESE, ONION, TOMATO, COLESLAW, PINEAPPLE & BAKED BEANS (PRAWN & CHEESE IS £1.00 EXTRA)

❑ **MEAT DISHES**

PRIME RUMP STEAK	£7.95
MEGA MIXED GRILL	£8.75
PRIME FILLET STEAK	£8.95
GAMMON STEAK & PINEAPPLE	£6.50

Our Chef will be delighted to serve either Chasseur or Diane Sauce to compliment your Grill. All the above served with a choice of potato, fried onions, mushrooms, grilled tomatoes & crispy salad

CUMBERLAND SAUSAGE Served with French Fries and Baked Beans	£3.75
CHICKEN FILLETS Served with French Fries & Salad	£5.95
HOMEMADE STEAK & KIDNEY PIE with a selection of fresh vegetables	£4.95
HOMEMADE MEAT LASAGNE Served with French Fries & Salad	£4.75

❑ **CHILDREN'S MENU**

CHICKEN NUGGETS & CHIPS	£2.50
SAUSAGE, BEANS & CHIPS	£2.50
SCAMPI & CHIPS	£2.50

☞ *DAILY SPECIALS ALWAYS AVAILABLE*

☞ *PLEASE ASK TO SEE OUR DESSERT MENU!*

Figure 13.2 Pub restaurant menu.
Source: The Pilot, Eastbourne.

one of these pub restaurants is illustrated in Figure 13.2. Five of the top-ten branded restaurants in the UK are such pub-based operations. The influence of the major UK brewers in developing the pub catering business is illustrated in Table 13.3. Some of these are the carvery-style operations as discussed in Chapter 11. The larger managed chains control costs by centralized cooking and production. In this regard, technology is being used in food production processes to ensure standard quality as well as to control

Table 13.3 Branded pub restaurants 1992.

Brand	Company	Outlets
Beefeater	Whitbread	250
Brewers Fayre	Whitbread	150
Toby Carving Rooms	Bass	98
Country Carvery	GrandMet	80
Toby Grills	Bass	80
Harvester	Fosters (leased to Forte)	79
Porterhouse Steak	Allied-Lyons	67

Sources: Various.

margins. Electronic point of sale (EPoS) technology, for example, has improved cash handling as well as providing management with accurate and accessible computer data. Such data can assist with unit and group menu planning, stock control and personnel planning. In addition, the larger managed chains are becoming more aware of the value of effective training in ensuring consistent quality and reducing staff turnover.

LICENSED HOUSE MANAGEMENT

As in many hospitality operations, the public house product includes such intangibles as atmosphere and warmth of welcome, and the professional licensee is fully aware of their importance. Traditionally, the acquisition of a licence was regarded as attractive to candidates with a service pension seeking a comfortable semi-retirement in congenial surroundings. Today, individual tenants or leaseholders too have become more business-oriented and professional. This section will consider how licensed premises are managed and what skills are required of its managers. These skills are becoming more important because the licensed trade is currently in a stage of transformation to cope with a hostile environment. So the professional licensee needs social, technical, business and marketing skills.

Social Skills

The public house licensee comes into contact with many different types of people and so an ability to 'handle' people is important. These include customers, staff, suppliers (local, regional and national) and agents of regulatory organizations (police, customs and excise, income tax, weights and measures, public protection, etc). Operationally, the licensee must be a good judge of character as his legal responsibilities include the duty to run an orderly house. This means that the licensee or an employee, should not serve persons who are in a state of intoxication. In practice, this judgement is difficult to make and demands training and experience. Additionally, the vigilant licensee must also be alert for banned substances such as drugs and for under-age persons in the bar areas.

Technical Skills

The service of food and drink in licensed premises demands special skills. Cellar skills, for example, are concerned with good practice in the hygienic dispensing of draught beers, minerals and wines as well as the correct storage of both empty and full bottled and draught containers. Similarly, skills in food preparation and service are those usually associated with restaurants which can help towards offering an attractive product which will encourage customers to return.

Business Skills

Although public houses are interesting, sociable and friendly places in which to work, the licensee must not lose sight of the fact that the business must make a profit in order to survive and grow. Public houses, unlike many other businesses, are prohibited by law to offer credit for the sale of alcohol. This means that pubs are not so much concerned with chasing account customers for payment as with maintaining and improving margins in maximizing profits. Profit margins for 'wet' sales range from 50 per cent to 65 per cent and for food from 55 per cent to 65 per cent.

Marketing Skills

Successful public house operations are those which have identified their target market and satisfy its needs, in the same way as alcoholic drinks manufacturers have done to good effect. This strategy demands flexibility and responsiveness from its management and staff which involves a closeness to customers and suppliers. It is important to monitor customers' expectations and perceptions as well as to keep in contact with materials suppliers so that input prices and quality may be controlled. Larger operations and multiple chains are able to obtain competitive advantage over independent sole traders in their ability to maximize volume quantity discounts, but all operators are currently aware that their retail prices need to be minimized.

CURRENT ISSUES AND TRENDS

Currently, operators of licensed premises are concerned with emerging trends which affect the viability of their businesses. These include:

- *Market trends*. Licensed house retailing has ceased to be recession-proof and has become a part of the wider leisure industry characterized by greater competition for disposable income. Turnover and profits are being adversely affected.
- *Costs*. Economies of scale provide larger organizations with the benefits of buying at advantageous quantity discount terms, but these are not available to smaller traders. The greatest cost for tenants or leaseholders is the rent paid to their landlord which is representing a greater proportion of their turnover. In the 1990s, this turnover has been, at best, static, but while many commercial rents have declined since the late 1980s, public house rents have increased. Fleurets, a licensed property company, suggest that rents in London have increased by 50 per cent since 1988.
- *Consumer trends*. Profitability is also being reduced by falling beer volumes and the increasing price sensitivity of consumers seeking value for money. Pubs in rural locations have been particularly affected by drink–driving legislation and have sought to attract customers by offering reasonably priced food. The

expectations of customers continue to rise. Pubs are providing better facilities such as family rooms, better decor and no smoking areas, but such improvements are often beyond the reach of sole-trader tenants or leaseholders whose profits are being eroded. Greater dietary concern is encouraging public houses to provide healthy alternatives on their menus, but many customers still expect pub food to be served in hearty portions of traditional British dishes.

- *Investment*. The capability to reinvest is linked to profits, especially for sole traders. Licensed retailing is currently regarded as a poor risk by banks and building societies because of the number of recent business failures in this sector. Many publicans have sought to maximize the peripheral income which may be derived from such sources as gaming machines, jukeboxes and pool tables. However, amongst the large chains there is considerable investment. For example, in 1995 Bass Taverns were expecting to invest £120 million in new pubs and pub conversions aimed at the family market, whilst Toby Restaurants had a £9 million investment programme.[20]

- *Operations*. Unit managers are concerned with ensuring the smooth operation of their house, but, wherever people are involved, unexpected events can occur. Although convivial places, public houses may attract the worst kind of staff and customers, and the licensee must be constantly alert for the breaches of law which are his responsibility. Individual leaseholders are now fully responsible for the whole of their leased pubs and, although this offers greater security of tenure, there is a stronger need for preventive maintenance of premises. Some operators have addressed this problem by greater control of energy costs; for example, with low-energy lighting or by recycling the heat produced in cellar coolers to produce hot water.

FUTURE OF THE LICENSED TRADE

In 1866, Capper wrote:

> There has of late years been a very large falling off in the consumption of the liquors in which he deals, due almost entirely to Parliamentary interference with the trade and to the demands of the National Exchequer. Duties and taxation have been maintained at so high a level during recent years that it has become increasingly difficult for the licensee, faced with rising costs and falling sales, to make a reasonable living. In these adverse circumstances the licensed victualler may well ask himself how he is to keep his head above water.[21]

Although this was written over a century ago, it could be applied to the present day. Similarly Capper's suggestions to overcome these concerns are equally relevant:

- professionalism: 'apply to the business of keeping a public house the principles that have been tested and proved sound in every other line of business'.
- scope: 'not to be content merely to sell the beers, wines and spirits which his licence permits, but to seek out profitable side-lines not dependent on the sale of alcoholic liquor – meals for example'.

It is clear that the licensed trade sector is experiencing major changes which provide opportunities to review traditional practices in the light of emerging trends. Economic recession has accelerated the rate of change and demanded greater professionalism and business orientation in an increasingly hostile market. Those licensed units which survive will be those which recognize that good-value food provides sales potential if supported by service training and target marketing. These changes may serve to alter the business direction of the British public house. The traditional image of the beerhouse will be replaced by multi-function licensed outlets which resemble a mixture between a continental-style brasserie, wine bar or restaurant and which more successfully meet the needs of their customers.

REFERENCES

1. Thompson, D. (ed.) (1993) *The Oxford Dictionary of Current English* (2nd edition), Oxford: Oxford University Press.
2. Sproat, I. (1994) 'Tourism – a ministerial view', in *The Innkeepers Yearbook*, British Institute of Innkeepers, p. 28.
3. Brewers Society (1992) *Pubs: The 'Best of British'*, London: Brewers Society.
4. Brewers Society (1992) *Beer Facts*, London: Brewers Society .
5. Medlik, R. (1978) *Profile of the Hotel and Catering Industry* (2nd edition), London: Heinemann.
6. Key Note Report (1992) *Public Houses* (9th edition), London: Key Note, p. 5.
7. Ibid.
8. Mintel (1992) *Britain Eating Out*, Drink Intelligence Report, London: Mintel, p. 59.
9. BMRB International (1992) *Target Group Index*, London: BMRB.
10. PAS (1992) *Drinks Market Survey*, London: Public Attitude Surveys Ltd.
11. Brewers Society (1992) *The Public's Attitudes Towards Pubs*, MORI, London: The Brewers Society, November.
12. Mintel op. cit.
13. Palmer, A. (1994) 'Industry report '94', *The Publican*, No. 470, January 10, p. 3.
14. Lang, S. (1994) 'The pub and social trends' at *The Pub in 2000* Conference, 5 November.
15. DTI (1992) *Catering and Allied Trades*, Business Monitor Series no. SDA28, London: HMSO.
16. Mintel op. cit., p. 59.
17. Jones, P. (1988) 'Licensed trade catering', in *Foodservice Operations* (2nd edition), Cassell: London.
18. Mintel op. cit., p. 62.
19. Thompson, R. (1994) 'Fast food's chain reaction', *Independent on Sunday*, 1 May, p. 3.
20. Dixon, S. (1994) 'Bar billions', *Hospitality*, December, pp. 23–5.
21. Capper, W. Bently (ed.) (1866) *Licensed Houses and their Management*, London: Caxton Publishing.

FOURTEEN

Fast Food

STEPHEN BALL

INTRODUCTION

Fast food has been one of the big success stories in the UK hospitality industry during the past twenty to thirty years. The incoming North American chains, their professional management and modern techniques and approaches, the franchise, the right locations and a number of converging social and market trends have made it so. Today the fast-food industry generates large revenues for its providers and is a valuable contributor to government income, economic growth, the balance of payments and employment. But the success of fast food is not restricted to the UK; it is a worldwide phenomenon with more people than ever consuming fast food both in their home countries and abroad. This seems set to continue with fast food's share of the world consumer catering market forecast to increase from about 19 per cent in 1991 to 25 per cent in 2000.[1]

With this rapid and dynamic growth fast food has made an increasingly significant impact upon our diets, our personal spending, our social life and the environment. The fast-food industry has also made a marked impression in the hospitality industry and other industries, being the impetus behind numerous modern technological, marketing and managerial developments. The multi-unit chains have spearheaded many of these developments.

WHAT IS FAST FOOD?

Fast food has been defined in a variety of ways with no single definition or interpretation gaining a consensus. Definitions of fast food tend to be product-based, process-based or place-of-provision-based. Each definition has its own distinct features,[2] application and values. Ball[3] reproduces a selection of fast-food definitions and suggests why it has proved difficult to construct a suitable widely used definition.

The definition of fast food used here is product-based and focuses on the physical composition of the product. It contains four features which must coexist for fast food to be clearly differentiated from other products. These features are:

- A finished product shelf life of usually minutes (e.g. hot fast food, ice cream) and on occasions hours (e.g. sandwiches). Rapid deterioration occurs beyond these times particularly without holding equipment. This perishability factor is consistent with that of service products generally.

- Fast product finishing (and in some cases total production) and service times. The range of fast foods, demand levels, production methods and system efficiencies mean that actual times will differ from between 2 to about 15 minutes for products provided to consumers on site to about 30 minutes for those delivered to consumers off-site.
- A hand- or fingers-held product often accompanied with disposable packaging and sometimes disposable cutlery.
- A low selling price relative to other restaurant products.

Because of its nature fast food can be consumed on the premises or off the premises as a take-away or a delivered product.

OPERATIONS IN THE FAST-FOOD SECTOR

Fast food is supplied to consumers through a diversity of sources and in both the private and public sectors (e.g. hospitals and schools). Some private sector outlets such as McDonald's restaurants, KFC outlets or fish and chip shops specialize in the sale of fast food, selling no or very few other products. In others fast-food sales comprise only a part of the outlet's overall sales. In such cases fast-food sales can be relatively significant (e.g. a Pizza Hut restaurant, or an ethnic cuisine restaurant such as an Indian or Chinese restaurant, with a take-away or home delivery service) or minor (e.g. a public house, a garage forecourt shop or a supermarket with a take-away facility).

Traditional Operations

Around the world the fast-food industry is operating at different stages of development.[4] In Britain fast food, in its traditional form, is a well-established part of the hospitality industry. Fish-and-chip shops, which sell what is considered by many to be the original fast food, have their origins dating back over a century. Some people claim that the first fish-and-chip shop was John Lee's in Mossley, Lancashire set up about 1863. Others consider it was Marlin's in the East End of London which also opened in the 1860s.[5] Ethnic cuisine take-aways also have a long history dating back to earlier in the twentieth century. The first Indian restaurant, for example, is believed to have been the Salut-e-Hand in Holborn which opened in 1911, but it was not until the 1950s that both Indian and Chinese take-aways moved into the mainstream. There are now estimated to be more than 7500 Indian and 6000 Chinese restaurants spread across the UK. Traditional operations also embrace other ethnic outlets and sandwich bars. A number of characteristics are common to the majority of these traditional operations. These include them being small single-unit, family-run and low-capital investment operations. They also tend to rely on rather traditional and fairly labour-intensive on-site food preparation and presentation methods and make little use of sophisticated technology and marketing techniques. Together these traditional operations comprise a large, fragmented and heterogeneous sector.

Modern Operations

Since the late 1970s the advance of fast-food chain operations, such as BurgerKing, McDonald's, KFC and Pizza Hut, has been relentless and widespread throughout Britain and is continuing unabated. The chains have expanded rapidly through franchising, and consequently have polarized the market between themselves and the traditional independent operations. A number of methods of involvement are used by the chains in the fast-food industry including company-owned and managed outlets, franchised operations and joint ventures. These are more fully explained in Ball.[6] The chains are strongly branded, largely US-influenced and modern operations with sophisticated technologies. Operations are designed around systems of catering that have been likened to manufacturing production lines, with the design and layout of outlets, the scheduling and procedures of work being carefully and systematically planned to produce consistent and standardized products. Modern operations increasingly offer a combination of eat-on-the-premises, take-away, drive-through or customer-delivery service types.

Convenience Stores

A new form of fast food to be developed in the UK is the convenience store. In 1987 there were about 2200 stores catering in Britain, with an estimated sales turnover of £882 million. Only a proportion of this turnover, about 10 per cent, is derived from catering sales, since a convenience store is essentially a typical, old-fashioned, neighbourhood corner shop that also sells food and drinks for consumption as take-aways. But for the retailer, catering sales have the advantage of about a 45 per cent gross profit margin, compared with 15–20 per cent on the other products they sell. About 10 per cent of the store floor-area of around 2500 square feet (232 square metres) is devoted to catering food-sales, usually located near the entrance. It is presented in a manner very similar to fast-food stores, through the use of illuminated, coloured menu boards and refrigerated display counters. But there are no staff providing service to the customer. The customers self-select food and drink items off the shelf or from dispensers, heat their food in the available microwave ovens if required, and take their items to a retail-type check-out. It is expected that the average customer spend will be around 95 pence. The range of food and drink items and type of menu on offer varies according to the location of the store. Full-concept units are usually found near office blocks or on major roads. Such units would have the full range of self-service drink dispensers, providing coffee, tea, hot chocolate and fruit juices, along with a range of self-service hot snacks, such as pot noodles, samosas, Cornish pasties and jacket potatoes. The American influence is also present in some chains that offer tortilla-style items, such as 7-Eleven's 'chimichanga'. Smaller units would provide fewer hot-food items, concentrating on sandwiches sold over a sandwich/deli counter. One chain is also experimenting with a new concept fast food: high-quality pastry pouches with spicy or sweet fillings, served hot – developed by a major food chain. Another distinctive feature of a convenience store is that it is open from early morning to late at night, seven days a week. The catering potential in this sector is great, since there are many chains operating on this principle, such as Spar, VG and the Co-op, that have as yet not introduced catering food sales into their units. The three major UK chains are Sperrings, 7-Eleven (part of the Guinness organization) and Circle K. Sperrings is the largest with 81 stores in 1987, of which 16 are franchised. It has also been investigating this idea with Total Oil in terms of locating the convenience-store concept on the forecourts of petrol-filling stations – 40 such stores are planned. Such forecourt retailing is becoming more sophisticated, although hot take-away food sales are yet to become widespread. Texaco and Murco have 140 outlets between them that have the potential for this development.

Table 14.1 Pattern of change in the take-away/fast-food industry.

	1980	1987	1988	1989	1990	1991
Number of fish-and-chip shop businesses etc.	22,715	28,686	29,124	29,928	30,921	29,319
Number of fish-and-chip shops, etc. as a percentage of all catering businesses	20.7	23.7	23.8	24.1	24.8	24.4
Turnover, including VAT (£m), of fish-and-chip shop businesses etc.	1,103	2,826	3,377	3,682	4,162	4,264
Turnover incl. VAT of fish-and-chip shops etc. as percentage of turnover (incl. VAT) of all catering businesses	8.9	12.2	13.3	13.3	13.8	13.7

Source: Central Statistical Office (1994) Catering and Allied Trades in Great Britain. *Annual Abstract of Statistics*, Government Statistical Service, London: HMSO.
Notes·
1. The full description of the types of fish-and-chip businesses included in this analysis is fish-and-chip shops, sandwich and snack bars, and other establishments selling food partly or wholly for consumption off the premises.
2. Only businesses registered for VAT are recorded.

SIZE AND NATURE OF THE FAST-FOOD SECTOR

In contrast to other industrial sectors in the UK, no government definition or classification of fast food, fast-food operations or the fast-food industry exists. This means that there are no government statistics for the fast-food industry in its entirety. However, there are government statistics which relate to parts of the sector. For example, Table 14.1 refers to take-aways and fish-and-chip shops. Furthermore the lack of any other universally recognized, accepted and used definition has resulted in different organizations and bodies producing varying figures of the size and value of the UK fast-food market. This means reference to the size data of any one source needs an understanding of the definitions used, the assumptions made and the data collection instruments employed. Any comparisons of size data from different sources must be treated with caution.

Any attempt to calculate the size of the fast-food industry in the UK is problematic for a number of reasons. The industry is fragmented and covers a large number of small geographically dispersed outlets and businesses. The industry comprises a variety of forms of business enterprise including companies and sole traders. In many instances fast-food business, as referred to above, is combined with other catering and business activity. These factors make the collection of size data difficult; a task which is further complicated by business failure and changes in ownership.

The size of the industry can be measured in a variety of ways, but probably the most useful indicators, and those which are used here, are the number of businesses and outlets, turnover, number of meals served and the number of employees.

Number of Businesses and Outlets

Table 14.1 provides some indication of the size and importance of the fast-food industry between 1980 and 1991. This data is extracted and developed from government statistics and relates to Division 6 Activity 6612 of the Standard Industrial Classification (SIC)

Table 14.2   Analysis of take-away/fast-food businesses by turnover, 1992.

Turnover (£000)	Number	Percentage of the total
1–25	1,119	3.8
26–49	7,773	26.3
50–99	12,175	41.2
100–249	6,865	23.2
250–499	1,164	3.9
500–999	311	1.1
1000–4999	148	0.5
5000 +	14	0.0
Total	29,569	100

Source: Business Monitor PA1003, 1992/Key Note.
Notes:
1. The full description of the types of businesses is as in Table 14.1.
2. The businesses are those registered for VAT.

which includes take-aways and fish-and-chip shops. These figures, whilst illustrative, understate the size of the industry as not all fast food is take-away. Some elements of fast food are contained in other SIC Activity categories. Statistics related to these fast-food elements are impossible to isolate from these categories. Table 14.1 shows how the number of take-away businesses, and their proportion in relation to all catering businesses, steadily rose between 1980 and 1990 but then dipped slightly as the recession took hold in 1991. In 1991 fish-and-chip shop businesses, etc. represented over 24 per cent of total catering businesses.

Most take-away business is in traditional operations. This is reflected in Table 14.2 which shows that over 71 per cent of all take-away businesses had turnovers of less than £100,000 in 1992. Marketpower[7] estimated there to be 228,970 commercial catering outlets in Great Britain and of these 18,227 were fast-food/take-away outlets.

It is estimated that over 3000 outlets are chain operated. Table 14.3 details some of the leading chain operators in 1992. Evidence of the rapidly changing situation can be seen regarding McDonald's who opened their 500th outlet in the UK during 1993. During the 1980s ownership became increasingly concentrated in the hands of the large companies who have both increased the outlets in their chains and increased their proportion of the total fast-food outlets. Conversely the independents have witnessed a decline in their share of total outlets. This trend is expected to continue.

Volume of Output, Meals Served and Numbers of Employees

Of the total turnover from all catering businesses in 1991 nearly 14 per cent represented the turnover from fish-and-chip shops, etc. (Table 14.1). The 1991 sales figure of £4264 million was almost four times as great as the 1980 figure of £1103 million. In 1993 Mintel estimated that fast-food sales in Britain were worth £5.2 billion. With the recent recession, growth has been more sluggish and the market remains fiercely competitive. Today hard-hitting promotions and heavy price discounting are hallmarks of the industry. In 1990 Marketpower estimated that the fast-food chains and take-aways accounted for 1397 million meals served, which as a proportion of all the meals served from commercial catering outlets represented about 25 per cent. Specific information about the size of

Table 14.3 Major operators of fast-food chains (number of outlets) 1992.

Operator/trading name	Ownership/franchiser	Number of outlets
McDonald's	McDonald's Corp (USA)	473
KFC	Forte/Pepsico	301
Pizza Hut	Whitbread/Pepsico	293
Wimpy	Wimpy International	230
Perfect Pizza	Scott's Hospitality	241
BurgerKing	Grand Metropolitan Retailing	202
Southern Fried Chicken	Fast Food Systems	150
Quicksnack	Travellers Fare	144
Pizzaland	Bright Reasons	106
Deep Pan Pizza	City Centre Restaurants	86
Domino's Pizza	Domino's Pizza	80
Baskin-Robbins	Allied-Lyons	70
Spud-U-Like	Jacobs Family	45

Source: Key Note Publications Ltd, 1993 and company information.

the fast-food industry according to the numbers of people employed is unavailable. However, recent Department of Employment statistics[8] suggest that fast-food businesses are significant employers. In September 1989, 295,400 were employed (excluding self-employed) in restaurants, cafés and snack bars combined with fish-and-chip shops, etc. Today it is estimated that between 150,000 and 180,000 work specifically in the fast-food industry.

MARKETS SERVED

In spite of the limitations of the many existing definitions of fast food, and the consequent shortcomings of any related size calculations, evidence clearly exists to show that the UK fast-food market is large, significant and growing. The current popularity of fast food is due to a combination of social and other factors. These include:

- Greater average real personal disposable incomes although the recent recession temporarily affected incomes.
- Trading down from relatively more expensive and more formal catering outlets during the recent recession.
- Less formal eating patterns and more casual eating – 'eating on the run' or 'grazing', as it is sometimes called, has increased.
- An increasing number of women going to work – women have less time at home to prepare meals and are more likely to be able to afford fast food.
- An increase in one-person households.
- Better access to private transport.
- Efforts of the industry to create demand by advertising heavily and offering a quick and efficient service at low prices.
- Increased international travel has increased desire for foreign fast foods at home.
- Increased urbanization of population.

Analysis of the fast-food market shows that in 1991 sandwiches had the largest share (see Table 14.4). Sales of hamburger meals were the next largest being responsible for

Table 14.4 Fast-food market by product sector (total spent in 1991 in £m).

	Take-away	Eat in	Total
Sandwiches	1019	108	1127
Burger Meals	291	479	770
Ethnic	424	310	734
Fish & Chips	562	92	654
Pizza Meals	276	330	606
Chicken Meals	261	105	366
Others			300

Source: Mintel International (1992).
Note: Total spent on 'others' is a personal estimate.

about 17 per cent of total fast-food sales. While there is growth in demand in the fast-food industry generally different parts of the industry have experienced different rates of growth. Market research has shown pizzas and ethnic meals in particular to have had the most rapid growth. The growth of the pizza segment has been helped by its healthy image and its ability to stand up to home delivery.

Growth in demand and consumption of fast foods is not uniform across all types of buyers. Total demand and consumption of fast food can be disaggregated into market segments with distinct buyer characteristics. Buyers vary by income, age, gender, socio-economic group, lifestyle, geographical location and other characteristics. Detailed consideration of these applied to fast-food customers is undertaken by West.[9] A profile of visitors to fast-food outlets[10] shows the highest proportion of visitors to be in the 15–24 year old age group. The proportions of visitors to fast-food restaurants steadily decline as age increases. In socioeconomic terms, a greater proportion of C1 respondents visit fast-food restaurants. The lowest proportion, by a striking margin, of visitors to fast-food restaurants is in the E group. By region, London and the South-East had the highest proportion of visitors to fast-food restaurants which was in contrast to the South-West and Yorkshire and Humberside. The regional variations in the proportions of visitors to fast-food restaurants may be due to the geographical distribution and density of fast-food restaurants rather than to any innate regional antipathy to fast-food restaurants.

LOCATION

One of the most important factors in establishing a successful fast-food operation is finding a suitable location. This is because fast food for most consumers is a low-involvement, convenience, often impulse, product for which they are not usually prepared to travel very far. This is unless perhaps the purchase of fast food is linked to other purchases (e.g., cinema tickets or other leisure products). Because traditionally fast-food chain operators have relied on relatively high volume sales of low-unit-cost food and drink items, to ensure financial success locations have been chosen where there are relatively large potential customer flows or concentrations of potential customers in close proximity. This helps to explain why fast-food chain outlets were originally located in prime high street locations but are now to be found in a wide variety of locations with similar customer flows or concentrations. As these locations become exhausted and their associated markets saturated newer locations will be sought.

The purchase, rental and rate costs relating to sites in areas of high customer flow are extremely high and competition for such sites is extremely keen from fast food competitors and other retailers. Hence it tends to be the large chains who can secure such sites whilst smaller, more traditional operations (e.g., fish and chip shops, ethnic cuisine takeaways and sandwich bars) tend more often to be on secondary sites. These areas do, however, still receive reasonable traffic flows.

Newer fast-food locations include shopping centres, either as stand-alone outlets or as part of a food court, in most airports; in railway stations and motorway service areas (e.g., KFC outlets can be found at certain of Forte Welcome Break service areas); increasingly in educational establishments including universities and large schools; in health care sites (e.g., McDonald's has an outlet at Guys Hospital in London); in sporting and leisure complexes (e.g., BurgerKing has outlets at caravan sites, Pizza Hut Express has a 3000 sq. ft pizza slice operations in Thorpe Park, while a mobile McDonald's fast-food restaurant is frequently seen at major sporting and other venues); in defence bases, office and industrial complexes. A recent development has been the tie-up of contract caterers with branded fast food. Compass, for instance, has acquired exclusive franchise rights to develop BurgerKing outlets at all its contracts in the health care, education, leisure, travel, business and industry markets. They have also recently acquired the Le Croissant Shop chain and have rights to run kiosk-style Pizza Hut operations, Upper Crust and Dixie's Donuts brands. Demand is therefore the most important influence on the location of fast-food outlets.

The decision about where to locate a fast-food outlet is basically comprized of two separate yet interrelated elements. The first of these is selection of a general trading area. Some of the factors determining the potential of a trading area include:

- Population and population density.
- Volume of traffic flows.
- Income distribution.
- Extent of house building.
- Nature and extent of competition.
- Job security of population.
- Health of local businesses.
- Presence of advertising media.
- Employee availability.
- Nearness of supply source.

Secondly, there is the selection of a specific site within the trading area. The key influencing factors on the potential of a site in terms of turnover, cash flow and profit can be categorized as:

- Convenience and approachability factors.
- Legal enactments.
- Physical conditions.
- Occupancy costs.

To find suitable trading areas and sites, to acquire sites and then to administer them, most of the major operators have their own properties division. Property developers, estate agents and others may also approach the operators with sites which they think may

Table 14.5   The main features of the fast-food chain restaurant offer.

Features	Description
Tangible Elements	
Food and drink	Traditionally limited menu. Consistent controllable quality, precisely specified, equally portioned. Relatively low prices.
Secondary items	Newspapers, children's partyware
Physical environment	Clean, bright, modern, carefully laid out. Air conditioning, washrooms, functional furniture, staff uniforms, parking.
Packaging	Food and drink is distinctively packaged (disposable), easy to handle and for some items temperature retaining.
Intangible elements	
Personal contact with staff	Encounters with customers are technology-led and usually very brief. An exception occurs with children's parties.
Service delivery	Often a combination of eat-on-the-premises, take-away, drive-through, or customer delivery.
Promotion	Emphasis is given to value for money, consistent quality and cleanliness. Food/drink items may be distinguished by originality, size, cost competitiveness, fillings, health factors, etc. Promotions are usually bold and colourful to gain attention. Emphasis on children's offers.
Outlet atmosphere	Often find bold colours, plants, music and noise. Other customers can be significant in eat-in contexts. Corporate identity prominent.
Location	Convenient for the customer whether on foot or in the car and to the customer for delivery; accessible.
Emotions felt by customer	Aim to satisfy with the offer.
Post-transaction service	Little emphasis as yet here. BurgerKing launched the 'BK Care Line' – a free phone customer information, complaint and enquiry service in 1991.

be suitable. The major operators use a variety of approaches and computerized databases to evaluate specific sites and identify potential target areas.

PRODUCT OFFERING

Fast-food outlets sell a total consumption package, or what is sometimes called the service package. This defines the offer and consists of a mixture of elements. The food – the burger and fries or the fish and chips – is only one part of this package. Armistead[11] considers that for a take-away food outlet the service package consists of physical items or 'tangibles' and service elements or 'intangibles' and that these two elements are about equal in proportions. Table 14.5 details the main features of the total fast-food offering related to a modern operation. It should be noted that these features will vary in their importance to different customer types and will vary between fast-food concepts. The image that a particular fast-food offering has will also vary according to the customer type.

Operators need to pay attention to both sets of elements if they are to succeed – a fast-food operation which sells food which is satisfactory to customers but which has a slow service in unacceptable conditions will fare no better than one that serves unsatisfactory food, quickly in pleasant surroundings. However some elements can be regarded as core (e.g., food), while others might be viewed as peripheral (e.g., newspapers and after-transaction services). Once a core element has done its job – met the primary needs – the peripherals of the service package feature next in the customer's decision-making. Often the core elements offered by fast-food operations are indistinguishable from one another in the eyes of the customer and it is only the peripherals which distinguish the offers of different operations.

The menus of fast-food restaurant/outlets have commonly been regarded as simple, restricted and built around core items such as hamburgers, fried chicken, fried fish, pizza, croissants, etc. This was indeed the case for most modern operations when they were launched in the UK in the 1970s and 1980s and in the introductory stage of the product life cycle. Product quality control, standardization, franchising and the internationalization of fast food were all aided by this strategy. Several menu trends can be observed, however, as the fast-food market has matured in the UK, as markets have become susceptible to customer fatigue and as operators have sought sales growth. These include additions to the product mix. KFC now also sells chicken burgers as well as fried chicken pieces. McDonald's has added sandwiches, salads, baked potatoes, chicken items, pizza and Mexican food in some if not all of its outlets. Menu extensions like these have blurred the product sector boundaries and are typical of the industry in its mature stage.[12] Other menu trends in the maturing fast-food market have been the introduction of healthy foods, more desserts, breakfast and children's menus.

ORGANIZATION AND STAFFING

Traditional hot fast-food operations utilize simple low technologies where the equipment is manually controlled and designed more for domestic than industrial use. They have relied heavily upon the social and technical skills: hard work, commitment and the attitude of their personnel[13] who in many cases have no qualifications and are self-taught. Outlets are normally small in area and cater for small volumes. Consequently, staffing complements are low and are often restricted to members of the proprietor's family and if needed to two or three hired staff. Where hired staff are used they are normally service staff; family members are usually responsible for production. Complements of more than ten workers would be a rarity. Production and service are both labour intensive and it is usual to find separate workers responsible for each with little overlap of workers into one another's areas.

Modern fast-food units are staffed and organized differently. Those which need high customer volumes and throughput to achieve acceptable returns (e.g., high street operations) are labour hungry and need staffing complements to cover long opening hours and probably seven-days-a-week operation. The standardized methods of operating enable unskilled staff to be employed and the use of part-time staff permits greater flexibility. The organization of a fast-food chain must combine strong control with flexibility. Figure 14.1 shows a typical staffing structure for a fast-food chain with likely lines of reporting up to an operations director. The number of regional managers and area operations executives will vary between chains according to such factors as the number of restaurants in the chain and their geographical distribution. Operative staff work closely as a team, with each member of staff having a specific task or set of tasks to undertake. Each team is organized and controlled like a finely tuned and well-disciplined ship's crew and hence in many fast-food outlets members of staff are referred to as crew members.

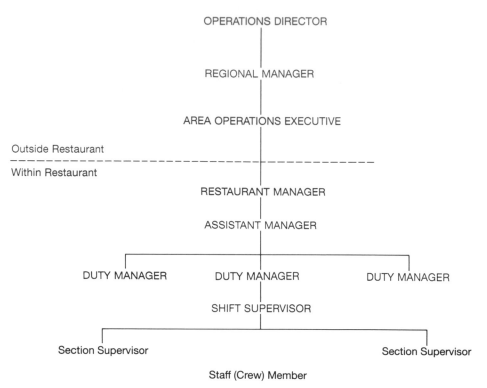

Figure 14.1 Organization chart for a fast-food chain.

OPERATING PROCEDURES

A fast-food outlet is a combination of a production and a retail service outlet. Modern outlets utilize manufacturing-style production methods and techniques similar to those commonly found in factories whilst simultaneously promoting themselves as food and drink retailers competing with other such retailers. They can thus be considered as both a small factory and a retail shop. Such operations, particularly those operated by the chains, have embraced the industrialization of service called for by Levitt[14] in that they use mass-production techniques, production-line principles and systematic approaches in design, planning, organizing and control throughout. These approaches enable customers to be served quickly and facilitate the efficient production of a standardized product of a reliable quality. Operations are driven especially by organized preplanned systems, or soft technology, rather than being reliant upon the discretion, attitude or skill of their workers. Operatives use advanced equipment and carry out simple tasks requiring little skill. Levitt argues that these technological elements have been key ingredients in the success of McDonald's. Table 14.6 draws on Levitt's work to show the main features and potential benefits of the production line approach in the context of fast-food operations.

Many modern fast-food outlets are built upon the operational target of closely controlling labour utilization and upon the scientific management principles of work organization, worker selection and training, performance monitoring and the use of scientific methods. These scientific methods can be seen in the way work activities are precisely

Table 14.6 Features and benefits of production lining fast-food operations.

Features	Potential benefits
Limited discretion of personnel	Standardization, order and quality
Substitution of personnel by equipment	Lower labour costs
Division of labour	Specialization of labour skills
	Better control of labour costs
	Simplified training
Standardization of service	Fast service at lower cost

defined and in the way the total job is broken down into a sequence of tasks which in turn are broken down into the smallest and simplest of steps. Each of these steps requires the minimum of skill. Figure 14.2 details the steps involved in the task of producing a hamburger in a typical fast-food outlet.

In many of the chains operators' standards and working activities are clearly defined in an operating procedures manual. These are comprehensive documents often comprising hundreds of pages and cover the whole operation. These manuals, as Ball[15] explains, are essentially guidelines for worker behaviour. Staff training is based upon them, work activity is conducted in accordance with them and performance is monitored and controlled according to them. The typical contents of a fast-food operations manual were discussed in Chapter 9 (see Table 9.2).

Fast-food operations use a variety of methods to produce food. These are shown in Table 14.7. The choice of method is influenced by the ability of the food production area to satisfy the volume of demand and by the shelf life of prepared food. Like food production the service process is systematized in modern fast-food operations. From the initial customer contact with an operation, whether by telephone, fax, computerized message or in person, the service sequence is queue, order, pay, assemble order, service and consume. An exception to this arises with fast-food 'home' delivery service to the customer where payment occurs after service. The control of food production to reduce spoilage is critical to fast-food operations. Limiting order takers, using a 'bin' person as in McDonald's, and using communication/information systems between the production area back-of-house and the service area front-of-house as in KFC and Arby's, are all ways used by fast-food operators to achieve this.

Staff training is vital for the production of a consistent product which satisfies customer expectations. The major chains place great emphasis on this whether it be intended for franchisees, managers or operatives. Operatives receive careful training. Just as operative tasks are broken down into small steps so training programmes for operatives are built from small modules of instruction. Once the instruction has been delivered the staff are required to complete a questionnaire to illustrate their grasp of the training. Cost and revenue control are rigorous in modern fast-food operations and, while often time-consuming and costly, are necessary to ensure that the very tight margins within which they operate are not jeopardized. Electronic point-of-sale (EPoS) and other microcomputer-driven management information systems are the norm and provide stock control, sales mix analysis, staff productivity data, staff scheduling information, etc.

The success of modern fast-food operations greatly depends on their ability to meet the documented standards of operating procedures. In franchised fast-food operations the franchisee is bound by the franchise agreement to operate the business according to the

Time in seconds	Task carried out by crew member			
	1	2	3	4
0	Call out order for six more	Place top half of bun in toaster		
5			Place frozen 1.6oz burger on grill	
20			Sear burger	
50		Remove top half from toaster Begin toasting base of bun		Begin dressing top half of bun
60			Turn burger	
80				Dressed bun to grill
90		Base of bun to grill		
100			Meat pulled and burger assembled	
110	Wrap-completed burger			

Figure 14.2   Production of a hamburger using a grill.
Source: Jones, P. (1988) *Foodservice Operations* (2nd edition), London: Cassell, p. 71.

documented procedures and is trained accordingly. Commonly, franchised agreements give franchisers the right to audit the franchisees performance based upon the laid-down operating procedures. The concept of inventory control is frequently used for auditing in both franchised and non-franchised fast-food chains. This is illustrated in Figure 14.3. McDonald's, like many other chains, has area advisers and performance audit teams who regularly visit outlets to check operating performance against standards. In McDonald's case they are especially concerned with performance related to QSV and C: Qual-

Table 14.7 Classification of fast-food production types.

Type of food production method	Description of method	Extent of tie with demand	Application
Batch	Short-duration activity	Unlikely to be tied to customer demand	Low volume outlets or periods
Ongoing	Continuous	Not directly tied to demand but some forecasting	Very high volume situations (i.e., busy outlet or peak meal periods)
To order	Short-duration activity	Directly tied	Low volume outlets or periods. For customized menu items

Source: Ball, S.D. (1992) 'Fast-food Technology and Systems of Operation', in S.D. Ball (ed.) *Fast Food Operations and Their Management*, Cheltenham: Stanley Thornes.

ity, Service, Value and Cleanliness. If a fast-food franchise is found consistently to be failing to meet standards the result can be that a manager is fined or the franchise removed.

CURRENT ISSUES

A number of contemporary issues, including those related to health, the environment and ecological matters, are in the ascendancy, and fast-food operators will have to confront them in the future. Those who ignore them will do so at their peril – if not from a social perspective then certainly from a commercial one.

Fast food has received nutritional criticism from many quarters in recent years. This will undoubtedly continue. Some of this has been unjustified, unwarranted and sensational; some has been deserved. Lawson[16] discusses why some of this criticism may be unjustified but also in common with Lobstein[17] and Silverstone[18] provides evidence to support the perception that fast food contributes to an unhealthy diet. High saturated fat, salt and sugar levels and low fibre content seem to have come under particular scrutiny. Some operators have responded to the nutritional issues positively and have made serious attempts to shed the unhealthy image of fast food. Nutritional information sheets are provided by the major chains while efforts directed at food include the development of new 'healthy' products – e.g., low-fat burgers by McDonald's and the experimentation of KFC with a Light 'n' Crispy product with 20 per cent lower fat content than the original, and the addition of more healthy items to menus. McDonald's in the US offers 99 per cent fat-free shakes, no-cholesterol muffins, frozen yoghurt and wholegrain cereals, Premier ice cream, gourmet versions of existing hot fast foods and more sophisticated ethnic cuisine dishes; these are just some of the other developments envisaged. The nutritional profile of fast food will also be enhanced by the continued shift towards the use of unsaturated fats, the development and use of new cooking methods, the continued search for healthy raw materials and the increased promotion and distribution of fast-food nutritional information. Perhaps these kinds of initiatives will result in criticisms being replaced by acclaim!

STORE DAILY RETURN

Store name –
Number –

Form No.					Transaction count –
Day		Date			Average check –
		D D M M Y Y			
S M T W T F S					

	Per system financial report (20)								£ £ £ £ £ £ p p
	Register 1		Register 2		Register 3		Register 4		
	A	B	A	B	A	B	A	B	
= TODAY'S SALES									
Less voids									
Less staff meal vouchers									
Less luncheon vouchers									
Less promotional coupons									
Plus other income									
Cash responsibility									
+/– Overs/ (shorts)									
Cash for banking									
Bankings confirmed									
Pick-up 1 – Banked									
Pick-up 2 – Banked									
Pick-up 3 – Banked									
Total banking									

CASH SPOT CHECKS					
Employee	Time	Reg/draw	Cash	Till reading	Over (short)

HOURLY READINGS			Employees		
Time	Hrly sales	Cum. sales	Crew	Mgrs	Sales per man/hr
8 a.m.					
9 a.m.					
10 a.m.					
11 a.m.					
12 noon					
1 p.m.					
2 p.m.					
3 p.m.					
4 p.m.					
5 p.m.					
6 p.m.					
7 p.m.					
8 p.m.					
9 p.m.					
10 p.m.					
11 p.m.					
12 p.m.					
1 a.m.					

Today's sales –	
Less voids –	
Less VAT –	
Less staff food –	
= Net sales –	

RETURNED DOCUMENTS– CHECKLIST	TICK HERE
DAILY	
Cashier fin. report	
System fin. report (20)	
Audit roll	
Bank slips	
Luncheon vouchers	
Staff meal vouchers	
Prom.coupons	
Other (specify)	
WEEKLY (with Sunday's report)	
Stock evaluation return	
Week's delivery notes	
Inter-store good transfers	
Weekly waste report	
Period-to-date report (41)	
Wages input (H/O copy)	
Inter-store labour trfrs.	
Store cash exps. claim	
Other (specify)	

LABOUR CONTROL				
	Open – 10am	10am – 3 pm	3 pm – 7 pm	7 pm – Close
Net sales –				
÷ Crew hours –				
= Sales p.M.H. –				

TOTAL LABOUR			
Net sales	Total crew hours	£'s per man/hour	Hours +/– schedule

COUPONS		
No	Type	Value

YIELDS (*Mon/Thur only)	
* Fish	
* Fries	
* Shakes	
* Coca-cola 5 – 1	
* Fanta 4.5 – 1	
* Shandy 4.5 – 1	
* Lemonade 13 – 1	

Figure 14.3 Fast-food inventory control sheet.
Source: Jones, P. (1988) *Foodservice Operations* (2nd edition), London: Cassell, p.

Figure 14.4 Typical fast-food outlet.
Source: Casey Jones.

Green pressures from fast-food consumers, the general public and others are increasingly being exerted on fast-food operations. These have been related to a variety of issues including the types of disposable packaging used, waste disposal, litter and the use of natural resources. Again some companies have responded positively to these issues and have adopted environmentally friendly policies, appointed environmental managers and taken other initiatives such as waste reduction measures, litter patrols, the use of recycled materials and energy management. Other ecological issues include the amount of land used for cattle farming compared to cereal farming, the matter of whether rain forests are being cleared for cattle pasture land, and the human health consequences associated with intensive animal rearing (e.g. the possibility of BSE being transmitted to humans). Those companies which pay attention to such issues for whatever reason – and their motives could be cynically interpreted as mere tokenism or as a means of gaining a competitive edge – will increase their appeal to an environmentally and ecologically conscious public and will improve their image.

FUTURE TRENDS

Future prospects for the fast-food industry both in the UK and worldwide are extremely bright and the industry is expected to continue its charge forward. The multi-unit branded operations will lead the way for the industry and the future of fast food will be strongly brand-related. One trend expected to continue is the increased diversity of fast-food locations. Fast-food outlets will continue to develop in non-traditional contexts and on new sites in the UK. Increasingly, fast food will be available in contract catering sites, pubs, hotels, restaurants, leisure complexes, petrol station forecourts, newsagents, and via in-store concessions and in-house operations in large supermarkets and stores both in urban areas and in out-of-town retailing parks. Some of this development will be aided by the development of franchised small fast-food bar units, requiring lower capital investment.

Opportunities remain for geographical growth by the chain operators in the UK. The more remote parts of the country and the smaller towns and urban suburbs offer particular opportunities. With the dismantling of border controls, the opening of the Channel Tunnel in 1994, which will improve the speed and ease of communication between the UK and continental Europe, and with the harmonization of European rules and regulations, opportunities for domestic and foreign fast-food operations are great. Geographical growth is therefore expected by increased internationalization.

Increased numbers of operations using the newer delivery systems (e.g. drive-through and home delivery), as well as the development of new systems (e.g. multi-drive-through systems), where outlets have multiple windows designed to cope with high volumes of cars, and customer self-service and self-pay systems, are anticipated. The home delivery market, which is still in its infancy in the UK, will continue to expand and new products which lend themselves to travel more easily than some existing products such as burgers will be developed – although even with burgers research work is being done to improve their transportability for delivery. The extent to which home delivery will threaten established high-street operations is not thought to be great; most of its locations are in neighbourhood areas. As the chains begin to develop in secondary locations in neighbourhood restaurants, they too will need to consider the implications of home delivery. Perhaps another new move will be for smaller street-side hot food carts to get into the lunchtime office delivery market, using mobile telephones to take the orders. The development by the chains of cheaper, fixed or mobile fast-food kiosks where space is at a premium (e.g. in sports stadia, cinemas) is also predicted.

The market share of the brands has increased from less then 1 per cent in 1974 to a point where today, excluding franchises, the major brands have 7.6 per cent of the value of meals served in the UK.[19] This increased market share of the brands will require a response from the small operators if they are to remain in the marketplace. The small operators may be forced to form marketing consortia, for example, or look to ways of chaining; at present there are no prominent chains of Chinese or Indian restaurants.

Further technological advancements are expected within the industry. The chains will be at the forefront of these developments and the major operators will especially continue to invest quite significantly in technological research. These advancements will be required to satisfy the ever-changing needs of customers. McDonald's, for example, is testing credit card payment, and BurgerKing is testing customer-operated ordering terminals.[20] Equipment, and particularly computerized system, innovations will increasingly focus on saving time and energy and facilitate productivity and profitability gains. Pressures upon fast-food operators are also likely to come from the 'green' movement who are expected to focus attention on the environmental consequences associated with the methods and equipment used in outlets. As fast-food operations fine-tune their activity even closer to particular market segments more sophisticated management information systems and better consumer databases are expected.

The issues and challenges confronting the fast-food industry in the twenty-first century will be significantly different from its predecessor. Steering the course of fast-food operations in the right direction will undoubtedly be a complex task and much pressure will be placed upon the industry's managers. Professional management at the corporate and unit level in the chain operations has played a major part in the success of the industry to date; it is they who will hold the keys to the future of fast food both at home and overseas.

REFERENCES

1. Euromonitor (1992) *The World Market for Consumer Catering*, London: Euromonitor.
2. Price, S. (1993) *The UK Fast Food Industry*, London: Cassell.
3. Ball, S.D. (1992) 'Understanding fast-food operations', in S.D. Ball (ed.) *Fast Food Operations and Their Management*, Cheltenham: Stanley Thornes.
4. Ball, S.D. (1994) 'Fast food gathers momentum in Europe', in A. Gordon (ed.) *Hospitality in Europe*, London: Sterling Publications.
5. Day, T. (1994) 'Frying tonight', *Guardian Education*, 15 February.
6. Ball, S.D. (1993) 'Productivity and Productivity Management within Fast-Food Chains – a Case Study of Wimpy International', M.Phil. Thesis, Huddersfield University.
7. Marketpower (1991) *Catering Industry Population File* (5th edition), London.
8. Department of Employment (1991) *CSO Employment Gazette*, May, HMSO.
9. West, A. (1992) 'Fast-food marketing', in S.D. Ball (ed.) *Fast Food Operations and Their Management*, Cheltenham: Stanley Thornes.
10. Key Note (1990) *Fast Food Outlets*. London: Key Note Publications.
11. Armistead, C. (1985). 'Introduction to service operations', in C.A. Voss *et al.*, *Operations Management in Service Industries and the Public Sector*, Chichester: John Wiley.
12. Parsa, H.G. and Khan, M.A. (1992) 'Menu trends in the quick service industry in the various stages of the industry life cycle', *Hospitality Research Journal*, Vol. 15, No. 1, pp. 93–107.
13. Gabriel, Y. (1988) *Working Lives in Catering*, London: Routledge and Kegan Paul.
14. Levitt, T. (1972) 'Production line approach to service', *Harvard Business Review*, Sept–Oct, pp. 41–52.
15. Ball, S.D. (1992) 'Fast-food technology and systems of operation', in S.D. Ball (ed.) *Fast Food Operations and Their Management*, Cheltenham: Stanley Thornes.
16. Lawson, J. (1992) 'Nutritional and environmental issues confronting fast-food operations', in S.D. Ball (ed.) *Fast Food Operations and Their Management*, Cheltenham: Stanley Thornes.
17. Lobstein, T. (1988) *Fast Food Facts*, London: Camden Press.
18. Silverstone, R. (1993) 'Whither fast food?', *International Journal of Contemporary Hospitality Management*, Vol. 5, No. 1, pp. 1–3.
19. Price, S. (1994) in J. Webster 'Fast food explosion', *Caterer and Hotelkeeper*, 1 September.
20. Bertagnoli, L. (1989) 'Arby's', *Restaurants and Institutions*, 13 November.

FIFTEEN

Employee Feeding

CLIFF GOODWIN

INTRODUCTION

Staff restaurants today bear little relationship to those originally set up in the industrial sector as 'staff canteens'. Those facilities, which began to be set up in the nineteenth century, were very much part of an employer's attempt to look after the physical welfare of employees. Further impetus to expand the sector arose during the Second World War, when the Emergency Powers (Defence) Factories Canteen order 1940 and 1943 made catering provision compulsory for all factories employing more than 250 workers. In the 1970s, governmental pay-policy restraint caused many organizations to develop alternative methods to reward their employees. In its simplest form this could be the issue of luncheon vouchers, but in order to give better perceived value to their staff, organizations often offered employee dining facilities. Today staff restaurants are often seen by employers as an important part of the employment package, and are sometimes used as a method of differentiating themselves from their competitors. A recent survey[1] indicated that the average benefit of a staff catering facility to an employee was around £300 per annum.

In this sector, foodservice facilities are ancillary to the main purpose of a business, which may be manufacturing, commerce or retailing. In spite of this, there could be a series of facilities ranging from a simple cafeteria service, perhaps supported by a vended beverage service, to a full range of self-service, buffet and table service, and executive dining rooms. Some large organizations have a range of facilities which can be used by employees of different seniority in the hierarchy. The culture of an organization, regarding the relationships between its employees, is often reflected within the dining-room arrangements. Hence some organizations may have totally unsegregated dining with directors and temporary staff all eating together, whilst others will have very complex structures for various grades of managerial and administrative personnel. In addition, many commercial organizations have high status dining facilities used for entertaining corporate clients.

The nature of the provision within this sector is changing too, both in response to customer tastes and from the influence of the high street. Several operators now use the ideas of branding of products, which will be discussed in a later section, and the increasing concern over diet and health has been reflected in the provision of salad bars and healthy options within menus. In an attempt to reduce costs and match customer require-

Table 15.1 Size and scale of contract foodservice sector in the UK, 1994.

	Outlets	Meals (millions)
Business and Industry	7,073	427
Government and agency staff feeding	347	27
State Education	4,603	163
Independent schools	579	99
Healthcare	459	77
Local authorities*	295	15
Ministry of Defence	267	86
Oil rigs	140	n/a
*includes town halls, police, fire, courts and welfare.		

Source: BHA Contract Catering Survey, 1995.

ments more closely there has also been an increase in the volume of automatically vended services, and in the provision of snack items.

SIZE AND STRUCTURE OF THE SECTOR

It is estimated that this sector accounts for 40 per cent of the total number of meals served in the UK foodservice industry.[2] The number of outlets and meals served (excluding snacks) in the foodservice management sector for 1993 is illustrated in Table 15.1. The two major methods of operation are self-operated (direct management) and contracted.

Marketpower[3] suggest that of the 18,545 outlets in the Business and Industry sector, the contractors operate some 60 per cent of them. This is well ahead of the 30 per cent achieved in other parts of Europe, but some way behind the 80 per cent operated by contractors in the USA. The biggest potential growth area for the contractors is in the cost sector, where they currently only operate 14.4 per cent of the 83,000 outlets. The Industrial Society Survey[4] suggests that there has been a significant rise in market penetration by the contractors who are said to be able to offer cost reductions and the ability to offer improvements in service quality when compared to in-house providers. The survey showed that 20 per cent of employers had switched to provision by outside contractors in the past three years. The survey also reported that the share of the number of outlets operated by contractors had increased by 27 per cent in the last year. Commercial pressures during the recession have also led to the increased use of contractors. Organizations who have been asked to reduce their head count, can do this simply by transferring their labour to a contractor. Whereas organizations may have been reluctant to do this in the past out of concern for their former employees, Transfer of Undertakings regulations now ensure that workers' rights will be protected.

Self-operated Facilities

In this case the parent organization is totally responsible for the catering provision and usually owns all equipment, has dedicated personnel, and is responsible for the entire operation. This means that a firm involved in commerce or engineering may be responsible for an area of operation outside its own normal field, with the responsibility for the operation often vested in the human resource department. This may present problems for the company, and they may not, for example, be able to benefit from large food-purchasing discount arrangements enjoyed by some contractors. However they will be fully in control of their operations. The extent of service provided will be determined by the company's policies. ICI for example, did operate their own facilities as part of their policy 'to ensure that, wherever practicable ... its employees have access to a good quality meal at a fair price in pleasant surroundings'.[5]

Contracted Services

In this option, the equipment is usually owned by the parent company (client), and the service is provided by the contractor. A contractor therefore is usually able to operate with little capital investment in the operation. The 1994 Catering Policies Survey by the Industrial Society[6] suggests that 76 per cent of catering operations are contractor operated, and that the average life of a contract with a particular contractor is eight years. After this time the client would usually offer the contract to another contractor rather than operate the catering in-house. The survey also looked at the reasons for changing the catering management arrangements, and these, in order of significance were:

- Need for cost reductions.
- Need for improvement in service/quality.
- Company policy change.
- Need to reduce headcount.

The market is dominated by a number of major contractors: Sutcliffe, which has recently been acquired by the Granada group; Gardner Merchant, formerly the contract catering division of Forte, which has now been the subject of a management buy out; and Compass, formed by the amalgamation of Bateman Catering and Midland Catering. These large corporations have constantly changing organizational structures, but the current trend is for them to organize themselves into specialist divisions serving particular market segments. In addition to these three large contract-catering organizations there are a large number of small to medium-size operators. These may operate in a number of markets or specialize in particular market segments. For instance 'High Table' serves the directors' dining segment, competing against a division of Gardner Merchant's known as 'Director's Table'.

CONTRACTORS AND CATERING CONTRACTS

A management contracting arrangement is defined by Sharma[7] as 'an arrangement under which operational control of an enterprise which would otherwise be exercised by the directors and managers appointed or elected by its owners, is vested by contract in a separate enterprise which performs the necessary management functions for a fee.'

In the contract catering business, this fee may be made up in several ways. These include a straight fee; one linked to the turnover of the business; one in which purchasing discounts are returned to the client organization to offset against the fee; a combination of the above. It is not uncommon for contractors to gain as much income from purchase discounts obtained, but not passed on to clients, as it is from the fees charged. This will result in local management following a strict policy of using authorized suppliers in order to maximize such discount earnings to the contracting organization.

Contracts are usually one of the following types, or occasionally may be a combination, dependent on the nature of the client's business:

- Management fee (sometimes called 'cost plus').
- Fixed cost.
- Full cost recovery (nil cost).
- Commercial return.
- Guaranteed performance.

Management fee contracts are the most common, and under this arrangement the contractor provides the services as required by the client and submits an invoice for all goods and services provided, and thus would include materials, labour and overheads such as disposables and cleaning materials. To this would be added an agreed management fee, hence the term 'cost plus'. The fee may be fixed in nature or a percentage of the expenditure. The client will have additional costs to pick up such as fuel costs, which are part of a building's overheads, and items such as depreciation on equipment. Clients may also incur heavy and light equipment capital expenditure costs.

The fixed-cost type of contract is less popular with contractors as they have to accurately assess all the catering costs for the period ahead and then bill clients with, for example, one-twelfth of the year's projected costs each month. If contractors underestimate the costs, they have to bear the losses. However if this does occur, the contractor is likely to want to renegotiate, usually on the basis that insufficient information was available on which to make a detailed assessment of costs. This form of contract is becoming increasingly popular with clients, as in this way they can be assured of their catering costs. Public sector organizations, such as local councils requiring a catering provision to the employees at a Town Hall often use this type of contract. This is often forced on them by the need to put their catering facilities contract out to tender as required by current legislation. By using fixed price contracts they are able to compare projected tender costs easily.

The full-cost recovery contract, which essentially dictates the pricing policy, is adopted where the client does not wish to subsidize the catering operation. If this is acceptable to local employee representatives, the contractor would provide services at commercial prices, and retain all income. The contractor has to operate them rather like any commercial restaurant, and hence runs the risk of making a loss if the management is ineffective. Such contracts may or may not include provision to cover overheads costs such as energy.

Commercial return contracts are a growing trend in catering operations, as contractors increasingly begin to run commercial operations. Again as part of a contract with a local authority there may be some public services in addition to those provided for the employees of the organization. Thus a contractor may offer a fixed sum of money, or a percentage of sales to the client in order to operate that part of the business.

Guaranteed performance contracts can take several forms, but it is quite common for the client to ask that the tariff charged recovers food costs, or food costs plus VAT. In this way such costs are not charged to clients, nor are takings returned to them. Essentially, it means that the client will only have to subsidize labour and overheads, and that is guaranteed. Such operations will usually involve a 'floating tariff' to customers as commodity prices fluctuate throughout the year.

Table 15.2 Types of catering contract in the UK, 1993.

	No. of outlets
Management fee (cost plus)	7958
Contracts with performance guarantees	529
Fixed price	3003
Partnership	72
Concession (rent)	1792
Total	13,354

The BHA Survey, whilst using a slightly different classification of contract types, showed management fee contracts, followed by fixed price contracts as the predominant forms of contract in the UK, as illustrated in Table 15.2.

A contract between a client and contractor would normally specify the following:

- A specification of the standards expected with regards to meals and beverages served. Contractors usually have standard portions sizes for catering operations, but will vary these according to individual client requirements.
- Operating times of the various facilities.
- Total budget available for the service provision (see contract forms above).
- Responsibility for cleaning and maintenance of equipment and facilities.
- Relationship for VAT purposes (i.e. the contractor acts either as a principal or agent for VAT purposes).
- Description of responsibilities for insurances and public liabilities.
- Financial arrangements regarding bill payments and possible client deposits.

An increasing trend is for contractors to offer a range of services in addition to catering, such as office cleaning and grounds maintenance, which will save a client having to deal with several different organizations for different services.

OPERATIONAL ISSUES

For all operators there is the need to provide an adequate service, yet to keep costs under control. For a contractor, there is a constant dilemma for the organization has to meet the needs of both the client and the customer in the various catering outlets. In order to facilitate this there has been a growth in the use of self-clearing systems, self-help systems, take-aways and cashless operations, which result in lower labour costs. Sometimes in an attempt to make facilities more attractive, and in improving the service, the usage of a facility may increase. In a commercial contract this would be good practice, as it would spread the overhead. However, if an operation were run in which each meal provided incurred a subsidy from the organization, then increased customers would mean an increased cash subsidy. Thus normal rules of operation do not always apply in this sector. This may explain the trend of providers to move to a nil subsidy situation with their catering provision.

Alternatively clients could give all employees a pay rise and scrap the meal service. Indeed contractors sometimes have to face this question too at the time of contract renewal. However, a number of organizations strongly believe in the need to provide catering facilities, based on a number of factors. Firstly, the provision of a catering ser-

Table 15.3 Breakdown of meal costs.

	Food cost (%)	Labour cost (%)	Other costs (%)
Industrial Society Survey	43	45	12
BHA Survey	40	43	17

vice reduces the time for beverage and meal breaks. In manufacturing industry this can make significant differences to productivity, since it shortens the time that machinery is shut down during breaks. In office environments, facilities such as vending machines cut down the amount of time people are away from their desks and can save energy from the use of numerous kettles, boilers and coffee percolators located within a building. Secondly, at times of high unemployment, the provision of good catering facilities may not apparently be necessary to attract or keep staff, but employee satisfaction may be enhanced by offering opportunities for social interaction and team building. Thirdly, once an organization has committed itself to capital expenditure on its facilities it will want the facilities to be used to provide some return (although not necessarily financial) on its investment. Finally, employee representatives may see catering facilities as an integral part of the employment package, and the continued provision of services can be used as a bargaining point for employers during wage negotiations. The Industrial Society 1994 survey[8] identified six main reasons for providing catering (in order of significance) as general company policy, staff morale, service/perk for staff, tradition/historical, lack of local facilities and keep staff on premises.

The current trend is for organizations to attempt to recover food costs in their tariff structures, and many attempt to add a margin to contribute towards the recovery of other operating costs. A breakdown of food, labour and overhead costs is illustrated in Table 15.3. In an attempt to react to the recession companies have responded by lowering the overall subsidy, raising prices, and offering more snack items.[9] The average annual subsidy per user of a facility was calculated at £373, or £210 per employee, indicating an average take up of 56 per cent.

In this sector, the careful control of food costs is essential to success. As a result most operators have a sophisticated menu-planning system which encompasses a mix of commodities in different price bands in addition to the usual menu-planning requirements of texture, colour and flavours. Such systems involve standard recipes and presentation standards clearly specified for each operation. Operational management have the task of costing the various menu items and ensuring that tariff recovery requirements are met. Food cost plus VAT is currently a common approach being adopted, and this involves the management in carrying out food costings on a regular and frequent basis with menu item prices changing regularly, perhaps daily, especially for vegetables. In sophisticated, high-volume locations, such systems are sometimes linked to automatic commodity requisitioning and re-ordering procedures. Further approaches to pricing could involve the banding of menu items with a 'regular' and 'economy dish' being available, with perhaps a 'premium' dish available at key times such as the end-of-month salary date.

It is also important to control labour costs. The employee feeding sector, like other catering operations, employs a large number of part-time employees. However, if we convert part-time staff into full-time equivalents (FTEs), the average number of staff per catering outlet is 7.9.[10] The Industrial Society survey identified that the average number of meals served per FTE in employee catering outlets is 25 for contractor-operated units and 20.6 for self-operated outlets, giving an overall figure of 23.9. The average number of meals served per catering staff hour was 4.7. Catering management continue to strive to keep operating costs to a minimum, and often resort to technology and mechanization to keep ever-increasing labour costs in check. This approach has led to the growing use of automatically vended services, especially for the provision of beverage services.

OPERATIONS

There are three main systems used for serving food and beverages in this sector. These are automatic vending, trolley service and cafeteria operations.

Automatic Vending

The Automatic Vending Association recognizes that the development of vending machines in Britain is closely related to the industrial catering sector. 'By the 1950s ... it was clear that the future [of vending] lay in servicing the worker and his [sic] refreshment needs.' The AVA list 82 different types of goods or services that may be vended by machine, but from the caterer's viewpoint, there are four main categories.

- Beverages – hot or cold. Hot can be further divided into 'instant' which is further divided into dried and frozen products, fresh brew, and capsule vendors which allow customers choice of particular blends of tea or coffee in encapsulated form. Cold drinks, too, may be dispensed by machine using concentrates, or alternatively by refrigerated can vendors.
- Confectionery and snacks. Usually a supply of common branded confectionery goods.
- Sandwiches. This includes items such as pork pies, Scotch eggs, quiche, etc.
- Meals – hot or cold. These are offered in refrigerated units, often adopting a carousel type of mechanism to deliver a range of products to the customer. Such machines are often sited next to microwave ovens which allow customers to reheat their food. These are used particularly in unmanned facilities, perhaps to provide a service for maintenance or computer staff who have to be on duty throughout the night.

Machines vending such products may be found in cafeterias, offices, factories, refectories, hotel corridors, student common rooms, clubs and pubs, and many other types of location. It has been estimated that there is a vending machine for every 100 people in the UK. The total annual turnover of all types of machine is more than £1000 million. The largest type of vend is from 175,000 beverage machines, which dispense over 3500 million drinks per annum. Another 100,000 dispense confectionery, and 70,000 food and drink. The employee feeding sector is a major user of such machines, with over 76 per cent of all UK companies having beverage vending.

The type of machine will depend upon the product being vended. Those vending pre-packaged goods, such as confectionery, soft drinks and sandwiches need only electricity supplied, whilst cup-vending machines need water supplied also. Machines are also temperature controlled and may be ambient, refrigerated or heated. The operating mechanism varies from machine to machine but they include cup, drop-flap, rotating drum, compartment, endless belt, lift, and column and drawer mechanisms.

Vending services can be provided through machines financed by outright purchase, lease and lease purchase, rental or supplier on a commission basis. Purchase requires a large capital outlay as sophisticated machines with many choices, and the capability of delivering freshly brewed products can cost in excess of £5000. Small operators therefore often opt for more simple machines which involve the customer carrying out some mechanical procedures such as placing a cup under the product, pushing a button, and then moving the cup to a water dispenser spout. In addition to the purchase, the operators would have to take out an annual maintenance agreement. Leasing has the advantage that large outlays are not required, and the agreement usually includes a maintenance plan. Rentals are usually for more short-term commitments, and allows a user to change machines more often, although rentals can be expensive. Many organizations simply contract out their vending operations, and within a catering contract, the vending section may be subcontracted, although the larger operators do have their own vending divisions. The final option is to consider supplying goods, usually on branded products such as Coca-Cola on a commission basis. Under this type of arrangement, the supplier provides the machine and the operator receives a commission on each can sold on a sliding scale according to sales volumes.

Since the caterer is not expected to be technically capable of maintaining or repairing these machines, the complexities of their mechanisms will not be dealt with here. In those cases where the machines are operated by a vending company on contract to the caterer, all maintenance, cleaning, restocking and control is likely to be carried out by the vending operator's staff. The caterer need only report a machine defect or failure if this should occur. Caterers operating their own vending machines must therefore have well-trained staff responsible for the regular cleaning, replenishing, maintenance and control of the machines. In 1975, 80 per cent of machines were self operated, but today there is a growing trend towards contract operation, reflecting US practice, where 95 per cent of all machines are on contract.

The advantages of installing vending machines include flexibility, accessibility, control, and labour saving. A vending machine, properly maintained, provides its product 24 hours a day. It allows workers in businesses of all types to take refreshment whenever they wish, according to their individual needs. So long as industry and commerce are prepared to accept their workers having flexible break times, there is no doubt that their performance is improved by providing tea, coffee or other beverages throughout their working day. Machines may be sited in close proximity to the workplace, be it factory or office, thus reducing the amount of time required by the user to get to and from the service point. This is particularly important in offices and factories covering several hundred square metres. The machine dispenses an exact measure or amount of the vending commodity for the correct value of coins or tokens, therefore wastage, pilferage and loss are eliminated and exact control is made possible, which was not always possible with trolley service. It is estimated that one machine can be serviced by a member of staff in 20 minutes each day. With the use of disposables, which reduces the need for washing up, this probably involves fewer work hours than a conventional food and drink service would necessitate.

The disadvantages of vending machines have been speed, quality, lack of personal contact and vandalism. A well-trained cafeteria operator can probably dispense teas more quickly than one machine, but even so a machine using instant ingredients takes only ten seconds to serve one customer. Where speed is particularly important, several machines located around the service area would be needed. Initially there was a great deal of resistance to tea-vending and coffee-vending due to the poor quality of the product, reinforced by its dispensing in a plastic or paper cup. This resistance has been eroded by definite improvements by the manufacturers of vending products and a change in consumer attitude towards the product and disposables. The vending machine has effectively replaced the tea-trolley (see below). It is a factor that vending manufacturers are aware of and have researched in order to design machines that reduce the impact of lack of personal contact. They believe that 'brightly coloured and well-lit machines can do much to overcome any resistance encountered from the "impersonal tag"'. In addition the public is becoming more used to partly self-help systems, the good customer reaction to the major banks' automatic telling machines (ATMs) being a good example. Perhaps because of the above, damage, malicious and otherwise, may be caused by frustrated consumers. No machine is entirely vandal-proof, but modern machines are very robust, despite their increasing sophistication. On contract-operated sites, the contractors have a vested interest in ensuring the security of takings, since they receive a share of them, while a damaged or broken-down machine affects the operators' or caterers' turnovers.

From what has been outlined so far, the catering manager in an operation where vending machines are installed must have three clear priorities. Machines must be sited effectively to maximize their use and provide the best possible service. Staff, if a self-operator, should be well-trained and capable of replenishing, cleaning and regularly maintaining the machines; and if it is a contract operation, that the contractor fulfils these same obligations properly. Finally, clear policies should be established with regard to customer dissatisfaction due to machine malfunction or breakdown. For instance, if a customer complains that the machine accepted money but failed to vend or refund the same, there must be a consistent policy with regard to refunding money or not. In any event, it is in everyone's interest to ensure that the machine is kept in proper working order, so it is advisable to place a notice on each machine that says who should be contacted in the event of any dissatisfaction.

Today payment systems are changing. A number of organizations operate 'free vend' periods for their staff, perhaps for one hour mid-morning and one mid-afternoon, with the rest of the day being on a tariff basis. Such a system would, of course, require the machine to have a timing mechanism. In order to overcome problems with coin mechanisms, so often the cause of vending machine complaints, many companies in the past adopted a total free-vend policy. This proved disastrous, with customers taking drinks indiscriminately, with many being left only partially consumed. Interestingly the introduction of any sort of payment, even as small as 5p, will cut down consumption to an average of around 3.5 cups per day per person. Increasingly, cashless systems are being introduced where employees are either issued with, or buy a 'smart card' which carries an amount of credit which slowly reduces in value as it is used, rather like a telephone card. The Industrial Society survey identified that of all beverages sold today, 71 per cent are vended, and the average number of beverages consumed per customer per day is 1.63.

Trolley Service

Despite the advent of automatic vending, some operators still operate a tea or beverage trolley that tours the factory or offices providing mid-morning and mid-afternoon refreshment. The principal advantage of such a service is that the refreshments goes to the employees rather than the employees having to leave their workplace to have refreshment. Also, staff representatives have tended to support the person bringing round the tea rather than make him or her redundant through replacement with machines.

Like any other form of service, there are essential features that the foodservice manager must be aware of. One trolley can serve approximately 200 people, if they are not dispersed over too wide an area or on too many floors. It should provide a choice of beverage and snack items, but choice should be kept to an acceptable minimum to simplify administration, control and stock turnover. From experience, a trolley on a regular route will establish a well-defined pattern of sales – so many teas, coffees, glasses of milk, and so on – which enables the operator to stock the trolley sufficiently to satisfy predicted sales without excessive waste. The trolley should be regularly cleaned and maintained so that beverages and food items are served hygienically and presented in an appetizing way. The route of the trolley should be carefully considered and reviewed regularly to take into account the starting, break and finishing times of staff, the distance to be travelled and any obstructions to a smooth schedule, such as lifts. No route will be ideal since it will take about 1.5 hours to serve 200 people, for some of whom the trolley will arrive too early, and for others it will be too late. Therefore the caterer should be in close consultation with management and employee representatives to maximize satisfaction with the service. The trolley operator should only serve from designated stops to ensure an efficient service, since experience has shown that it takes longer to serve people when they stop the trolley to purchase than if the trolley stops for a while to serve several people. This also helps to establish a routine so that employees who move around the building know where to find the trolley at any given time.

The control of trolley service is just as demanding as any other food service system. Items may be easily pilfered and cash is particularly vulnerable. Much depends on the security-consciousness and honesty of the operator and, in some cases, caterers have adopted a procedure whereby stock is 'sold' to the attendant before the service, which he or she then pays for out of receipts, less any returned stock. The attendant is therefore much more likely to guard the stock and cash than otherwise. This system is particularly used outside the employee feeding sector when trolleys are used for refreshment services at sporting events, such as hot-dog stands at football matches and so on.

Cafeteria Operations

There are three main variations of the cafeteria system: in-line counter; free-flow; and carousel.

The *'in-line' cafeteria* consists of a single counter along which customers pass to select food and beverage. It is sometimes described as the 'straight-line' cafeteria, but not all such counters are in fact straight, although there are advantages in ensuring that the counter is straight – primarily because customers pushing trays along the counter may be distracted enough to push the tray either off the rail where it changes direction away from them or into the counter, thereby spilling items, where it turns towards them. This style of cafeteria can serve between four and eight customers per minute depending upon those factors mentioned above such as speed of the service staff, proficiency of the cashier and the menu display, and also the customer's familiarity with the unit and the order of

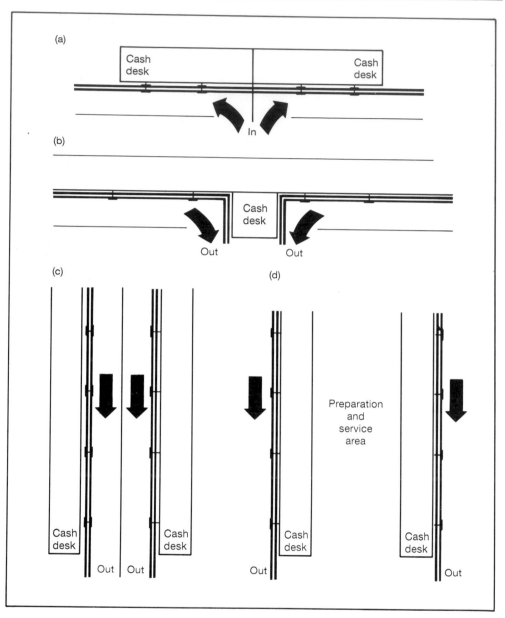

Figure 15.1   In-line cafeteria layouts.
Source: Jones, P. (1988) *Foodservice Operations* (2nd edition), London: Cassell, p. 88.

presentation of items along the counter. Some experts believe that the counter should be arranged logically in the order of the menu so customers select a starter, main course, a sweet and beverage in the 'correct' sequence, while others advocate that all those items served at room temperature or chilled should be at the beginning of the counter, so that hot items are served last and therefore have less time to cool before they are eaten.

Figure 15.2 Typical free-flow servery.
Source: Gardner Merchant.

Whichever method of presentation is adopted, it is important to be consistent so that customers will become familiar with the layout, and will know at which point along the counter they will find particular items.

The length of the cafeteria counter will depend upon the number of menu items, but will be between 6 and 15 metres (20 and 50 feet). The longer the counter, the slower the service is likely to be. This has led to some modifications of the basic idea. The counter may be divided into two, with both halves serving the same selection of items. Customers may start at either end and move towards the cash points located at the midpoint of the counter, or start at the midpoint and move towards either end, as illustrated in Figure 15.1. Alternatively, there may be parallel counters, with the customer flow between the counters on either side. Finally two counters may be placed either side of a central service point running in parallel with each other.

The *free-flow system* is also known as the 'scramble system' or 'hollow square'. Whereas in-line cafeterias usually comprise one counter in whatever configuration thought suitable, the free-flow system has several counters each serving different meal items, such as hot foods, sandwiches, salads, desserts and beverages. The major advantage of free-flow is that it avoids the necessity to queue, and although short queues may form at periods of high demand, the number of customers that can be served may be as high as 15 per minute. Customers prefer this layout because the service is quicker, there is less queuing, and the customer who only wants a snack does not have to use the same counter as someone who requires a three-course meal. Additionally, a wider selection of menu items may be offered. In particular, it is possible to operate a call-order counter for grills that is impracticable in a conventional cafeteria. From the caterer's point of view, the free-flow layout has the advantage of flexibility. During periods of slack demand, some counters may be closed, counters may be removed in the event of breakdown and

Figure 15.3 Carousel servery.
Source: Middlesex Polytechnic.

greater use may be made of self-service by customers since the flow of the entire system is not held up by one slow customer.

There are two main types of layout of the free-flow cafeteria. The hollow square has counters placed around three sides of the service area in a U-shape, with the customers entering and leaving via the open side, as illustrated in Figure 15.2. This is used particularly in operations where there is a steady flow of customers throughout the service period, such as in department stores. The echelon design has counters arranged at an angle next to each other. This is used particularly where there are a large number of people to be served, as in the industrial sector. With both layouts it is important that the counters are well signposted so that customers can easily identify the particular counter they wish to use, and counters should be arranged so that as little cross-flow takes place as possible.

The *carousel* was first introduced into Britain some years ago and has been a limited success. It comprises a large rotating arrangement of shelves, approximately two metres in diameter, on which food and drink are presented, as illustrated in Figure 15.3. Thus customers remain stationary as the carousel revolves once every minute to enable them to select items from it. Only one-half of the carousel is in the service area, so that as items are removed, the shelves can be replenished in the serving area behind the unit. Trays, cutlery, napkins and beverages are usually separately available from dispensers so as to avoid congestion at the unit. Cashiers are situated between the carousel and the dining room. As a method of self-service, it has a customer throughput of between eight to ten per minute, which is higher than the traditional in-line counters. It requires less space than many other self-service layouts, particularly in the service area of the operation. However, operators must be well trained to re-stock the shelves quickly and efficiently to maintain a steady flow-rate of customers, and customers may cause delays waiting for a complete revolution of the unit before making their selection. In this respect, the carousel is most suited to operations where there is repeat custom on a frequent basis. Use of carousels over a number of years has shown that they are of less use where hot food is being offered as there are problems of maintaining food temperature and quality. They have had greater success in dispensing items such as pre-prepared cold dishes and sweets. Visitors to the Kennedy Space Center in Florida will no doubt be familiar with the carousel used there.

Food Production Systems

Food production in this sector tend be very traditional, although it is influenced by technological change. Currently, influenced by customer requirements, particularly in relation to 'healthy eating' as described in a later section, there has been a return to these traditional approaches. Whilst other sectors may have progressed to decoupled approaches such as cook-chill, *sous-vide* and cook-freeze, the employee feeding sector is returning to traditional production, involving the use of batch cooking to help ensure retention of essential nutrients. This is partly a result of the fact that an average size operation serves approximately 250 meals a day, which does not lend itself to viable high levels of capital expenditure. The idea of centralized production with delivery of food to satellites is only really appropriate in large industrial locations. A later section discusses the influence of the high street, and how this is leading to a 'food court' type of approach being considered in large operations, as opposed to the traditional approach of mass production of a limited number of menu items. There is still, however, the need for large volume production, and this tends to be reflected in the type of production equipment used. It is common to see the use of Brat pans, pressure steamers and combination ovens in large-scale operations to facilitate batch cooking.

MARKETS AND BRANDING

The customers using in-house facilities are almost exclusively employees of the host organization. Visitors may also use the facilities, and high-ranking visitors such as potential customers, financiers and sometimes politicians and foreign dignitaries will usually be served in executive dining-rooms. The bulk of the clientele will effectively be in a semi-captive market, and in extreme cases such as on board an oil rig will be totally captive. Many industrial sites are in isolated locations, or are far from commercial outlets, and their employees would therefore have little choice other than to bring their own food. Commercial operations often exist with large numbers in a single location, and hence numbers of diners can vary dramatically according to weather conditions. A 10 per cent swing in demand in a location with 3000 employees would cause a variation in meal

Table 15.4 Major UK catering contracts and brands.

	High Street brands	Own brands
Compass	Pizza Hut, Taco Bell	
	BurgerKing, Dixie's Donuts	
Gardner	McDonald's, Dunkin Donuts	Pizza Gusta
Merchant	KFC	'Lincolns' (Burger)
		'Strollers Deli' (Sandwich)
Sutcliffe		'Hampers' (Sandwich)
		'Zefferelli's' (Pizza, burger)

requirements of 300 in one meal service. This indicates the need for good records of sales trends, and also the ability of the production area to respond quickly to change in demand. This leads to a need for systems and equipment that can be responsive to such changes and hence the use of equipment such as pressure steamers, and steamer/ovens and the use of cook-chilled, and cooked-frozen items to meet these fluctuations.

Essentially customers in such establishments are generally using the facilities to meet a basic need for food, which is supplied to a good quality at an acceptable price in the amount of time available. Whereas many public catering outlets, such as one in a motorway service area, may only change the menu quarterly, menus in this sector usually change daily in order not to cause menu fatigue. As more establishments turn to flexible working methods and the use of 'flexi time', the opportunity to have a wholesome meal quickly may be seen as a great advantage to an employee. As a result, seat turnover can be quite high and will be determined by the style of the meal provision. Large free-flow serveries in cafeteria style operations will allow customers to get through quickly and return to their work, whereas the executive dining-rooms will allow a meal to be enjoyed at a more leisurely pace, perhaps whilst concluding an important business deal. Cafeteria seat turnover may be two to three times an hour, and snack bars up to six, whereas executive rooms may be as low as 0.33 per hour.

Taking a main meal at work may allow employees more time in the evening for social and recreational activities as they may not have the burden of having to prepare an evening meal. Increasingly, the staff restaurant is becoming a location for more social meal experiences. This has been reflected in the branding of some staff restaurant outlets, in an attempt to reflect catering outlets in the high street, as illustrated in Table 15.4. This has either taken the form of high-street brands, such as Pizza Hut and Taco Bell being adopted by the contractor, Compass. In other cases the contractors have adopted their own in-house brands – a strategy preferred by Sutcliffe and Gardner Merchant. High street brands need large customer numbers to make the capital investment viable. A Taco Bell has recently been installed by Compass in Birmingham University at a cost of £30,000. A small Pizza Hut module offering six types of pizza can be installed for £15,000 and several multi-branded outlets have been installed in hospital contracts, where Compass offer Pizza Hut, Burger-King, Dixie's Donuts and Café Select. However, smaller operations, such as in large banks in the city of London, have also seen such brands introduced.[11]

In some larger operations a range of branded outlets are being sited together to offer a range of facilities to customers, rather like you would find in a large retail centre's food court. Ian Daley, Managing Director of Compass's 'New Famous Foods' division, claims that:

WIGGINS TEAPE WEEKLY MENU

MONDAY	TUESDAY	WEDNESDAY	THURSDAY	FRIDAY
Celery soup	French onion soup	Asparagus soup	Mushroom soup	Tomato soup
Ratatouille Vol-au-vents	Curried eggs with rice	Vegetable lasagne	Mixed pepper quiche	Baked jacket potato, coleslaw and cheese
Sauté beef and vegetables	Lamb stew and dumplings	Corn beef hash	Tandoori chicken	Deep fried cod with lemon poached cod in white wine sauce
Ham 'n' egg	Haddock with prawn sauce	Home-made scotch egg	Grilled lambs liver with onions	Lamb chop lyonnaise
Paella 75p	Chicken Maryland 75p	Roast sirloin of beef 75p and yorkshire pudding	Pork escalopes 75p	Beef carbonnade 75p
Baked beans French beans Cauliflower Chipped potatoes	Sliced courgettes Mixed vegetables New potatoes	Buttered cabbage Sliced carrots Roast potatoes	Sweet corn Sliced green beans Lard potatoes	Tomatoes Garden peas New potatoes
Gammon ham Prawn and pineapple Cheese	Gala pie Scotch eggs Cheese	Cold chicken Egg mayonnaise Cheese	Cold roast beef Tuna and apple Cheese	Assorted meats Cheese
Coffee and walnut sponge and custard	Lemon meringue tartlet and custard	Bread-and-butter pudding and custard	Baked apple and custard	Mixed fruit cobbler and custard
Alpine rice	Sago	Semolina	Tapioca	Creamed rice

ICE CREAM IS AVAILABLE ON REQUEST

SENIOR STAFF DINING ROOM

MONDAY	TUESDAY	WEDNESDAY	THURSDAY	FRIDAY
Celery soup	French onion soup	Asparagus soup	Mushroom soup	Tomato soup
Orange and melon cocktail	Hors-d'oeuvre	Prawn cocktail	Wardorf salad	Stuffed mushroom with garlic
Grilled sirloin steak garni	Chicken Maryland	Roast sirloin of beef and yorkshire pudding	Pork escalopes	Fried cod with lemon
New potatoes Sauté potatoes French beans Grilled tomatoes	New potatoes Jacket potatoes Sweet corn and peppers Cauliflower with butter	Roast potatoes New potatoes Buttered cabbage Baton carrots	Lard potatoes Croquette potatoes Mixed vegetables French beans with almonds	New potatoes French fries Petits pois Sweet corn
Gammon ham Smoked mackerel Cottage cheese with walnuts	Smoked trout Gala pie Roast turkey	Tuna and apple Scotch egg Gammon ham	Roast beef Salmon and cucumber Pork pie	Gammon ham Sardines Smoked chicken

Figure 15.4 Typical industrial catering menus.
Source: Wiggins Teape.

'well known brands offer their clients several advantages, foremost being the ability to raise prices in an environment where customer expectation of low-priced food is well established. Customers are more comfortable paying a higher price for a brand they know at a price they expect'.[12]

Gardner Merchant has its own in-house pizza, burger and deli brand operations and has agreements with McDonald's, KFC and Dunkin Donuts, but has yet to find many establishments large enough to justify the installation of these high street brands.

Sutcliffe offers in-house brands too but feels that high street brands would be inappropriate according to their Group Marketing Director. She feels that as employee feeding establishments serve the same market every day, then a variety of menus must be offered. She also believes that better-value brands are more suited to the institutional environment, where a meal is seen as a benefit or perk and states, 'With high street brands, there are franchise fees to be paid, and too many people trying to take a cut'.[13]

Caterers in this environment have realized that what they have been offering in the past may have been more than the customer wanted, and as a result the operation may have been incurring unnecessary costs. Lynette Eabourne of Sutcliffe states 'The traditional meat and two veg. meal is not what people want now … so why not offer them pasta or a good baguette, which suits them better and costs a lot less to provide than a roast or boeuf bourguignon.'[14] The most successful brand of Sutcliffe is 'Hampers', a sandwich bar operation which allows staff restaurants to compete with the high street. Where such operations have been introduced they have increased sales by up to 20 per cent.

Other trends have been determined by the changing nature of the gender mix of the workforce. The obvious implications of this are the development of menus which reflect a workforce which has an ever-increasing mix of different ethnic groups, and a substantial increase in the proportion of the female workforce. This, combined with a growing interest by the public in diet and health, has resulted in a trend towards people eating less, and towards a more 'healthy diet'. The contractors use this as a selling point with campaigns such as the Gardner Merchant 'Look after your heart' promotion. This is given greater emphasis by some employers who feel that they have a responsibility towards their workforce in promoting a more healthy diet.

CURRENT ISSUES AND FUTURE TRENDS

The Transfer of Undertakings (Protection of Employment)

A major growth of employee feeding has been in the public sector. This has been as a result of government legislation enacted during the 1980s requiring local authorities and health authorities to put their catering services out to tender. However, the expansion of The Transfer of Undertakings (Protection of Employment) regulations (known as TUPE) were originally introduced in 1991 to accommodate the so-called 'Acquired Rights Directive' from the European Union and have been the cause of controversy for some time. These regulations have now been clarified by rulings in the House of Lords, and essentially they mean that at the time of transfer of a business, the contract of employment immediately prior to the transfer will be maintained after the transfer. Hence the transfer of employment of a worker from an in-house catering provider to a contractor or between contractors means that the employment will remain protected. Also the employee will be entitled to terms and conditions of employment no less favourable than those previously enjoyed. The terms relating to occupational pension schemes do not apply, and are subject to agreement by the parties. This will have considerable significance in public sector contracting, where contractors were previously able to offer staff lower salaries and hence be in a strong position when bidding for contracts brought about by competitive tendering requirements.

Cost Control

This sector has a great emphasis on cost, as it is an ancillary service to an organization's main business. Operators are constantly trying new approaches to keep costs under control such as the further development of the use of self-clearing systems, take-away foods, self-help counters and single-status dining. Technologies such as belted systems like 'Cidelveyors' to transport trays of dirties into the wash-up area, and the use of cashless systems, will also be used to reduce staffing and hence improve productivity. However, at the same time, the consumer is beginning to require products (or clones of the products) that are available in the high street. This may allow providers to set more commercial pricing, and hence help reduce subsidies.

Contractor Diversification

Regarding contractor operations, 1994 has seen significant changes in the UK foodservice management industry with a number of mergers and acquisitions taking place. The dependence on traditional business and industry to this sector has declined. The trend is increasingly for contractors to develop businesses in providing meal services for the public. The number of contractor-run outlets in state education has risen sharply, partly brought about by the introduction of Compulsory Competitive Tendering (CCT) legislation. Health care and Ministry of Defence have seen slight growth, whilst the number of outlets in Business and Industry have declined due to current economic conditions. Those offering in-house services seem to be switching to the contractors whose knowledge, expertise and resources are better able to respond to changing customer needs.

Internationalization

In 1993 the overseas turnover of UK-registered companies increased from £277 million to £458 million (£293 million EC and £115 million USA). This represents some 23 per cent of the total turnover in the UK.[15] Contractors are expanding into Europe and North America, and at the same time there has been a growth in UK business operated by overseas-based organizations such as ARA (USA) and Sodexho (France). Take-overs would seem to be inevitable, with a small number of large operators. Some form of oligopoly may then operate in this market in the future.

CONCLUSION

Employee feeding is a very large sector of the UK foodservice industry. In catering for large numbers of people, it uses systems, such as cafeterias and vending. Whilst these systems are not exclusively used in this sector, we have dealt with them here due to their significance. The sector is constantly evolving, and branding has become the emphasis towards the end of 1994. We can see the likely expansion of this, perhaps with the introduction of 'coffee and pastry' type outlets. It would appear that change seems to be increasingly consumer-led, and the sector will have to respond with appropriate changes in production and delivery systems.

REFERENCES

1. Anon. (1994) 'Staff restaurants save workers £300', *Caterer and Hotelkeeper*, 10 November, p. 9.
2. British Hospitality Association (1994) *Contract Catering Survey*, London: Marketpower.
3. Ibid.

4. The Industrial Society and Touche Ross (1994) *A Survey of Catering Policies, Costs and Performance*, London: Industrial Society.

5. Jones, P. (1988) *Foodservice Operations* (2nd edition), London: Cassell, p. 81.

6. The Industrial Society and Touche Ross op. cit.

7. Sharma, D.D. (1984) 'Management contracts and international marketing in industrial goods', in E. Kaynack (ed.) *International Marketing Management*, New York: Praeger.

8. The Industrial Society and Touche Ross op. cit.

9. Ibid.

10. British Hospitality Association op. cit.

11. Anon. (1994) 'All aboard the band wagon', *Caterer and Hotelkeeper*, 10 November.

12. Ibid.

13. Ibid.

14. Ibid.

15. British Hospitality Association op. cit.

SIXTEEN

Welfare Catering

NIGEL HEMMINGTON

INTRODUCTION

Definition of the welfare catering sector is not simple. It is an area that was previously know as institutional catering and was closely related to charitable and state social provision in areas such as education, health and the penal system. In these areas profit has not normally been the primary motive and for this reason it is often grouped with employee feeding and identified as cost sector catering. Details of the size and scale of this sector were provided in Chapter 1.

Any contemporary definition of the sector is perhaps best guided by application of the general definition: 'the provision of meals for those unable to provide for themselves' – inability resulting from age, both the very young and the elderly, illness and all other types of infirmity. Welfare catering is thus generally seen as including foodservice in education (schools, colleges and universities), health care (public and private hospitals), and social care (meals on wheels, day centres, care homes), and prisons.

Because of its origins in charity, for many years welfare catering had a rather impoverished image. In recent years, however, this has changed, particularly in response to competition but also as a result of legislation that has led to the building of improved purpose-built facilities and the development of advanced technical food service systems such as cook-chill and *sous-vide*. Concomitant with these developments has been the enhanced status of foodservice managers who play a fundamental role in the success of the systems and who must therefore be professionally qualified and technically competent.

The significance of the welfare catering sector is perhaps best illustrated by its size. On the basis of the number of schoolchildren, patients, prisoners, attendance at day centres and the number of meals on wheels served, the sector represents over 2 billion (2000 million) meal opportunities per year, the equivalent of nearly 6 million meals per day.[1] When compared with the fact that the whole of contract catering industry served just over 1 billion meals[2] in 1994 it is clear that welfare catering is one of the major sectors in the foodservice industry.

THE LEGISLATIVE CONTEXT

With its history of state provision the welfare catering sector has been subject to perhaps more legislation and government policy than any other foodservice sector. The provision of meals in schools and hospitals was an integral part of Britain's social policy after the Second World War. In school meals, for example, all education authorities were required to provide midday meals, suitable as the main meal of the day, at all maintained schools for all pupils who desired them. These services, having been established in the 1940s, remained largely unchanged until the 1980s. Change was signalled, however, in 1970 by the White Paper, *New Policies in Public Spending* which outlined efficiencies expected by the government in state spending. Despite imposing stringent financial restrictions on government spending during the 1970s the expected efficiencies were not achieved. This led to a number of significant legislative changes in the 1980s.

In the school meals sector, the *Education Act 1980* (section 22) removed the requirement that meals should meet minimum nutritional standards and empowered local authorities to determine the nature and extent of the school meals service they would provide and to set the charges to be made for them. The only remaining requirements were that meals should be provided for pupils whose parents received supplementary benefit or family income support, and facilities should be provided for those pupils bringing their own lunch-time food to eat at school. The *Social Security Act 1986* replaced family income supplement with family credit and replaced supplementary benefit with income support. Under this legislation free school meals were restricted to children whose parents receive income support whilst those whose parents receive family credit lost their entitlement to free school meals but receive cash compensation instead.

A key development in hospital catering was the circular, *Competitive Tendering in the Provision of Domestic, Catering and Laundry Services 1983–HC(83)18*, which advised health authorities to invite tenders for the provision of catering and other services. There was, however, a great deal of resistance from the health authorities, the hospitals and the unions with the effect that implementation was slow and in many cases the tender documents so complex and detailed that there were few bids from contractors.[3] By 1988 over 300 district health authorities had invited tenders but only nine had actually been won by outside contractors.[4]

In light of this lack of response, the *Local Government Act 1988* was introduced to ensure that it was more likely that catering services would be contracted out. The rationale behind this legislation was that by exposing services to competition and market forces they would evolve into more efficient, financially self-supporting operations. Although the response of outside contractors was still slow – Compass stating that most of the tender specifications were too restrictive and did not allow 'commercial flair to develop the service'[5] – the years since have seen a steady growth in interest from the commercial sector to the extent that in 1994 welfare catering, particularly education, represented the major growth area for contract caterers accounting for 38 per cent of outlets.[6]

During the 1990s, the focus has moved towards food safety and customer service. The *Food Safety Act 1990* and, more recently, the *Food Safety (General Food Hygiene) Regulations 1995* build on previous legislation and contain some new requirements, including the requirement to identify, control and monitor critical food hazard points in the specific food operations employed; the need to ensure that food handlers are supervised and instructed/trained in food hygiene matters 'commensurate with their work activity'; changes in temperature control requirements; and requirements for the transport of food in the course of catering operations. In addition to the requirements of the legislation, a new initiative has been the development of a *Guide to Compliance by Caterers* published by the Joint Hospitality Industry Congress (1995). This guide gives comprehensive information about legal requirements as they would be interpreted in catering operations and has the status implied by Regulation 20 of the 1995 Regulations – that is, that enforcement officers (Environmental Health Officers) must give 'due consideration' to the guide when assessing compliance with the regulations.

The Citizen's Charter concept has also required welfare caterers to be very much more aware of their provision. For instance, the *Patients' Charter 1995* requires that patients in hospital receive a written explanation of the hospital's 'patient food policy and the catering services and standards they can expect during their stay'. The charter identifies the standards as a choice of dishes, meals suitable for all dietary needs, a choice of portion size, no need to order more than two meals in advance, readily available help to use the catering services and the provision of the catering manager's name.

THE COMPETITIVE ENVIRONMENT

The Local Government Act 1988 was to have a profound affect on the welfare catering sector. Although interest from commercial companies was slow to develop, largely because of the complex tender documentation and the cost of tendering, the recession in the late 1980s and early 1990s encouraged contract catering companies to look more closely at the opportunities offered by the public sector. Indeed, by 1994 welfare catering and particularly education catering, represented the major growth area for contract caterers.

Most contract caterers now see the welfare sector as the major growth opportunity for the future and are therefore pursuing contracts much more aggressively than ever before. Several have set up specialist divisions to bid for and operate welfare contracts. The Compass Group, for example, has set up two divisions, Chartwells for education and Bateman Catering for health care. BET has followed a similar course of action establishing specialist divisions for education and health care contracts.

Another indication of the contract caterers 'more aggressive approach is their introduction of strongly branded and themed restaurants. These include some very powerful international brands such as Pizza Hut and BurgerKing. This strategy is more fully discussed in the section on marketing.

Whilst contract caterers have moved more towards catering in the welfare sector, they have not limited themselves to catering and several have also won other support services such as cleaning, domestic services and portering – Sodexho is perhaps the leading company in this multi-service provision. This trend raises the question of whether in the longer term contract catering companies will move more towards facilities management rather than just specifically catering management.

From the above it is clear that the government's desire to see a more competitive commercially oriented environment in welfare catering has to a large extent been achieved. How this develops and how the direct service organizations (DSOs – the original public sector providers) fare in this environment remains to be seen. Whilst established contract caterers are able to withstand the loss of contracts and return to compete in the future, single contract DSOs are unlikely to survive such losses, with the result that competition in the future will be reduced.

Table 16.1   UK population by age, 1993 to 2041.

Year	< 16	16–39	% 40–64	65–79	> 80	Total (millions)
1993	20.6	34.9	28.8	11.9	3.9	58.2
2001	20.7	32.9	30.6	11.4	4.3	59.8
2011	19.2	30.0	34.1	11.9	4.7	61.3
2021	18.3	29.7	32.7	14.3	5.1	62.2
2031	18.2	28.4	30.5	16.3	6.6	62.2
2041	17.6	27.8	30.1	16.8	7.8	61.2

Source: Central Statistical Office, 1995.

DEMAND FOR WELFARE CATERING

For the purposes of planning services such as welfare catering it is essential to project the future size and demographic nature of the market. With knowledge of birth-rates, death-rates, net immigration and the current age profile of the population, it is relatively simple to predict the numbers in particular age groups into the future. Table 16.1 shows the age profile of the UK population in 1993 with predictions to 2041. The groups of particular interest to the welfare catering sector are those under 16 and those over 64. These two groups are identified as the dependent population in that they represent that proportion of the population who are supported by those of working age. They are also those who make the greatest demands on the educational, health and care services – nearly 40 per cent of total government expenditure on social protection is spent on the elderly.[7]

The dependency ratio, the number of children and pensioners per 100 people of working age, is a key statistic. The ratio was 63 in 1992 but it is expected to peak in 2036 at 82 when the baby-boom generation reaches retirement age and the number of pensioners is projected to be 17 million – by comparison in 1993 there were 9 million people over 64. This future burden has clear implications for the provision of health care services and certainly indicates substantial growth in the demand for catering services within the sector regardless of whether it is state or commercially based. Another factor that is likely to have a substantial affect on the demand for welfare services such as meals on wheels and day centres is the 1991 Care Programme Approach which details the government's policy of providing care for as many people as possible in the community. Finally, the proportion of one-person households gives an indication of potential dependency on health care services. Whilst in 1961 the proportion of one-person households was 11 per cent it rose to 27 per cent in 1993.[8] This clear upward trend shows the increasing numbers of people who have little or no family to support them in times of illness and who are therefore likely to need health care support at various times in their lives.

CONSUMERS AND THEIR NEEDS

The operational characteristics of the welfare catering sector are largely determined by the nature of the consumer groups it serves, the most significant factor being that as an ancillary service to other activities (e.g. education, health), welfare catering has to serve a predetermined market created by the primary service with which it is associated. This often leads to extremely varied markets made up of a range of different consumer groups, the best examples being large general hospitals where a whole range of capabilities (physical and mental), age, socioeconomic and lifestyle groups will be present. It is these two factors, the predetermined market and the variety of consumer groups, that present the major challenges to the welfare catering sector.

Despite the above, it is nevertheless possible to identify a number of general consumer need characteristics in the welfare catering sector. These include nutrition, social role, variety and location.

Nutrition

More than in any other sector, the nutritional needs of consumers are given particular attention by welfare caterers. The nutritional role of any welfare provision will however be determined by the contribution it is expected to make to the overall diet. With school-children, for example, the school meal is only one of a number of feeding opportunities during the day and should therefore be seen within the context of the child's whole diet. Care homes providing 24-hour care on the other hand, provide the resident's whole diet and should therefore plan to meet the appropriate nutritional standards for that type of person and their lifestyle. Despite this, the primary role of any meal programme must be a nutritional one and, conscious of this fact, operators within the welfare sector generally try to balance the need to encourage people to eat whilst responding to nutritional guidelines such as the NACNE (National Advisory Committee on Nutritional Education) Report 1983, the COMA (Committee on Medical Aspects of Food Policy) Report 1984 and more recent reports such as The Health of the Nation 1994 and Nutritional Aspects of Cardiovascular Disease 1994.

The nutritional role of welfare meals has been most vigorously debated in the school meals service. Although guidance on nutritional standards had been given prior to the 1944 Education Act, it was not until the Provision of Milk and Meals Regulations of 1945 that specific nutritional requirements were made. These remained largely unchanged until the 1980 Education Act when the government removed the requirement to provide meals of a defined nutritional standard (except for the children of parents who received supplementary benefit or family income supplement). There has been much debate about this policy ever since and there have even been questions asked in the House of Commons. Despite this there are still no minimum nutritional requirements for school meals.

In hospitals, meal programmes often play a significant part in the overall medical care. For this reason special diets play a significant role in hospital catering and most hospital kitchens include a special diet bay where meals to meet the particular needs of specific patients can be produced. In addition to diets for conditions such as diabetes and coeliac disease and other more specialist diets such as low-potassium diets, reducing diets and renal diets are also provided. An example of how advanced the provision of special diets has become is the provision of sterile diets for patients in isolator tents. Patients suffering from severe combined immune deficiency disease or aplastic anaemia have to be treated in sterile environments, provided by isolator tents, and any food introduced into the tent must be either aseptic canned foods or irradiated foods.

Social Role

The social role of meals in the welfare sector has been recognized for some time. The social psychological support provided by meals, particularly in terms of security, is identified by McKenzie who stated that; 'Food acts as an aid to security. Thus when everything seems to be going wrong we comfort ourselves that things are "alright really" by turning to established favourite dishes.'[9] As long ago as the 1950s Dichter (1954) identified that

> The cold cup of coffee ... has deep emotional meaning. To the insecure patient it is a sign. Good hot coffee is symbolic of the home away from home, of being welcome. Bad coffee is the perfect symbol that he is a stranger, that he is receiving what amounts to the orphan's negligent care.[10]

Clearly the role of meals goes beyond the purely nutritional to include wider concepts of care. In health and social care, meal times often represent the only fixed points in the day and frequently the only opportunities to socialize. This has also been recognized in the meals-on-wheels service where in many cases the delivery of meals is one of the few regular forms of contact for the recipient and thus plays a social and monitoring function. In school meals the social role is somewhat different. A study in Gloucestershire[11] established that parents identify the social role of school meals as a key strength of the service. Specifically they identified that they provide one of the few occasions when children can eat together in a fairly formal traditional manner so that children develop social skills.

Choice and Variety

As well as providing nutritionally sound meals it is essential that caterers provide a choice of meals to ensure that all consumers have an alternative that is acceptable to them. Without choice it is likely that some people would find the offered meal unacceptable for reasons of preference, medical condition, religion or beliefs. Without the provision of an alternative some consumers may fail to eat meals, and certainly uneaten meals make no contribution to the diet regardless of their nutritional content.

In the longer term, variety is also important in maintaining interest and enthusiasm for meals. The extent to which variety needs to be offered is largely a function of the frequency with which meals are taken and length of time for which the meals are required. In hospitals, where the average length of stay is eight days,[12] two-week cyclical menus are normal. In situations where meals are required more long-term however, such as schools and care homes, more variety is likely and four-week cyclical menus would not be unusual.

Location

Unlike other foodservice sectors, welfare caterers have to plan for the fact that because of limited physical or mental capabilities, many of their consumers will not be readily able to feed themselves and that in many cases they will not be able to go to restaurants or other central meal locations. This characteristic of the welfare sector requires that in these situations, meals on wheels and hospitals for example, the prepared meals have to be transported to the consumers, who are sometimes in remote locations distant from central production facilities. A number of systems have been developed to address the problems associated with the transportation of meals and these are discussed later in this chapter.

Consumer Orientation

Foodservice operators have recognized that the key issue in welfare catering has become one of market needs analysis rather than market segmentation. Through analysing the specific needs of their consumers operators seek to identify the key factors that need to be satisfied with a view to tailoring their product/service to match these needs. In this way it is anticipated that effectiveness and consumer satisfaction can be maximized. This focus on consumer needs is illustrated by the fact that many hospitals conduct regular surveys of consumer attitudes to the food service provision. The Gloucester Royal Hospital, for example, conducts regular questionnaire-based surveys which are supplemented by personal discussions with individual patients. Indeed the hospital seeks to meet individual needs by actually encouraging patients to discuss their requirements with the catering management team.

Similar approaches have been adopted in other parts of the welfare catering sector including school meals and meals on wheels. The school meals service in Gloucestershire, for example, commissioned a major study of consumer attitudes to primary and secondary school meals in the county. As a result of this study it made a number of changes to its operational and marketing strategies.

MARKETING

It is often assumed that because welfare catering deals with a captive market there is no need for marketing. This is a commercially dangerous assumption, particularly in light of the current competitive environment as described earlier. Recent experience has shown that marketing planning is an essential component in the provision of quality meals services. Whilst market segmentation is not necessarily appropriate, market analysis in terms of needs is essential to the development and provision of a consumer-oriented service. Marketing plans in terms of product/service specification, price (where appropriate), location and distribution, and promotion should then be generated in response to the findings of the market needs analysis. By following market-orientated strategies it should be possible to maximise uptake and thereby benefit from economies of scale. Maximizing the uptake of nutritionally balanced meals should also contribute to improved diets in the target consumer group. Apart from these reasons, the fact that contracts are invariably monitored by client organizations should persuade contractors that a market-oriented approach is appropriate.

The development of branding is perhaps the clearest indication that market orientation is going to be a key factor in the future of contract catering. The Compass Group has introduced its own Famous Foods brands including Upper Crust and Café Select, but perhaps more significantly it also has exclusive agreements with Pizza Hut and BurgerKing. Gardner Merchant has introduced McDonald's, Pret a Manger and Dunkin' Donuts to some of its contracts, whilst Sutcliffe has developed its own brands including Stripes American Diner, La Bonne Baguette, Zefferelli's and Jackets-no ties.

OPERATIONAL SYSTEMS

The challenges of catering in the welfare sector, particularly in terms of large volumes and the transportation of meals, have led to the development of a number of sophisticated foodservice systems. Whilst the systems adopted in each of the welfare areas are different there are a number of general themes common to several of them. These common themes include central production, meal preservation, meal distribution, and meal regeneration.

Central Production Facilities

Perhaps the most fundamental decision in many situations is whether to centralize or decentralize meal production. Decentralization involves the development of multiple production and service units located close to the point of consumption. Centralized systems involve the development of a large-scale central production unit (CPU) which produces the meals in one central location. Meals are then either distributed hot, direct to recipients, or in a preserved form (chilled or frozen) to a number of satellite end-kitchens, which are located closer to the point of consumption, and where the meals are regenerated and then served locally.

The centralization–decentralization question has been an issue in hospital catering for many years, the debate centring around assumptions of economic efficiencies in centralized systems and quality advantages in decentralized systems. A study by Thompson *et al.* helped resolve the debate by making a direct comparison between centralized and decentralized systems operating under similar conditions at the Stamford Hospital, Connecticut.[13] They concluded that although there were no significant differences in customer satisfaction or service temperatures, they calculated that there were possible labour cost savings of 20 per cent with the centralized system. This led to the widespread adoption of centralized systems in both the USA and the UK.

There are nevertheless a number of advantages and disadvantages associated with the use of centralized systems which should be fully considered before their implementation. The advantages include:

- Higher labour productivity as a result of mass production techniques.
- Lower labour costs – reduced by as much as 20 per cent for large units.
- Higher productivity from facilities and machinery which can be utilized for extended periods.
- The need for fewer skilled staff, most of whom are located at the CPU. Skilled staff are not normally required at the satellite kitchens.
- Savings in materials costs through bulk purchasing and closer control at the central unit.
- Improved control over quality and food safety systems – particularly in terms of the ability to demonstrate due diligence.
- Greater standardization leading to improved reliability and consistency of product.
- Lower capital investment per meal produced.
- More social working hours for most of the production staff.

The disadvantages of centralized systems include the following:

- The need for locating, purchasing and obtaining planning consent for an appropriate site for the CPU.
- In the event of contamination the number of consumers affected will be many times that of a single cook-serve location.

- Any breakdown of the system or problems with staff (e.g. labour relations) is likely to have major implications.

An alternative to the development of CPUs, and yet one that retains the advantages of centralized production systems, is the purchasing of ready meals in either frozen or chilled form. A number of National Health Service hospitals have adopted this approach as have several meals-on-wheels services including the London Borough of Bromley and Oxford County Council who have both opted for frozen meals.

Central production units have become less fashionable in the 1990s, particularly in the sector that adopted them in the 1980s, namely the hospital sector. It is estimated that the average CPU cost £3 million to set up. For a district health authority with five or more hospitals, such investment was acceptable, even though 'some of the claims and costings made for cook-chill CPUs at the time of commissioning were optimistic in the extreme'.[14] The government's recent health reforms, however, have resulted in 90 per cent of hospitals opting out of health authorities by adopting or seeking to adopt trust status. This has left many CPUs, located at one hospital, without the demand from the other hospitals they were previously catering for, except in a 'handful' of cases. It was estimated in 1993 that there were 39 big cook-chill CPUs operating at capacities well below their optimum levels.[15] By definition, all centralized systems require the support of delivery systems and preservation methods, the nature of which will be determined by the delivery distances and times. The range of alternative approaches is shown in Figure 16.1.

Meal Preservation

The second major strategic choice for welfare caterers (after centralization) is to select the most appropriate form of meal preservation. Initially, welfare catering systems depended on the warm-holding of foods during delivery. This was usually achieved through the use of various types of insulated or heated containers. Early meals on wheels were delivered using a range of insulation-based methods including wooden hay boxes, wrapping in old blankets and virtually anything else that would retain heat. In hospitals delivery systems have been based on plates with heat store elements, electrically heated trolleys and insulated trays.

Warm-holding is most suited to situations where consumption takes place within a short time of production (i.e. where the delivery times are short). This is because with increased warm-holding the palatability, appearance and nutritional value of meals deteriorate rapidly. In terms of food safety the critical factor for these meals is that the food temperature should be maintained at over 63°C from cooking to final service to the consumer. For this reason insulated systems are usually limited to situations where meals can be loaded at a minimum temperature of 80°C and delivered within 30 minutes. Where these requirements cannot be met heated delivery systems are necessary.

Preservation systems that extend the delivery/storage time include cook-chill, cook-freeze and *sous-vide*. Each of these approaches has a number of advantages and disadvantages in terms of meal production, delivery and quality.

Cook-freeze is based upon preservation through the blast freezing of meals down to below −18°C. Meals preserved in this way can be stored for several weeks which gives much greater flexibility and in their solid state these meals are easily handled and transported. A significant advantage with frozen meals is that with their extended storage

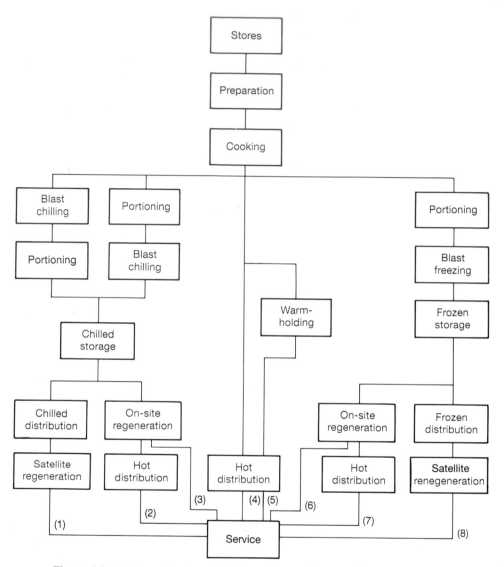

Figure 16.1   Alternative hospital foodservice systems.
Source: Jones, P. (1988) *Foodservice Operations* (2nd edition), London: Cassell, p. 104.

times it is possible to deliver several meals in one delivery and therefore reduce the frequency of deliveries. This is a particular advantage for the meals-on-wheels service where deliveries can be made once a week to those recipients with freezers. Regeneration can be either from the frozen state or after thawing. Regeneration from frozen requires that thorough reheating throughout must be ensured whilst defrosting must be achieved in a temperature-controlled environment. Another advantage of frozen meals is that evidence of thawing makes it obvious when the systems fails. There are however some drawbacks with cook-freeze. Some food items are not suitable for freezing, these include eggs, salads, soft fruits and some sauces. Recipes may need modification; some sauces for example may separate and will therefore need modified starch to bind the emulsion. Finally, the costs of freezing and low-temperature storage are greater than for chilling.

Cook-chill systems are based on the rapid chilling of meals down to 3°C (within 90 minutes) and storage at between 0°C and 3°C. Under these conditions meals can be stored for up to five days including the day of production and the day of service. The advantages of this system are that there is little or no adverse affect on meal presentation, palatability or nutritional value, and it can be used for all foodstuffs, although there may need to be modifications for some menu items such as sauces. The disadvantages with cook-chill are fourfold. Firstly, the whole system needs very close control and monitoring to ensure that health risks are minimized. This is particularly critical in terms of demonstrating due diligence. Hazard analysis and management will become key issues for such systems with the implementation of the Food Hygiene Regulations 1995. Secondly, the critical and narrow range of temperatures involved demands extremely high operational standards. There is also the risk of large-scale loss of meals where temperature requirements are not met. Thirdly, because of adverse publicity in the early years of its implementation there is some consumer resistance to cook-chill systems. Finally, unlike for frozen meals, there is no easy way to detect breakdowns in the storage system. In the USA temperature-sensitive coloured tags are used to detect rises in temperature above 5°C.

Sous-vide is the most recent alternative for meal preservation. It is based on the packing of meals in high-barrier plastic pouches that look similar to the vacuum packaging used in food retailing. Raw, blanched or semi-cooked foods are placed in the bags and are then cooked, chilled and stored at 0°C–3°C. The advantages of this process are that it extends the storage time of the meals to up to 21 days; minimizes food deterioration (particularly that due to dehydration); reduces cooking loss; reduces nutrient loss; and protects food from contamination. Despite these advantages, *sous-vide* has not been seen as applicable to the welfare catering sector largely because of costs. The capital costs associated with establishing the system are significant and there are also revenue costs associated with the packaging which make meals expensive.

Distribution Systems

The distribution requirements of meals will be largely determined by the type of preservation adopted. As previously discussed, where hot meals are being transported they will either have to be insulated or placed in heated containers to ensure maintenance of the meals above the minimum temperature of 63°C. With storage time critical to the quality of meals in these systems, distribution networks must be designed to minimize delivery times.

Chilled meals present a similar problem of temperature control during distribution. Indeed, the problem is accentuated by the very narrow band of permissible temperatures (0°C to 8°C) which are unlikely to be maintained by merely insulating the meals. For this reason it is essential that chilled meals are distributed in refrigerated transport with temperature monitoring equipment. It should be noted that although the legal maximum storage temperature is 8°C, it is good practice to store meals at 0°C to 3°C.

Frozen meals should also be distributed at their storage temperature (i.e. frozen). It might be tempting to allow these meals to thaw during delivery but thawing without temperature control is an unacceptable hazard. Delivery in a chilled condition would also create potential problems since such meals would have to be regenerated and consumed on the day of delivery thereby reducing flexibility at the local level. There is also the risk that they may be refrozen or stored at the satellite location.

Regeneration

One of the advantages of hot meal delivery is that it requires no regeneration and therefore no heating equipment at the point of consumption. Systems that employ preservation techniques, however, inevitably require some form of regeneration at the local level. Suitable technologies for the regeneration of meals include infra-red ovens, convection ovens and combination steam ovens. Microwave ovens are only suitable for the regeneration of individual meals, meals on wheels for example, and therefore have limited use in high volume-feeding situations such as hospitals, schools and luncheon clubs.

The regeneration of frozen meals from the frozen state requires particular care in terms of ensuring that the whole food mass is thoroughly heated to an acceptable temperature; that is, above 63°C. Frozen meals present particular problems for microwave ovens which can tend to leave ice pockets whilst heating the rest of the food mass. The solution is to heat the food slowly allowing conduction to stabilize the heat distribution through the food and therefore thaw any ice pockets.

SCHOOLS

Although the provision of school meals was encouraged by the Education (Provision of Meals) Act 1906, no statutory requirement to provide school meals was made until after the Second World War when the Education Act 1944, implemented by the Provision of Milk and Meals Regulations 1945, required all education authorities to provide meals at all maintained schools for all children who desired them. The Act also laid down minimum nutritional standards, namely 20g of protein, 25–30g of fat, 630–1000 kilocalories and suitable amounts of other nutrients including vitamins and minerals. This legislation provided the basis of the national school meals service that was to prevail in the same basic form until 1980. As discussed earlier, the Education Act 1980 empowered local authorities to determine the nature and extent of the school meals service they would provide and to set the prices for them (although they were still required to provide free school meals for those eligible for them). This legislation has had a radical affect on the nature of the school meals service in the years since 1980 and led to considerable debate about the continued need for minimum nutritional standards and the wider role of school meals in children's diets.

Within the context of government requirements to reduce expenditure, individual local authorities exercised their autonomy in a variety of ways. Some reduced their provision to the statutory minimum, Buckinghamshire, Dorset and Lincolnshire for example, whilst others such as Merton and Croydon contracted the service out to commercial operators. Many authorities however chose to maintain the service through reducing costs, charging prices that would cover costs and providing foods that children would buy. These policies led to a major change in style of service where traditional set meal arrangements were replaced by cash cafeteria systems which were defined by the Inner London Education Authority as 'a service where items on the tariff are separately priced, the charge being related to the standard meal charge, and where pupils have the freedom to buy as much or as little as they wish. In each cash cafeteria it is possible for children to buy items

Table 16.2 School pupils in the UK by type of school (000s).

	1970/71	1980/81	1990/91	1992/93
Public sector schools				
Nursery	50	89	105	109
Primary	5,902	5,171	4,955	5,077
Secondary	3,555	4,606	3,473	3,606
Non-maintained schools	621	619	613	607
Special schools	103	148	114	115
Total	10,230	10,633	9,260	9,513

Source: Central Statistical Office, 1995.

equivalent to a full school meal ...'. The cash cafeteria is now the dominant style of food service system in the school meals service at secondary level. Whilst it brings a number of benefits in terms of cost/revenue and in encouraging pupils to eat, there are also concerns particularly in terms of the affect such systems have on children's diets.

The School Meals Market

Table 16.2 shows the number of school pupils in the United Kingdom from 1970/71 to 1992/93. The total number of schoolchildren in the UK reached a peak in 1977 when there were 11.3 million pupils. Since then the number fell to 9.2 million in 1990 rising again in 1992/93 to 9.5 million. Regardless of these variations the potential school meals market is clearly very significant and it this potential volume of business in a captive environment that has been attracting commercial operators to the sector in recent years.

Table 16.3 shows the number of meals served in public sector schools 1979 to 1993. These figures show that despite the large potential market discussed above, only 45 per cent of children had school meals in 1993. In fact the proportion of children taking school meals has declined from 64 per cent in 1979 to a low of 43 per cent in 1989/90. In the light of discussions on schoolchildren's diets (see below) it is interesting to note that 'other arrangements' such as chip shops and cafes accounted for just under a quarter of all lunch time meals in 1993.

With the publication of the NACNE (National Advisory Committee on Nutritional Education) Report 1983 and the COMA (Committee on Medical Aspects of Food Policy) Report 1984 concern focused on the nutritional aspects of school meals. The policy of allowing choice had led to concern about the effects it would have on the diets of children. The issue was referred to the Sub-committee on Nutritional Surveillance of COMA which carried out a study examining the contribution of school meals to the overall diets of schoolchildren. The study concluded that there were 'no significant differences between the average energy or nutrient intakes of children taking school meals from outlets offering a free choice cafeteria style service and those obtaining a fixed price school meal'.[16]

Nutrition education had already been identified as a key factor in improving the eating behaviour of children[17] and the role of school meals as a vehicle for such education has also been identified.[18] In response, many local authorities developed their operational and marketing plans around the theme of healthy eating. East Sussex Education Authority

Table 16.3 School children's lunch-time meals in Great Britain.

	1979 (%)	1986 (%)	1991 (%)	1993 (%)
Packed lunches	12	31	31	32
Paid school meals	52	31	31	29
Free school meals	12	17	12	16
Other arrangements	24	21	25	23
All pupils	100	100	100	100

Sources: Central Statistical Office 1995, Department of Education and Science 1979, Chartered Institute of Public Finance and Accountancy 1986.

produced a promotional campaign to promote school meals and raise children's awareness of the nutritional implications of food choice; in Durham a 'Right Bite' theme was developed offering wholefood, low-fat and low-sugar menu items. Group 90, the school contract caterers on the Isle of Wight, have introduced a healthy eating system based on a traffic light theme where children are advised to choose only one red coded meal item, up to two amber items and as many green items as they like.

What Do Consumers Want?

A key factor in the provision of quality services is an understanding of consumer needs. Gloucestershire County Council commissioned studies of consumer attitudes to school meals in primary and secondary schools.[19] Whilst in secondary schools pupil attitudes were investigated, for the primary school study the attitudes of parents were investigated. The findings of these studies provide an interesting perspective on what school meals consumers want.

The parents of primary schoolchildren identified a number of key issues. Healthy eating was by far the most significant issue for parents who specifically identified the need for less convenience food, chips to be offered less frequently, more wholefoods, no tuck shops or ice cream vans and more guidance for children on food choice. The social role of school meals was a significant issue, parents identifying that school meals provide one of the few opportunities for children to eat together in a fairly formal, traditional manner. They were also of the opinion that social skills should be taught and that the dining environment should be kept quiet and peaceful. Other issues identified by parents were value for money, the impracticality of going home, and the extra work associated with making sandwiches.

The study of secondary school pupils, on the other hand, revealed another set of issues. The dining environment is a major determining factor in pupils' perceptions of school meals. Where dining-rooms are perceived to be boring, cramped and oppressive pupils prefer to spend their lunch-time elsewhere. With regard to quality of meals, many pupils said that they would pay more for meals outside school, or even save their money, rather than have school meals. Choice and variety of foods was the third most important issue, whilst traditional meals service was perceived to offer limited choice, cash cafeterias were seen as a positive improvement.

The school meals response to these findings was to develop both operational and marketing plans to address the issues raised. These included the development of a 'Healthier

Eating Manual' to advise catering supervisors, the introduction of a new preformed plastic-tray based service and a marketing and promotional campaign. The result of these strategies was that uptake rose from 27 to 32 per cent despite a price increase during the period.

HOSPITALS

The modern hospital catering service was created as a result of concerns about patient diets during the Second World War. The Briscoe Committee 1943 identified extreme nutritional inadequacy in the diets of patients in London hospitals and recommended that specialist catering departments be set up within hospitals. This recommendation was implemented as part of the National Health Service Act 1946 along with the appointment of professional full-time catering officers who introduced meal choice and the use of recognized recipes and methods of food preparation. Although significant improvements were made in the service up to the 1970s, the provision remained below the expected catering standards of the time and a number of critical reports, including the Egon Ronay Organization and the Consumer Association, were published during the 1970s and 1980s. This and the government's demands for efficiencies in public spending led to legislation requiring competitive tendering.

Size of the Market

The size of the hospital catering market is indicated by the number of in-patients and day-case attendance. In 1992/93 there were 7.8 thousand in-patient cases in England with an average stay of eight days. This equates to a total of 62.4 thousand patient days for which catering services would be required. In addition to this day-cases would add around 2.7 million patient days [20] Assuming an average of two meals per day, these figures would indicate a total market of something like 5.4 million meals per year. As with school meals, this is clearly a very significant captive market that commercial contractors are now looking towards as an opportunity to expand their businesses.

Operational Systems

All the operational issues previously discussed – centralization, preservation, distribution and regeneration – apply to hospital catering systems. Centralization brought with it the problems associated with the transportation of meals, particularly the maintenance of food temperatures. Early delivery systems were based on bulk delivery using electrically heated trolleys. Continuing problems with the quality of food delivered in this way led to the development of highly specialized systems specifically designed for hospitals.

Tray-service systems

The development of tray-service systems has perhaps been the most radical development leading to a number of variations on the basic tray theme. The first of these tray systems was the *Ganymede* system which was based on plates with heated metal pellets that release heat into the plate over the period of delivery. A number of other similar heat store systems have been developed including the Grundy *Finessa* and the *Heatrex* system.

Day 1 Monday	Day 2 Tuesday	Day 3 Wednesday	Day 4 Thursday	Day 5 Friday	Day 6 Saturday
Vegetable Lasagne	Vegetable Pizza	Roast Lamb	Chicken Sweetcorn Pie	Fried Fillet of Fish	Minced Beef Lasagne
Grilled Ham Steak & Pineapple	Beef Casserole	Spinach Potato Bake	Vegetable Hot Pot	Poached Fish	Cheese & Tomato Flan
Shepherd's Pie	Poached Fish	Minced Chicken	Grilled Sausages	Vegetable Curry	BBQ Spare Rib Chop
Gravy	Parsley Sauce	Mint Sauce	Parsley Potatoes	Sweet & Sour Pork	BBQ Sauce
		Gravy			Minced Beef
Sautéd Potatoes	New Potatoes	Roast Potatoes	Creamed Potatoes	Rice	Jacket Wedges
Creamed Potatoes	Creamed Potatoes	Creamed Potatoes	Sliced Green Beans	Chipped Potatoes	Creamed Potatoes
Sliced Green Beans	Carrots	Cauliflower	Baked Beans	Creamed Potatoes	Sweetcorn
Sweetcorn	Peas	Mixed Vegetables		Peas	Courgettes
				Carrots	
Eve's Pudding	Lemon Meringue Pie	Apple Pie	Apricot Crumble	Fruit Flan	Fresh Fruit Salad
Custard	Low Fat Yoghurt	Fresh Fruit	Custard	Milk Pudding	Cream
Fresh Fruit	Fresh Fruit	Fresh Fruit	Apricots in juice	Fruit Cocktail	Milk Pudding

Day 7 Sunday	Day 8 Monday	Day 9 Tuesday	Day 10 Wednesday	Day 11 Thursday	Day 12 Friday
Roast Chicken	Chicken Fricassé	Steak & Kidney Pie	Roast Turkey	Lamb & Vegetable Casserole	Fried Fillet of Fish
Seasoning	Vegetable Sauce with Pasta	Chilli Bean Casserole	Vegetable Milanaise	Cheese & Broccoli Flan	Poached Fillet of Fish
		Honey Roast Ham	Poached Fish with Cheese Sauce	Minced Beef Lasagne	Cheesy Ratatouille
				Gravy	Beef Curry
					Tartare Sauce

Custard
Milk Pudding
Fresh Fruit

Day 13   Saturday

Shepherd's Pie
Cheese & Tomato Pizza
Sausages
Gravy
Mashed Creamed Potato
Chipped Potatoes
Mixed Vegetables
Baked Beans
Fresh Fruit
Pineapple Upside-down
 Sponge
Custard
Milk Pudding

Milk Pudding
Low Fat Yogurt

Day 14   Sunday

Roast Beef
Cauliflower Cheese
Savoury Minced Beef
Gravy
Yorkshire Pudding
Roast Potatoes
Creamed Potatoes
Carrots
Green Vegetables
Trifle
Fresh Fruit
Milk Pudding

Milk Pudding
Yogurt

Milk Pudding

Figure 16.2   Hospital lunch menu cycle.
Source: Gloucester Royal NHS Trust Hospital.

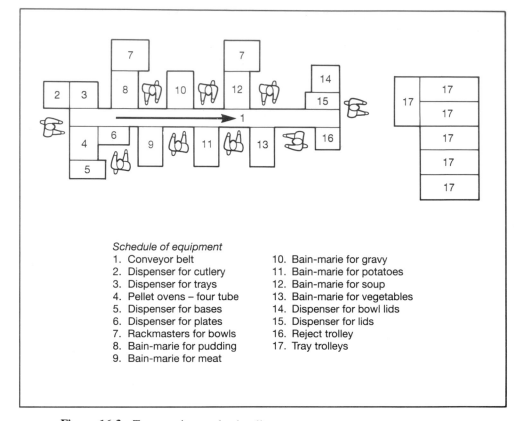

Figure 16.3 Tray-service production line.
Source: Jones, P. (1988) *Foodservice Operations* (2nd edition), London: Cassell, p. 115.

These systems have been successful in keeping meals hot but have tended to suffer from the problem of drying foods out.

Another approach to tray delivery has been the use of heated trolleys as opposed to heated plates or plate bases. Southmead Hospital in Bristol uses the *Traymeal* system for the delivery of 750–800 meals per day with maximum delivery times of 20 minutes. This system is based on trolleys which have hot and ambient compartments for different meal components. The hot compartment is heated by a heat store which is electrically charged for 40 minutes before delivery.

A third approach to tray delivery is based upon insulation rather than additional heat. These systems are based on insulated moulded plastic trays which contain two to four bays for meal items. Because there is insulation between the different bays it is possible to place hot and cold foods adjacent to each other in the same tray with them remaining hot or cold as originally loaded. *Temprite*, which is probably the leading system of this kind, has been installed in both the Gloucester Royal NHS Trust Hospital and the Cheltenham General Hospital. Experience indicates that these systems are suitable for deliveries of up to 30 minutes where loading temperatures of at least 80°C can be achieved.

All the above tray systems depend upon the same logistical support system. Menus are sent to wards in advance to allow patients to make their choice of meals – examples of lunch and supper menus are shown in Figure 16.2. These menus are then returned to the catering department and used as the basis for subsequent meal production. Food is then portioned and plated on trays using a conveyor belt system, as illustrated in Figure 16.4. As trays are completed and reach the end of the conveyor they are placed into trolleys and immediately conveyed to the ward. The logistics of this system are critical and precise timings have to be met to ensure that meals are delivered in time and in an acceptable form. Normally the meal service will be staggered over a period of one to two hours with each ward being processed over a specific time slot. On arrival at the ward the meal trays should be immediately distributed to patients to ensure receipt in an acceptable condition.

Cook-chill systems

Cook-chill meals can be chilled in either individual portions or in bulk multiple portions depending on the desired food service style. At Frenchay Hospital in Bristol, for example, bulk chilled meals are produced at the hospital's CPU which are then loaded into insulated trolleys and are then regenerated at ward level in convection ovens. The reason for bulk meals in this situation is primarily in order to facilitate family-style service in the ward. Whilst this is acceptable for the majority of patients, for some it is not suitable and for these patients meals are plated from the original bulk supplies. Individual chilled meals can be portioned either before chilling, which increases storage space requirements, or after chilling which creates problems of temperature control during the portioning process. The regeneration of pre-portioned meals can also create problems in terms of the varied rates at which different foods heat up.

Ready meal systems

A number of hospitals are now adopting a ready meals system based on either frozen or chilled meals. This approach removes the need for a CPU and the associated problems of food manufacturing allowing the hospital to concentrate on regeneration and service. The use of specialized food manufacturing companies enables hospitals to benefit from highly advanced technical facilities that they would be unlikely to be able to provide or operate themselves. The choice of appropriate suppliers could also be beneficial in terms of demonstrating due diligence.

CARE HOMES

Demographic trends in the UK population have already been discussed. In particular the dependency ratio was identified as 63 in 1992 and is expected to rise to 82 by 2036 when the number of pensioners is expected to reach 17 million, accounting for approximately 23 per cent of the population. This growth in the elderly dependent population has led to a growing need for long-term care in residential homes of which there are now around 17,000 in the UK.[21] Table 16.4 shows that there were a total of 323,000 residents in homes in Great Britain with 264,000 in homes for the elderly and 8000 in homes for the physically disabled. The number of people in these homes has increased by over 40 per cent since 1981. Care homes are either operated by local authorities, voluntary organizations or the private sector (as discussed on p. 87).

In Gloucestershire, for instance, there are 124 registered care homes with an average

Table 16.4 Residents in homes and hostels in Great Britain (000s).

	1981	1991	1993
For the elderly	198	272	264
For the physically disabled		8	8
For those with learning difficulties		33	37
For the mentally ill		10	12
All residents		323	321

Source: Central Statistics Office.

occupancy of 23 people. Given that the average amount of money spent on food is £17 per person, per week, the total market is worth around £345 million per year in raw materials alone.[22] With the sector being so fragmented in terms of the proportion of small units averaging around 25 residents, and with no dominant players and virtually no structure in terms of associations, it is not an area of any great interest to commercial catering organizations.

In virtually all establishments lunch is the main meal of the day and most offer a choice of meal at lunch-time. It is normal for homes to have at least one designated cook who has primary responsibility for the menu. It is usual, however, for residents to have an input into menu planning either through informal expressions of meal preferences, through more formal meetings and in some cases suggestion boxes. The most common food production system in this sector is cook-serve where meals are prepared ready for serving between 5 and 30 minutes before service.

MEALS ON WHEELS

The meals-on-wheels service was started in the 1930s by the Invalid Kitchens of London. It was further developed during the Second World War by the National Old People's Welfare Committee (NOPWC) and the Women's Royal Voluntary Service (WRVS) largely in response to the inability of the elderly, sick and frail to attend communal feeding centres of the time. After the war, the NOPWC largely concentrated on the development of luncheon clubs, whilst the WRVS was the leading organization in the development of meals-on-wheels. By the 1960s a national network of meals-on-wheels schemes had been developed. This was helped by the National Assistance Act 1962 which had permitted local authorities to provide meals for old people in their homes and to help voluntary organizations by allowing the use of local authority premises and equipment. Over time, local authorities generally assumed control over meals provision, with the WRVS largely concerned with delivering the meals.

Market Size and Demand

Consistent with the demographic trends already discussed, the demand for meals on wheels has been steadily rising. The number of meals served rose from 13 million in 1969 to 38 million in 1992/93. The number of meals served to the elderly and physically disabled served elsewhere, i.e. in luncheon clubs, in 1992/93 was 15 million.[23]

In terms of what users of this service expect, a number of studies have examined the attitudes of the elderly to meals on wheels. One of the most recent investigated the attitudes of recipients in Leicester.[24] The main findings of the study were as follows:

- Most recipients (86 per cent) were either satisfied or very satisfied with the service. This could, however, be the result of fear that criticism would lead to withdrawal of meals.
- The key determinant on the perceived quality of meals was the quality of the protein element (usually meat or fish). Sausages and beefburgers were considered to be inferior substitutes for meat.
- The 'easy to cook' meal, delivered weekly or monthly, was not a popular alternative. Such meals require suitable storage and cooking facilities in the home.
- The most acceptable delivery time was 12.00 to 12.30 p.m., with most complaints from those who received meals before 11.30 a.m. and after 1.30 p.m.
- Evening meals were not popular. Most elderly people see lunch time as the principal meal time of the day, and probably have some concerns about opening their doors on dark evenings.
- Mashed and croquette potatoes were particularly disliked. In view of the fact that the potato is an important source of ascorbic acid in the diet, meals-on-wheels menu planners need to think of other ways in which this nutritional element may be provided, for instance by offering cabbage as a vegetable, or orange juice.

These findings provide useful guidance on the provision of meals on wheels. Research indicates that the service achieves far more than just feeding people. The daily visit to deliver the meal also enables a check to be made on the well-being of recipients and also fulfils a social role in terms of enabling people living on their own to meet and talk with someone, however briefly, every day.

Nutritional Aspects of Meals of Wheels

As identified above, welfare catering in general is particularly concerned with effective nutrition. Until the DHSS circular 'Organization of Meals on Wheels' in 1970, nutritional objectives in this sector had not been very clear. With the involvement of local authorities however, a concern for diet and nutrition emerged. This 1970 circular noted that meals on wheels would only make a significant contribution to nutrition if at least five hot meals a week were served; protein intake was important and could be supplemented by the addition of dried milk; fats and carbohydrates in excess should be avoided; fruit should be provided once a week to boost ascorbic acid in the diet; and delay should be avoided in delivery due to the loss of vitamin content.

A number of studies[25,26,27] have investigated nutritional aspects of provision and the role of meals on wheels in diets of the elderly. They identified a number of important nutritional points as follows. Meals on wheels are only part of the total diet of the elderly, many of whom receive meals from friends, neighbours and family as well. The diets of the house-bound elderly exhibit a number of characteristics such as low intakes of vitamin D and ascorbic acid. Although average portion sizes, energy values and protein content of meals are adequate, there are often wide variations between meals and the nutritional value of the meal is considerably reduced if there is extended warm-holding of the finished meal and/or if plate waste is high. Despite such research, there are no specific nationwide nutritional specifications for meals on wheels, although in 1992 the Advisory

Body for Social Service Catering did recommend quality standards, including nutritional guidelines, in their publication *A Recommended Standard for Community Meals*.

Another feature of this service is the need to recognize and serve the needs of people with a range of dietary needs. Some of these needs relate to medical conditions which may require salt-free or low-sugar content. Other dietary needs relate to ethnic origin and may necessitate the provision of kosher or halal dishes, for instance, 10 per cent of meals served by the Westminster Meals Service are kosher.[28]

Operational Systems

The meals-on-wheels service has traditionally focused on the delivery of hot meals. The actual transportation of meals was originally on foot, with the first 'wheels' being those of bicycles and prams! Maintaining meals at an acceptable temperature was a problem and a number of improvised insulation methods were adopted, including the use of hay boxes, old blankets, Canadian Red Cross dinner pails, and virtually anything else that would retain heat. After the war, these methods were replaced by either heated systems, such as Food Conveyor's 'Hotlock' which maintained heat through the combustion of charcoal, or by insulated containers. In the 1980s, the traditional Hotlocks were phased out and replaced by electric alternatives such as Corsair and Excelarc. Despite its widespread usage there has always been concern about hot meal delivery in three main areas – acceptability (delivery temperature and food quality), nutrition, and hygiene. Delivered meal temperature has frequently been an issue of concern. One study of meals on wheels[29] found that the temperature ranged between 30°C and 62°C, with no meals meeting the required temperature of 63°C. Warm-holding also affects the nutrient content of meals. Ascorbic acid loss of over 75 per cent was found in creamed potatoes during the first 30 minutes of storage.[30]

In view of these problems, a number of alternative meals-on-wheels systems have been investigated. The University of Leeds looked at systems based on the delivery of partially prepared meals (frozen, pouch sterilized and raw-ingredient packs) which could be temporarily stored and then regenerated in the home.[31] The same study also investigated a delivery system based on the regeneration of frozen meals in a specially adapted delivery vehicle, but it was found to be around 40 per cent more expensive than the traditional approach. Although not suitable for all recipients, these systems do offer higher nutrition content and improved acceptability. More recently, the delivery of chilled meals has also been tried, however, the narrow margins for food safety have largely prevented its widespread adoption.

Despite these investigations into alternatives, most meals-on-wheels programmes still transport and deliver hotel meals, using insulated or electrically heated systems. Some authorities, including Bromley, Westminster and Oxford, have moved to a combined system, where those capable of reheating meals are delivered frozen meals weekly, while the less able continue to receive hot meals daily. Those on the frozen meal system are provided with storage and cooking equipment. The amount of choice varies from authority to authority, but one frozen meal system does offer a choice of 60 alternative dishes. Cost savings in terms of fewer deliveries, however, are unlikely to be realized since many meals are still delivered by voluntary organizations and most delivery runs have to be maintained for those still receiving hot meals.

PRISON CATERING

This is not a sector of the hospitality industry about which much is known! However, there clearly are features of provision that are unique to this sector. Firstly, 'hot food served at regular times helps keep prisoners calm and potentially riot free'.[32] Secondly, the approach to how prisoners are served will depend on the nature of the prison. These range from so-called 'open prisons' which allow inmates a fair degree of freedom, up to high-security operations with a much higher level of supervision. For instance, Glenlochil prison, fairly typical of the 20 prisons in Scotland, houses 330 prisoners. Like other sectors, costs are a major constraint. The catering budget in Scottish prisons in 1994 was just £1.50 per prisoner per day. Another distinctive feature of prison catering is that prisoners may often play a role in the preparation of food. Thus 23 prisoners in Glenlochil perform tasks such as potwashing, vegetable prepping, bakery, butchery, and kitchen portering. In some cases this is tied into enabling prisoners to gain qualifications as part of their rehabilitation. Likewise, for some prisons, the foodstuffs used are actually grown by the prisoners on prison farms and market gardens. As with other sectors of welfare catering, meal choice is often limited and in many cases prisoners select from a menu planner one or two weeks in advance in order to reduce waste.

CURRENT ISSUES AND FUTURE TRENDS

Between 1945 and the late 1970s, the welfare catering sector as a whole was relatively stable. Even the introduction of new technologies such as tray-serve systems or CPUs seemed to have little impact on the nature of the customer experience or meal product offered. However, since the early 1980s, legislative change has had a major impact on catering provision in all parts of the welfare sector. Therefore, with this unstable environment, predicting what is likely to happen in the future is extremely difficult. Two major trends are apparent however, based largely on the large scale of production undertaken in this sector. These same trends are also apparent in the flight catering industry (see p. 234). These are the impact of information systems on logistics, and the forward integration of food manufacturers into catering provision.

The evolution of computer-based information systems has led to the development of sophisticated real-time information systems in parts of the foodservice industry, particularly the fast-food sector. The welfare sector has been slow to realize the benefits such systems can bring to its large-volume, logistically complicated situations. This looks set to change, however, with contract caterers introducing their information systems to welfare contracts DSOs will have to follow suit to remain competitive. Indeed Highland Catering Services (DSO) have already introduced a system in their school meals service which provides half-hourly reports from all schools on the numbers of items sold, sales volume, number of customers by age group, the mix of paid and free meals and the average spend per customer. The system provides managers with comparative information which can then be used to monitor performance at each unit relative to other units.

With better information about consumption, welfare caterers are also better able to manage their supply chain. The development of catering products by the large-scale food manufacturers, such as the major frozen food brands like Findus and Birdseye, means that meal items can now be bought in totally ready prepared condition. Since many hospital and school kitchens have been converted into 'assembly kitchens' designed to regenerate food delivered from a CPU, it requires little change to eliminate the CPU and buy directly from manufacturers. Thus, Yorkshire Food Services, which provides meals to a large number of hospitals in the county, is increasingly buying chilled and frozen foods direct from manufacturers; whilst Brakes, a major UK supplier of prepared meals, is setting up three distribution centres in Plymouth, Aylesbury and Kettering dedicated to serving hospitals.[33]

CONCLUSION

The welfare sector of the foodservice industry differs significantly from the other sectors in three main respects. First, it has been largely part of the public sector. Employers have either been central government departments, local authorities or the National Health Service. Even though the sector has experienced great change in the last 15 years, largely related to moving provision out of the public into the private sector, many of the features that derive from a public sector history remain. For instance, this public sector tradition meant that many if not most catering workers in this sector belonged to a trade union, with all the industrial relations implications that arise from this. Secondly, the sector exists to fulfil a social purpose. The welfare caterer is still concerned with feeding very large numbers of people with standard nutritious meals, in the context of a moral duty of care as well as meeting customers' needs. Many employees have resisted 'privatization' because it appears to introduce the need to make a profit from providing a welfare service. Such resistance has not been uninfluenced by the fact that some workers have found themselves re-employed by contract caterers who have won contracts, but at rates of pay and with conditions of service less attractive than those previously offered by their public sector employer. Finally, welfare caterers serve 'consumers' with meals that are paid for by 'clients' other than the consumer. It is not unusual for these consumer and client groups to have divergent views about provision. For instance, although schoolchildren consume school meals, often the parents that pay for them have very different views as to what should be provided. As one recent survey of over 1300 parents and secondary school children identified, 'in the league tables of taste, pupils' preferences contrast strongly with what their parents would like them to eat, illustrating the difficulties school caterers face in trying to keep everyone happy all the time'.[34]

REFERENCES

1. Central Statistical Office (1995) *Social Trends 25*, Government Statistical Service, London: HMSO.
2. British Hospitality Association (1995) *Contract Catering Survey 1995*, London: British Hospitality Association.
3. Cumming, M. and Hill, B. (1992) 'Competitive tendering for National Health Service domestic services', in Teare, R. (ed.) *Managing Projects in Hospitality Organisations*, London: Cassell, pp. 77–100.
4. Jones, P. (1988) *Food Service Operations* (2nd edition), London: Cassell.
5. McDermid, K. (1989) 'In-house bids win contracts', *Caterer and Hotelkeeper*, 18 May, p. 14.
6. British Hospitality Association op. cit.
7. Central Statistical Office op. cit.
8. Ibid.
9. McKenzie, J. (1979) 'The eating environment', in Glew, G. (ed.) *Advances in Catering Technology*, London: Applied Science Publishers, pp. 474–81.

10. Dichter, E. (1954) 'A psychological study of the hospital–patient relationship', *The Modern Hospital*, Vol. 83, November, p. 61.

11. Hemmington, N.R. and Chapman, F. (1992) 'Planning in a regional school meals service', in Teare, R. (ed.) *Managing Projects in Hospitality Organisations*, London: Cassell, pp. 33–76.

12. Central Statistical Office op. cit.

13. Thompson, J.D., Hartman, J. and Pelletier, R.J. (1960) 'Two types of tray service studied side by side, Hospitals', *JAHA*, Vol. 34, 1 February 1960, pp. 82–8.

14. Gledhill, R. (1993) 'The NHS carve-up', *Caterer and Hotelkeeper*, 19 August, pp. 30–3.

15. Ibid.

16. Committee on Medical Aspects of Food Policy (1989) Sub-committee on nutritional surveillance, *The Diets of British Schoolchildren*, London: HMSO.

17. British Dietetic Association (1980) 'School meals policy statement', *Journal of Human Nutrition*, Vol. 34, pp. 316–18.

18. Ruxton, C.H.S., Kirk, T.R., Belton, N.R. and Holmes, A.M. (1993) 'School meals', *British Food Journal*, Vol. 95, No. 8, pp. 9–12.

19. Hemmington, N.R. and Chapman F. op. cit.

20. Central Statistical Office op. cit.

21. Jordan, F. (1992) *A Research Project Investigating the Relationship between Contract Catering and the Residential Care Homes Sector*, Cheltenham and Gloucester College of Higher Education.

22. Ibid.

23. Central Statistical Office op. cit.

24. Tilston, C.H., Gregson, K., Neale, R.J. and Tyne, C. (1992) 'Meals-on-wheels service in Leicester: A marketing study', *British Food Journal*, Vol. 94, No. 2, pp. 29–36.

25. Stanton, B.R.D. (1971) *Meals for the Elderly*, London: King Edward's Hospital Fund.

26. Turner, M. and Glew, G. (1982) 'Home delivered meals for the elderly – a nutritional study', *Journal of Food Technology*, Vol. 36, No. 7, pp. 72–9.

27. Davies, L. (1981) *Three Score Years ... And Then?*, London: Heinemann Medical Books.

28. Clavey, J. (1994) 'Westminster meals service', *Caterer and Hotelkeeper*, 26 May, pp. 48–50.

29. Turner, M. and Glew, G. op. cit.

30. Hill, M.A., Baron, M., Kent, J.S. and Glew, G. (1977) 'The effect of hot storage after reheating on the flavour and ascorbic acid retention of precooked frozen vegetables', in Glew, G. (ed.) *Catering Equipment and Systems Design*, London: Applied Science Publishers.

31. Armstrong, J.F., O'Sullivan, K. and Turner, M. (1980) *The Housebound Elderly – Technical Innovations in Foodservice*, Huddersfield Polytechnic.

32 Webster, J. (1995) 'An inside job', *Caterer and Hotelkeeper*, 9 February, pp. 70–71.

33 Gledhill, R. op. cit.

34. Collings, R. (1994) 'Lessons on lunch', *Caterer and Hotelkeeper*, 23 June, pp. 34–5.

SEVENTEEN

Travel Catering

DAVID KIRK AND TREVOR LAFFIN

INTRODUCTION

Travel catering is a relatively well-defined sector of the foodservice industry, which has shown modest growth in the last few years. In 1991, travel catering represented some 6–7 per cent of the total number of meals served in the UK.[1] According to the same report, the market for travel meals increased by 46 per cent between 1985 and 1991. During this same period the growth rate of meals consumed outside the home as a whole grew by only 27 per cent.

Although rail, airline and ship catering differ in terms of the types of food they offer and the systems they use to provide the service, they have many factors in common. In particular, passengers who are travelling long distances cannot make the same choices about where to eat or drink that are open to people travelling by private car. Organizations also have the operational constraints of providing staff and raw materials to a unit which moves from one location to another. This requires a sophisticated logistic planning system for the allocation of staff and distribution of materials. In this chapter each sector of travel catering will be looked at in turn – airline, rail, ferry, cruise ship and terminus catering.

AIRLINE CATERING

One of the unique aspects of airline catering is that the cost of the catering service is usually included in the price of the airline ticket. The nature of in-flight catering is fundamentally related to the airline, flight type and class of ticket. There are a number of different dimensions to this. These include the duration of flight – either long-haul or short-haul; the type of route – domestic or international; the type of flight – charter or scheduled; and class of service – budget/economy/tourist, club/business/executive, or first. Foodservice varies from a cold beverage and a pack of nuts or crackers on a short domestic flight to two or three meals served on china and accompanied by wines and liqueurs, as is found on a first-class long-haul flight. One of the main determinants of the nature of the cabin service provided is related to the duration of the flight. For example, a domestic flight from London to Manchester takes less than one hour whereas a long-haul non-stop flight from London to Los Angeles or Hong Kong takes around 13 hours.

Size and Nature of In-flight Catering

The market for in-flight meals is obviously closely related to the growth in the number of people travelling by air. In spite of the increased competition from road and rail, particularly for short-haul flights and despite changes in methods of conducting business because of electronic mail and teleconferencing, the number of air flights has increased by 7 per cent per year.[2]

However, the nature of in-flight catering is changing because of marketing, financial and operational pressures on airlines. Particularly in the case of short-haul flights, where there is competition, not only with other airlines but also with rail, airlines have responded to this pressure in different ways. Some airlines have chosen to compete on the basis of low costs and the fact that passengers need a simple and efficient journey from airport to airport. To this end, some airlines have reduced the cabin service to a simple cold snack, a trolley buffet service during the flight, or the provision of a buffet in the departure lounge to allow passengers to select their requirements for the journey.[3] In the USA, where competition on price is fierce following deregulations, many domestic flights provide no cabin service, or simply a packet of peanuts or biscuits and a non-alcoholic drink. In contrast, on many long-haul flights, airlines often choose to use the quality of their food service as a way of differentiating themselves from the competition. Even here there has been a simplification of the meals provided and an experimentation with alternatives. For example, on some transatlantic flights which take place overnight, a dinner is provided in the departure lounge prior to take-off. This allows passengers to sleep during the flight without the disturbance of cabin service.

There is a growing interdependence of airlines, particularly in the area of linking domestic networks to major intercontinental routes. This can include sharing ground production facilities, logistics and even styles of service. For example KLM and Northwest Airlines have developed a new business class for people travelling from Europe to a large number of destinations in the USA.[4] Airlines such as Virgin Atlantic are developing very strong brand-names which can be franchised to smaller airlines. These brands can also be applied to catering and other cabin services.[5]

Airlines are developing interrelated timetables to promote links between international carriers and domestic networks.[6] This has been available in the USA for some years, but is also being developed in Europe, such as the link between the domestic routes of Air UK and the international routes of KLM. British Airways is developing similar links with a number of airlines. These flights are operated as part of the British Airways timetable and operate with staff in British Airways uniforms and British Airways catering products. Many airlines are forming strategic alliances which cover not only routes but also other related activities including the joint development of flight kitchens.[7]

Markets Served

In discussing the market for airline food, we can differentiate between two different markets: that of the airlines competing for passengers on routes, and that of the in-flight catering companies seeking contracts with airlines through the price, quality and reliability of the service. As far as the airlines are concerned, the nature of the cabin service is closely related to the class of ticket. For the USA the breakdown of ticket sales[8] is Economy/Tourist (71 per cent), Business/Executive (16 per cent), and First (8 per cent).

In terms of the supply of food, beverages and other cabin requirements many airlines operate their own in-flight catering companies, with units at major airports on their routes. However, many airlines are either selling off their catering production facilities or setting them up as independent operating companies.[9] As production technologies develop, the cost of providing a catering service becomes closely related to the volume of production. Modern facilities, which can produce 40,000 meals per day, can supply the requirements of a large number of airlines.

Location

The location of in-flight operations is clearly driven by the need to service airlines and therefore facilities will develop in line with the distribution of international travel routes and destinations. Airlines may, in some circumstances, supply aircraft with enough supplies for both the outward and return leg of a flight, but it is more common for aircraft to carry supplies for a single journey. This requires that the airline secures the provision of appropriate supplies at all major airports on their routes. They may do this through their own subsidiaries or by establishing contracts with in-flight catering companies servicing each airport. In extreme cases, where a reliable contractor is not available, airlines may supply all of the food for both the outward and return leg. As new international destinations open up, there is an expanding need for new catering facilities. For example the development of international flights to the Yemen as a result of the discovery of new oil reserves has led to the need for a new catering company to operate a flight kitchen.[10]

Product Offering

The service of food and drinks to passengers on an aircraft has become a standard feature for many airlines, even on short-haul flights of less than two hours' duration. There is a case to be made for all airline passengers to be served a non-alcoholic beverage because of the dehydrating effect of flying. But many services are considerably in excess of the level of provision needed to satisfy basic physiological needs of passengers for food and drink. Another of the original functions many have been to entertain and distract passengers from what could be a tedious or frightening experience, but this function has now, to a considerable extent, been superseded by in-flight entertainment systems. However, the function of food and beverage service on aircraft has become a way of defining a unique characteristic of an airline – it is a means of product differentiation in what is otherwise a fairly standard way of covering long distances in a short period of time. Particularly where there is competition on a route, airlines may use the cabin service as a means of marketing their product.

Both the taste of food and drink and the appetite of passengers change when flying at altitude. This affects the nature of food offered and the time of service. For example, the flavour of foods become less distinct and the aroma of wines is reduced. At high altitude, many people react more strongly to alcohol and caffeine. A further effect of long-haul flights is that the body becomes dehydrated and therefore passengers are encouraged to drink non-alcoholic beverages and water at regular intervals. Because passengers are restricted in the amount of movement and exercise they can take, heavy foods and those which are difficult to digest are avoided. Many airlines, in their business and first-class service, offer a choice of light and easy-to-digest meals for those passengers who react adversely to more substantial meals whilst in the air. For example, British Airways have a 'Well-being' menu choice on many flights. The cabin service can play a large part in countering jet lag. The timing and nature of meals served is designed in relation to the time of arrival at the destination so that the flight finishes with a meal that is appropriate to the time of day at the destination.

Menu planning plays an important part in the process of providing airline meals. There are severe limitations on the service (tray size, etc.), on the technology (selecting foods and recipes which are tolerant of the time/temperature process involved) and on the needs of captive and sedentary customers. Planned menus are converted to standard recipes which are used as the basis of the in-house or contract specification to control quantities, quality and cost. Photographs are often used to communicate precise information about both the meal and tray layout. Because of the importance of meal service as a means of breaking up the monotony of a long flight journey, particular emphasis must be placed on the appearance of the meal. Attention also needs to be paid to satisfying the requirements of specific groups such as vegetarian and vegan customers and those with particular ethnic requirements. For example, in order to satisfy international customers, it may be necessary to provide kosher and halal meals.

Organization and Staffing

Flight kitchens are now being developed which have capacities in excess of 40,000 meals per day and service flights for up to 40 different airlines – for example the new facility provided by KLM at Schiphol airport. These modern in-flight kitchens are designed for year-round, 24-hour-per-day operation (17 to 18 hours for production, 4 to 5 for cleaning and maintenance) and therefore employ up to 1000 staff. The production units are divided into a number of departments, such as goods reception, central warehouse, preparation kitchens (meat, fish, vegetables), hot kitchen, cold kitchen, pastry/bakery, packing, tray assembly, trolley assembly, dispatch and waste disposal. In addition to these production areas, a number of ancillary areas are required, such as offices, changing rooms, product development kitchens and quality-control laboratories.

In all in-flight catering systems, hygiene plays an important part because of the use of high-risk products such as meat, fish and dairy products which are stored at chilled temperatures for long periods of time. Strict quality control is required, based on the principles of risk assessment, precise time temperature control, microbiological testing of products and hygiene audits of all storage and production areas. In-flight production kitchens either have their own laboratory or send materials to a commercial laboratory for testing. This testing includes the quality of all raw materials and finished dishes and the hygiene standards of all production areas. Samples of all meals produced are kept until one week after the flight has ended, in case there have been any food-related illnesses or complaints reported.

Standard Operating Procedures

Operating procedures can be divided into a number of activities: those which take place in the production unit; the transportation to the airport; the loading of materials on to the aircraft; the service of food and beverages to customers and crew; and the transfer of waste and materials for washing back to the production unit. Services for a flight may be provided by a catering operation owned by the airline or flights may be serviced by an independent contractor. Typically, the service provided is much more than just the food and beverage requirements of the flight and also includes duty free sales, blankets, pillows, linen, toiletries, newspapers, magazines, children's games, baby food, first-aid kits and printed menu cards.

Whether the service is provided by a subsidiary of the airline company or by a contractor, the basis of the service will be a detailed specification for each flight. Initial production planning is done one to two weeks before the flight, when an estimate is made of material requirements for each flight, to allow the ordering of materials. Four days before departure production plans are prepared for each department. Final adjustments are made on the day of the flight, when the detailed planning sequence is commenced. For each flight there is a planned sequence of preparation of meals, assembly of materials and printing of labels for trolleys and containers. This includes all the special meal requirements, such as vegetarian, special diets and one of requirements for First Class and VIP customers. An inventory list of all items required on the flight is printed out to allow inspectors to check for the correct assembly of items for each flight. A full load for a 747-400 consists of 6.5 tonnes of materials, including over 800 laid-up meal trays. Checking is essential to ensure that all of the requirements are present.

A computer system is used to link the production facility with information from reservations and check-in. Food items are produced to a schedule based on the estimated time of departure of the flight and on the projected number of passengers in each class. The majority of items are provided using a sophisticated cook-chill system. All foods, whether to be served hot or cold, are prepared in advance and chilled to below 5°C and held in chilled storage until they are ready for service. During transportation, dry ice is used to maintain the temperature of food items. Not all foods are produced in this way. For some flights, hot meals may be packed in insulated trays whilst still hot and kept above 60°C until they are served to the passenger. This system may be used on short-haul flights where the meal must be served as soon as the aircraft is in the air.

The majority of hot food items are cooked in bulk, using large-scale equipment such as convection ovens, combination ovens, pressure cookers and continuous fryers. The cooked dishes are then portioned into bulk containers and rapidly chilled. Following this, they are then held in chilled storage until required by the assembly department. In a similar way, all baked items such as breads and desserts are prepared in advance and chilled.

A few hours before the flight is due to depart, the process of packing, assembly and loading begins. Meals which are to be served hot are taken from chilled storage and packed into oven-proof containers, which may be foil, plastic or china. The foods are portioned into oven containers in accordance with the flight specification, which will lay down the weights of each of the components of the meal and the appearance of the meal. The oven containers are then loaded into oven racks and kept in chilled storage until they are required for assembly. Food assembly areas require control of temperature if hazardous foods remain in this area for any length of time out of refrigeration. Temperatures of 10°C or less are recommended.

The next stage is referred to as 'tray setting', which consists of assembling all of the items needed on a meal tray. For large operations a conveyor belt is used to carry the trays past a series of assembly points. At the end of the conveyor, assembled trays are then placed into trolleys. There are many different sizes of trolleys used by the airlines and it is important that the correct trolleys are used to suit the type of aircraft used on a specific flight. Labels are placed on the outside of the trolley, indicating the flight number, the contents of the trolley and its location on the aircraft.

Two to three hours before a flight, all of the trolleys and containers are assembled in the dispatch bay. At this stage checks are made to ensure that all requirements are complete. These materials are then loaded into special delivery vehicles. The vehicles are designed to have pneumatic elevators to raise the height of the platform of the truck to that of the loading door on the aircraft – this is 9 metres above ground level in the case of a 747. At the last minute ice and newspapers are added to the load. The complete load for a long-haul Boeing 747-400 aircraft is made up of over 40,000 items which must be supplied by the catering company. This load occupies over 60 square metres of space.

The journey of the trucks is planned to coincide with the requirements of the airline. Communications links are vital. Flight times are subject to delays and cancellations and there is often less than two hours to unload, clean and reload an aircraft. Before loading can begin, the used trolleys and containers must be removed from the aircraft into an empty truck and returned to the in-flight catering unit. To cope with last-minute needs, the catering company will have a fleet of small vans which can be used to facilitate last-minute changes which arise after the trucks have started their journey.

After they have been loaded onto the aircraft, materials and equipment are stowed in the galley areas. Small aircraft may have two galleys, whereas a 747-400 may have six galleys. The precise configuration will be specified by the airline. All trolleys and containers must be stowed in the correct location in each of the galleys on the aircraft, so that cabin crew do not have to search through a number of trolleys before finding what they want. To this end, catering staff liaise with the cabin staff to check that all materials are on board and that materials are located in their correct storage areas. All equipment and supplies must be securely fastened ready for take-off. A typical galley is illustrated in Figure 17.1.

At this stage, cabin crews have more to think about than just food and drink, since they need to ensure that all passengers are correctly seated, that their cabin luggage is securely stowed and that safety instructions are completed. However, even with all of these other activities taking place, cabin service may have started with the service of a complimentary drink to first and business-class passengers while the aircraft is still on the ground. Also, the first meal to be served may be loaded into the on-board convection ovens, if the meal is to be served as soon as the flight is in the air.

The planned service of food and drink starts as soon as the plane is in the air. The exact sequence depends on the time and duration of the flight. A short domestic flight may have a full hot breakfast or dinner service in the short time that the aircraft is in the air. A charter flight may have only a beverage and chilled snack service. A long-haul flight may serve two or three hot meals during the flight, together with frequent drinks to reduce the effects of dehydration and jet-lag.

Whatever the nature of the flight, the sequence of service is similar. The pattern of service will be largely dictated by the configuration of the aircraft, taking into account factors such as the number of aisles and the number of seats in each section. Oven racks with pre-loaded hot meal containers are placed in the ovens 15 to 20 minutes before they are required for service. Cabin crew then start service according to a planned sequence, which will vary from one airline to another. For a given meal there may be one trolley for meal trays and hot meals and a second for beverage service. In addition to this, items such as bread rolls and hot beverages may be required. At the end of the meal, trays are

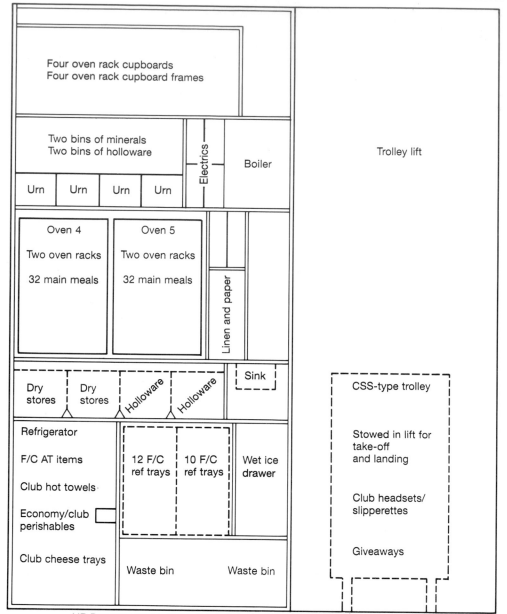

NB Dustbin and brush for this galley stowed behind crew seat, door 2 left.

Figure 17.1 Stowage galley on a Boeing 747.
Source: British Airways.

returned to the trolleys which in turn are relocated in the appropriate galley storage area and made safe for landing.

When the aircraft has landed used trolleys and containers are transported to the local in-flight unit for sorting and cleaning. Conveyor belts are used to allow staff to separate glasses, china and cutlery from all of the waste material. There are now many initiatives to reduce the volume of waste and to maximize recycling of materials. In some operations, this activity has been automated, with magnets used to remove cutlery and powerful water sprays to rinse off waste food, plastic materials and napkins. Large flight dishwashing machines are used to wash all of the glasses, china and trays. These are then returned to store until needed for the next flight. In order to service an aircraft, three sets of all equipment are required, one set on the aircraft, one at the start of the flight and the other at the destination.

Current Issues and Future Trends

Because of the effect of the recession on business travel, a number of airlines have had to rethink the nature of what they offer to customers. This is based on quantitative and qualitative market research.[11] In particular, there has been pressure on First Class service during the recent recession. A number airlines have eliminated their First Class service and upgraded the Business Class. There is a move towards simple fresh food with an emphasis on service.[12]

As was described earlier, there have been a number of approaches developed to control the cost of in-flight meals, but this is proving quite difficult in practice.[13] One way of controlling cost is to reduce the amount of labour required. This can be done, for example, by buying in ready prepared food items which will reduce the number of catering staff required. Purchase of ready to assemble food products can include: ready portioned meats; ready prepared sauces; and cook-freeze/cook-chill products. In addition to catering staff, a large number of people are required to pack and assemble meals, trays and trolleys. The use of robotics is being introduced in order to reduce the cost of some of these activities.[14]

RAILWAY CATERING

The provision of food and beverages on the railways has undergone dramatic changes in the last few years, not least due to the restructuring of the railways in line with recent government policy and the provisions of the Railways Act (November 1993). The institution that was once British Rail is now no longer, although the name lives on. Names such as British Transport Hotels, Travellers Fare and, more recently, InterCity On Board Services have all disappeared, although some still operate under a new mantle.

The full impact of privatization, started in April 1994, has yet to be realized. The industry is now fragmented but this in itself offers scope for individuality and competitive spirit to create new catering ventures. On 1 April 1994 Railtrack was set up as a separate government-owned company and the then existing passenger businesses (Network South East, InterCity and Regional Railways) were replaced by 25 passenger train operating units which were to be franchised. However, in the light of the recent spate of one- and two-day national strikes further franchising attempts may be hindered. It is therefore against this backdrop of dramatic change that British railway catering must be viewed.

Prior to privatization rail catering was the responsibility of InterCity On Board Services (ICOBS) on all InterCity and Network South East trains. Catering on other routes was open to tender from other catering operators. Since privatization each of the InterCity routes is responsible for its own on-train catering with the newly formed On Board Supply (OBS) company responsible for the provisioning of food and equipment on the

InterCity routes and for the operation of on-board services for charter trains, Network South East, regional railways and the Cross Channel Catering Company (CCCC).

The Market

Recent statistics from the newly privatized companies are difficult to obtain due to their short period of existence. However, in the year to March 1994 a total of 713.2 million passenger journeys were made (British Rail Annual Report 1993/94). This offers tremendous potential for the caterer, be it OBS or any of the other private companies who tender for the supply of catering services. In an attempt to increase their share of the catering market, improvements have been made to the services offered, the styles of food, the physical equipment on-track and even extends to the opening of catering facilities on board 20 minutes prior to the departure of the train to entice business away from station caterers and to make better use of staff time.[15]

Product Offering

The type of catering facility a passenger may expect when travelling by rail may be viewed from two perspectives: in-terminal catering and on-board catering. With regard to the latter, this is dependent upon the duration of the journey, the class of ticket purchased and the time of day. On-board catering can range from a beverage served from a trolley to a silver-served three- or four-course meal in the Pullman car. Certain types of service will only be operated on the longer journeys and only passengers in possession of specific classes of ticket are eligible to use the clearly designated catering facilities. Certain services are only available at specific periods of the day, although it is now perceived as necessary to provide some form of catering facility at all times on longer journeys, for example in the buffet bars, in an attempt to provide a good customer service.

The types of service offered on board are as follows:

- *Trolley service:* this is an at-seat service offering hot and cold beverages, sandwiches and snacks from a trolley pushed through the carriages and stopping at the customers request. This form of service is generally not available at weekends.
- *Buffet bar:* the buffet bar service offers, in addition to hot and cold beverages and snack items, a limited range of hot food such as burgers, pizzas, lasagne and stews. These are reheated in the galley behind the buffet and the customer takes them to his/her seat for consumption. This service also includes a breakfast tray and an afternoon tea pack.
- *Restaurant Car:* these services operate a more formal menu for both lunch and dinner. For some time the provision of food on trains was limited to either a snack from the buffet or a very formal, relatively expensive silver-service affair. The gap between the two has now been filled by the Express Diner menu operating after breakfast and replacing the first-class menu on non-Pullman services. A range of individually priced items encourage one-course dining with an average spend of £8.50 for a main course.

  A first-class service also operates in the restaurant cars at both lunch and dinner periods. Passengers choose from a selection of four appetizers, three hot

Figure 17.2 First-class restaurant car.
Source: Travellers Fare.

main course dishes plus one cold choice, two desserts and a selection of cheeses, followed by coffee and chocolates for a price ranging from £15–£20 excluding wine. This is illustrated in Figure 17.2.

- *Pullman service:* on the InterCity East Coast there are approximately five of these services operating daily between Edinburgh and London. Pullman services are targeted at the first-class and Silver Standard sectors and provide an at seat service, both for refreshments and full meals. In terms of choice the menu is similar in structure and price to first-class but offers more choice. Complimentary service of tea and coffee is made available to all first-class Pullman customers.

- *Sleeper service:* operating only on designated night services, mainly from the south of England to Scotland, this is an 'at berth' service of refreshments at the end of the journey. Additionally, first class passengers may choose from fruit juice and croissant or a cooked breakfast.

Staffing

Staffing on board will vary in accordance with the type of services being offered. On services operating a buffet service only, one member of catering staff would be required. Where both buffet and trolley service are in operation, a minimum of two staff members would be required, with up to 7–8 members required for the provision of the above plus full restaurant and Pullman services. The chief steward is responsible for the catering services on board, whilst a purser is responsible on trains with Pullman services provided.

Generally, staff work approximately 39 hours per week over 7 days, although on the Glasgow/Edinburgh to London routes they may work a set of four 10-hour shifts, making the return journey in each case. Catering staff are not normally expected to rest overnight away from their base station except in the event of unforeseen circumstances. Each Inter-City route has an appointed trains manager who is responsible for the whole operation, helped by a number of assistant managers and clerical support staff.

Operational Procedures

Prior to any catering services being provided there is a complex system of ordering food items to be done. On InterCity East Coast this is done on a weekly basis using a computerized system. Passenger loads for specific journeys are calculated, often based on previous sales data, and the trains manager places the orders a week in advance with OBS for each train. OBS then supply the commodities as required. Based on past sales figures, the required amount of food stock is delivered to the respective trains. Staff are then issued with this stock, for which they are responsible and any shortages at the end of the journey must be accounted for. Should extra supplies of certain foodstuffs be required en route due to excess demand, staff can phone ahead to the next pick-up point and supplies collected there upon arrival. This additional stock must also be reckoned for in the closing inventory. On the Edinburgh to Kings Cross route, for example, these pick-up points would be Newcastle, Doncaster and York.

On most InterCity routes the main catering vehicles used are of the Mark IV type. InterCity East Coast deploys a fleet of 30 Mark IV vehicles, backed up by ten recently refurbished Mark III vehicles. The kitchens on board are of a modular design, allowing pieces of equipment to be removed as required; for example, allowing ambient sections to be replaced by chilled units. Electricity is the type of energy used in these modern galleys, although refrigeration is still a problem with the kitchen moving at speeds of up to 125 m.p.h.

In the restaurant car, operating the Express Diner, first class or first-class Pullman menus, most menu items will be prepared using conventional cooking methods as far as possible with food being brought on board in its raw state. Steaks, for example, will be purchased in vacuum packs and cooked to order but items such as roast beef would be delivered in a pre-prepared state. Likewise with some of the hot dishes served in the buffet bar.

A high degree of control is maintained in the provision of food and beverage, irrespective of the route operated. All commodities are logged out to trains and the catering staff are responsible for this. Issues to the staff are recorded at the beginning of the journey and a closing stock taken at the end. The staff member must then submit the relevant cash sum for the stock consumed. This system applies to all types of service. Due to the nature of the food items, the trolley services and buffet bar are 100 per cent controllable. Here most items are prepacked (even tea and coffee come in sealed containers) and stock is easily reconcilable. Control over fresh produce does pose more of a problem, but accurate forecasting and strict production and portion control are implemented.

There are a number of problems which are inherent in the provision of food and beverage on trains aside from the fact that the kitchen is moving at high speed.[16] Water, electricity and refrigeration supplies are expensive and revenue losses can be costly if they fail. In order to achieve the high standards of service, staffing levels must also be high. Whilst breakfasts and evening meals are profitable, there is less uptake in the restaurant cars at midday where staffing levels have to be as high as for the more profitable periods.[17] Additionally, timetabling has to be accurate so that staff are not away from their home depot overnight, yet providing enough staff to deal with a busy breakfast service could leave the train top-heavy with staff on other journeys.

Current Issues and Future Trends

Aside from the privatization of the British Rail network and its associated services, the single most important issue in contemporary rail travel is the opening of the Channel Tunnel. This has already had a significant impact on both the airlines and ferry companies which operate on the short-haul continental routes and once the rail services are operating at full capacity the competition for business on the London/Paris/Brussels routes will become even more fierce.

At the present time only one of the two forms of rail transport through the Tunnel is available to the travelling public. EuroTunnel's 'Le Shuttle' train carries drivers and their vehicles between Folkestone and Calais in 35 minutes. These specially designed trains transport both private and commercial vehicles but there are not catering facilities provided on board. Passengers are free to move between carriages, but the only seating accommodation available is in their vehicles. Food and drink may be purchased at the terminal prior to the departure of the train, and commercial vehicles have the additional facility of a 'truck stop' at Ashford in Kent. This catering outlet, owned by EuroTunnel, provides HGV drivers with a wide range of facilities including accommodation (for those prohibited from driving at the weekends) and can issue tickets for the Tunnel journey.[18]

For foot passengers there is the Eurostar train. Whilst in the Tunnel, these high-speed trains share the tracks with 'Le Shuttle'; however, dedicated tracks will eventually be made available on both sides of the Tunnel enabling Eurostar to travel the distance between Waterloo International, Paris Nord and Bruxelles Midi in approximately two hours.

Catering on board the Eurostar services presents a tremendous opportunity for the caterer. The on-board services on Eurostar are provided by Cross Channel Catering Company (CCCC), an Anglo-Continental partnership between Wagons-Lits (France), Sabena (Belgium) and InterCity's On Board Services.[19] Eurostar's main competitors are the airlines and it is to airline standards of catering and on-board services that CCCC works. There are two standards of catering provided dependent upon the type of ticket purchased. First-class passengers, whose meal is included in the ticket price, are catered for in a similar style to an airlines club class, with a full range of meal occasions catered for dependent upon the time of day. Contrary to the practice currently operated by OBS, the food on board Eurostar first class is cook-chill rather than freshly prepared, reflecting both the airline-style image and the company's pursuit of consistency of product. Staff are required to regenerate the food on board, with the production of this food taking place in central production kitchens similar to those operated in airline catering. The menus served reflect a mix of French, Belgian and British tastes. A further dimension is that staff working on Eurostar are required to be bilingual.

For services other than first class the catering facilities are similar to those offered by InterCity's existing operation – a buffet car offers a restricted range of simple items and a trolley service of snacks and beverages is available for those who wish to remain at their seats.

The success of this project is dependent upon convincing the public that it can offer a competitively priced alternative to the existing forms of air and sea travel. Competition from the airlines will inevitably increase as they strive to improve their own product in a number of ways, which in the end can only be good for the consumer.

MARINE TRAVEL CATERING – SHORT SEA ROUTES

The classification of commercial catering within marine travel encompasses two distinct sectors – passengers on short sea routes and clientele on board cruise ships for an extended duration of five days or more. Each of these sectors presents different demands on the foodservice operator as the customer expectations across these sectors will vary; indeed, within one sector there may be a broad range of expectations and needs which the caterer must address. These may range from the basic physiological need for a substantial filling meal in the case of a commercial vehicle driver to providing corporate entertainment in a silver-service restaurant at the other end of the spectrum. This is highly evident in the provision of catering on the short sea routes operated in the English Channel and the Irish Sea.

It is in the short sea route sector of marine catering that the most significant advances have been made in the last few years, spurred on by the opening of the Channel Tunnel. Today competition between ferry operators in this sector is fierce with a number of types of transport available to carry passengers on the relatively short crossings in the Channel and the Irish and North Sea to continental Europe. These include roll-on/roll-off ferries, hydrofoils and, more recently, high-speed catamarans. The type of catering facilities offered is limited by the size of vessel in which it is being offered and the duration of the crossing. Thus, on certain routes the facility may range from a kiosk offering hot and cold beverages, sandwiches and snacks to a full à la carte, waiter-service restaurant, or a combination of these and other facilities.

Size and Scale of Sector

There are relatively few operators in the short sea sector of the market.[20] The market is dominated by P & O European Ferries and the Swedish-based Stena Sealink Line, each with approximately 30 per cent share of the market. Other operators with a significant impact include Brittany Ferries (French-owned with approximately 12.4 per cent), Sea Containers subsidiary Hoverspeed (5.1 per cent) and Sally Line (4.2 per cent).[21] Within the short sea sector there are a number of markets served by these operators. The short sea sector had approximately 19 million ferry passengers in 1993.[22] Analysis of these markets shows three distinct types. There are holiday-makers or clientele travelling by sea for pleasure purposes; commercial vehicle drivers; and the business community.

Each type of market will present the caterer with their own specific needs. Recognition, and fulfilling their needs, as in any catering operations, is the key to success. Some operators, for example P & O, provide concessionary restaurants for commercial vehicle drivers, recognizing that their particular needs are quite different to those of the pleasure traveller or the business executive. Most operators offer a business or club-class package, with waiter service of complimentary tea and coffee in clearly designated lounges, designed specifically to meet the needs of the busy executive, with facilities on some of the multi-purpose 'superferries' extending to on-board conference rooms and associated services. According to P & O, Club class is seen as 'symbolising our determination to satisfy the needs of our passengers'.

The period spent on board a ferry can be viewed as a pause in the journey which is totally under the passengers' control. Increasingly, it is being marketed by operators as being 'part of the holiday experience' and, importantly, a time of relaxation for the passenger, be it as a holiday-maker or commercial vehicle driver. Passengers, therefore, must be provided with catering facilities commensurate with their needs. Indeed, P & O have established in a recent survey that the provision of catering facilities is the third most important service as requested by their passengers. Moreover, often two ferry companies will operate on the same route at a similar fare structure so the standard of on-board catering can often be a deciding factor in their choice of operator.

All of the major operators in the short sea sector are located at the main seaports of the south-east of England (Southampton, Dover, Newhaven amongst others) as well as Fishguard in Wales and Stranraer in Scotland. A number of other services operate from the north-east of England and from the north of Scotland. The location of quayside facilities to service the catering operations on boardship is a key feature of most of the major operators. The logistics of supply of food commodities to a variety of locations, timings and so forth is complex, with the larger companies operating a system of central purchasing of all food items with a distribution to all ports on a daily basis.

Product Offering

The number and types of catering facilities on board ferries vary according to the physical constraints of the vessel, the number and type of passengers it carries and, importantly, the duration of the journey. Many modern ferries are more akin to floating hotels with 'a myriad of services available to make the trip relaxing and entertaining'.[23] Food and beverages are provided in outlets ranging from kiosks for simple snacks to self-service style restaurants seating up to several hundred people on the new 'superferries'. Silver-service restaurants still feature on many vessels, especially those offering a premium-class service although this style of food service system tends not to be found on the very short sea crossings due to constrictions of time. Fast food has also established itself firmly as an on-board product, especially on the newer, larger ferries, with P & O operating their 'First Base' outlet and Stena Sealink their first outlet with one of the major high street brands, McDonald's, on board the Stena Fantasia, one of the largest vessels on the short sea route. On average, there tends to be from 3–5 various food and beverage outlets on most ferries, obviously dependent upon size, not including staff feeding facilities. The immediate potential market, whilst captive for the period of the journey, is not totally dependent upon the on-board catering facilities (unlike airline catering they are free to bring their own refreshments), with an average passenger uptake of the catering facilities ranging from 32–60 per cent dependent upon the time of day.

Organization and Staffing

Staffing on board ferries will vary according to the time of day, the facilities offered and the type of vessel. It is difficult to generalize about staffing structure as not all operators will manage their vessels in the same fashion. Generally each vessel will have a purser who is responsible for the provision and service of all 'hotel facilities' and to whom the staff report. Other key members of catering staff on board are the assistant purser and the senior chief cook. On a ferry with a complement of 100 staff up to 60 of them may be primarily involved in catering but they may also be called upon to perform other duties. At the less senior levels, staff may work a variety of shifts, for example two weeks continuously day on, day off, followed by one week of night shift followed by six days off.

Standard Operating Procedures

Computerized central purchasing is common practice given the scale of some of the operations. At P & O, for example, the food requirements for the short sea fleet are handled through Dover, with designated large-scale suppliers of meat, vegetables and frozen produce being used. Individual food items are sourced by management and their supply to the company's dockside warehouses is dealt with by one of these designated suppliers (who will purchase the item from the manufacturer and negotiate prices with P & O). Each vessel must carry sufficient supplies for the return journey as victualling of vessels takes place only in the home port. However, specialist items such as patisserie may be delivered to the ship in France.

In keeping with consumer demand there is a greater emphasis now placed on the use of fresh produce, with many of the dishes being prepared on board. To facilitate this, cook-chill production systems are also used, with regeneration of dishes on board ship, whilst other food items, especially fast-food products, are prepared in much the same fashion as they are in their shore-based counterparts.

With regard to service to food, this is similar to restaurant operations based on shore, incorporating self-service, buffet, waiter-service, silver-service and kiosk styles of service. The supply of food and beverages to passengers usually takes place port to port in order to maximize sales and to provide efficient customer service. Meal provision is therefore less restricted than it may be in other forms of travel catering.

Current Issues and Future Trends

One of the major issues affecting the short sea sector is the opening of the Channel Tunnel linking mainland Europe and Britain. This has had, and will continue to have, a major effect on the Dover–Calais route, although the Tunnel's competitiveness in relation to ferry traffic will naturally decline the further the ferry routes are located away from the Tunnel. However, the prospect of the Tunnel has led ferry operators to invest heavily, with new 'superferries' being added to some fleets and the upgrading of ships being common practice.

In 1991 approximately 16 million passengers travelled by ferry on the short sea route, growing to 19 million by 1993. By 1995 it is estimated that this will increase to 24–25 million with the Tunnel expected to take up to 50 per cent of this market. It is evident that competition between operators will become even more fierce. Ferry operators must continue to offer an ever-increasing standard of product, in every sense, if they are to remain in business. The provision of catering is intrinsically linked with this quality product as operators compete with each other for a potentially shrinking market.

There are other issues which may have an impact upon travel catering in a marine environment. The provision within the next year of a new type of high-speed ship (HSS) by Stena Sealink will mean a change from the current concept – due to the speed at which these vessels can travel the journey times on HSS routes will be significantly reduced with greater emphasis placed on quick dining outlets such as fast food.

CRUISE SHIP CATERING

After a period of decline in the 1970s, the world cruise market is growing at a tremendous rate. Estimates show[24] that the market is due to double by the year 2005, with a worldwide increase from 5.3 million passengers to 11.5 million passengers. Several of the large companies are investing heavily in new cruise ships with this growth in mind, with P & O due to take delivery of the *Oriana* (67,000 gross tonnes) in 1995, the *Sun Princess* (77,000 gross tonnes) in 1996 and two further superliners in 1997. In addition to liners such as the *Canberra* and the *Sea Princess*, P & O will be in a strong position to capture this increase in both the UK and the worldwide cruise markets.

Product Offering

The logistics of provisioning a cruise ship are rather more complex than those of a cross-channel ferry. In addition to the vast amount of equipment required, the liner may be at sea for an extended period of time and will often have to restock in foreign ports. However it must have sufficient supplies at all times to maintain a full catering service to high paying, often demanding, passengers.

Irrespective of the category of the ship, or the ticket price, it is often the quality of the food which determines the success of a voyage.[25] The price of the food (and in some classes often the beverages) is included in the ticket price and for this reason a variety of restaurants are operated. Thus the facilities may range from one (or several) full silver-service fine dining-rooms through to self-service restaurants and coffee shops. In many respects the facilities offered on board resemble those in a large luxury hotel with a full array of leisure and shopping facilities, staffed and managed in very much the same manner.

Staffing

Generally, the passenger–crew ratio on most ships is very high, with an average of one crew member to every two passengers. However, on the most luxurious ships this ratio can almost be 1:1.[26] As in a luxury hotel, all grades of staff are employed; however, working hours are long with up to 14 hours a day not being unusual. Coupled with working seven days a week, often for several months, shared accommodation with work colleagues and living at sea make working in this sector of marine catering rather arduous. The financial rewards are high, often with tax-free wages and substantial tips, and the opportunity to travel the world makes this a particularly interesting field in which to work.

TERMINUS CATERING

In addition to the provision of a food and beverage service during the journey, the availability of restaurants, coffee shops and bars is a common feature of the airport, railway station and port terminal buildings. These facilities are most fully developed at airports, where airport operating companies are well aware of the importance of income from catering and other retailing concessions to the financial performance of the airport. The service has been expanded from the provision of food and beverages, to include large retailing operations, largely through the leasing of space to concessionaires.

Retailing has been most fully developed at airports, where very large numbers of people visit major international airports and are often there for long periods of time waiting for flights or waiting to meet friends and relatives. For example, Heathrow Airport receives over 40 million visitors and passengers each year, which represents a large potential market. In a modern airport, great care is taken over the location of catering and retailing concessions and integration with seating areas, check-in desks and transit lounges. Refreshments are required both on the landside (before security checks/emigration control) and airside (after security checks/emigration control and for passengers in transit).

The recognition of the importance of retailing activities has resulted in the development of large retailing areas in airports. A large international airport may receive 50 per cent of its revenue from retailing concessions. Concession income is much more significant for airports with a large proportion of international travellers, as compared with commuter airports.[27] The trend is towards the provision of a large number of small units rather than a few large concessions. Also, we have seen the introduction of familiar high street brands into these retailing areas. A good example of this is in The Village of Gatwick.

CONCLUSION

This sector of the hospitality industry faces the unique challenge of feeding people whilst they are travelling between destinations. There are therefore some unique challenges to overcome. Firstly, the mode of travel needs to be designed in such a way as to enable foodservice to take place. On board aircraft, space is very limited so that galleys are kept as small as possible. On the railways and on board ships, there is more space so that kitchen layouts more closely resemble the production areas found in more conventional surroundings. Secondly, there may be significant logistics problems in terms of effectively supplying 'outlets' that do not always directly return to their point of origin. This necessitates setting up a complex supply chain that enables aircraft, trains or ships to be provisioned in a number of different ways at different stages of their route. Finally, food and drink are not the sole or even the main reason for the customer purchase, they are simply a part of a 'travel package'. Such packages are often based on a combination of price and time of departure and/or arrival, and not on the quality of food served. However, if the foodservice standard is unsatisfactory, despite its low level of importance in the purchase decision, it can cause high levels of customer dissatisfaction. Foodservice providers therefore need to be aware both of the marketing and of the operational implications of this.

REFERENCES

1. Key Note (1993) *The U.K. Catering Market*, Key Note Report, London, p. 116.
2. Boberg, K.B. and Riley, L.A. (1993) 'International airlines and tourism', in *Encyclopaedia of Hospitality and Tourism*, Khan, M., Olsen, M. and Var, T. (eds) New York: Van Nostrand Reinhold, pp. 851–60.
3. Reed, A. (1992) 'The Greening of Europe', *Air Transport World*, Vol. 29, No. 1, pp. 87–9.
4. Shifrin, C.A. (1994) 'KLM, Northwest unveil new business class', *Aviation Week & Space Technology*, Vol. 140, No. 9, p. 44.
5 Shifrin, C.A. (1994) 'Virgin fleet expansion key to growth strategy', *Aviation Week & Space Technology*, Vol. 140, No. 1, pp. 39–40.
6. Shifrin, C.A. (1993) 'British Airways builds U.S.-style regional network', *Aviation Week & Space Technology*, Vol. 139, No. 6, p. 34.
7. Anon. (1994) 'Airline unit seeks to buy catering business from SAS', *Wall Street Journal*, 29 May, p. 10.
8. Boberg, K.B. and Riley, L.A. op. cit.
9. Hill, L. (1993) 'Trimming fat from food costs', *Air Transport World*, vol. 30, No. 5, pp. 96–8.
10. Vandyk, A. (1994) 'Oil-fueled expansion', *Air Transport World*, Vol. 31, No. 5, p. 108.
11. Pedrick, D., Babekus, E. and Richardson, A. (1993) 'The value of qualitative data in quality improvement efforts', *Journal of Services Marketing*, Vol. 7, No. 3, pp. 26–35.
12. Graham, A. (1994) 'Care in the air', *Hospitality Industry International*, No. 3, pp. 41–3.
13. Henderson, D.K. (1993) 'Airline catering outstrips cost cutting', *Air Transport World*, Vol. 30, No. 5, pp. 99–100.
14. Jones, P. (1995) 'Innovation in flight catering', in Jones, P. (ed.) *Flight Catering*, London: Longman Publishing.
15. Anon. (1994) 'Catering on track', *Hospitality Industry International*, No. 3, p. 40.
16. Webster, J. (1994) 'Truckers take a break', *Caterer and Hotelkeeper*, 29 September, pp. 60 1.
17. Jenner, G. (1992) 'A signal for change', *Caterer and Hotelkeeper*, 15 October, pp. 36–9.
18. Tarpey, D. (1994) 'A taste for tunnel travel', *Caterer and Hotelkeeper*, 24 March, pp. 33–5.
19. Webster, J. op. cit.
20. Key Note Report (1992) *A Market Sector Overview: Cross Channel Ferries* (3rd edition), London.
21. DRMD (1991) Market Survey.
22. Stena Line A.B. (1993) *Annual Report*.
23. Hillier, C. (1992) 'Ferries fight British Airways', *Caterer and Hotelkeeper*, 30 July, pp. 30–4.
24. Murray, M. (1994) 'High class on the high seas', *Hospitality*, No. 146, pp. 24–5.
25. Sall, B. (1993) 'Do the waves still rule?', *Hospitality*, No. 141, pp. 12–14.
26. Harmer, J. (1993) 'When the boat comes in', *Caterer and Hotelkeeper*, 4 November, pp. 33–5.
27. Doganis, R. (1992) *The Airport Business*, London: Routledge, pp. 131–57.

EIGHTEEN

Outdoor Catering

PETER JONES

INTRODUCTION

This specialized sector of the food service industry is probably one of the most difficult to operate successfully and one of the most speculative. Unfortunately it is extremely difficult to estimate the size and turnover of this sector since, by the very nature of things, outdoor catering is not a permanent operation. The kind of events vary from garden parties for just a few people up to a few thousand at royal garden parties; fêtes and other fund-raising events; exhibitions, either on permanent sites such as the National Exhibition Centre or Olympia, or on a much smaller scale at other temporary events; agricultural and county shows; air shows such as Farnborough and Biggin Hill; sporting events of all kinds, the British Grand Prix and the Grand National are examples; private functions such as wedding receptions, clan gatherings, anniversary parties and other social occasions.

There are few statistics on the size and nature of this sector due to the temporary nature of these events and the type of operator involved in the business. Much of the Standard Industrial Classification is based on information relating to licensed premises, VAT registration or other sources. In this sector, no licence is required to operate as an outside caterer; there are no premises except possibly a base store and kitchen; and there are many small operators who may not be registered for VAT. Broadly speaking there are three or four major outside caterers who operate throughout the UK – firms such as Searcy, Payne & Gunter, and Ring & Brymer; a number of medium-sized firms with a regional base; and a very large number of small operators.

CUSTOMER DEMAND AND TYPES OF OUTSIDE CATERING

Outside catering can be broadly divided into two main types of function: contracted and speculative.

Contracted Functions

In this case, the operator agrees to cater for a specified and guaranteed number of customers. In this respect it is very similar to banqueting, except that instead of providing food and refreshment in a banqueting suite, the setting is likely to be a semi-permanent

Figure 18.1 Outdoor catering chalets at Wimbledon (centre left).
Source: Hunting Aerofilms Ltd.

chalet, as in the case of many agricultural and county shows, or a marquee on the lawn for 'one-off' events such as wedding receptions or garden parties.

Speculative Functions

The outside caterer in this instance is not assured of any custom, but contracts to provide refreshment on a site for members of the general public attending the event, as in the case of many sporting events. If the attendance at such meetings is high, then the rewards are great, for the caterer can achieve a very high turnover in a very short space of time. But the risks are high too, for attendance is often subject to the vagaries of the weather, to the extent that many outside caterers will insure themselves against losses due to adverse weather conditions affecting business. The relationship, though, is not always obvious. For instance, during tennis matches at Wimbledon, as illustrated in Figure 18.1, breaks during play due to rain or bad light can increase food and drink sales!

A major source of demand is known as 'corporate hospitality'. Many companies invite their stakeholders to events as part of their marketing effort. In the case of customers such hospitality is effective promotion and public relations; for employees it may be part of an incentive package; for suppliers it is largely public relations; and so on. Until recently most corporate hospitality was at spectator events. The firm would hire a box or marquee at major sporting events and provide meals and drinks before, during and after the event. For instance, the National Westminster Bank, sponsors of the one-day cricket competition, have a large marquee for invited guests when the final is held at Lords Cricket ground. In 1993, the cost of attending the British Grand Prix or a Five Nations rugby match at Cardiff Arms Park was nearly £400 per person per day.[1] Increasingly, firms are devizing participative events in which the invited guests are able to take an active part. Such events may include rally driving, parachuting, paintballing or golf. For instance, Viceroys, based in Kent, offer 'action experiences' which include clay pigeon shooting, quad bikes, dune buggies, and war games.

Such is the size and scale of this activity that in 1988 the Corporate Hospitality Association was formed in the UK. Members of the association are of three different types. *Principal suppliers* are either outdoor catering companies; or the venues, such as Wembley Stadium or Alton Towers, at which the event takes place. Such a package might include parking, meals, drinks, and entrance tickets for an all-inclusive price. *Agents* buy hospitality from such suppliers and sell it to their customers, sometimes having added value to the package by including guest speakers, celebrity guests, flowers, and other ancillaries. Such agents may be able to negotiate discounts with suppliers due to their 'bulk' purchase of hospitality. *Brokers* are hired by clients to find suitable hospitality packages. They purchase these, often on a commission basis, from suppliers or agents. Some operators may be both supplier and agent, or agent and broker. In 1990, the principal firms in the corporate hospitality business[2] were Keith Prowse, Cavendish, and Mike Burton (agents/brokers), and Payne & Gunter and Ring & Brymer (suppliers/agents), with an estimated annual turnover of £500 million.[3]

During the 1980s, corporate hospitality had a 'bad press'. For instance, an article in *Management Today*[4] refers to 'send-it-to-Ascot-and-bugger-the-expense mode of most British corporate entertainers'. This and the recession of the early 1990s and the Gulf War caused purchasers to modify their demands and select alternatives to spectator-based events.[5] The BMSL Survey of 1990 had predicted strong growth in the market which did not materialize. In 1991 business was down by about 30 per cent.[6] Keith Prowse, who had been the market leader with £10 million annual turnover, nearly twice that of the nearest competitor, collapsed due to cash-flow problems.[7]

OUTSIDE CATERING OPERATORS

Just as there are two main types of catering in this sector, so there are also two types of caterer engaged in this business – the professional outside caterer and the non-specialist outside caterer.

Professional Outside Catering Firms

These range from sole traders with their mobile ice-cream vans or hot-dog stalls up to very large firms. The larger firms are very much specialists, with a great deal of experience. Such firms not only cater for the functions noted above, but also undertake catering for firms and organizations on the clients' premises, providing food and refreshment at meetings, seminars and conferences. This type of catering helps to even out the somewhat seasonal nature of their business, as true *outside* catering is obviously only undertaken in the summer months in most cases. Such specialist outside caterers operate very much like any other type of caterer. They have a management team in charge of sales, operations, personnel and administration, which forms a nucleus of permanent staff, fully trained and familiar with the operating standards and organization of the firm. In addition they employ as many part-time staff as they require for a particular function, since it is uneconomic to employ waiting staff permanently due to the fluctuating nature of the business. None the less, the part-time staff, more often than not, have regularly worked for the firm at the same annual events year after year. It is usual for full-time employees to fill the key personnel roles such as control clerks, chalet managers, chefs and storekeepers, while the part-time staff work under their supervision.

There are also a very large number of small operators. One study[8] has looked at small businesses in this sector in Sussex. Eighty-three caterers were identified, with nearly every town of a significant size having at least one operator. Nearly three-quarters of these were sole traders, one-fifth were partnerships, and over 90 per cent employed less than ten full-time staff. Amongst this sample, over 40 per cent had no catering qualifications and a further 20 per cent had only gained such qualifications after setting up the business. Many of these businesses are operated from home and the most significant market served was wedding receptions.

Non-specialist Outside Caterers

Outside catering is often undertaken by hoteliers, restaurateurs and others who are not regularly in the business of catering outdoors. During the early 1990s, many such caterers began to operate in this market in an effort to sustain their businesses during the recession. For instance, Susan Richardson of the Eglantine restaurant in Kent began outdoor catering in 1991 and by 1993 it was generating three times as much revenue as the restaurant itself.[9] She states: 'the overheads and fixed costs [of outside catering] are much lower – we only hire staff for specific functions and we charge clients for the hire of any special equipment. The purchase of a refrigerated van has been our main additional cost.' Other restaurateurs with outside catering activities include Anton Mosimann in London, Tracy Hedgecock in Brighton and David Watson in Yorkshire.

In these cases, non-specialist outside caterers have been successful, but there are pitfalls awaiting the unwary. Such operators are usually prompted to take on outside functions for two reasons: first, they are aware that the rewards for success are high; and second, because regular clients of their hotel or restaurant specially request them to 'do' the local fête or a daughter's wedding reception. The pitfalls are twofold. In attempting to cater elsewhere, the regular business is deprived of key personnel and equipment which results in a lowering of the hotel's or restaurant's standards to the dissatisfaction of customers. Likewise, due to a lack of trained staff, inexperience in outdoor catering, shortages of equipment, and so on, the quality, presentation and service of the food is not up to the standards expected by the client, who expects the restaurateur to be as successful on the back lawn as in his or her own restaurant.

OPERATIONAL ISSUES IN OUTSIDE CATERING

There are problems associated with outside catering that are specific to this particular sector of the industry. On permanent or semi-permanent sites some or all of the essential *services* are plumbed in (i.e. sanitation, running hot and cold water, electricity and gas). But in outside catering, more often than not, cooking has to be done on Calor-gas stoves, water transported from a distance and lighting provided by gas or paraffin lamps (although the light is not such a serious problem as most outdoor functions are held in the longer summer evenings). In view of this and the sometimes primitive accommodation, it is extremely difficult for the outside caterer to meet the *hygiene* regulations. In addition, many semi-permanent sites are subject to regulations, conditions and specific requirements laid down by the local health authority's sanitary department. The outside caterer must ensure that the storage of foodstuffs, cleaning and washing of kitchen and service equipment, practices and activities of staff are all of the highest standard – not just because at all special events (like the Farnborough Air Show or Ascot week) health inspectors visit the catering units on site, but because the good name and reputation of the firm depends upon the quality of the food and service that it provides.

Security is a major headache for the outside caterer. Foodstuffs, cellar stocks and equipment all have to be stored, often in canvas marquees or tents that are extremely difficult to make secure. At the same time, it is necessary to hold relatively high stocks of everything as the caterer is usually miles from base and would not have the time or opportunity to leave the site to replenish stocks or to provide for some unforeseen eventuality. Thus theft and pilferage are not unknown. The public attends the larger events in its thousands, so that inevitably there are dishonest elements who will take advantage of the crowds and circumstances to remove anything that is not secure. At the same time, in order to staff the event, caterers have no option but to employ part-time and casual staff about whom they know very little. Such staff may not physically steal items from the site, but they may consume food and drink while at work or break equipment due to malpractice, both of which will affect caterers' profits.

Apart from the security problem, two aspects of *staffing* are problematic. First, it may be extremely difficult to obtain the required numbers of staff and, second, staff may require some training. At an event like Farnborough Air Show, several thousand staff are required for a period of nine days. Usually, firms have well-established links with casual staff and they can find enough staff from such contacts, but for the larger events they employ housewives and students, particularly those studying hotel and catering subjects. This may necessitate bringing the staff in on the day before the event or some hours before it starts to brief them fully on the style of the operation and train them up to the required level of service.

Finally, *acts of God*, a term borrowed from the insurance companies, adequately describes the unforeseen and unpleasant things that can befall the outside caterer. The most obvious factor is the weather. In the UK one tends to think of torrential rain, but very hot weather can have as much impact, placing an enormous strain on coolers and portable refrigerators and making it very difficult to serve the type of food demanded by the consumer, namely crisp salads, ice cream and cool drinks. There is also the problem of insects, particularly in the summer months. Flies and wasps not only increase the risk of contamination by cross-infection, but also are extremely unsightly around beautifully presented foodstuffs or circling the heads of hot, thirsty customers and may also upset staff trying to prepare or serve food.

OPERATIONAL ASPECTS

Generally speaking, the prices of food and refreshments at outside catering functions are higher than those usually charged in regular outlets such as public houses and restaurants. The reason for this higher pricing policy is the need to cover the additional costs of catering outdoors. Such costs include the following.

- *Marquees*. Although some catering firms may own their own tentage, usually it has to be hired from firms specializing in this area. The costs of this may be borne directly by the client or it may have to be passed on to the customer through prices.
- *Transportation*. All foodstuffs, beverages and equipment have to be transported to the site either in the firm's own vans or in hired transportation so there are the running costs of petrol, drivers' wages and hire charges and the possible capital costs of depreciation, insurance, and so on, to take into account.
- *Fuel*. Where the caterer has to provide his own fuel for the operation, particularly for cooking, the costs of this may prove to be greater than usual.
- *Equipment*. The caterer must take great care to ensure the safe transportation of equipment, particularly crockery and glassware, that may have a value of several hundred pounds even for a relatively small function. This may require the use of special packing cases and boxes designed for such purposes which add to the cost. But in addition, whatever the equipment is packed in, staff are involved in the considerable task of packing and unpacking on site and in stocktaking to assess losses and breakages.
- *Insurance*. Many outside caterers have the additional cost of insurance against unforeseen events, in addition to the normal insurance costs relating to equipment and employees' protection. It is likely that the premiums are higher for out side caterers than for those who operate under normal circumstances.
- *Depreciation*. Large sums of money are tied up by the large stocks of equipment needed for peak-season business.
- *Losses*. Finally, caterers will probably find that despite all the care they have taken they will still have relatively high losses of equipment due to breakages, misuse and pilferage; certainly far more than on a secure site. Such losses, of course, have to be passed on to the customer.

Due to the very wide range of catering events that may be undertaken and the wide variety of firms engaged in the business, no detailed analysis of operating procedures can be given. In many respects an outside catering function is no different from a 'banquet' function. Full details of the client's requirements should be taken and in addition the caterer should visit the site to establish means of getting to and from the site and how close transport can get to the unit before, during and after the event; services available on site and requirements with regard to power supplies, portable generators and gas bottles; size of floor area and storage space in both preparation and service areas in order to plan the siting of cooking equipment, tables and chairs, buffet tables and service points; availability of premises before the event for the setting up of equipment and *mise-en-place*, and after the event to close down and remove equipment; levels of stock that will be required and can be stored securely on site, and the provision of security personnel should they need to be left overnight; and other security arrangements concerning the admission of catering staff and personnel to the site during the event.

During the function itself the preparation and provision of food at outside catering events may be carried out in three basic ways. All food can be centrally prepared and sent out to be reheated and dressed on flats or plates on site; all food can be prepared and served on site; or a combination of the two. There is no doubt that there are sound reasons for using a central kitchen or commissary. Standards of food are maintained since the cooking of food is either carried out or monitored by the firm's permanent staff. Wastage may be reduced due to bulk production. Centrally prepared dishes may be more impressive than it may be possible to prepare on site. Stricter control of foodstuffs is made possible. Storage of raw materials is eliminated on site. Less equipment is required on site. Staffing levels on site can be reduced and fewer skilled personnel are required there.

The disadvantages of a central kitchen are the degree of organization required to ensure that all the outside units receive the food that they require; difficulties associated with transporting prepared foods safely; problems of reheating or reconstituting dishes on site, with all the possible dangers of contamination; staff on site may not have the experience or know-how to cope with any of the problems that may arise; there is little or no chance of food being returned if too much is allocated, despite strict supervision. Thus, there can be no doubt that it requires a great deal of skill and expertise to organize an outdoor catering event successfully and achieve a profit.

A typical example of a large-scale outside catering event is the Farnborough Air Show held every two years. It is a multi-million pound venture attended by all the major aerospace manufacturers and aviation firms who exhibit their hardware in the exhibition halls. They also entertain their clients and personnel in chalets arranged in rows overlooking the runway to give the best possible view of the air show itself. These chalets are semi-permanent in that supply roads, concrete bases and essential services, such as sanitation and water, are *in situ*. But the chalets themselves are only erected for the show and are essentially marquees and tenting fixed to scaffold poles, although the client firms renting them go to considerable trouble to make their interiors as plush and comfortable as possible, as illustrated in Figure 18.2. A large catering firm at the show may be catering for over 40 different companies, ranging from one chalet unit up to the largest of the show comprising seven chalet units joined together, from a central compound on site.

For purposes of administration and control, chalets are divided into zones of approximately equal size, with a zone manager acting as trouble-shooter for the five or six chalets under his control. Likewise, vans and drivers are allocated to carry all stores and provisions for each zone from a central compound. Both zone managers and drivers may be equipped with short-wave radios to keep in constant touch with each other and the compound as telephone lines are limited and always busy. The compound, built primarily for security purposes, contains all administrative offices, the stores, cellar, linen 'room' and staff canteen. It is likely to be staffed 24 hours a day for the entire eight days of the show by full-time employees of the company and provides back-up services in all areas such as staffing, training, hygiene, public relations, and so on. Each chalet has its own manager in charge of the unit. Each manager is fully briefed before the show and given a dossier containing all the information he or she may require, including names and telephone numbers of key personnel at the compound, notes on administrative procedures, stock control and staffing, security procedures, general hints on staff training, Calor-gas safety instructions, copy of the occasional licence granted for the sale of intoxicating

Figure 18.2 Chalet interior at major event (Ferranti plc at Farnborough Air Show).
Source: Ferranti plc.

liquor in the chalet, function sheet and menus, and so on. In most cases menus have been determined in advance in consultation with the client, so food would be issued each day according to the specification. Some items could be blast-frozen at a central commissary off-site, others prepared in the compound, but it is left to the chefs in each chalet to put the finishing touches to the dishes and to present them attractively. Liquor stores are likewise predetermined for the chalet's bar, with enough stock to last three or four days to minimize the movement and requisitioning of new stock. Most clients dispense their refreshments free of charge (although they were careful to control access to the chalet so that only bona fide guests were entertained) so that bar stocks are provided on a sale or return basis. Equipment is delivered to each chalet on the day before the show opens and checked against a stock sheet. It is returned on the last day, again after a stock check, so that breakages and losses can be calculated. Staffing for a typical chalet serving 100 customers a day, for morning coffee, lunch and afternoon tea, might comprise one chalet manager, two chefs, two bar stewards, six waiting staff and two kitchen porters.

During the course of the show, the large outside catering firm will be responsible for the service of tens of thousands of meals and employ many hundreds of staff, most of whom are working for them on a part-time basis and travelling up to 60 miles (96 kilometres) each day to get there. Every member of staff has to be provided with a uniform and passes to get into the show, and they have to be directed to a particular chalet and eventually paid at the end of it all. Chalet managers are responsible for the standards and performance of staff and are given guidelines concerning this.

CONCLUSION

Outside catering is a specialized sector of the food service industry covering a wide range of functions and events. Although the Farnborough example highlights an event much larger than most outside catering events, it illustrates the essential point – it is a risky business that requires a great deal of forethought and planning down to the last detail with regard to all aspects of the operation. And once the function is under way, it is essential to *control* very closely the movement of stocks and performance of staff, for without strict control the potential profit from an outside catering function may not be realized. In many respects this type of catering provides a real challenge to the professional caterer and a great deal of his job satisfaction is to be gained from the diversity of operations and difficulties surmounted.

REFERENCES

1. Law, J. (1993) 'Trying to be different', *Executive Travel*, January, pp. 45–6.
2. BMSL Report (1990) *The Effectiveness of Corporate Hospitality*, London: BMSL Publications.
3. Darwent, C. (1990) 'The party's over', *Management Today*, August, pp. 82–3.
4. Ibid.
5. Woolgar, T. (1990) 'Turning work into a memorable event', *Marketing Week*, 2 March, pp. 41–4.
6. Furness, S. (1992) 'Sportsworld hospitality', *Hospitality and Entertainment*, Spring, p. 20.
7. Bryant, S. (1991) 'Hospitality: a state of emergency', *Meetings and Incentive Travel*, October, pp. 10–12.
8. Cappell, J. (1993) 'Outside Catering in Sussex', Unpublished dissertation, University of Brighton.
9. Harmer, J. (1994) 'Branching out', *Caterer and Hotelkeeper*, 31 March, pp. 40–2.

Index

Note: Page numbers in italics indicate significant entries.

accommodation experience 25–29, 42–44, 55–56, 63, 65
accommodation operations 10, 11, 12, 32–33, 58–59, 69–70, 92–94, 102–104
Accor 29, 34, 40, 64
acoustics 114
airline catering *234–241*
air conditioning 113
airport hotels 40, *41–42*
average speed 39, 53, 132, 144, 242

banqueting 140, 147–150
Bass 170
bed spaces 31, 52, 64
Beefeater 124, 131, 132, 168
billing 33
branding 34, 40, 151, 166, 188, 190, 203, 215
breakfast 145
Brewers Society 9, 161
British Airways 235
British Hospitality Association 1, 3, 9
British Tourist Authority 3, *10*
budget hotels *61–71*
buffet service 148–149, 242
BurgerKing 2, 154, 173, 177, 179, 189, 204, 211
business travellers 22–24, 36–37, 39, 40 42, 64

cafeterias 154, *199–203*
CAMRA 164
Campanele 37, 64, 66, 69
care homes 88, 227–228
carvery 141
Center Parcs 51, 52, 53, 54, 58
central production kitchens 216–217, 227, 231, 238, 258
cleanliness 93, 111
Compass 2, 192, 204, 211, 215
competition 17
compulsory competitive tendering (CCT) 87, 207, 210
computerized reservation systems 22, 32, 39, 47
concessions 194, 250
conference delegates 22, *41*, 98
conference facilities 43, 44, 98
consortia 47, 84
consumer demand 22, 27–28, 75, 97, 107–109, 146, 154, 157, 163, 169, 178, 212, 221, 222–223, 228, 234, 235, 242, 247

consumer spending 7
convenience stores *174–175*
corporate hospitality 253
country-house hotels 38, 50
country resort hotels *51*, 53

decor 112–113, 125, 126, 127, 166
decoupling 14
demographic trends 28, 212, 228
deregulation 153, 154
De Vere hotels 51, 58
disposables 187
drive-through 188

employment 6, 31, 132, 154, 163, 177
environment 187
ethnic restaurants 5, 129, 130, 136, 173, 178
Eurostar 245

family restaurants 136
family service 120, *134*, 148
fast food *172–188*, 205
ferry catering 246–249
fish and chip shops 173, 175, 178
food 109–110, 178, 210, 213
food production systems 13, 118, 183
food service operations 10, 11, 13, 117, 119, 155, 158, 165, 182–185, 216–220, 223–227, 230, 237–241, 244–245, 255–259
Forte 29, 38, 40, 63, 64, 144, 153, 154, 179, 192
franchising 29, 64, 135, 144, 154, 184, 188, 235
Friendly Hotels 63
furnishings 114, 166

Gardner Merchant 2, 192, 204, 215
grading, hotel 75
Grenada 63, 64, 154
gueridon service 120, 135
guest houses 21, *73–84*
guides 75, 78

Happy Eater 1, 63, 129, 156
Harvester 124, 131, 168
health awareness 15, 185, 206, 221, 237
Hilton International 29, 34
Holiday Inn 21, 29, 39, 71
holiday villages 50, *51–52*
home delivery 188

hospitals 25, *86–95*, *223–227*
hostels 25, 96–104
Hotel and Catering Training Company 3, 6, *10*
hotel bedrooms 26, 27, 28
Hotel, Catering and Institutional Management
    Association 1, *9*
hotel chains 21, *30*
hotel development 4, 37–38
hotel facilities 26, 40, 55, 69, 99
hotel operating costs 31, 76
Hotel Proprietor Act (1956) 73
hotel reservations 22
housekeeping 33
Hyatt 30
hygiene 256

industrial catering 5, 191
information technology 16, 183, 231, 238

Kentucky Fried Chicken 2, 132, 154, 173, 177, 179,
    185, 204

legislation 15, 73, 129, 162, 206, 209, 213, 241
leisure travellers 24–25, 65, 77
licensed trade 129, *161–171*
Little Chef 1, 63, 129, 132, 153, 156
local authorities 87
location, foodservice 133, 155, 157, 178–179, 214,
    236
location, hotels 36, 37–38, 54, 66–68, 78–79
lounge service 140, *144*

management contracts 29, 90, 191, *192–194*, 211, 238
marine catering 246–250
market segmentation 26, 77–78
Marriott 29, 38, 40, 48, 64
McDonalds 2, 130, 132, 154, 173, 176, 177, 179,
    185, 189, 204
meal experience 109–116, 213
meals on wheels *228–231*
menus 123, 143, 147, 159, 167, 181, 204, 205, 214,
    224, 237
motorway service areas 153, *154–156*, 160
Mount Charlotte Thistle 37, 51

NACNE 213, 221
nutrition 185, 213, 220, 229, 230

occupancy rates 31, 52, 69, 76
organization, accommodation *44–47*, *56–58*, 70,
    81–82, 89, 102, 103
organization, foodservice 150, 181, 237

Pizza Hut 126, 131, 132, 135, 173, 177, 179, 204,
    211
plate service 120, 134, 141, 148
prison catering 231
product mix 140, 154, 163, 222
product offering 43, 55, 68, 79, 88, 99, 180, 236,
    242, 247, 249
production lining 14, 183, 226
profit margins 169, 195

public houses 4, 129
public sector catering 193, 209–232

quality 94, 95

railway catering *241–246*
reception 32
recycling 187
reservations 32, 59
residential care 25
restaurants 7, *122–137*, 140–144
room rates 21, 40, 64
room service 140, *144–146*

sales turnover 8, 176
school meals 5, *220–223*
security 256
self-employment 7, 76, 81, 163, 181, 255
self service 14, 120, 174, 194, 199–204, 247
service standards 43, 55, 68, 79, 111, 180, 183, 194
short break holidays 59, 77
silver service 120, 134, 142, 148
socioeconomic change 28, 87, 169, 177, 212
Sodexho 207, 211
sous-vide 15, 203, 209, *219*
staffing accommodation 45–47, 56–58, 70, 81, 89,
    92–93, 102, 103
staffing foodservice 181, 237, 243, 247, 249, 256
Standard Industrial Classification 2, 117, 161, 175,
    252
steakhouse 126
structure, industry 7, 74, 154, 165, 191, 246
suite accommodation 23, 47
suppliers 16, 82, 151, 231, 236, 244, 248
Sutcliffes 2, 204, 215
Swallow Hotels 36
systems 11, 183, 215, 218, 223, 230

take-aways 176
technology 15, 47, 121
terminus catering 250
TGIFridays 17, 124, 126, 131, 135
theme restaurants 136
Toby Restaurants 131, 168, 170
tourism spending 30, 39
tourists 22, 77, 97
trading area 179
Travelodge 2, 63, 64, 71
tray-service systems 223–227, 238–239
trolley service 198–199, 242, 244
TUPE 206

vending 174, 195, 196–198

warm holding *217*, 230, 238
waste disposal 187, 241
Wimpy 6, 122, 128, 154, 177
workforce 7, 181, 206

Youth Hostels 96, 100, 104
YMCA 25, 96, 100
YWCA 25, 96, 101